I'll See You Again

The Bittersweet Love Story
and Wartime Letters of
Jeanette MacDonald
and Gene Raymond

**Volume 1:
The War—and Before**

D1453231

Maggie McCormick

I'll See You Again: The Bittersweet Love Story and Wartime Letters of Jeanette MacDonald and
Gene Raymond
Volume 1: The War—and Before
© 2019. Maggie McCormick. All rights reserved.

Published in the USA by:
BearManor Media
P O Box 71426
Albany, Georgia 31708
www.bearmanormedia.com

Printed in the United States of America
ISBN   978-1-62933-436-3 (paperback)
          978-1-62933-437-0 (hardcover)

Book and cover design and layout by Darlene Swanson • www.van-garde.com

Contents

In memory of Roy,

the most tragic figure in

the Raymonds' story.

He deserved a longer, happier life and

Gene and Jeanette deserved more time with him.

Acknowledgments

This book could not have been written without the help of the following people: Becky and Jeremy Armstrong, Armstrong Family Estate Services; Diane Bachman, Bentley Historical Library, University of Michigan; Garland Baldwin; Kaye Berger; Jack Clark; Ned Comstock, Doheny Memorial Library, University of Southern California; Tara Craig, Head of Public Services, Rare Book & Manuscript Library, Columbia University; Irene Daligga; Keith Davis; Richard De Coursey; Ann Diedelot; Claire M. Dinkelman, the University of Wisconsin–Milwaukee Libraries, Archives Department; Connie Elliott; Simon Elliott, UCLA Library Special Collections, University of California, Los Angeles; Robert A. Frank, Administrator, The Andre Kostelanetz Royalty Pool; Sue Garland; Deborah Goerz; Eric M. Graf, Public Service Office, Motion Picture, Broadcasting, and Recorded Sound Division, Library of Congress; Molly Haigh, UCLA Library Special Collections, University of California, Los Angeles; Rosemary Hanes, Reference Librarian, Moving Image Section, Library of Congress; Claire Harmon; Elizabeth Hensley; Milla Ilieva; Julie Illescas; Jamie, Lawnview Cemetery, Rockledge, Pennsylvania; Jennifer Evans Joseph, Reference and Instruction Librarian, Geneva

College; Mary Klein, PhD., Director, Office of Research and Technology Development, Albert Einstein Healthcare Network; Derek Klezmer, SOFA Entertainment; Frank Labrador; Dr. Karen Lacy; Fay La Galle; Wayne Lawless; Maureen Lynch; Genevieve Maxwell, Reference Librarian, Academy of Motion Picture Arts and Sciences; Alicia Mayer; Vicky McCargar, University Archivist & Special Collections Librarian, Coe Library–Chalon Campus, Mount Saint Mary's University; Gary McMaster, Chairman and Curator, The Camp Roberts Historical Museum; Lisa Mozeley; Melissa Mueller, Washington Park, Milwaukee, Wisconsin; Patrick Mundt, Baron-Forness Library; Tal Nadan, Reference Archivist, The Brooke Russell Astor Reading Room for Rare Books and Manuscripts, The New York Public Library; Roger P. Noonan; Scott O'Brien; Ben Ohmart, BearManor Media; Julie Osborne, Yankee Air Museum; James Robert Parish; Bill Park; Andrea Parker; Tim L. Pennycuff, Associate Professor and University Archivist, University of Alabama at Birmingham; Sandra Reed; Toni Reinke; Barry Rivadue; Nevin Robb; Joan Halford Rohlfing; Brittany Rubino, NBCUniversal Media LLC; LaManda Scott; L. Richard Scroggins; Daniel Mayer Selznick; Bill Stewart; Larry Stouch; Laura Stroffolino, Curator, Print and Picture Collection, Free Library of Philadelphia; Vincent Terrace; Robert W. Thom, Trustee of the Gene Raymond Trust; Edward Baron Turk; Brenda and Mark Working; and others who prefer to remain anonymous. They shared materials, helped with research, and offered support in a variety of ways.

I am grateful to the legions of fans who wrote about their experiences with Jeanette MacDonald and Gene Raymond in fan club publications and private correspondence, giving very special insights to those who never had a chance to meet them. Without their reports on radio and TV broadcasts, and meeting the Raymonds backstage, a tremendous amount of information would be lost.

Several people deserve special acknowledgement.

Dale Kuntz generously shared photos, as well as fan club journals, from his vast collection. They were a tremendous help in researching the many facets of the Raymonds' lives and careers that weren't always mentioned in the press. Dale's longtime love and enthusiasm for Jeanette and Gene is inspiring.

I appreciate Brent Perry for sharing his memories, which put many things in perspective. His photo restoration talents greatly improved the appearance of some of the pictures used in this book. I am extremely grateful for his help and friendship.

Enormous thanks to Kayla Sturm for sharing one of the drafts of Jeanette MacDonald's autobiography. She generously plans to upload the book so it is available online for Jeanette's fans to read, free of charge.

I am grateful to the late Eleanor Knowles Dugan, as well as to her daughter, Jill Coogan, and Eleanor's friend, Ginny Sayre, for sharing Eleanor's collection and research, including items given to her by the late Ken Richards. Eleanor was one of the first to encourage me to write this book and I regret that she passed away before it was finished.

I owe very special thanks to Teri Parker for her invaluable assistance with researching, proofreading, and offering suggestions on how to improve this book. I appreciate being able to discuss ideas with her throughout the writing process and having someone share my enthusiasm when things fell into place. Although we sometimes agree to disagree on certain matters concerning Jeanette MacDonald, without Teri's knowledge and help, this book would not be possible. She is a true friend through thick and thin and I can never thank her enough for all of her support.

Finally, I am thankful for my late parents. My dad introduced me to old movies, including *Sweethearts*, *Three Daring Daughters*, and *Flying Down to Rio*. My mom shared my love of Jeanette and Gene, and let them take over our house and our lives. My parents taught me the importance of respect and truth, values that also were important to the Raymonds. I'll always appreciate their support, encouragement, and love.

Preface

In the 1930s, Jeanette MacDonald was queen of the screen, singing her way through a series of operettas and musicals, with and without her frequent co-star, Nelson Eddy. Like many stars of the Golden Age of Movies, she began her career on Broadway and went to Hollywood during the early days of talkies. In the early 1930s, she was known as The Lingerie Queen, making successful musicals and comedies at Paramount–Publix Corporation (Paramount), where she frequently co-starred with French entertainer Maurice Chevalier, and Fox Film Corporation (Fox). Several of the songs that she introduced at Paramount became standards, including "Beyond the Blue Horizon," "Isn't It Romantic," and "Lover."

In 1933, Jeanette signed with Metro–Goldwyn–Mayer (MGM) and it was there that she became a superstar. Two years later, she was teamed with screen newcomer Nelson Eddy in the operetta *Naughty Marietta* (1935), which became a surprise sensation, launching America's Singing Sweethearts into immortality. During the Depression, their films were perfect escapist entertainment. The team of Jeanette MacDonald and Nelson Eddy helped save MGM from bankruptcy, just as child star Shirley Temple saved Twentieth

Century–Fox Film Corporation (Twentieth Century–Fox), and dance team Fred Astaire and Ginger Rogers saved RKO Radio Pictures Inc. (RKO).

Jeanette and Nelson introduced a generation of moviegoers to operetta, opera, and classical music, proving to the uninitiated that it was far from boring or intimidating. While Warner Bros. Pictures (Warner Bros.) was known for gangster movies and Universal Pictures (Universal) for monsters, ask any film buff which studio made the best musicals and they are sure to answer MGM.

Jeanette was the first classically trained singer to make more than just a few movies; however, she left her mark on more than operettas. Without her, the classic 1936 film *San Francisco* would not have been produced. Idea man Robert "Hoppy" Hopkins had little luck trying to interest studio executives in his story about the 1906 earthquake as a vehicle for Jeanette and Clark Gable. She stepped in and convinced the studio of the picture's possibilities, even turning down projects and remaining off salary until Gable's schedule was free. The movie earned six Academy Award nominations, including Best Original Story. Jeanette introduced the title song, which became one of the California city's official anthems. Her tenacity in getting the film produced led Hopkins to dub her The Iron Butterfly, describing her delicate beauty and shrewd business acumen. At first, Jeanette laughed over the nickname; however, over time, she came to dislike it. Part of her business savvy included having her manager and attorney negotiate short-term contracts with story approval, something few stars had at the time.

In Jeanette's favorite film, *Maytime* (1937), she proved her acting ability, aging from young woman to elderly matron. Her performance was honored by the Screen Actors Guild (now SAG–AFTRA); many film buffs thought that she should have received an Oscar nomination as well. In *The Firefly* (1937), she showed off her dancing talents, in addition to her vocal skills. When tenor Allan Jones sang "The Donkey Serenade" to her, she spoke volumes with her eyes, although she never opened her mouth. It became Jones' signature song and he never failed to thank Jeanette for giving him equal screen time.

Jeanette was a true motion picture pioneer. Her singing of "March of the Grenadiers" in *The Love Parade* (1929) was the first use of prerecording on film. In *Oh, for a Man!* (1930), she sang one of the earliest opera excerpts in a sound film. MGM co-founder Louis B. Mayer promised that Jeanette would star in the studio's first three-strip Technicolor feature; he kept his word with *Sweethearts* (1938), the fifth of her eight films with Nelson Eddy. Jeanette also starred in Paramount's first complete two-color Technicolor talkie, *The Vagabond King* (1930), and MGM's *The Cat and the Fiddle* (1934), in which the finale was the first use of Technicolor's three-strip color process in a live-action/non-cartoon film. Both critics and fans wish that she had made more color films, as her beauty, peaches and cream complexion, expressive sea-green eyes, and stunning titian hair were made for Technicolor.

Author/TV panelist John Kieran wrote, "It wasn't what the poet had in mind when he wrote it, but whenever I hear Jeanette MacDonald sing, I think of [William Cullen] Bryant's line—'a voice of gladness, and a smile and eloquence of beauty.' There is a lilt to her loveliness. Like the birds, she was born to add music and merriment to a sad world."[1] Jeanette was one of the first singing stars to appear in all forms of entertainment: Vaudeville, Broadway, movies, opera, concerts, radio, records, nightclubs, summer stock, and television. She even appeared with the circus in a pair of benefits (1948 and 1955). From 1939 to 1959, she gave recitals around the country, accompanied only by a piano, as well as numerous concerts with symphony orchestras. According to a 1978 article in *American Classic Screen,*

"She broke records in every house she appeared for five successive years and proceeded to shatter her own records in houses to which she returned."[2] She even sang at the White House (1954) and at two inaugural balls (1953 and 1957). In the 1940s, she tried her hand at opera, singing *Romeo et Juliette* (1943–1945) in the United States and Canada, and *Faust* (1944, 1945, and 1951) in several American cities. In the 1950s, she performed a successful nightclub act (1953, 1954, and 1957), as well as summer stock runs in *Bittersweet* (1954, 1955, and 1959) and *The King and I* (1956).

Producer/director Cecil B. DeMille said that Jeanette could hold a high C for fifty-five seconds without cracking. At her peak, her range ran from low A to high E flat. Although some critics said that Jeanette's voice was small, compared to other classical singers, there were few complaints about being able to hear her without a microphone, even in enormous venues like New York's Carnegie Hall and London's the Royal Albert Hall.

Those who saw Jeanette's red-gold hair, sea-green eyes, and enchanting smile up close insisted that she was even more beautiful in person than she appeared on screen. Makeup artist William Tuttle, who worked on some of Hollywood's most glamorous stars, said, "I thought Jeanette was one of the most beautiful women on the screen, really. And you know, I never heard many people say that."[3] Critics often compared her to a Dresden china figurine. Producer Florenz Ziegfeld said "that if he had to typify the American Beauty, he could do it only with Jeanette MacDonald."[4] Film historian John Kobal wrote, "Jeanette MacDonald's chin may have been a bit too large for her face, her shoulders too broad, her singing possibly affected by too many tremoloes [sic], but she had enormous charm. This, plus a sparkling sense of humour [sic], large deep green eyes, an abundance of red-gold hair, and a totally bewitching smile, made her one of the great musical stars of the decade." He continued, "It is the delightful MacDonald that makes the film [*Maytime*]; sparkling with wit and warmth, she can do more than anyone with the lift of an eyebrow, the crinkling of her chin in thought or humour [sic]. She turns effortlessly from 'throw-away' laughter to heartbreak with no need of wringing hands or gulping sobs."[5] Despite Jeanette's fame and accolades, she remained modest about her appearance. She often described her titian hair as carroty and, in 1964, when a fan asked about her beauty, she said, "GOLLY, I never thought I was even pretty til [sic] years after I was in movies!"[6]

Many said that Jeanette's inner beauty shone through, for she was as kind and generous to behind-the-scenes personnel and her fans as she was to the Presidents, celebrities, and royalty she encountered. Each morning, when her car dropped her off at the studio, she cheerily said "good morning" to other stars' chauffeurs. During the Depression, she anonymously gave money to the extras on her films, knowing that they were struggling. At the end of the day, she often purposely flubbed lines so the extras would get overtime pay. She appreciated the studio crew and insisted on the same directors, cameramen, hairstylists, and other personnel to work on her movies, fully aware of how their jobs contributed to her success. Jeanette said, "The best friends I made in that time were the working crews on my pictures. They could count on me to go to bat for them with the front office whatever the odds. They never thought of me as a prima donna—I was just Jeanette."[7] She was a loyal friend and, long after she became a movie star, she remained in touch with people that she knew from childhood and her Broadway days. Actress/dancer Ginger Rogers, one of Jeanette's bridesmaids, said, "Jeanette has been one of the happy experiences of my life."[8]

At the height of Jeanette's fame, her face and voice were recognized in countries that didn't know the name of the President of the

United States. Even those who never had the opportunity to meet her in person recognized a special quality in the singer. In 1989, Susan Rogers Cassidy, who was a child when Jeanette died, summed up many fans' feelings: "Jeanette was a beautiful and classy lady who expressed her love through her glorious voice. Her twinkling eyes and delightful mannerisms show us her keen intelligence and fine sense of humor. She's someone you would have liked to have known."[9]

In 1965, Jeanette's death made front-page headlines around the world and the testimonials were heartfelt. At her funeral, composer Rudolf Friml, whose music was used in Jeanette's films *The Vagabond King* (1930), *The Lottery Bride* (1930), *Rose-Marie* (1936), and *The Firefly* (1937), told columnist James Bacon that Jeanette had done more to popularize his songs than any other singer. Friml said that he did not send flowers to Jeanette's funeral because he had given her "Only a Rose," recalling the song that she sang in *The Vagabond King*.

Many entertainers grew up seeing Jeanette on screen, dreaming of following in her footsteps. World leaders, from Presidents Franklin D. Roosevelt, Harry Truman, and Dwight Eisenhower to Chancellor Adolf Hitler, also expressed their admiration for her. Columnists and TV hosts commented on the loyal devotion of her fans, both before and after her death.

Although both Jeanette MacDonald and Nelson Eddy preferred to be remembered for their individual accomplishments, their names continued to be linked in the minds of many fans and film historians. Long after their deaths, their names and images remained a part of popular culture. Writers, who grew up watching their movies, regularly mentioned them or spoofed them on TV, in commercials, on Broadway, and on screen. They were imitated by a plethora of performers and given tribute concerts, featuring the songs that they popularized, alone and together.

Gene Raymond was a handsome blonde leading man who con-quered all mediums with his clean-cut looks and cheerful personality. In the 1920s, he was a successful juvenile actor on Broadway and on tour. In the 1930s, he starred with many film legends, including Bette Davis, Joan Crawford, Barbara Stanwyck, Carole Lombard, Loretta Young, Dolores del Rio, and Jean Harlow. He showed his versatility on stage and screen in comedies, dramas, and musicals. He also was a talented songwriter and director. Like Jeanette, he was part of a screen team, appearing in five 1930s movies with Ann Sothern.

Anticipating the United States' entry into what would become World War II, during the spring of 1940, Gene took flying lessons. In October 1940, over a year before the United States entered the war, he was one of the first celebrities to register for the draft. In January 1942, he enlisted, turning down a civilian defense job because he knew that, as a licensed pilot, he could better serve his country in the Army Air Force. His exemplary service in the military and the Air Force Reserve, not only during World War II, but during the Vietnam War, led to many honors. In the 1940s through the 1970s, he com-bined work on stage, radio, movies, and television with service on a variety of military, show business, and charitable boards.

Like Jeanette, Gene was loyal to his family and friends, making sure that they were provided for, both physically and financially. He arranged for several members of the Raymonds' extended family to get care at the Motion Picture and Television Country House and Hospital, where he was later a trustee, and made sure that both of his wives were able to remain in their homes, despite declining health. Many of his friendships dated back to his Broadway days, his arrival in Hollywood, and his service during World War II.

For years, Jeanette MacDonald and Gene Raymond were touted as one of the happiest couples in show business. Their friends called them the MacRaymonds and they adopted the nickname themselves. Although they co-starred in only one film, *Smilin' Through* (1941), they often worked together, touring for five months in the play *The Guardsman* (1951), and appearing on numerous radio and television shows. Columnists noted how the couple spoiled each other and how affectionate they remained over twenty years after their wedding. Jeanette once described her husband as a combination of "Mickey Mouse, Santa Claus and Superman all rolled into one."[10]

From the Raymonds' June 16, 1937 wedding, when a reported fifteen thousand fans lined up in front of the church, until Jeanette's January 14, 1965 death, when her last words to her husband were "I love you," their lives sounded like a romantic fairytale. They each admitted that marriage had to be worked at and that they didn't always get along. In Jeanette's unpublished autobiography, she wrote candidly about problems that they had after the war, when both were struggling with their careers and adjusting to changes in the entertainment industry, as well as the country. However, they persevered and remained together for over twenty-seven years, until Jeanette's death.

In the 1970s, rumors began circulating that the Raymonds' happy marriage was a sham. Stories spread about Jeanette having a secret thirty-year affair with her frequent co-star, Nelson Eddy, and questioning Gene's sexuality, with unsubstantiated evidence to support them. Many incidents where Jeanette and Nelson allegedly were together have been disproved, as the stars could not have been in two places at once. Books, blogs, and web sites quoted letters that few people, aside from one author, had seen. Private conversations were reported that only someone hiding under the bed, or in the closet with a tape recorder, could repeat. Many off-screen "Jeanette and Nelson" sightings were really Jeanette and Gene sightings, since fans, and even newspapers, often confused the two actors because of their Jeanette connection and the fact that they slightly resembled one another. Still, the myths are perpetuated, and, in the twenty-first century, these fantasies are more prevalent than the truth on mainstream web sites and in print.

In 1958, Jeanette said, "I have a phobia about telling lies, and will have nothing to do with people once I have found them to be liars."[11] Although she often followed the show business tradition of shaving a few years off her age, only a hypocrite would speak so vehemently against lying and lead a double life. And, given the opposition and continual abuse from Gene's mother, no woman would have married Gene—and remained with him for over twenty-seven years—unless she truly loved him. Similarly, in an effort to defame Jeanette and separate the couple, Gene's mother wrote many negative things about Jeanette's reputation and past love life. Why wouldn't she threaten to expose Jeanette's affair with Nelson Eddy if, as some claim, it was common knowledge in Hollywood, both before and after the Raymonds' marriage? She made it clear that she had no qualms about ruining her son's career, publicly embarrassing him, or suing him to stop the wedding.

The war and the Raymonds' work often kept them far apart, forcing them to communicate by costly telephone calls, telegrams, and through the mail. The fact that, from their courtship days through the 1960s, both Jeanette and Gene saved letters, cards, and telegrams, speaks volumes about how much they cherished their correspondence. Jeanette planned to reproduce some of them in her autobiography, saying, "On the assumption that everyone likes to take a peek at the letters of another, I'm including herewith some of our wartime communiques [sic]; deletions done by that common enemy, THE CENSOR."[12]

The Raymonds' story was too big for just one volume. The purpose of this trilogy of books is to present Jeanette and Gene's relationship in their own words, through their correspondence, interviews, and drafts of Jeanette's autobiography; set the record straight on various matters that have been reported erroneously elsewhere; and show how the war affected their lives and careers. It is divided into three volumes.

The first traces the lives of Jeanette MacDonald and Gene Raymond, from their modest beginnings through their meeting, marriage, and their activities during World War II. It shows how they each worked hard to gain worldwide fame, found love, and created an idyllic home together. Always patriotic, both Raymonds gave their all during World War II, both overseas and on the home front, but to the detriment of their marriage and careers. The picture on the cover was from the Raymonds' last photo shoot before Gene was sent overseas in 1942. It was taken on the outdoor steps at their home, Twin Gables.

Volume two is made up of transcriptions of letters written during World War II, giving an insight into Jeanette and Gene's everyday lives. Their wartime letters are touching, full of tenderness, concern, humor, and, occasionally, passion. They shared their mundane every day experiences and asked each other for advice. One can tell that they respected each other, as well as loved each other. Like all couples, they didn't get along 100% of the time. They were human and it is that human side that is so endearing.

The third volume examines the Raymonds' lives after the war, when changes in the entertainment industry affected their careers. Many planned projects never materialized. The strain and frustration they faced put stress on their marriage. They often were apart, due to their work and Gene's service in the Air Force Reserve. Additionally, Jeanette had many health problems, which led to her untimely death. In later years, Gene faced rumors about his marriage and sexuality, handling both with dignity. Although he remarried nine years after he was widowed, he never stopped loving Jeanette. He kept her legacy alive by attending her annual fan club banquets, taking flowers to her crypt, and promoting her career in TV and print interviews. The third volume includes the bibliography for the series.

All three books feature some photos from the Raymonds' personal collection, now in possession of the author. The biographical volumes include quotes from private letters and various drafts of Jeanette's unpublished autobiography. Letters have been quoted as they were written, with punctuation, grammar, and spelling errors intact and noted with [sic]. Occasionally, punctuation was added in brackets for clarity. Hopefully, readers will see the real Jeanette MacDonald and Gene Raymond through their writings and realize what a solid foundation they had.

During the books' production, several people remarked that Jeanette and Gene are forgotten today. With their movies airing on television, screening at film festivals, and available on DVD and for streaming, many younger people are discovering their talents. Fans of all ages discuss the Raymonds' lives and careers on multiple Facebook groups, Twitter, Instagram, in blogs, and on podcasts. Although their efforts during World War II have been neglected in many sources, this volume should remind readers all that the Raymonds did for their country, overseas and on the home front.

There have been numerous books written about Jeanette MacDonald, including biographies, filmographies, cookbooks, and novels. This series does not purport to be a complete look at Jeanette MacDonald and Gene Raymonds' lives or careers or an analysis of their films. It concentrates on the years that they were together. Most movies made before they met are mentioned only by title; those made in 1935 and later generally include a brief synopsis. There is an overview of the Raymonds' radio and TV appearances; it would take another book to list all of them and describe them in detail. An effort has been made to concentrate on material that is not available in other books in hopes that the series will appeal to seasoned fans, as well as readers who know nothing about the Raymonds.

To learn more about Jeanette's movies, I suggest Eleanor Knowles Dugan's *The Films of Jeanette MacDonald and Nelson Eddy* (Grand Cyrus Press, 2011). For a complete biography, I recommend *Hollywood Diva* by Edward Baron Turk (University of California Press, 1998) and a draft of Jeanette's unpublished autobiography, which will be available as a free download at longtime fan Kayla Sturm's web site.

A portion of the proceeds from all three volumes will be donated to Sierra Delta, formerly known as Service Dogs for Heroes, a non-profit organization that trains and places service dogs with veterans who have visual, hearing, or mobility impairments, or Post Traumatic Stress Disorder. The Raymonds loved their country, as well as their dogs, and were enthusiastic supporters of the men and women who served in the military. It seems only fitting that books that utilize so much of their wartime correspondence will help those who served the United States.

The title, *I'll See You Again*, relates to the Raymonds on several levels. Jeanette sang the Noel Coward song in *Bitter Sweet*, both on screen (1940) and on stage (1954, 1955, and 1959), and, in 1947, she recorded it for RCA Victor. Like the musical from whence it came, the Raymonds' lives often were bittersweet, full of highs and lows in their careers and marriage, but their love was everlasting. They were married twenty-seven years, but separated by death for thirty-three.

"I'll See You Again" was Gene's favorite song. In 1942, while he was stationed in England, Jeanette sang it on the radio on *The Pause That Refreshes on the Air*, slightly altering the lyrics to address their wartime separation. Since the show wasn't broadcast in England, she sent him records of the program. The lyrics expressed the tone of the

Raymonds' correspondence, as they both focused on the future and their plans of making a life together after the war. Gene even quoted the lyrics in one of his letters. Through the years, their careers often separated them geographically, but they kept in touch by telephone, letters, and telegrams.

Gene chose "I'll See You Again" as one of the songs that the organist played at Jeanette's funeral, where it took on a deeper meaning. Although Gene wasn't terribly religious, he believed that he'd see his wife in heaven someday. Hoping that her autobiography would be published after her death, he wrote a foreword, concluding, "I shall never forget one minute of our union. Jeanette, my wife—all mine and I loved her with all my heart. I'm sure she is waiting for me."[13]

Chapter One

Jeanette MacDonald and Gene Raymond both grew up in show business, helping to support their families when their fathers could not, but the similarities in their backgrounds ended there. Jeanette came from a happy, stable home and lived in one place until she was sixteen. Gene's parents frequently fought and eventually separated; he moved so much that he attended eleven schools in one year. These differences affected their personalities, as well as their thoughts on marriage and children.

On June 18, 1903, Jeannette Anna McDonald was born at 5123 Arch Street in Philadelphia, Pennsylvania to Daniel and Anna Wright McDonald. When Anna went into labor, she almost didn't make it from the bathroom to the bedroom, and Daniel, a shipping clerk and salesman for a doorframe and mantel company, who wanted to be a physician, was forced to deliver his impatient third daughter, who arrived before the doctor. It was one of the few times in her life that perpetually late Jeannette was early. She was named after her paternal grandmother, Jeannette Johnston (spelled Johnstone or Johnson in some sources) McDonald, and her mother. On April 8, 1904, almost-ten-month-old Jeannette Anna was baptized at Olivet Presbyterian Church.

Anna Wright and Daniel McDonald, year unknown. Jeannette inherited her father's large eyes, red hair, and engaging sense of humor.

Sometime between 1910 and 1920, Daniel changed the spelling of the family name to MacDonald to better reflect their Scottish heritage. It's doubtful that he ever went to court to make it official, since both the *New York, New York Death Index* and his cemetery marker spell his name McDonald. In the 1920s, while Jeannette was working on Broadway, she dropped an N from her very long first name so it would fit better on a marquee. According to her longtime friend and secretary, Emily Wentz, Jeannette changed the spelling when a New York numerologist told her that "she would have greater success if the number of letters in her name added up to the number '8.'"[14] Early Playbills and reviews inconsistently spelled her first and last names in various combinations. In the remainder of this book, her name will be spelled Jeanette MacDonald, no matter the year being discussed.

Jeanette had two older sisters: Elsie Wallace McDonald, born December 17, 1893, and Edith F. McDonald, nicknamed Blossom, born August 21, 1895. Although many sources claimed that Edith's middle name was Blossom, or Blosem, allegedly, a family name from the Wright side, 1900 and 1910 census records, as well as the October 25, 1896 baptismal record from Olivet Presbyterian Church, clearly list her middle initial as F. What the F stood for is unknown.

Although Jeanette and Blossom frequently fought when they were young, they were particularly close as adults. Blossom often referred to her as "my baby sister,"[15] "my little sister,"[16] or "my kid sister."[17] Blossom also was close to Gene, especially after Jeanette's death.

All three MacDonald girls inherited Daniel's red hair. Jeanette's often was described as red-gold; some sources said that she enhanced it with a henna rinse. When asked about her hair color, Jeanette unpretentiously called it carroty.

During Jeanette's early years, the household also included Daniel's widowed father, Charles, who died in 1910. He encouraged little

Jeanette to perform, and shared a daily drop of rye with her, much to the horror of teetotaling Anna.

At the age of three, Jeanette made her musical debut, singing "O That Will Be Glory" at Tennent Memorial Presbyterian Church. When no one applauded, she clapped for herself and urged the congregation to join her. In 1939, Jeanette said, "Now mind you, I don't remember this, but I am told on good authority that it actually happened. I'm afraid I rather shocked the congregation."[18]

Jeanette had happy memories of her childhood in Philadelphia, playing with a toy piano on the porch, making homemade ice cream with her father every Saturday, and seeing sights with her mother while her sisters were in school. Often, the family went on picnics in the country, with Jeanette usually getting sick during the ride home. Throughout her life, she continued to be plagued by motion sickness, extremely difficult for someone whose occupation involved so much travel by plane, train, ship, and automobile. In 1946, she told columnist Erskine Johnson, "I'm a living argument for the fact that man was meant to travel on his own two feet."[19] Jeanette described her home life as "very normal. I have no home scars. I grew up in a happy atmosphere. I have enjoyed life because of that."[20]

Although Jeanette said that her mother had a lovely singing voice and several people praised Daniel's story-telling abilities, neither of the MacDonalds had show business aspirations. Anna's nephew, Charles Wright, thought that Jeanette inherited some of her talent for captivating an audience from her father. Wright said, "Uncle Dan was my 'fun' uncle with a flair for performing. He would tell a succession of stories, acting them out with gestures which would provoke continuous laughter from his audience of relatives. Jeanette could not help but be influenced by his love of the theatrical."[21] In a 1932 interview,

Jeanette said, "I owe much to my father. . . . He had a splendid personality, and always was ready for fun."[22]

All three MacDonald daughters had natural musical talents and studied dancing and piano when they were young. They often performed for their parents and their guests, with Elsie playing piano, Blossom dancing, and Jeanette singing. In an effort to keep their daughters modest, Anna and Daniel were cautious offering praise. Later, Jeanette understood their reasoning, but blamed their lack of praise for her own self-doubts about her career.

While young Jeanette was doing chores, like scrubbing floors or washing dishes, she routinely sang. She recalled that, whenever she discovered that she hit a new note, she would find it on the piano then dash off to tell her mother. Jeanette also phonetically sang along with the opera records on her neighbor's Victrola.

Jeanette wasn't pushed into show business, but performed because she liked it. Her cousin, Charles Wright, recalled seeing five-year-old Jeanette sing and dance a highland fling in a Scottish costume during amateur night at Philadelphia's Twentieth Century, a nickelodeon above Freihofer's Bakery. She beat the adult contestants, winning the $5 prize, now equivalent to about $133.

Jeanette begged to go to dancing school like her sisters and quickly won leading roles. After entertaining at amateur shows and lodges, by age eight, she was performing in Al White's children's revues, *Six Sunny Song Birds* and *Seven Merry Youngsters*, touring Vaudeville in the eastern states. At age eleven, Jeanette temporarily retired after New York's Gerry Society stopped her from performing because she was under sixteen. The MacDonalds saved what she earned, which helped pay for further musical study.

From around 1911 through 1914, young Jeanette performed in Al White's children's revues.

Early on, Jeanette knew that she wanted a career as a singer. Her sisters recalled how Jeanette said that she wanted to become famous so she could buy their mother a solid gold bed—and herself a pony. When Jeanette was twelve, she wrote an essay for school titled "Why I Want to Be a Grand Opera Star." After she became a movie star, she often said that her greatest aspiration was to do recitals, singing only with piano accompaniment, with no costumes or props, and she denied wanting to sing opera. It was only after she conquered every other medium that, during World War II, she challenged herself by studying operatic roles and singing opera. In later years, when asked what occupation she would have pursued if she hadn't gone into show business, Jeanette said that she would have liked to be a teacher, joking that it was because she liked to boss people.

From a young age, Jeanette was adamant about learning things in private so she could practice without putting herself up for public critique if she was not perfect. She learned to ride her bicycle in the backyard of the family home so her friends couldn't see her. Composer/conductor Nat Finston, who worked with Jeanette at the Capitol Theatre, Paramount, and MGM, remembered her as "a very talented woman" and "a quick study." He praised her tone production and called her "the most natural voice I've ever heard." He also recalled her desire to rehearse in private. "Whenever Jeanette had to learn something new, she'd go into her dressing room with [vocal coach Grace] Newell and stay there until she'd learn it, and then come out and do it perfectly," he said.[23] During her movie career, Jeanette took home the acetate recordings that the studio made of her songs and, while looking in the mirror, she practiced singing to them. Finston explained that she did it "to look at herself so she would be synchronized perfectly and look beautiful while doing it. She was afraid of looking ugly while she sang."[24] It was something that she learned from her early vocal coach, Ferdinand Torriani, who stressed looking beautiful while singing. Jeanette never minded visitors coming to the set when she was filming musical numbers, but preferred just the cast and crew when she did dramatic scenes.

Throughout Jeanette's life, if anyone criticized her appearance, she believed in working to improve herself. When schoolmates nicknamed her "Broomstick Legs" and teased her about her skinny limbs, she exercised by climbing stacks of books to develop her calves. After critic George Gerhard made disparaging remarks about Jeanette's on-screen appearance in *The Love Parade* (1929), she contacted cinematographer Victor Milner, who photographed her in the film. Together, they experimented on their own time. Jeanette learned the most flattering lighting, camera angles, and makeup techniques. Later, she invited Gerhard to lunch to thank him for pointing out her flaws so she could fix them. Throughout her career, she used what she learned from Milner in her movies, recitals, and stage performances, usually doing her own makeup and sometimes even fixing the lights herself. In the early days of television, she often instructed the lighting and camera technicians, and they continued to use her tips on future broadcasts.

Jeanette's philanthropic nature also developed early. During the First World War, while she was attending West Philadelphia High School for Girls, her 1B class raised money to help French and Belgian mothers and children who were left homeless and destitute after the retreat of the Huns. She also was part of a committee that sold tickets for a December 16, 1918 benefit for the Overseas Educational Reconstruction Fund.

In the fall of 1919, while Jeanette was attending high school in Philadelphia, Blossom was working as a chorus girl in *Ned Wayburn's Demi Tasse Revue*, the first stage show at the four thousand-seat Capitol Theatre, which opened on October 24 in New York, New

York. At the time, large theaters, like the Capitol, had long, elaborate performances on stage in between screenings of silent movies. When Blossom told Wayburn that he ought to see her sister, he said to bring her in for an audition. Because Blossom couldn't afford a telegram, she sent a special delivery letter to Jeanette, and she and Daniel soon arrived in New York, telling Anna that he was looking for a job there. Dolled up in makeup and her sister's clothes, sixteen-year-old Jeanette auditioned. Wayburn wasn't that impressed with her singing; however, after she fell into the orchestra pit while doing a time step and a high kick, he thought that she was an excellent comedienne. He gave her a job in the chorus for $25 a week, now equivalent to about $364. Jeanette talked him into letting her understudy prima donna Lucille Chalfant. Blossom recalled, "Imagine, in three minutes, after I'd been rehearsing the same thing for five weeks. In five minutes she put the bee on him to let her understudy for the prima donna, a fast worker. She's always been sure of herself."[25]

Jeanette appeared as an Indian girl in the musical number "In Arizona," while Will Crutchfield spun a rope and threw coffee cans at her; she also was a twinkling star in the revue's finale, "Come to the Moon," a song written by George Gershwin, Lou Paley, and Ned Wayburn. The show played four shows a day, seven days a week. Coincidentally, in 1924, the Capitol was acquired by entertainment magnate Marcus Loew; it became the flagship of the Loew's Theatre chain and premiered many MGM films, including Jeanette's.

Anna MacDonald objected to her youngest daughter moving to New York and launching a stage career. She recalled, "No matter what objection I raised, Jeanette had them over-ruled [sic]. I asked her father, and, like most fathers where girls are concerned, he left the matter up to me. I didn't want to be a foolish mother and stand in her way—maybe this *was* an opportunity—surely she must have something or she would not have been *offered* a chance when so many girls were *begging* for one. I finally let her go."[26]

The MacDonalds agreed that Jeanette could try out a career for a few weeks. Eventually, they sold the house on Arch Street and joined Jeanette and Blossom in New York. Elsie, who eloped with Earle Krout in 1911 and with Albert Ward in 1919, remained in Philadelphia with her second husband and son Earle Krout, Jr., who later changed his name to Earle Wallace. Following her second divorce, in 1934, Elsie opened The Elsie MacDonald School of Dance in Upper Darby, Pennsylvania, a western Philadelphia suburb, where she taught until 1958.

Jeanette always gave Blossom credit for helping her get started. She said, "It was Blossom who persuaded Father to let me show what I could do and it was Blossom who helped convince Father that I wasn't too young to start a career."[27]

According to biographer William Bass, when Jeanette fell off the stage during her audition, she injured her back in the area of her kidneys. A doctor told her to stop drinking coffee and the pain would go away. She stopped; however, for the rest of her life, she was plagued with back problems, often getting relief from a masseuse or chiropractor. In the Raymonds' wartime correspondence, Gene alluded to a persistent kidney or bladder infection, as well as Jeanette disliking his coffee breath.

In Philadelphia, Jeanette attended Thomas Dunlap School through eighth grade and spent three terms at West Philadelphia High School for Girls. At the time Jeanette attended, there were separate buildings for boys and girls on the same campus; later, when it became coeducational, it was known as West Philadelphia High School. Jeanette studied a commercial course, which included stenography and bookkeeping. Her stenography training may have influenced some of the spelling in her correspondence, particularly words that she repeatedly wrote phonetically, like "thot" for "thought" and "wotta" or "watta" for "what a." In high school, she participated in musical productions and was a member of the sorority Phi Sigma Alpha. She was proud of her membership and, after she moved to New York, she continued to use their stationery. In 1950, she attended a reunion of her sorority sisters.

In New York, Jeanette's parents insisted that she continue her education while she worked, and Ned Wayburn agreed. In the mornings, she attended high school and, in the afternoons and evenings, she performed onstage. In between the matinee and evening shows, she took lessons at Wayburn's dancing school, where she learned many of the expressive hand, face, and torso movements that she utilized on screen. Later, she studied with choreographer Albertina Rasch, who staged the dances for some of Jeanette's MGM films. During this time, Jeanette also worked with several voice teachers, including composer/conductor Wassili Leps, the first coach she studied with in Philadelphia. In her unpublished autobiography, she detailed some of the other voice teachers' strange methods, like balancing a full glass of water on her head during practice and holding a mirror to her lips as she sang.

Additionally, while Jeanette worked, she began a habit of absorbing all she could about lighting, staging, and choreography, often having long discussions with Ned Wayburn about his experiences in show business. William Bass noted, "[Wayburn] became the first of many such loyal male friends within the profession she would cultivate."[28] In an effort to learn as much as possible, while Jeanette worked in the theater, she befriended numerous producers, directors, actors, composers, and musicians. She said, ". . . [I] talked with them about their work and their problems. I talked until men would talk to me and I listened— listened eagerly—absorbing the masculine philosophy. I learned that men cherish friends—that is why they are so careful about making friends. They dont [sic] want to be hurt by losing a friend. And because I was not interested in any of these men as men, but only in what they could teach me, we became friends. And I found that a feeling I always had was true—that a girl of today can have men friends, good staunch men friends with no nonsense about them—if the girl is interested in them as fellow human beings and not as potential husbands."[29] During her movie career, she befriended many of her male colleagues, including singers Nelson Eddy and Allan Jones, directors Ernst Lubitsch, W.S. "Woody" Van Dyke, and Robert Z. "Pop" Leonard, makeup artist William Tuttle, and recording engineer Mike McLaughlin..

In New York, Jeanette attended two different high schools. On November 11, 1919, she transferred from West Philadelphia High School for Girls to New York's Washington Irving High School, where she was enrolled for one term in the commercial course. In February 1920, she was admitted to Julia Richman High School, where she studied commercial and academic subjects. She was a poor student in classes that she disliked, particularly math. On June 16, 1920, she quit school for the term because she was supposed to turn in written reports on nine books, but only did three. She told her friend, Florence Gleason (later Florence Gleason Robb), ". . . the teacher told me my marks and as the reports are all made out what's the use of going on till the 30th. I flunked English. Isn't that disgraceful?"[30]

On September 24, 1920, Jeanette was discharged from Julia Richman to transfer to an unnamed high school in Boston, Massachusetts, where she was playing in the touring company of *Irene*. Jeanette never returned to school; instead, she educated herself by avidly reading on a variety of subjects. Later, Jeanette said, "It was obvious, since I knew so definitely what I wanted to do, that finishing school would have been a waste of time for me. They make a girl spend so much time at studies that doesn't [sic] interest her. I particularly hated mathematics. I enjoyed geography and languages, but you can learn so much more by travel than you ever could learn from text books."[31] She studied French, anticipating that she would need it in her career. In the early 1930s, Jeanette hired a maid and chauffeur from Belgium, which helped her maintain her fluency in conversational French.

Although Jeanette didn't graduate from West Philadelphia High School for Girls, in July 1950, during a visit to her home city, she received a plaque from Joseph L. Pollack, President of the West Philadelphia High School Alumni Association, honoring her as the school's "Most Outstanding Alumna." Jeanette was modest about the honor. "Very embarrassing because I never graduated," she laughed. "I only went there six months [sic]. I explained that to them, but they said it was all right because many of their most outstanding alumnae have never graduated."[32]

Loyalty was a strong point with Jeanette; once someone was her friend, he or she usually was her friend for life. Through the years, she kept in touch with many of her Philadelphia classmates, encouraged them to visit her in New York and California, and joined them for several class reunions. Presumably, she would have been in the class of 1922. During a 1952 reunion, a reporter asked Jeanette what year she would have graduated. Always sensitive about her age, she said, "I think it's a good idea for us not to tell. It's a woman's privilege. Let's see. Say 1935. Yes, that's a good date. Make it the class of 1935."[33] Never mind that, in 1935, Jeanette was thirty-two years old and had been a movie star for six years.

Classmate Rose Landesberg Devon recalled how, despite Jeanette's fame, she remained down-to-earth: "There was never anything withheld. She was always cheerfully candid about herself and grew older (or more mature) as frankly and as openly as anyone in the theater or public life. . . . As much as anyone can leave a scene and be a part of it, Jeanette did. . . . Haughtiness was not in her. We loved her."[34] Long after Jeanette left Philadelphia, Devon's husband, Louis, owned the drugstore where Jeanette bought ice cream as a child. He recalled that, whenever he saw her during her visits to Philadelphia, she asked about former neighbors and sent them her regards. Some of Jeanette's childhood friends were invited to her wedding and were remembered in her will.

During Jeanette's early days in New York, she had few friends, which may be one of the reasons that she appreciated her Philadelphia chums. After she confided in one New York high school friend about her job, she learned that her classmates weren't allowed to associate with anyone in the theater because their parents thought that a chorus girl was one step above a prostitute. She also didn't fit in with the chorus girls, who looked down on Jeanette because of her naiveté and laughed at her cotton underwear. Later, Jeanette recalled that she spent her first paycheck on lacy lingerie to be more like her co-workers. One can't help wondering what the chorus girls thought when Jeanette went to Hollywood and became known as The Lingerie Queen. In 1937, when asked about the real starting point of her career, Jeanette recalled the cotton underwear incident. She said that the teasing from the chorus girls made her swear to show them, adding, "I think I've been trying to show them ever since."[35]

After *Ned Wayburn's Demi Tasse Revue* closed, Jeanette and Blossom were in *Ned Wayburn's Song Scenes* (1919), another revue at the Capitol Theatre. Jeanette was one of twenty dancing four-leaf clovers in a number called "Say It with Flowers." She also appeared in the production number "A Little Bit o' Scotch" as part of the ensemble.

Jeanette parlayed the chorus jobs with Wayburn into minor parts on Broadway and on tour, eventually graduating to ingénue roles. She appeared on Broadway in *The Night Boat* (1920), *Irene* (1920), *Tangerine* (1921), *A Fantastic Fricassee* (1922), *The Magic Ring* (1923), *Tip-Toes* (1925), and *Yes, Yes, Yvette* (1927), sometimes touring in the shows as well. Her chorus role in *The Night Boat* included a number with three other girls and four of Jud Brady's Famous Collies, ideal for the lifelong dog lover. In a letter to her friend, Florence Gleason, Jeanette drew a diagram to illustrate how they stood.

Jeanette often understudied the leading ladies in her shows and bemoaned the fact that they didn't miss performances so she could do their roles. Later, she was glad that she never went on for Stella Hoban in *The Night Boat*. "I used to think I should have one of those overnight successes if only I got my chance," she said. "It was lucky for me that the chance never arrived. I was still in my teens and the star role was that of a sophisticated married woman. I would have looked too ridiculous."[36]

In August 1922, *Variety* claimed that Jeanette planned to replace Edna Bates in a tour of the musical *For Goodness Sake* (1922); however, subsequent newspaper reviews did not list Jeanette in the cast. Presumably, she went into the Broadway company of *A Fantastic Fricassee* instead. In 1926, she briefly toured in the musical *Bubbling Over*, which closed before it reached Broadway. She is pictured in a bubble on song sheets from the show.

Usually, Jeanette's performances garnered positive notices, but the shows closed quickly. At the time, productions often had lengthy engagements in Chicago, Illinois, and sometimes toured to other cities before or after their Broadway runs. In the case of *Irene*, which held the record for long runs for eighteen years, the show's Broadway success led to several touring companies, which played other cities at the same time as the musical's New York run. In early August 1920, Jeanette joined the Broadway cast, appearing in the chorus for a week while she learned her first big part, Eleanor Worth, a secondary character who sang two songs. She briefly appeared in the role in New York before joining what was called the Chicago Company a few weeks later. That way, press agents could advertise that she was from the Broadway cast. The first city that she played was Boston, replacing Bernice McCabe, who played Eleanor on Broadway before and after Jeanette. On tour, Jeanette also was understudy for Helen Shipman, who played the title role.

Jeanette inscribed this mid-1920s portrait to Edith Martin, who was in the chorus of *Tip-Toes*. It read "To Edith. We're bound to have a third season together and I hope so for you're a dear. Lovingly, Jeannette." When she signed photos, Jeanette tended to use fans' first and last names, but often used only first names with friends and family.

During Jeanette's brief engagement in the Broadway production of *Irene*, she met actress Irene Dunne, who, for a short time, played the title character in New York, before joining another touring company.

Jeanette and Irene became lifelong friends and, after both became movie stars, they often socialized, along with their husbands. In 1936, Jeanette played the title role in a *Lux Radio Theatre* adaptation of *Irene*.

During the 1927 tour of *Yes, Yes, Yvette,* Jeanette was involved in various publicity campaigns to promote the musical. In March, she modeled "Victrix" Hats with chorus girls from the show at The Fair, a Chicago department store. The hats were made of felt and were styled close to the head, like a cloche. In April, Jeanette and cast member Amy Revere, who sometimes roomed with Jeanette on the road, drove the Electric Red Bug, a small, economical open-air car, through the streets of Boston, with a sign promoting the show. In May, Jeanette flew with Lieutenant R.E. Cobb, dropping flyers over Boston for "Rose Day," which raised money for the Soldiers and Sailors Club to help wounded veterans.

In 1923, in the midst of Jeanette's Broadway career, her singing voice almost was destroyed by a botched tonsillectomy, which damaged one of the muscular pillars in her throat. At the suggestion of Phoebe Crosby, who played her mother in *The Magic Ring,* Jeanette began studying with vocal teacher Ferdinand Torriani, and her voice was restored. After his 1926 death, Jeanette worked with his assistant, Grace Adele Newell, who continued teaching his technique, which involved exercising the muscles in the throat and diaphragm.

Through the years, Grace became like a second mother to Jeanette, and Grace, who never married, said that she thought of Jeanette and Gene as her children. During the lessons, Jeanette and Grace often argued; however, they always ended each session with a hug. Jeanette took Grace to Hollywood with her, where director Ernst Lubitsch jokingly called her Jeanette's morals teacher because Grace insisted that smoking, drinking, and late hours could harm her pupil's voice. According to singer Ken Richards, a fan who became Jeanette's friend, Grace was fond of Early Times bourbon and didn't practice what she told her students.

Although Jeanette followed Grace's rules when she was working, she was not the teetotaler that she was portrayed as in the movie magazines, where her image was dictated by the studio. In her unpublished autobiography, she admitted to smoking several cigarettes once and getting drunk once, both of which made her sick. In 1920s correspondence with ex-boyfriend Irving Stone, she mentioned drinking port wine. She also smoked briefly in her first movie, *The Love Parade* (1929). Although Jeanette usually asked strangers not to smoke around her, before or after a recital, she never objected to Blossom, Gene, or friends like directors Ernst Lubitsch, Woody Van Dyke, and Robert Z. Leonard, singer Nelson Eddy, actor Frank Morgan, secretary Emily Wentz, or business manager/fiancé Bob Ritchie smoking. She also didn't object to drinking. Jeanette kept a well-stocked bar and plenty of cigarettes for guests, and often gave friends and crew members alcohol for Christmas. In a 1935 letter to Gene, she jokingly called Woody Van Dyke "such a drunkard"[37] and, in her unpublished autobiography, she recalled how the *Rose-Marie* (1936) crew played a practical joke on the director by substituting mineral oil for his customary gin. She told reporter Ida Zeitlin, "I've been known to take a glass of sherry. But sherry makes my nose itch, and you can't be talking to someone at dinner, and rubbing at your nose the whole time."[38] In a 1956 interview, Jeanette said that one of her voice teachers told her, "A voice is one thing that cannot be preserved in alcohol." She also claimed, "It makes me sick."[39] As noted in Jeanette and Gene's wartime correspondence, she drank socially, but not to excess, and seldom when she was working.

When Jeanette moved from Paramount to MGM, she convinced the studio to hire Grace Newell. She coached many famous pupils, including Irene Dunne, Bebe Daniels, Allan Jones, and Jane Powell. In addition to taking vocal lessons at Grace's studio, when Jeanette was filming, she often took lessons in her dressing room during her lunch hour. She was loyal to Grace and continued to study with her until the voice teacher retired in the 1950s, when she was well into her eighties. In 1952, Jeanette said, "She is an older woman now, but one of the youngest people I have ever known in outlook and interests."[40] After Jeanette stopped performing publicly, to keep her voice in shape, she continued to vocalize and learn new songs. In a 1937 interview, she said, "A voice is simply a musical instrument. To use it correctly requires constant practice, just as does playing a violin or piano. A singer can never afford to get the idea that she has learned and practiced all she needs to."[41] Grace often celebrated holidays with Jeanette and Gene, and was part of their surrogate family, along with Jeanette's longtime friend and secretary, Emily Wentz.

In the early 1920s, Jeanette met Emily through their mutual friend, Eleanor Uehlinger, when Jeanette and Emily both were appearing on Broadway. Emily was born in Brooklyn, New York, exactly two weeks before Jeanette. Coincidentally, Emily's middle name was Macdonald. They sometimes dined together between the matinee and evening performances of their shows and frequently double dated. Emily had a fine contralto voice and often worked for theatrical impresario Samuel "Roxy" Rothafel, who produced live shows at New York's Roxy Theatre and Radio City Music Hall. Emily preferred singing in groups, as solo work made her nervous. Like Jeanette, Emily studied with Grace Newell. The two pupils frequently joked about Grace's order to "vitalize."[42]

In December 1936, Emily and her mother went to California to spend Christmas with Emily's older brother. They planned to stay through Jeanette's June wedding; however, Emily's mother liked California so much that they decided to make it their permanent home. Jeanette helped Emily find work as a singer and extra at MGM and as a singer in the chorus when Jeanette appeared on the radio. Although Emily said that the extras tried to hide their faces so they could appear in multiple scenes, a quick eye can spot her in *Sweethearts* (1938), *New Moon* (1940), and *I Married an Angel* (1942). She also can be seen as a member of the church choir in a still from *Smilin' Through* (1941). Emily recalled, "Of course, the Studios [sic] have their 'regulars' and would try to skip calling me. However, Jeanette would look around the set and if she didn't see me she would have them call me to be on the set immediately. Her loyalty in this respect was evident, as you would see the same people on each picture. This applied to her stand-in, hairdresser, wardrobe, etc. Everyone loved to be on her pictures as they loved her and the work usually ran for months."[43] Emily said that she appeared in all of Jeanette's pictures through 1942, beginning with *The Firefly* (1937).

Emily also worked part-time for Jeanette, helping her secretaries, Sylvia Grogg (later known as Sylvia Grogg Wright), Eleanor Payne, Grace Smyth, and Britann Laymon, with fan mail at their Sunset Boulevard office. In 1942, when Grogg left to help Jeanette's concert manager, Jeanette convinced Emily to become her full-time head secretary, although, by then, Emily had a wartime job at Douglas Aircraft. Since Jeanette was planning a recital tour to benefit Army Emergency Relief, she called Colonel Stevenson, head of the personnel department at Douglas. Despite the fact that all war plant employees were frozen in their jobs, Jeanette pulled strings and obtained Emily's release. Emily said it helped that Colonel Stevenson was a Jeanette fan. Having been in show business herself, Emily understood how to handle many situations that the average secretary would not. Interestingly, Emily worked for—or with—all three MacDonald sisters. In the 1930s, she was in a stage show with Blossom and, in 1936, Emily worked briefly at Elsie's dancing and dramatic school in Pennsylvania.

Jeanette (right) helped Emily Wentz (left) get singing jobs before Emily became her full-time secretary. In 1937 and 1938, she was part of the vocal ensemble on Jeanette's radio series *Vicks Open House*. Here, they relaxed before a broadcast.

On March 11, 1943, Emily's mother died. Jeanette invited Emily to move into one of the apartments above the Raymonds' garage, where Jeanette's personal maid, Rose Coen, and her husband, Henri, who sometimes acted as Jeanette's chauffeur and hairdresser, also lived. For the next twenty years, Emily resided there. From the 1940s through 1959, she traveled with Jeanette, handling secretarial duties, arranging press conferences, acting as a liaison with fans, and sometimes serving as Jeanette's dresser. Emily often acted as the fall guy backstage, reminding Jeanette of other commitments when she was too polite to tell fans that she needed to leave. Beginning in 1945, Emily used the professional name West because she found Wentz was too hard for many people to understand, particularly over the telephone, and she tired of spelling it for them. Through the years, Jeanette and Emily became as close as sisters. When Emily died, Gene reiterated that she was family to the Raymonds.

There was always lots of humor and music in the MacDonald home, even when their finances were unstable. Daniel, who had been in building construction and dabbled in Philadelphia politics, had a difficult time finding a job in New York, so Blossom and Jeanette often supported the family.

In the 1920s, Emily spent many pleasant times at the MacDonalds' New York apartment, enjoying Daniel's delightful sense of humor, a trait his youngest daughter inherited. Emily recalled, "He was always cracking jokes and trying to make us laugh. Sometimes he'd tell slightly naughty, harmless stories and jokes, but nothing vulgar. I remember many times at dinner seeing Mrs. MacDonald's stomach jiggling under the table from laughter when she tried not to laugh at such jokes."[44] As evidenced in the Raymonds' wartime correspondence, Jeanette also appreciated double entendre.

Herbert Ohmeis, younger brother of Jeanette's first fiancé, was less impressed with Daniel, whom Herbert met at the age of nineteen when the MacDonalds visited the Ohmeis family in 1923. Fifty-five years later, he described Daniel as "a pleasant enough man but rather on the mediocre side. I gathered he had a managerial position with a building supply company and sort of fit the image. Not too self-possessing and was dominated by Mrs. MacDonald. When he and Dad were alone, conversing, he did not lend much to the conversation, was somewhat ill-at-ease and appeared a bit out of his element. He loved his family, was proud of his daughters and was providing for them all to the best of his ability. But he was a plain man, and did not project a particularly successful image. Jeanette and he did not seem to be very close, for some reason."[45] Despite Ohmeis' assessment of the father/

daughter relationship, when Daniel died, there was only one photograph in his wallet: a picture of Jeanette. In her autobiography, she told several sweet stories about her father, and she regretted that he did not live to see her success on screen.

According to William Bass, the MacDonalds were "very conservative, religious and clannish, traits that would stay with Jeanette throughout her life. . . . She rarely confided in anyone unless they were clan, or adopted by friendship into the clan. Very few people would ever get to know Jeanette MacDonald intimately. Her cautiousness in friendships and intimacies grew out of her nature, the family tradition, and out of her own personal discipline."[46] One can't help wondering if she also was cautious about confiding in casual friends because of her experience with her New York high school classmates.

Additionally, Bass said that the MacDonald women all were very opinionated and frequently got into heated discussions on a subject, with none of them agreeing. Daniel wisely tried to stay out of their arguments. Bass added, "Despite this tendency to disagree completely and vociferously among each other, there still grew a deep and lasting bond of love and devotion among the four women. In later years, husbands and friends could never get over the fact that two, three, or all four of the MacDonald women could get heated about a subject under discussion, only to later sit down to dinner and laugh all the way through it as though they had not ever had any disagreements."[47] These friendly arguments influenced Jeanette's feelings on how to handle problems in her marriage. She liked to openly discuss issues to work through them, while Gene preferred to ignore them.

Jeanette also was very straightforward, a trait she inherited from both parents. Although some thought that she sometimes was too blunt, Maurine Loomis, who worked as an extra on Jeanette's

Paramount films, as her lighting stand-in at MGM, and later as her portrait photographer, admired the trait. She said, "You always knew where you stood with Jeanette."[48]

Despite the fact that Jeanette later said that her parents were not demonstrative—to each other or their daughters—it was clear that they cared a great deal for one another. On August 1, 1924, Daniel died of myocarditis, an inflammation of the middle layer of the heart wall, at the age of fifty-five. Three days later, he was buried in the Wright family plot in Philadelphia's Mount Peace Cemetery, Section N, Lot 242, Grave 4, #1. Anna's parents, brother, and paternal grandmother also are interred there. The marker lists Daniel's birth and death years, along with those of Anna's parents. After Jeanette heard Anna call Daniel "darling" for the first time when she kissed his corpse, Jeanette realized just how much her parents loved each other. Touched by their deep but unspoken affection, Jeanette vowed to herself never to casually call anyone "darling." She often described herself as undemonstrative, unable to kiss, hug, or act effusive with casual friends like Gene did. However, as photos prove, she seemed to have no problem hugging, kissing, or showing affection with close friends or colleagues, like Grace Newell, Irene Dunne, Jane Powell, Ernst Lubitsch, Nelson Eddy, James Stewart, Louis B. Mayer, and Johnny Mack Brown.

Another event that affected Jeanette's views on love and marriage was her sister Elsie's 1911 elopement. Despite Jeanette's young age, she understood how much the secret marriage hurt her parents. Anna assured Jeanette and Blossom that she never would try to stop them, but made each of them promise that they never would run away to get married. Jeanette observed, "I gained some early knowledge of the importance of a good marriage and the agony of a bad one. When the inevitable divorce put an end to Elsie's marriage, Mother's embarrassment at the disgrace of divorce, too, impressed me with the need for making a marriage stick."[49] In 1920, Jeanette advised one of her Philadelphia high school friends, Florence Gleason, not to marry without first consulting her mother—and Jeanette. Gleason waited six years to get married; it isn't known if she confided in Jeanette. Later, when Elsie eloped and divorced a second time, Jeanette said that she began to fear falling in love.

In 1926, Blossom married her Vaudeville partner, Clarence Warren "Rocky" Rock; Jeanette sang at the wedding. The Rocks remained together until his death in 1960. After he retired from acting in 1942, he became Night Manager at the Beverly Hills Hotel. From 1956 to 1958, he was Managing Director at the Hollywood Knickerbocker Hotel. Because of his job, he sometimes missed family holiday celebrations. Like Jeanette and Gene, the Rocks had no children.

After Daniel's death, Jeanette said that she became closer to her mother. When Jeanette appeared in touring shows, Anna sometimes went on the road with her. When Jeanette moved to Hollywood, Anna joined her and, until Jeanette's marriage, they shared a series of rented houses. Anna also accompanied Jeanette to Europe twice.

In 1939, Jeanette told a reporter, "I could always talk over anything with my parents—my mother. Anything at all."[50] In a 1936 interview, she said, "Mother trusts me, and I believe in her. Naturally, I handle my own business affairs now that I'm grown up, but I consult her almost always, confide in her. My career has always been the most important thing for me, and her keen judgement and complete confidence have helped make it possible."[51] In 1941, Jeanette said, "She hasn't interfered or bossed. She has been a wise, guiding mother. She's always been there the few times I've really been in trouble and needed her help."[52] Before Jeanette's marriage, she often included Anna when she went to movies or parties, with or without a date. After her marriage, while Gene was working or serving in the military, Jeanette occasionally traveled or vacationed with Anna. According to William Bass, Jeanette frequently boasted, "She was more than my mother—she was my friend."[53]

Before air conditioning was prevalent, theaters usually closed for the summer. In between stage jobs, Jeanette modeled for Bergdorf Goodman department store and furrier C.C. Shayne & Co. for print ads that would run later in the year. When her finances were more secure, she took a tip from Mitzi Hajos, star of *The Magic Ring*, and, once a year, bought herself an elaborate gift. Mitzi, who usually was billed without her last name, told Jeanette that she bought herself an expensive "I–Owe–Me" present every year, "That way, no dirty old man will ever have an I.O.U. on me!"[54] In addition to a mink coat and various pieces of jewelry, Jeanette bought herself a custom-made Packard car. She also admired the way that Mitzi was kind to her fans, and Jeanette adopted the same attitude.

Jeanette realized that show business could be financially precarious. She reasoned that, if she could give an agent 10% of her income, she also could put away 10% for herself. Aside from her first mink coat, which she charged, she tried to pay cash for everything so she would not spend beyond her means. She frequently joked about her frugality, a trait stereotypically attributed to those of Scottish descent. Through the years, Jeanette was generous to a great many people, often anonymously, but even as one of the highest paid actresses in Hollywood, she maintained her frugal outlook and cut corners whenever she could. Longtime fan Betty Bradley recalled Jeanette sending Emily out to buy a dress between the matinee and evening performances of *The Guardsman* (1951) because Jeanette knew, if she went in the store, they would charge her more. Ken Richards said that, when Jeanette needed Spanish lessons, she had Emily call for a price, not mentioning that the lessons were for Jeanette.

In the 1920s, in the summer, between Broadway assignments, Jeanette modeled fur coats. This photo was for New York furrier C.C. Shayne & Co.

From the 1920s through the 1960s, Jeanette appeared on many radio broadcasts, including musical shows, like *Paramount–Publix Hour* (1929 and 1930), *The Camel Pleasure Hour* (1930, 1931, and 1932), and

The Electric Hour (1945 and 1946), and dramatic programs, like *Lux Radio Theatre* (1936, 1937, 1942, and 1944) and *Screen Guild Theater* (1939, 1946, 1947, and 1950). She also was on charitable broadcasts and was interviewed to promote her movies, records, recitals, and stage performances. Some were national broadcasts and others were done while she was on tour. Interestingly, in the early 1930s, she sang songs, like "Italian Street Song" and "Songs My Mother Taught Me," that she later sang on screen. Her earliest documented radio appearance was on May 12, 1927, when she sang with other *Yes, Yes, Yvette* cast members on Boston's WNAC to promote the show. On October 13, 1927, the cast also appeared on *Broadway Nite* [sic] over New York's WMCA. It isn't known what she was paid for her early broadcasts; however, in the 1930s through the late 1940s, she generally earned $2,500 to $5,000 per broadcast, depending on the length and how much she sang, now about $26,000 to $91,000 per show.

In the fall of 1927, Jeanette's positive reviews in the Broadway and pre-Broadway touring productions of *Yes, Yes, Yvette* led to a contract with producing brothers Jacob J. "J.J." and Lee Shubert, whose theater empire was the largest in the twentieth century. On November 7, 1927, two days after *Yes, Yes, Yvette* closed, she signed a contract that ran through September 1, 1928. It also gave the Shuberts an option for a nine-month renewal. The contract guaranteed her twenty-five weeks' work at $700 a week and $900 a week if her option was renewed. Those figures are now about $10,000 and $13,000 a week. It meant that she no longer had to audition for roles or model fur coats since she would receive a weekly paycheck. The contract also had the stipulation that she could not perform on radio or in the movies without the written consent of the Shuberts.

Jeanette in a scene from *Sunny Days* (1928) with Carl Randall. Photo from the Brent Perry collection.

A week after Jeanette signed the contract, she opened in Philadelphia in *The Studio Girl* (1927), a musical version of George Du Maurier's novel *Trilby* that closed before it reached New York. During the time that she was with the Shuberts, she worked almost continuously. She appeared on Broadway in *Sunny Days* (1928), *Angela* (1928), and *Boom-Boom* (1929), touring in the shows as well. She was featured in ads for Lux Toilet Soap (1928), Fralinger's Original Salt Water Taffy (1928), C/B a la Spirite Corsets (1928), and Flash De Luxe Hand Cream (1929), each of which mentioned her current show.

While Jeanette was working on Broadway, she made screen tests for Warner Bros. (December 1927), Paramount (December 1928), and Fox (January or February 1929); however, the Shuberts refused to release her from her contract. In later years, Jeanette was vocal about her affection for Lee Shubert and her dislike for his brother, whom she had to deal with more often since J.J. handled the musical productions. When actor Richard Dix wanted her to appear in the film *Nothing but the Truth* (1929), the Shuberts asked $75,000, now about $1.1 million, for her release. Paramount thought that was too much to risk on a newcomer and passed on the offer. Jeanette blamed J.J. Shubert for the missed opportunity. Shubert wasn't picking on Jeanette; he was angry about the Hollywood studios raiding his Broadway casts for the movies.

Jeanette also disliked J.J. Shubert for casting her in *Boom-Boom*, as she felt the show was risqué and unfunny, and the role did not suit her image. In it, her character was described as having been born with a silver flask in her mouth, implying that she came from a wealthy family and liked to drink, and she was forced to become her sweetheart's stepmother.

Archie Leach, one of the actors in *Boom-Boom*, appeared with Jeanette in her Fox screen test. Although the studio wasn't interested in either actor, later, like Jeanette, Leach went to Hollywood, where he changed his name to Cary Grant and had a long and successful screen career. He and Jeanette generally did not travel in the same social circles; however, he attended a December 1945 party that she and

Gene hosted in honor of General Jonathan Wainwright, as Grant was one of the General's favorite actors.

On April 29, 1929, the day after *Boom-Boom* opened in Chicago, Jeanette wrote a letter to J.J. Shubert, telling him that she was quitting the show when her contract expired on May 30, giving him plenty of time to replace her. In various other sources, including Jeanette's autobiography, she claimed that her contract expired June 1. After she sent the letter, she was slightly concerned, as she didn't know how leaving the Shuberts would affect her Broadway career and feared that the producers might spread rumors that she was temperamental. A few days later, she received a call from her manager, Bob Ritchie, who told her that director Ernst Lubitsch had seen her Paramount screen test and wanted to discuss a movie role with her over breakfast the following Sunday on his way back to Hollywood.

Lubitsch had been in New York, looking for a leading lady to star opposite French entertainer Maurice Chevalier in Lubitsch's first sound film, *The Love Parade*, which also was the screen's first original operetta. *The Love Parade* was about a queen who married a rogue and, as prince consort, he revolted because he had nothing to do. Lubitsch attended Broadway shows and viewed screen tests, searching for a star for his film. He rejected many actresses, but saw a quality that he liked in Jeanette's test. When he heard her sing, he knew that he had found his queen.

Around May 8, Lubitsch stopped in Chicago for a couple of hours, reserving a suite at the Blackstone Hotel. He arranged for breakfast to be served in his suite so that he and Jeanette could talk privately about *The Love Parade*. He not only told her the plot, but acted out various roles and sang some of the songs for her. After their conversation, she gave Lubitsch an oral agreement to be in the movie. Lubitsch thought that she was too thin and ordered her to gain ten or fifteen pounds. Jeanette wondered how she would have time to spend several weeks at the New Jersey milk farm she previously visited to gain weight, since her Shubert contract didn't expire until May 30 and Lubitsch wanted her in Hollywood in early June. Nevertheless, she told Bob Ritchie to negotiate a contract with Paramount, which she signed after she returned to New York. Her salary was $2,500 a week for *The Love Parade*, now about $36,800, and the contract included an option for a second movie.

In her autobiography, Jeanette said that she was so worried about getting permission from the Shuberts to leave early that she made herself half-way sick. Jack Garrity, the Shuberts' Chicago General Manager, sympathized with her and told J.J. Shubert that she was very ill, which led to the producers releasing her from her contract a few weeks early. Correspondence to ex-boyfriend Irving Stone implied that she feigned illness with the help of a doctor to expedite her release. Had she left while still under contract, she would have been required to pay the Shuberts 25% of her movie salary and they could have banned her from working for a year. It is unclear exactly when Jeanette left *Boom-Boom*; however, the May 22, 1929 issue of *Variety* noted that she was replaced by Marcella Swanson. Both Garrity and Lubitsch remained close friends and were mentioned in the Raymonds' wartime letters.

While Jeanette was at the milk farm, she developed what she described to Irving Stone as a cold in her kidneys and in her autobiography as colitis, an inflammation of the inner lining of the colon; she ended up losing more weight than she gained. She suggested to Irving that it might have been divine retribution for lying about her health to the Shuberts. In early June, Jeanette and Anna headed to Hollywood by train. In Jeanette's autobiography, she said that she always had a soft spot in her heart for Chicago because it was where her life changed forever.

Chapter Two

Jeanette had no great aspirations to go into the movies and admitted that she was motivated solely by the money, which was $1,600 a week more than she was making with the Shuberts. Currently, that would be over $23,000 more a week. According to some reports, she flipped a coin to decide whether or not to go to Hollywood.

Jeanette started her film career at the top, as the lead in a major hit musical. *The Love Parade* was nominated for six Academy Awards: Best Picture, Best Director (Ernst Lubitsch), Best Actor (Maurice Chevalier), Best Cinematography (Victor Milner), Best Art Direction (Hans Dreier), and Best Sound Recording (Franklin Hansen). It lost all six nominations. The movie catapulted Jeanette to fame, landing her on magazine covers all over the world. In addition to the United States, through the years, she was on covers in England, France, Belgium, Hungary, Yugoslavia, Spain, Sweden, Brazil, Finland, Italy, Portugal, Argentina, Romania, Austria, Canada, Czechoslovakia, Japan, Croatia, Denmark, Germany, Australia, and the Netherlands—and probably many other countries.

Interestingly, around the same time that Lubitsch signed Jeanette to a contract, director James Cruze tried to get the Shuberts to release her to appear in *The Great Gabbo* (1929) opposite Erich von Stroheim, and MGM also tried to put her under contract. One can't help wondering if Jeanette would have achieved the same early popularity without Lubitsch guiding her screen persona, which often involved playing royalty or upper class women. Under his guidance, she appeared naïve yet sexy, always showing a joie de vivre on screen. He was able to bring out her natural ability for playing the absurd.

Jeanette never failed to credit Lubitsch for her success. "I started right at the top in pictures, which I have sometimes thought might have been a disadvantage," she said. "However, it was a great advantage, because had I started with any other director other than the wonderful Lubitsch, I might not have fared as well as I did. I had the advantage of his greatness."[55] Maurine Loomis claimed, "Jeanette's personality in the Lubitsch films was more like she was in real life."[56] Although Loomis did not elaborate, many thought that Jeanette's non-Lubitsch characters took themselves too seriously and lacked the light humor found in the films he directed. Both Jeanette and Gene often remarked on the importance of humor in marriage.

In 1931, when Jeanette was asked about her career, she said, "I feel my metier for the screen is romance with comedy. I'm more interested in stories than salary. Given good stories the salary just naturally follows."[57] Throughout her career, Jeanette continued to focus on solid stories and complained about the bad scripts that she was offered.

From June 1929 to October 1930, Jeanette was under contract to Paramount, where, in addition to *The Love Parade* (1929) with Maurice Chevalier, she made *The Vagabond King* (1930) with Dennis King, *Let's Go Native* (1930) with Jack Oakie and Kay Francis, and *Monte Carlo* (1930) with Jack Buchanan and ZaSu Pitts. Additionally, Jeanette filmed scenes for the all-star revue *Paramount on Parade* (1930); however, all but a long shot were cut before the film's release.

There is some debate over whether she remained in foreign issues of the movie. The UCLA Film & Television Archive restored the revue, including some Technicolor scenes, but several sequences remain lost.

Between 1929 and 1958, Jeanette recorded over fifty songs for RCA Victor and its British and French affiliates, His Master's Voice (HMV) and Disque Gramophone. Some songs later were reissued on LPs on RCA's Camden label. Her first selections were "March of the Grenadiers" and "Dream Lover" from *The Love Parade*. Her contracts allowed her to choose the material that she recorded, usually a mixture of songs from her movies and pieces that she performed in her recitals, subject to RCA's approval. Professional loyalty was important to Jeanette. She remained with the label for the rest of her career.

The early 1930s were a difficult time for the motion picture industry. With the advent of sound, many theaters closed, and a plethora of silent stars lost their popularity because they had thick foreign accents, their voices were not pleasing on screen, or their voices didn't match their images. After the foreign release of *The Love Parade*, Nat Finston recalled sitting in on a production conference, where studio founder Jesse Lasky told financial advisor Sam Katz, "We're keeping open the doors of Paramount because Jeanette is singing!"[58] Despite that statement, and the fact that Jeanette was one of the screen's first female singing stars, when musicals declined in popularity, Paramount lost interest in her. The studio didn't pick up her option because executives couldn't imagine her in a non-singing role.

After Jeanette left Paramount, she made *The Lottery Bride* with comic actors Joe E. Brown and ZaSu Pitts, which was released by United Artists in 1930. The melodramatic operetta had a Technicolor finale. Between December 1930 and May 1931, Jeanette was in three films for Fox: *Oh, for a Man!* (1930) with Reginald Denny and a pre-*Dracula* Bela Lugosi, *Don't Bet on Women* (1931) with Edmund Lowe, and *Annabelle's Affairs* (1931) with Victor McLaglen and Sally Blane. As of this writing, *Annabelle's Affairs* is considered lost, as all that remains is one reel of the eight-reel comedy. Although *Oh, for a Man!* featured one of the earliest opera excerpts in a sound film, Jeanette's singing of "Liebestod" from Richard Wagner's *Tristan und Isolde*, none of these pictures advanced her career.

Interestingly, part of Jeanette's contract with Fox included the clause that MGM could borrow her for a remake of Franz Lehár's operetta *The Merry Widow*. However, MGM didn't make the movie until 1934, after Jeanette already was under contract. In 1931, there also was talk of her doing *The Merry Widow* on stage in Paris, a project that never materialized.

In Jeanette's autobiography, she said that, when she was young, she alternated between pretending which of two neighborhood boys was the father of her dolls; however, in high school, she wasn't popular with the opposite sex. In a 1937 interview, she recalled how a boy stood her up when he was supposed to escort her to a birthday party. The next day, when she met him on the school grounds and asked where he was the night before, he told her to go to hell. Some years later, when Jeanette was on the stage, he called her for a date. When he asked if she remembered him, Jeanette countered, "Do *you* remember what you yelled at me one day at school?" He responded, "I told you to go to hell, didn't I?" Jeanette got in the last word: "And that's what I'm telling you" and hung up the phone.[59]

During Jeanette's Broadway years, she called herself "a confirmed face slapper." She claimed that she refused to kiss any man unless she loved him. "If I was attracted . . . then I'd enjoy his kisses. But if any man thought I must be 'easy' because I was in the theatre, then I fought like a hellcat." She recalled, "I picked up my share of marriage proposals, too. Most of them came from men older than I was, men I suspected didn't love me. They wanted to latch on to me, a girl with a future, and make something out of it for themselves. I despised them more than the out-and-out propositioners [sic] who ran like rabbits at the idea of marrying anybody."[60]

In the 1920s, Jeanette was involved romantically with three men, all of whom were handsome and clean cut, like Gene Raymond. Around 1922, she met New York University architecture student John "Jack" Marcellus Ohmeis (November 25, 1901–September 18, 1967) at the Beaux Arts Ball, a raucous costume party that sheltered Jeanette compared to an orgy. Jack turned out to be one of the few gentlemen there, and they began dating. He was the son of a wealthy bottle manufacturer and introduced Jeanette to society life. Eventually, they became engaged, although, throughout much of their relationship, Jeanette was on the road with various musicals. She refused to give up her career for marriage. In a 1936 *Photoplay Magazine* interview, Jeanette said that Jack asked her to elope, but, since she promised her parents that she would consult them first, she refused. After being away from Jack for a year while she was on tour, she realized that her feelings had changed and she was glad that she had not married him. In the spring of 1927, they broke their engagement, although occasionally, they still dated.

In a 1937 interview, Jeanette recalled the romance. "When I was very young I fell deeply in love. It was a question, then, of fulfillment of this love or giving it up for a career I had planned and always dreamed about. Looking back now, I don't think I would have been happy with that man. We always see things more sanely if we wait until the first wild glamour has left us. . . . I regard marriage as important . . . therefore, before I ever take such a serious step, there will be much to ponder and consider."[61]

In the mid-1920s, Jeanette was engaged to Jack Ohmeis, son of a wealthy bottle manufacturer.

After the 1929 stock market crash, Jeanette loaned Jack $2,500 (now equivalent to about $36,800), which he repaid in the 1950s. For many years, Jack owned a Chevrolet dealership in Oneonta, New York. In late 1949, he moved to the Virgin Islands, hoping that the climate would help his wife's health. In 1959, Jeanette last saw Jack in New York, presumably, to make sure that he had no objections to being mentioned in her autobiography. In some earlier magazine interviews, she gave him a pseudonym to protect his privacy. Jack's sister, Elizabeth "Lee" Ohmeis Batchelder, loaned Jeanette photos of Jeanette and Jack for use in the book. Both women were surprised that there were not more pictures of the couple together.

In September or October of 1924, during the Chicago run of *The Magic Ring*, Jeanette met Irving Calvin Stone (December 22, 1901– January 3, 1968) at a North Shore society dinner dance. At the time, she was still engaged to Jack Ohmeis, and Irving was a newlywed. A few months earlier, on April 17, 1924, he married Rosina Wolff, the daughter of a wealthy druggist, in Crown Point, Indiana, a popular elopement spot for Chicago residents, since there was no waiting period for a marriage license and Crown Point is right across the Illinois border. There was nothing clandestine about Jeanette's relationship with Irving, as she knew his wife, parents, sister, and cousins, and he affectionately called Anna "Aunt Annie."

From the tone of the earliest surviving letters from Jeanette to Irving, it sounded like they began as friends, as she mentioned Jack Ohmeis, as well as Irving's wife. It is unclear whether Jeanette and Rosina also were friends, as the Stones divorced in 1927, around the time that Irving began saving Jeanette's correspondence. In a letter dated April 26, 1927, Jeanette wrote that she was sorry that Irving's marriage was ending—unless he was not, and then she was happy for him. In two August 1928 letters, Jeanette implied that Rosina might want to reconcile with Irving, and Jeanette seemed jealous, but in a letter dated August 24, 1929, she suggested that Rosina call her while she was visiting in California. Rosina remarried in 1932; Irving remained single.

When Irving met Jeanette, he was a real estate broker in Chicago. In 1925, he moved to Milwaukee, Wisconsin, where he and his brother-in-law, Charles Wirth, operated Wirth–Stone & Co., a real estate and investment firm. In 1928, Irving began working in the personnel department at the Boston Store, a Milwaukee department store co-founded by his uncle, Nat Stone, who was then President. Presumably, Irving continued to sell real estate, as, in the 1930 census, he listed real estate broker as his occupation. After Nat's 1931 death, his nephew, I. Stanley Stone, succeeded him as President. Stanley and his cousin Irving were close and, later in 1931, Irving became one of two Merchandise Managers at the store; eventually, he served on the Managing Committee.

In the 1920s, Irving Stone, Merchandise Manager of the Boston Store in Milwaukee, dated Jeanette. Photo courtesy of the University of Wisconsin–Milwaukee Libraries, Archives Department.

During Jeanette's relationship with Irving, she was honest with him about dating other men. It was even more of a long distance relationship than the one between Jeanette and Jack Ohmeis, as

Jeanette and Irving only saw each other when she played Chicago or Milwaukee, or he visited New York. In 1930, after she became engaged for a second time, she and Irving remained friends. They continued to correspond, even after her marriage to Gene, her third fiancé. She also kept in touch with Irving's parents. Interestingly, long before she met Gene, she told Irving that she never would marry an actor or get married in June, fearing her husband would give her one gift for her birthday and anniversary.

Jeanette invited Irving to her wedding, but he did not attend. At the end of 1937, Jeanette and Gene sent Irving a telegram, wishing him a happy New Year. On March 9, 1938, Irving was a guest at a dinner party that the Raymonds hosted at their home. The Stone family was mentioned in one of Gene's wartime letters, replying to a disapproving comment that Jeanette made about their war efforts. On September 7, 1947, Irving attended a party that the Raymonds gave in honor of General Ira Eaker, Commander of the VIII Bomber Command, in which Gene served during World War II. Through the 1950s, Irving attended some of Jeanette's Chicago and Milwaukee performances, and she often saw him when she visited both cities. According to William Bass, "The Boston Store employees always knew when Jeanette was in town for Stone would stroll up and down every aisle in the store with Jeanette on his arm showing off to his gawking employees and customers that he was a friend of Jeanette MacDonald."[62]

Although Irving's birthday was still listed in Jeanette's 1963 date book, she did not mention him in her autobiography. It isn't known whether he refused to give permission, if she felt that the relationship was not significant enough to discuss, or if she didn't want to look like she had too many beaus before she met Gene. It also isn't known if religion would have been a problem for Irving's family or Jeanette's if the couple had been more serious, since he was Jewish and, at the time, many people disapproved of marrying outside one's faith.

In the 1920s, Jeanette paid a dental bill for Irving and clearly was more successful than he was. In 1968, when he died of a heart attack at the age of sixty-six, he left an estate valued at $351,630, now equivalent to over $2.5 million.

In April 1928, during the Broadway run of *Sunny Days*, Jeanette met stockbroker Robert "Bob" George Ritchie (February 11, 1896–July 15, 1972) at a Mayfair Club party at New York's Ritz–Carlton Hotel. They began dating, often meeting at the apartment that he shared with his best friend, Steve Kroeger, and hiding their relationship from Anna because she disapproved. She thought that Bob was too old for Jeanette and too reckless; she also didn't like anyone usurping her role as Jeanette's confidante.

A little less than six months after Jeanette and Bob started dating, he wrote a letter to Jeanette, then on tour with *The Queen's Taste*, renamed *Angela* before its Broadway opening. In the letter, Bob confessed that he was engaged to Gertrude Laird, called Florence in Jeanette's autobiography so Jeanette wouldn't have to have her sign a release to use her name. He explained that, by the time Jeanette received the letter, he would be married because he felt obligated to Laird; however, he insisted that he always would love Jeanette. On October 4, 1928, Bob followed through with the marriage and Jeanette was heartbroken. According to correspondence, during Bob's marriage, Jeanette seemed more serious about Irving Stone, probably turning to him on the rebound. However, less than two months later, on December 3, Bob returned on the night of *Angela's* Broadway opening, telling Jeanette that he was getting his marriage annulled. Despite her plan to ignore him, eventually, they began dating again. By April 1929, Bob edged out Irving as top man in her life.

Bob had a reputation as a playboy. According to Jeanette's biographer, Edward Baron Turk, Bob kept a list of the names and dates of his sexual conquests, which, between 1927 and 1960, included over four hundred different women. In an outline for her autobiography, Jeanette wrote, "Discretion was thrown to the wind when I met Bob Ritchie. I was ready, willing and able to be seduced, but he was gentleman enough to refuse me."[63] However, according to Bob's list, on April 7, 1928, shortly after they met, Jeanette was noted for the first time, with forty additional marks during their seven-year relationship. Post-divorce correspondence with Irving Stone implies that they also were more than friends. In her autobiography, Jeanette said that she turned down Jack Ohmeis' advances; however, they spent time at his family's summer house in Lake Hopatcong, New Jersey with friends, sans chaperone, so it is not known if they also were intimate.

Jeanette worried about Bob's extravagant spending, the opposite of her own frugal tendencies. Bob proposed multiple times and, in December 1930, despite some misgivings and Anna's dislike of him, Jeanette announced their engagement to the press, claiming that they had been engaged for some time. In Jeanette's autobiography, she said that she trusted Bob with her career and finances, but that his marriage to another woman made her distrust him romantically. However, in letters that she wrote to him, and to Irving Stone, she sounded like she truly loved Bob and that she planned to marry him, although she obviously had doubts or she would have followed through with their engagement.

Bob often gave Jeanette business and career advice, and helped negotiate her contracts, including her Paramount and MGM salaries. Some, including Maurice Chevalier, said that Bob was verbally abusive to her and they couldn't understand why she put up with him.

Although Bob often traveled with Jeanette and shared a home with her and her mother in Hollywood, Jeanette vehemently denied rumors that she and Bob were secretly married. In Anna's 1931 diary, she worried that Jeanette and Bob would get married and use Jeanette's European recital tour as a honeymoon, and Anna would miss the trip. In 1933, Jeanette joked to Irving Stone that she would let him know when she married Bob because she expected her ex to send a wedding gift. Notoriously frugal Jeanette even bet columnist Walter Winchell $5,000, currently equivalent to almost, $92,000, if he could prove that she was married, as he insisted, but he never found evidence of a marriage. In a 1935 letter to Gene Raymond, after Winchell said that she and Gene had split, Jeanette brought up the columnist's inaccuracy to Gene, recalling that Winchell also had been wrong about her marrying Bob. When Jeanette's close friend and attorney, Louis Swarts, asked Jeanette if she and Bob ever were married, she said that his question hurt her more than any of the gossip.

In Hollywood, Ernst Lubitsch also fell in love with Jeanette, although she did not reciprocate his feelings. During the filming of *Monte Carlo*, at a party, he cornered her in the bathroom and proposed to her. Jeanette was so stunned, by both the proposal and the location, she laughed in his face. Lubitsch was hurt by her rebuff, but eventually, they became close friends, and Jeanette often counseled him on his love life.

Many film historians think that Lubitsch was Jeanette's best director, bringing out a combination of sophistication, innocence, sexiness, and humor in their four celluloid collaborations that was not seen in her other pictures. She was his favorite leading lady and appeared in four of the five musicals that he directed. (Lubitsch died eight days into filming a sixth musical.) Some film historians called her the quintessential Lubitsch heroine. In 1930, David O. Selznick, then Assistant Production Head at Paramount, didn't think that Jeanette was a big enough star to carry *Monte Carlo*; Lubitsch flatly refused to make it without her. *Monte Carlo* was a big hit, and was praised for integrating story and songs. Jeanette introduced "Beyond the Blue Horizon," which not only became one of her signature songs, but a popular music standard. Jeanette and Lubitsch last worked together on *The Merry Widow* (1934) at MGM, but remained lifelong friends. According to writer/director Walter Reisch, Lubitsch always kept two photographs on his piano: one of his daughter, Nicola, and one of Jeanette in *The Love Parade*. The piano was a gift from Jeanette. Lubitsch also included a framed photo of Jeanette on a shelf in his romantic comedy *The Shop Around the Corner* (1940).

In the early days of Jeanette's movie career, she was involved in an international scandal, through no fault of her own. The stories originated in Europe when some audiences thought that *Monte Carlo* was filmed on location. Rumors began circulating abroad that Jeanette had been involved with Prince Umberto, heir to the throne of Italy and husband of Belgium's Princess Marie-Jose, and that Jeanette had been disfigured or killed in a car crash in Belgium while driving with him. Another story claimed that, after Princess Marie-Jose caught Jeanette cheating with Prince Umberto, the Princess shot Jeanette or doused her with sulfuric acid. The rumors became wilder, with claims that, after the real Jeanette was disfigured, she committed suicide, and Blossom had been masquerading as her sister.

During the filming of *Oh, for a Man!*, Jeanette heard about the stories from a fan in Belgium, who sent her a newspaper clipping. Jeanette wrote to the fan, asking her to send any other articles that appeared. Jeanette then subscribed to a foreign clipping service and learned more about the rumors, which seemed to get more sensational as time passed. When she didn't sing in *Don't Bet on Women*, the gossipmongers used it as proof that the Jeanette on screen was a substitute.

Despite the press printing the truth, the rumors continued. The story also was perpetuated in the 1931 French novel *Jeanette MacDonald?* by Maurice Privat. Concerned that the publicity would affect the success of her films in foreign markets, and, with her American career at a crossroads following the three Fox films, with the help of Bob Ritchie, Jeanette set out to prove that she was alive and well and not her sister. Bob arranged for Jeanette to perform on stage in Paris, France and London, England for a pair of two-week engagements. Jeanette and Bob believed that her live singing would prove to audiences that she was really Jeanette MacDonald. On August 1, 1931, she sailed to France with State Department letters, impressions of her fingerprints, and affidavits stating that she previously never had set foot on European soil. She was not allowed in Belgium or Italy until she proved that she was not an imposter.

When Jeanette's ship arrived, there were demonstrators at the dock. The authorities examined her credentials for hours before letting her debark. The French press was sure that she planted the rumors herself to garner publicity, and the French government planned to take 40% of her $5,000-a-week salary, now almost $83,000-a-week, as income tax. While Jeanette was in Paris, she visited a group of French veterans who were wounded during World War I, and contributed a hefty sum for their care. The French government was so touched by her goodwill gestures that they refused to withhold any taxes. When asked about the rumors, Jeanette told the press, "It is utter nonsense. One of the reasons for my European variety tour is to show myself in person, and thereby disprove the wild rumours [sic] that I am blind, disfigured, or dead!"[64]

Jeanette wisely included several French songs in her act at Paris' Empire Theatre and spoke to the audience in their native tongue. Before opening her mouth, she gave the audience the enchanting Jeanette

MacDonald smile. Her actions endeared her to the crowd, and their acceptance assured the future success of her films in European markets. After her initial performance, Maurice Chevalier even came on stage and kissed her. In a 1942 interview, she recalled the opening: "It was the longest, hardest, and most chilling moment of my life. And it is as clear today as it was then."[65] She never found out who started the rumors.

During Jeanette's 1931 trip to Paris, she visited veterans injured during the First World War. Manager/fiancé Bob Ritchie was pictured far left.

As for Prince Umberto, in 1946, he became King Umberto II, ruling for only thirty-four days before the citizens of Italy voted to eliminate the monarchy. He lived the rest of his life in exile in Cascais in the Portuguese Riviera. Although he and Princess Marie-Jose separated while they were in exile, they never divorced.

During the first four nights of Jeanette's Empire Theatre engagement, a thousand people stood and, for the first time in the theater's history, a matinee was offered. The first week's take was 487,500 francs, about $23,500, currently equivalent to over $389,000. Paris journalists called her "the greatest sensation since [Charles] Lindbergh,"[66] the aviator who made the first solo nonstop flight across the Atlantic Ocean and landed in Paris in 1927. The French were so impressed with Jeanette that they asked her to start the Grand-Prix de Paris. On September 13, 1931, she launched the thirteen-kilometer walking race by singing "March of the Grenadiers."

Jeanette repeated her stage triumph at London's Dominion Theatre, where the authorities had to install iron railings between the curb and the side entrance to hold back the crowds at the stage door. Jeanette recalled Anna's pride over the reception: "I saw Mother moved to tears for one of the few times in her life when she came into my dressingroom [sic] after my first night. My invariably calm and sedate Mother hugged me until my ribs bent, sobbing, 'This is the most wonderful thing that's ever happened to me.'"[67] While Jeanette was in London, she recorded four songs for RCA Victor's British label, His Master's Voice.

Jeanette's international success sparked a renewed interest from Paramount. Although she also received offers in Europe, in November 1931, she returned to her original studio for two of her best early films: *One Hour with You* (1932) with Maurice Chevalier, and *Love Me Tonight* (1932) with Maurice Chevalier and Myrna Loy. *One Hour with You* (1932), a romantic musical farce about infidelity, reunited her with Ernst Lubitsch and was nominated for an Academy Award for Best Picture. It originally was released with blue and gold color tints, which the UCLA Film & Television Archive restored and preserved.

Love Me Tonight, a musical retelling of *Sleeping Beauty* about a princess (Jeanette) and a tailor (Chevalier), is greatly respected by film historians for its use of music as part of the plot and Rouben Mamoulian's direction. It appears on many lists of "best musicals" and, in 1990, it was named to the National Film Registry for preservation in the Library of Congress. It was Mamoulian's favorite movie. Jeanette did all of her own riding and stunts, including the dramatic race to stop a train near the end of the film. Among the songs she sang were Richard Rodgers and Lorenz Hart's "Isn't It Romantic" and "Lover," both of which became standards. Mamoulian recalled, "Jeanette had the most wonderful sense of humour [sic]. It is regrettable that her later films gave her so little opportunity to exercise her superb sense of comedy."[68] Many film historians called her one of the great comediennes of the 1930s and agreed that it was a shame that she later was typecast in operettas.

In December 1932, Jeanette returned to Europe, where, in 1933, she played to ecstatic audiences in France (Paris, Lille, Lyon, Marseilles, and Strasbourg), the Netherlands (Amsterdam and Rotterdam), Belgium (Brussels), and Switzerland (Geneva and Lausanne). Her two-week engagement at the Rex Theatre in Paris garnered $175,000 in paid admissions, currently equivalent to almost $3.4 million. She received congratulatory telegrams from a plethora of celebrities, including Ernst Lubitsch, Maurice Chevalier, comedians Stan Laurel and Oliver Hardy, actor/filmmaker Charles Chaplin, and actors Mary Pickford and Douglas Fairbanks, Claudette Colbert, Buddy Rogers, and Joan Crawford and Douglas Fairbanks, Jr. "My trip to France did a great deal towards giving me confidence," Jeanette recalled. "I was given quite an ovation over there. They say I represent their idea of a real American girl because I do not smoke or drink. I have no inhibitions about smoking or drinking, but I think to [sic] much of my voice to place it in jeopardy."[69] Her arrival in Brussels caused a traffic jam and riot when over five thousand people greeted her at the station. In 1939, when Jeanette began touring the United States, she found the same reaction, with fans clamoring to get a glimpse of her wherever she went. In Paris, she recorded three songs in French for RCA Victor's French label, Disque Gramophone.

During Jeanette's second European trip, she continued to defend her reputation, suing reporter Andre Ransan and *Fantasio*, a Paris humor weekly, for defamation of character. Ransan wrote an imaginary interview with Jeanette that offended her. In it, he claimed that he was the anonymous press agent that started the rumors that she was a scarlet woman. Several American newspapers, including the New York *Daily News*, the *Chicago Tribune* , and the *Pittsburgh Post-Gazette*, printed a translated excerpt from his article. It said, "Our interview was intimate, intoxicating, sensual and delicious. She let me go as far as I liked. I cut off a lock of her hair. I counted the twenty-five lashes she has on each eyelid. I breathed on the down of her neck. I ran my little finger on her bare arm. I measured her calves. I tickled the palm of her bare hand."[70] Jeanette demanded 200,000 francs in damages, then approximately $8,000, currently almost $155,000. Ransan insisted that he was trying to be funny. In July 1933, Jeanette won the entire $8,000 in damages, but, at the judge's suggestion, she accepted Ransan's apology rather than collecting the money. Jeanette told the press, "It was outrageous! Why I'd never seen the man. He claimed he wrote it as a joke."[71]

According to a 1934 article, Jeanette's movies were more popular in Europe than any other films. Theaters even revived her older pictures, in preference to showing new ones featuring other stars. Both *One Hour with You* (1932) and *The Merry Widow* (1934) were filmed simultaneously in English and French, with Jeanette and Maurice Chevalier in both versions and different supporting actors completing the casts. Jeanette was fluent in French and did all of her own speaking and singing. *The Merry Widow* was MGM's most expensive film at the time, costing $1.6 million, over $30 million today.

Through the years, Jeanette maintained her popularity outside the United States. Early in her film career, composer Juan Giterman and lyricist Franco Amenabar wrote a song "Oh, Jeannette [sic]!," which was published in Buenos Aires, Argentina; she was pictured on the sheet music. In 1933, because Jeanette was the most popular American picture star in France, the French Consul presented her with a scroll, appointing her to a Vice Presidency in the Alliance Française, one of the oldest French fraternal organizations. In Australia, she was billed only as Jeanette and, in 1939, Australians named her the most popular feminine star. In 1940, columnist Jimmie Fidler said that, throughout the entire Orient, Jeanette was the number one box office favorite. In a 1943 international poll by *Motion Picture Herald*, in the midst of World War II, she was named the foreign theatergoers' favorite star. In 1954, when the British magazine *Picturegoer* asked readers what movies they would most like to see again, after *The Wizard of Oz* (1939), Jeanette and Nelson Eddy's films were the most requested musicals. In 1989, her *Bitter Sweet* (1940) co-star Edward Ashley reported that, when he was in Hong Kong, they advertised a Jeanette MacDonald film festival.

While Jeanette was overseas, she obtained two of her dogs. During her 1931 stay in London, Ye Olde English Sheep Dog Society gave her a year-old English Sheep Dog. She named him Captain because he was the only member of her entourage who didn't get seasick on the ship back to the United States. On Jeanette's second European tour, she took him with her, not realizing that he would have to be quarantined. She visited him every day. While he was abroad, he bit several people, including Jeanette. He was very jealous of other dogs and extremely protective of his mistress. Back in the United States, Captain frequently was in the news for terrorizing Jeanette's guests or other dogs, or damaging her rented homes. In May 1936, Captain bit Jeanette's secretary, Gladys Searles, and she sued Jeanette for $25,627, now equivalent to over $464,000. Jeanette insisted that it was Searles' fault and that she should make her claim under Workers' Compensation rather than a lawsuit. Newspapers did not report the results; however, later that year, Jeanette sent Captain to a farm run by the dog kennel Happyland because of the suit and because he didn't get along with Gene. She continued to call to check on the Sheep Dog.

During Jeanette's 1933 tour, she was given a nine-month-old Skye Terrier as a birthday gift. Always one to play with words, Jeanette said that she named him Stormy Weather, Stormy for short, because he was a grey Skye. Jeanette adored her dogs and defended their some-times questionable behavior. In 1936, when silent film actress Corinne Griffith sued Jeanette for $1,018 (now over $18,000), claiming Captain and Stormy damaged Griffith's house when Jeanette rented it, Jeanette insisted that her dogs were "perfect gentlemen."[72] Griffith won $547.45 in damages, now about $10,000. Stormy disliked Captain be-cause the English Sheep Dog routinely put his big paw on the little Skye Terrier. After Captain was sent to the farm, Jeanette still teased Stormy by bringing up Captain's name to scare him. Jeanette often said that Stormy was her favorite and, occasionally, he joined her on her recital tours. In 1942, while Gene was stationed in England, Stormy had to be put to sleep, shortly before his tenth birthday.

During Jeanette's second trip abroad, she met MGM producer Irving Thalberg and his wife, actress Norma Shearer, then queen of the MGM lot. Jeanette cleverly loaned Shearer her hairdresser, Henri, lead-ing to a lasting friendship between the two women. Jeanette's acquain-tance with Thalberg led to her moving to MGM in 1933. According to Jeanette's autobiography, Bob Ritchie advised her to sign with studio co-founder Louis B. Mayer, rather than Thalberg, as there was a great rivalry between the two men, and Mayer was more powerful. However, a letter from Thalberg, dated April 18, 1933, confirmed their oral agreement and was signed by Jeanette and witnessed by Bob Ritchie. A letter to Louis B. Mayer, dated September 1, 1933, also referred to this agreement. It's possible that Jeanette incorrectly remembered the details when working on her book or her co-writer, James Brough, dramatized the situation, as he did other events. In any case, once she arrived at MGM, she made sure to balance her loyalty between Mayer and Thalberg, knowing that friendship with both could only help her career.

An unsigned contract from June 1933 called for Jeanette to make two pictures at $30,000 each, with options for three more films at $35,000 each and an additional three movies at $45,000 each, now about $581,000, $657,000, and $827,000. One of the points she argued over was to get the studio to provide her shoes, stockings, and underwear. They finally agreed—if the items were seen on screen. It is unclear when Jeanette signed the contract or who signed representing MGM; her 1933 contract is not among the MGM documents at the Academy of Motion Picture Arts and Sciences' Margaret Herrick Library. On July 25, 1933, Jeanette returned to the United States on the S.S. Ile de France.

Jeanette was very unhappy with her first MGM picture, *The Cat and the Fiddle* (1934), and in a September 1, 1933 agreement with Louis B. Mayer, she demanded that Anita Loos or another competent screenwriter rewrite several sequences in the film. The agreement also allowed Jeanette to terminate her contract within a week of completing the picture or within a week of completing any other movies that she found unsatisfactory. It was signed by Jeanette and Mayer in September 1933.

Jeanette was smart to leave Paramount when she did, as, in 1933, the studio went into receivership and, in 1935, Paramount–Publix went bankrupt. The following year, under the leadership of Adolph

Zukor, the studio reorganized as Paramount Pictures, Inc. and was brought out of bankruptcy. Through the years, it went through a series of owners, including Gulf and Western Industries, Inc. and Viacom.

Since 1929, around the same time that Jeanette signed with Paramount, Louis B. Mayer had been trying to woo her to MGM. In 1932, Irving Thalberg tried to sign her, with one planned project being *The Merry Widow*, starring Ramon Novarro and Jeanette. In 1933, when she finally arrived at MGM, she was thrilled to join the studio, already known for publicizing its stable of glamorous stars and making quality musicals. MGM's first full-fledged talkie, *The Broadway Melody* (1929), won the Academy Award for Best Picture. The studio motto was "More stars than there are in heaven."

Louis B. Mayer liked to think of his studio as a family, with himself as the father figure and his players as obedient children. He encouraged Jeanette to think of him as a friend and confidante. Before Jeanette began filming any of her movies, she always stopped in Mayer's office for him to wish her luck. He loved operettas and wanted his movies to have happy endings. One of the most famous Mayer stories involved him getting down on his knees to sing the Jewish lament "Eli, Eli" to show Jeanette how he wanted her to put more schmaltz in her voice to sing "Ah! Sweet Mystery of Life" in *Naughty Marietta* (1935). Because she was the boss' favorite, Jeanette occasionally received perks that no other star on the lot did, like having a telephone in her portable dressing room. In 1935, she accompanied the studio head to the Academy Awards and, in 1938, she sang at an Association of Motion Picture Producers dinner honoring Mayer .

Most film historians acknowledge that Mayer was infatuated with Jeanette. Nat Finston said that the inner circle at Paramount always talked about Mayer never giving up on signing her. "It was somewhat sexual," Finston claimed. "He was crazy for her."[73] According to Joseph Newman, assistant director on *The Merry Widow* (1934), *Rose-Marie* (1936), *San Francisco* (1936), *Maytime* (1937), and *The Firefly* (1937), "Mayer was always around during the making of her pictures and that was very unusual for him, because he didn't hang around sets. I think he was very attracted to her, but I don't think there was any reciprocation on her part."[74] Although some speculated that Jeanette and Mayer were more than friends, if there had been anything sexual between them, it's doubtful that she would have socialized with his wife and daughters.

On April 25, 1940, Loew's, Inc. head Nicholas Schenck, Louis B. Mayer's wife, Margaret, and Louis B. Mayer congratulated Jeanette backstage after her Los Angeles recital debut. Mayer's grandson, Daniel Mayer Selznick, called this picture of his grandmother "the most glorious photo of her I have ever seen."[642]

In a 1936 interview, Jeanette described her relationship with her boss: "Mr. Mayer is a genuine friend of mine. He has advised me, wisely, inspirationally, about my work. I go to him with any problems I may have, talk everything over with him, tell him frankly whatever is on my mind. He gives me his man's reaction, his wise, masculine advice."[75]

Many claimed that Jeanette was Mayer's pet, although she later said that, during her years at the studio, their relationship was sometimes tumultuous. He was displeased when Jeanette went over his head on several matters, like contacting MGM's General Manager of Sales and Distribution, Felix Feist, to convince the studio to make *San Francisco* with Clark Gable. In 1937, Mayer was even more upset when she went over his head and talked to Nicholas Schenck, head of MGM's parent company, Loew's, Inc., when Mayer objected to her dubbing her vocals in other languages for her films' foreign releases. Jeanette argued that her voice was her stock-in-trade and Schenck agreed with her. Mayer became jealous of her rapport with Schenck, particularly when Schenck misquoted Jeanette, claiming that she preferred to negotiate with MGM General Manager Eddie Mannix than with Mayer, and that Mannix was her confidante at the studio. In reality, Jeanette said that she *liked* dealing with Mannix, not that she *preferred* dealing with him. Mayer also was jealous of Jeanette's relationship with attorney Louis Swarts, as Mayer wanted to be her only father figure.

Jeanette said that Mayer became angry over petty matters, like when he learned that she gave him and Eddie Mannix the same Christmas gift, a box of pears, and, for years, he held a grudge over the incident. In 1946, when Jeanette planned to return to the studio, Mayer brought this up to her. She reminded him that he never gave her a Christmas gift at all, causing him to laugh and forget any past problems. Through the years, Mayer attended many of Jeanette's Los Angeles recitals; in 1948, after her appearance at Philharmonic Auditorium, he hosted a party for her.

Early in her movie career, Jeanette was
known as The Lingerie Queen.

Jeanette's screen career was divided into two distinct periods. In
the early 1930s, in her films for Paramount and Fox, she was known
as The Lingerie Queen, an epitaph she disliked. She wore so many
filmy negligees and so much lingerie in her movies that, when fans
wrote for autographs, they began to request photos of her in her
nightgown. What bothered her most was the feeling that she was being typecast. She observed, "I'm sure that people must say about me,

on the screen, 'Good gracious, is Jeanette MacDonald going to take off her clothes—again?'"[76] Although tame by today's standards, her movies were slightly naughty, with Jeanette often appearing in sexy lingerie or the bathtub or both, and speaking dialogue full of double entendres. Ernst Lubitsch's light touch had a way of making slightly risqué films acceptable to the general public. Jeanette observed, "He could suggest more with a closed door than all the hay-rolling you see openly on the screen nowadays, and yet he never offended."[77] Despite Lubitsch's German heritage, she said, "Ernst had, not a German, but an American sense of humor. The most American sense of humor I know of."[78] Lubitsch biographer Joseph McBride said that Lubitsch combined the best of both cultures. "In fact, his enthusiasm for American culture blended with his tendency to keep a certain satirical distance from it. That, along with his continental attitudes toward sexuality and other social issues, combined to help make Lubitsch so special in the film business and a role model for other filmmakers."[79]

On July 1, 1934, the Motion Picture Producers and Distributors of America (later known as the Motion Picture Association of America or MPAA) began strictly enforcing the Production Code, which eliminated risqué costumes, four-letter words, and vulgar situations on screen. The studios themselves established the Code to avoid government censorship. Often referred to as the Hays Code, after Will Hays, the first Chairman of the Motion Picture Producers and Distributors of America, the Code had been in effect since 1930, but mostly was ignored. On June 13, 1934, an amendment was adopted that established the Production Code Administration and required films released after July 1, 1934 to obtain a certificate of approval. Joseph Breen was appointed head of the Production Code Administration.

The result of the enforcement of the Code was that Jeanette's image at MGM became more sedate than in her early films. Gone were the lingerie and double entendres. Replacing them were a series of mostly costume pictures, where she became the queen of operetta, introducing classical music to a generation of moviegoers. After appearing with Ramon Novarro in *The Cat and the Fiddle*, which was released before the crackdown, and with Maurice Chevalier in *The Merry Widow*, which made it past the censors with minor changes, before her 1937 marriage, she sang her way through four blockbuster films: the not-so-naughty *Naughty Marietta* (1935), *Rose-Marie* (1936), *San Francisco* (1936), and *Maytime* (1937).

Prior to a 1984 screening of *The Love Parade* and *Monte Carlo*, a critic noted, "Saucy is the word for Jeanette MacDonald at her best—and at her best she flirted opposite Maurice Chevalier. Jeanette MacDonald, you ask? Forget about the corseted iron butterfly who sang to Nelson Eddy so she didn't have to kiss him. Think of Jeanette MacDonald before she was a virgin."[80] In 2017, author Richard Barrios commented on Chevalier and Jeanette in *The Love Parade*. "Maurice Chevalier is perhaps most familiar to audiences for films, like *Gigi* (1958), that he made as a senior citizen. Jeanette MacDonald, for her part, is known far better for her later films with Nelson Eddy, not as a sexy star who runs around in her underwear. Thus, along with its many other virtues, *The Love Parade* is valuable for presenting both stars as audiences first knew them: he as a devastating lady-killer, she as the complete opposite of a buttoned up prima donna."[81] Despite comments like these from critics and film scholars who preferred pre-Code Jeanette, the post-Code films with Nelson Eddy were what made her a legend.

Jeanette never let fame go to her head. As a 1930s article noted, "Jeanette developed her voice, but she did not develop into a Voice. She retained her personality, her gaiety, her humor. She continued on as the same show-must-go-on trouper which she has always been. She emerged with a great Prima Donna voice, but without any of the Prima Donna characteristics."[82] Throughout her life, she acknowledged gifts with thank you notes; if she could not attend a party, she sent flowers or a note of regret. Reporters, as well as friends, remarked on her good manners and graciousness. She rose when an older person entered the room. She frequently helped people, giving from the heart, not to get recognition. During the Depression, Jeanette and Woody Van Dyke anonymously fed and paid rent for the families of about thirty studio workers. In the late 1930s, Jeanette became angry when the press reported that she bought blind fan Hazel Hurst a guide dog, as she hoped to keep the gift anonymous. Later, Hurst and her dog visited Jeanette at MGM and summed up the feelings of many: "Miss MacDonald's success has gone to her heart, not her head."[83]

In the early days of musicals, songs were performed live, with an orchestra a few feet away off camera. The only time Jeanette sang to a prerecorded soundtrack was "March of the Grenadiers" in *The Love Parade*, the first use of prerecording on screen. By the time she made *The Merry Widow* at MGM, sound film techniques had improved. Beginning with "Tonight Will Teach Me to Forget" (also known as "The Diary Song"), all of Jeanette's songs were prerecorded, usually at least a week before filming. Jeanette was given records of the takes that the studio planned to use so she could practice matching the phrasing at home. Although many stars lip-synched to the tracks during filming, Jeanette didn't approve of that practice. Instead, she sang with the prerecorded tracks, often in a lower key, so audiences could see the muscles in her throat moving, not just her lips. The playback was so loud on the set that some cast and crew members complained. Jeanette cheerily supplied earplugs for her co-workers.

Jeanette was a perfectionist and her own harshest critic. If co-stars forgot their lines and required retakes, she was patient, but she became furious with herself when she made a mistake. During the filming of *The Love Parade*, Jeanette had problems with the long train on the silver lamé gown that she wore when singing the reprise of "Dream Lover." She threw a tantrum, insisting it was impossible to walk in the dress. Ernst Lubitsch proved her wrong by donning the gown himself and sashaying around the set. He also filmed her outburst, making her realize how silly she looked. At MGM, when she was angry, Woody Van Dyke often gave her a chair to kick, sometimes going so far as to nail it to the floor to keep it from flying across the room.

Most of the time, Jeanette wore wigs in her movies because she was too impatient to sit still while someone worked on her hair; it also allowed her to arrive at the studio later and protected her hair from the hot lights. MGM hairdresser Sydney Guilaroff recalled her throwing a wig that she didn't like in a fit of temperament. MGM makeup artist William Tuttle said that Jeanette was a perfectionist who usually did her own makeup then would have someone check it. He remembered her warning him and her maid, Rose, to get out of the way when she discovered a flaw while preparing to shoot a scene for *Smilin' Through*. She then threw a mirror across the room in frustration. Given Jeanette's number of superstitions, it's surprising that she also didn't believe that breaking a mirror was bad luck.

Jeanette explained her behavior: "When I was at Paramount, they said I was temperamental. Well, it's true I'd always fight for anything I thought was right. But I always fought with those who held positions more important than mine. I'd fight with producers and directors and executives, but I never raised Cain with cameramen or electricians or stand-in girls."[84] She later added that the only time she was temperamental was "when there is someone around me who is thinking unlovely thoughts. It makes my tummy turn upside down."[85]

Early on, Jeanette learned that it was better to be considerate of her co-workers. She told Betty Bradley, "When I was in the theater, and touring with the stage shows, there was a star, one of the bigger stars, who was always mean to everybody. She was just mean all the time. And I told myself, 'If ever I get to be a really big star, I'm going to be nice. I'm not going to be like that.' And that's why I try to be nice."[86]

Despite the fact that Jeanette preferred to be considered an actress on her own merit, she was part of two screen teams. From 1929 to 1934, she made four films with Maurice Chevalier. Their chemistry was so convincing that many thought that they were a real-life item off-screen, despite the existence of Chevalier's wife and Jeanette's manager/fiancé Bob Ritchie. The reality was Jeanette's relationship with Chevalier was rocky, variously reported as civility to hatred, and they seldom socialized off screen. Jeanette called her co-star "the biggest bottom-pincher I have ever come across"[87] and Chevalier complained to singer Frank Sinatra that "it was the second saddest day in the history of France"[88] when Jeanette turned down his advances. One would think that the saddest day for a Frenchman would be when the Nazis entered Paris; however, when Sinatra asked Chevalier, he said that it was when soprano Grace Moore refused to go to bed with him. During Jeanette's 1931 trip abroad, Chevalier invited her and her entourage to stay at his home; however, he didn't want to work with her in their final film, *The Merry Widow*, jealous that her fame had surpassed his. In an outline for her unpublished autobiography, Jeanette called Chevalier "a cold professional twice my age" and said that her romantic interest in him was "nil."[89] In reality, Chevalier was fifteen years her senior, but it was clear that she had no attraction to him.

Chevalier always maintained that Jeanette had no sense of humor and that she objected to anyone telling risqué stories. However, her correspondence with Gene proved that she often used slightly naughty double entendres. A fan recalled an ashtray in the guest bath at the Raymonds' home that read "Old golfers never die; they just lose their balls."[90] If Jeanette were offended by it, she certainly wouldn't have displayed it.

For two years during the First World War, Chevalier was a prisoner of war in Germany. During World War II, he performed in a Paris revue, reassuring the public that France was still France under the Nazi occupation. In 1943, when Jeanette was asked about his pro-Nazi tendencies, she was quick to defend him. "I do not want to be thought in the slightest bit pro-Nazi," she told reporters, "but I do think that we ought to recognize the instinct of self-preservation that might motivate Chevalier's actions at the moment."[91] Some French citizens never forgave him for performing in Nazi-occupied France. Ernst Lubitsch, who was German-born and Jewish, came to hate Chevalier, and said that he thought the Frenchman collaborated with the Nazis during World War II.

Through the years, Jeanette attended a few of Chevalier's performances, as well as a 1957 birthday party for him on the set of *Gigi*, but seemed miffed when she heard that he did not want to reunite with her on screen or television. It was rumored that he signed to do *Gigi* on the condition that Jeanette would not co-star with him; yet, in 1958, he told a reporter that he hoped that they would make another movie together. "Part of the world has seen us young and handsome," he said. "Now they would see us no longer young, but perhaps still handsome."[92]

From 1935 to 1942, Jeanette was paired with baritone Nelson Eddy in eight films at MGM. Two of their pictures, *Naughty Marietta* (1935) and *Sweethearts* (1938), won the *Photoplay Magazine* Medal of Honor, the first significant annual movie award, which began in 1920. *Rose-Marie* (1936) lost to another one of Jeanette's movies, *San Francisco* (1936). Jeanette and Nelson also starred in *Maytime* (1937),

The Girl of the Golden West (1938), *New Moon* (1940), *Bitter Sweet* (1940), and *I Married an Angel* (1942). When asked about the team's popularity, Jeanette said, "I believe our operettas were so successful because our two voices had a timbre that was compatible."[93]

Once again, moviegoers were so convinced that the actors' screen chemistry was real that some protested to MGM when Jeanette married Gene Raymond. Despite evidence to the contrary, some fans still believe there was an off-screen romance between the co-stars and insist that Jeanette and Nelson weren't acting. In 1935, Jeanette told a reporter, "Just because two people play love scenes on the screen is not an indication that they are in love."[94] In 1940, she said, "We're friends, and it is much better that way for our work. But never sweethearts!"[95] In 1956, when the pair reunited for a TV appearance, she told the press, "Nelson and I used to date each other before I married Gene. We always have been good friends, but, well, it was just never a romance."[96] It's an insult to Jeanette's acting ability to say that she didn't have the same chemistry with other co-stars. During the filming of *San Francisco*, she didn't get along with Clark Gable, who openly disliked her, but audiences never knew it from the way she looked at him when the cameras were rolling.

Nelson and his wife, Ann, often socialized with Jeanette and Gene, and the couples had many mutual friends. Jeanette and Ann also occasionally socialized without their husbands. Ann attended a 1945 tea at the Raymonds' home in honor of Argentine Cooper, wife of the former Speaker of the Tennessee House of Representatives, William Prentice Cooper, and mother of Tennessee Governor Prentice Cooper. In several letters to Nelson and his fan club, Jeanette mentioned talking to Ann while Nelson was on tour. When Jeanette wrote to Nelson for permission to use a story in her autobiography, she also mentioned speaking to Ann about it while Nelson was on the road. The Eddys frequently were included in the Raymonds' anniversary celebrations and, in 1949, the couples attended a screening of Gene's movie, *Zoo in Budapest* (1933). When Jeanette died, Nelson said that he knew that she was ill, but didn't know the severity. He told reporters that, the week before, they had spoken about having dinner with their spouses.

Occasionally, there were rumors in the media that Jeanette and Nelson didn't get along. However, through the years, they both insisted that they always were friends, though, like most colleagues, they didn't agree 100% of the time when they were working. Blossom addressed the rumors in a 1941 letter to longtime fan Clara Rhoades, who later became President of one of Jeanette's fan clubs. Clara, who was a fan of both stars, told Blossom that she heard rumors that Jeanette and Nelson were making movies with others because they didn't get along. "That's a lot of hooey (pardon my slang)," Blossom answered. "The whole family likes him including J. I think the only reason they are using other names with Miss Mac Donald [sic] is because Mr. Eddy is a big enough draw now to bring the people into the box office on the strength of his own name. Isn't it strange how those silly stories get about?"[97] In an interview ten days before Nelson's 1967 death, he dismissed rumors of a feud as "silly," but admitted, "We didn't like the way each other sang, actually."[98] A 1954 inventory of the Raymonds' record collection included discs by friends like soprano Lotte Lehmann and tenor James Melton, but none by Nelson, except some radio broadcasts that Jeanette did with him. According to screenwriter DeWitt Bodeen, "[Jeanette] was respectful, but not filled with admiration for Nelson Eddy. Sometimes his lack of musicianship annoyed her; he could not transpose from one key to another at sight."[99]

In 1934, two events greatly affected Jeanette's life and career. In August, she planned to go on a motor trip through Yosemite National Park with Kitty Marin (wife of MGM producer Ned

Marin), Belle Stebbins (wife of agent Arthur Stebbins and niece of Twentieth Century Pictures co-founder Joseph Schenck, who was later Chairman of Twentieth Century–Fox, and Loew's, Inc. head Nicholas Schenck), and three of their children. When the Production Code Administration demanded that some scenes for *The Merry Widow* be re-filmed in order to be approved for release, Jeanette dutifully remained in Hollywood. On August 30, on the way home from Yosemite, a truck, driving on the wrong side of the road, crashed into the women's car, killing Marin, Stebbins, and Stebbins' two children and seriously injuring Marin's daughter. On September 3, Jeanette attended their joint funeral, with the realization that, had she not been filming retakes and gone on the trip, she would have been injured or killed. Bob Ritchie was one of Marin's pallbearers. That fall, Jeanette planned to tour South America and return to Europe; however, pre-production work for *Naughty Marietta* interfered. Had she accepted the tour instead, neither the on-screen team of Jeanette MacDonald and Nelson Eddy, nor the off-screen team of Jeanette MacDonald and Gene Raymond, would have been introduced.

Interestingly, Gene and Nelson were friends long before either really knew Jeanette, going camping and playing tennis together shortly after Nelson arrived in Hollywood. In a 1935 interview, Nelson said, "I'm going to [Lake] Arrowhead, [California] this week-end [sic] with Gene. I like him. He reads books. He can talk about a few things other than personalities and local gossip."[100] Gene and Nelson came from similar backgrounds: children of divorce who were close to their mothers and who, from a young age, financially supported their families. Gene was a natural blonde who occasionally dyed his almost-platinum hair for film roles. Nelson was a redhead whose hair turned prematurely grey and photographed blonde in black and white. Composer/lyricist team Robert Wright and George "Chet" Forrest, who worked on many of Jeanette and Nelson's movies, dubbed the unusual shade "Nelson Eddy grey." Wright said, "I never saw anyone else whose hair was quite that color—sort of blondish golden grey, almost like platinum."[101] Both Gene and Nelson had athletic builds and enjoyed horseback riding. Both drank, smoked cigarettes, and loved dogs and music. Both were fascinated by electronics and had recording machines to preserve radio broadcasts and performances by their party guests.

Gene and Nelson Eddy were friends long before either really knew Jeanette. At an October 1933 party, hosted by Nelson and his mother, Gene and Nelson were photographed with actress Sheila Terry, who was in *The House on 56th Street* (1933) with Gene.

Through the years, Gene and Nelson good-naturedly joked about the confusion of fans thinking one was the other. In 1933, when Nelson first came to Hollywood, autograph seekers repeatedly mistook him for Gene, presumably because they both had near-platinum hair at a time when most other blonde actors had hair of a darker shade. A 1938 column called Gene "the screen's only violently blonde leading man."[102] Apparently, some also thought that Gene and Nelson had a similar demeanor. Shortly after Nelson signed a contract with MGM, a movie magazine described him as "a blond giant with the charm of Jack Buchanan, the virility of Eugene O'Brien . . . and the boyishness of Gene Raymond."[103] A review of Gene's 1936 film *Love on a Bet* called Gene the "handsome screen star with the Nelson Eddy profile if not the Nelson Eddy voice."[104]

Gene and Nelson often laughingly compared how many autographs they signed under their own names and how many as the other. In a 1958 *Person to Person* interview, Jeanette and Gene told journalist Edward R. Murrow about how, when Jeanette and Gene were out walking, he was identified as Nelson; Gene signed Nelson's autograph to avoid a scene.

Jeanette didn't see the resemblance. In 1950, she told a reporter, "They're both blond, both big, and both seen a lot with me, but other than that, they're not alike. They say if you live with a person or work with them, you get to know them. To me, they don't look alike or act alike."[105]

Jeanette, Gene, and Nelson often played up the confusion to amuse their fans. Prior to a 1946 radio broadcast of *Sweethearts*, starring Jeanette and Nelson, the announcer introduced "America's most beloved singing sweethearts" to the audience, only to have Jeanette and Gene emerge holding hands, with Nelson chasing after them, then hurrying Gene backstage while Jeanette convulsed with laughter.[106] Whenever Nelson was asked why he never married Jeanette, he joked that he did—eight times on screen. When the Raymonds appeared on a 1951 episode of *Toast of the Town*, Gene asked Jeanette a series of questions, ending with "On your tours—or any other time—what is the question most often asked you?"[107] A fan described his wife's reaction. "Jeanette, with the most provocative look which just seems to say ('All right, brother, you've asked for it!'), replied, 'Why I did not marry Nelson Eddy!' Quickly Gene quipped, 'Well, why didn't you?' Our gal just couldn't hold back any longer, and just burst out laughing, and turned around, blushing to beat the band."[108] Gene couldn't contain his laughter as he told the audience, "I got her. I got her on that one."[109] In 1956, Jeanette appeared on the radio program *Juke Box Jury* with dancer Gene Nelson, causing her to look at him and say, "You know, I'm a little confused—having both Gene and Nelson sitting on one side of me!"[110]

In 1963, Gene tried to explain the confusion. "Through the years, you know, Nelson and I have cultivated quite a sense of humor about this because he's frequently mistaken for me, and I'm frequently mistaken for him. And when we're asked to sign each other's autographs, why, we cheerfully do so. And this results in satisfaction to all concerned, and they go away none the wiser. I don't know why this should be, because in actuality Nelson and I don't look anything alike. He's big and robust, and handsome, and magnetic, and I'm not even a robusto baritone. But we've survived over the years, and it's really, I think, solely because of Jeanette that this mistaken identity occurred."[111]

Even the press occasionally confused them, like the 1941 *Boston Daily Record* article that correctly identified Gene in a photo, but the headline said Jeanette was entertaining soldiers with Nelson. In 1943, columnist Dorothy Kilgallen reported that, in an article on stars' salaries, a New York daily erroneously listed Nelson as Jeanette's husband. In 1954, actress Faye Emerson confused them when she wrote a column about Jeanette and Gene's appearance on *Masquerade Party*, stating that Jeanette was on the show with Nelson. A 1958 story on the *Gigi* premiere mentioned Jeanette and Nelson signing autographs together when photos of the event clearly showed her with Gene. A member of Jeanette's fan club was amused when she overheard two audience members at a showing of *Smilin' Through*, insisting that

Nelson was on screen, despite Gene being listed in the opening credits. Even a 1997 Israeli CD of Jeanette and Nelson songs mistakenly pictured Jeanette and Gene on the front and back. Given all of this, it's probable that most, if not all, of the off-screen "Jeanette and Nelson" fan sightings through the years were really Jeanette and Gene.

In the 1970s, further proof of the public's ignorance came when Gene often was confused with brunette game show host Gene Rayburn because of their similar surnames. Gene Raymond laughed that even the Bel-Air Country Club, where he had been a member since 1934, routinely mixed up their reservations. In the 1980s, fans watched reruns of the TV series *Hawaii Five-0* and mistook blonde actor Richard Denning, who played the Governor, for Gene. He learned it was best to laugh. Through the years, his sense of humor would be tested many times.

Chapter Three

On August 13, 1908, Gene Raymond entered the world as Raymond Francis Guyon in Brooklyn. When he was eleven, his parents, Mary Schmidt and LeRoy "Roy" Guyon, separated; however, they didn't file for divorce until 1928. Mary, who worked as a necktie maker before her marriage, had delusions of grandeur and was discontent with Roy's lack of success in the business world. Roy preferred working with his hands and received more pleasure in accomplishment than making money. Gene's earliest childhood memories were of his parents fighting, and of trying to protect his brother, Charles Leonard Guyon, known as Leonard, seven years his junior. Throughout their lives, Gene continued to look out for his brother. While Gene was overseas, he appreciated Jeanette taking an interest in him as well. Coincidentally, Gene's brother was born on Jeanette's sister Blossom's twentieth birthday, August 21, 1915. After Jeanette and Gene's marriage, the family often celebrated both birthdays together.

Just like Jeanette's happy childhood colored her views on marriage and family, Gene's memories of his parents' disagreements influenced him as an adult. When he and Jeanette had a problem, he preferred to ignore it, rather than talk about it, afraid a discussion would turn into an argument. His parents' fights also made him reluctant to have children.

Gene remembered moving frequently during his early childhood, attending eleven different schools in one year. Because of the frequent moves, he was unable to form childhood friendships, feeling he was always the outsider. Many of the Raymonds' closest friends were people that Gene met through Jeanette or through his work. She said that this background led to him "being an introvert in a business where extroverts abound. As an actor, on stage or in front of cameras, he could suddenly become an entirely different personality. But in his heart he was a remote and lonesome man."[112]

Early on, it was clear that Gene recognized the differences in his parents. In the summer of 1919, he visited a Freehold, New Jersey farm and wrote separate letters to Mary and Roy. Although both were signed "Love and kisses Raymond," the letter to Mary, whom he addressed as Mother, was all business: sending her photos, thanking her for some books she sent, and asking her to bring him another pair of shoes because his only pair ripped in the back. The letter to Roy, whom he addressed as Papa, was twice as long and full of news of what Gene had been doing, including getting an ice cream cone every time he went to the market. Like Jeanette, Gene had a lifelong love of ice cream. During the war, when Gene's brother wrote to Jeanette and Gene, he continued to use the "Love and kisses" closing. Gene also occasionally used it with Jeanette.

Religion was one of many matters on which the Guyons differed. In later years, when Gene was asked about his father's religion, he said that Roy was a Protestant, but didn't elaborate on the denomination. In 1935, Roy was a member of the Men's Club of Christ Lutheran Church in Great Kills, Staten Island, New York. His funeral was held at the Methodist Episcopal Church at Woodrow Cemetery in Staten Island, where most of the Guyon family is buried.

Roy and his sons, circa 1920.

Although Mary claimed to be a devout Catholic, she also was a devotee of astrology and numerology. She said that she planned both of her sons' births so that they would be born under the sign of Leo. After the separation, she changed her name to Mary Kipling, based on numerology, and because she fancied herself a writer, like Rudyard Kipling. Later, Gene said that all she wrote was letters, hinting at the trouble that she tried to cause between Jeanette and Gene with her vitriolic correspondence. Sometimes, Mary also went by Marilyn or Marylin Kipling. She also Anglicized her maiden name to Smith. Before putting young Raymond on the stage, she changed the spelling of his name to Guion. Through the years, his mother alternated between calling him Gene and Ray; however, his father and brother always referred to him as Ray. Later, Mary changed Leonard's name to Robert Marlow (sometimes spelled Marlowe), also based on numerology, and, thereafter, he was known as Bob.

According to Roy, Mary went to a great deal of trouble to reinvent herself and make him sound like a villain. She was the daughter of Austrian and German immigrants, and, since they arrived in America in 1882, the year that she was born, neither Roy, nor his sons, ever were sure if she was born in New York City, as she claimed, or Germany. Roy told Gene that she insisted that they marry at New York's Church of St. Brigid because she was baptized there; however, in 1938, when Roy inquired about it for Gene, the church could find no record of her baptism. According to census records and *New York City Marriage Records, 1829–1940*, she was born in New York; however, she was not listed in the *New York, New York, Extracted Birth Index, 1878–1909*. A 1934 passenger list placed her passport number under naturalized citizens on the ship, indicating that she *was* born in Germany. She also lied about Roy having his mother committed when, in fact, in 1931, Roy's mother died the day after Mary removed her from the New York City Farm Colony, a poorhouse in Staten Island, where she voluntarily moved and was getting care.

Around 1919, after Roy left the family, Mary went to work and, for a while, she and her sons lived with her widowed father and brother.

She scoffed at novels, but was a voracious reader of newspapers, as well as publications dealing with numerology and astrology. Through the years, she sent Jeanette and Gene clippings from a variety of sources, including dailies, trade papers, and scandal magazines. Mary always was interested in social and political issues, including the welfare of the aged, and was a leader for women's suffrage. In 1937, she toured homes for the aged in Hondo and San Francisco, California; Portland, Oregon; and Seattle, Washington. She planned to write an extensive report on her findings and present it to the League for Political Education at a radio symposium at New York's Town Hall. In 1936, there were rumors that Mary wanted to run for Congress; for what party is unknown.

A series of photos used to help Gene get childhood work in the theater.

At the age of five, Gene made his stage debut in a stock production of *Rip Van Winkle*. Blonde and blue-eyed, he personified a casting director's idea of the ideal all-American boy. Gene said that his mother took him to the stock company as an experiment because she thought that he had talent for the stage; however, Roy also occasionally performed in amateur theatrics. In a 1936 movie magazine interview, Gene claimed that he was fascinated with the theater and stood in the wings every night, watching the adult performers and memorizing their lines. However, in a 1986 interview for Southern Methodist

University, he said that, when he was young, he had no particular desire to perform and that he would rather have been playing, like other children. In 1936, when asked what occupation he would have chosen, had he not gone into acting, Gene said that he would have liked to be a lawyer.

A few years after Gene's debut, it was Mary who pushed him into show business to help support the family. He played children's parts in stock and with the Bramhall Players, a Brooklyn repertory group. After two years at Holy Cross School (now known as De La Salle Academy), in 1920, Mary enrolled Gene in the Professional Children's School in New York City. At the time, the school did not teach acting, but allowed students to continue their studies while they were working, often via correspondence courses. Like Jeanette, Gene studied a business course. In 1923, he explained his plans to a reporter, sounding far wiser than his fourteen years. "You see, while I love the theater and shall always follow it, I am not blind to its uncertainties. It is wise to be prepared for uncertainties. You see, first of all, I want to make money to buy a home in some small but thriving suburban town. Then I want to establish a community theater. I believe that there is plenty of talent in small places that needs to be brought out. So if I have business training I shall know how to raise the money to build the community theater."[113]

In 1918, Gene met actress/playwright Jane Cowl, when he appeared with her in a small role in the Broadway play *The Crowded Hour*. She remained a friend and was mentioned in his wartime correspondence. In 1946, he last worked with her when they prepared for a Broadway play that she co-wrote, *That's for Remembrance*, which was cancelled before rehearsals began. Cowl was considered the greatest Juliet in the American theater, playing a record number of performances of *Romeo and Juliet* during the 1922/1923 theater season. She also co-authored the play *Smilin' Through* (1919), which Jeanette and Gene filmed in 1941. In 1962, Jeanette called Cowl her favorite actress.

In 1920, Gene was chosen to play one of the children in *The Piper*, a stage show about the Pied Piper of Hamelin, directed by Augustin Duncan. Gene's brother, Bob, also was in the production. Duncan later played an important role in Gene's career.

During this time, Gene appeared in *The Difference in Gods* (1921) for the Bramhall Players, and had small roles on Broadway in *Eyvind of the Hills* (1921) and *Why Not?* (1922). In 1922, he made his motion picture debut in *Make It Yourself*, a silent instructional film that ran on a bill with a feature and other shorts. In it, he showed how to build a crystal radio set for $6, currently equivalent to about $90. After Gene became a screen star, he never mentioned this movie. On February 5, 1923, he made his radio debut when New York's WOR broadcast the play *Why Not?* in its entirety.

Augustin Duncan gave Gene his first important break, casting him in the Broadway play *The Potters* (1923). Initially, Gene was an extra in a scene that took place on a trolley. During rehearsals, when the other actors went out in the alley to talk and smoke until their scenes came on, he sat in the front of the theater, watching the play. Within a few days, he knew everyone's lines, and, when the juvenile lead was fired because he looked too old for the part, the director asked Gene to replace him. Both Gene and the show were big hits. In 1923, he joined Actors' Equity and, three years later, at age eighteen, he bought a house in Beechhurst, a northeast section of Queens, New York. Presumably, he sold it when he moved to Hollywood.

In a 1986 interview for Southern Methodist University, Gene recalled how he was left to his own devices during this simpler, safer time. It explained why Jeanette later described him as self-sufficient. As a teen, after his 11:00 p.m. curtain, he not only rode the subway by himself, but routinely stopped at the automat for an after-performance supper of a chicken pot pie, a cup of coffee, and a dish of chocolate ice cream, all for the princely sum of 30¢, now a little over $4.00. At the time, there were child labor laws that forced producers to get work permits for actors under sixteen years of age, but no rules about them having a parent or guardian accompanying them home from the theater at night.

In March 1927, Gene posed with his mother during the Chicago run of *Cradle Snatchers*. Her inscription on the back indicated that she liked being mistaken for Gene's girlfriend, hinting why she later was so jealous of Jeanette. "Taken on our stoop. No one believes I'm Raymond's mother, they think he's kidding. He's always doing that anyway."

After over two hundred performances on Broadway in *The Potters* and a lengthy, successful tour, in 1925, Gene returned to Broadway in *Cradle Snatchers*. The play was co-written by Russell Medcraft, the actor that Gene replaced in *The Potters*, and it was Medcraft who suggested that producer Sam Harris hire Gene. The comedy ran for a year, with a cast that included Edna May Oliver, Mary Boland (who later worked with Jeanette in the film *New Moon*), and Humphrey Bogart. When the Broadway production closed, it also went on tour.

Gene continued in a succession of plays, usually playing a handsome juvenile; none were as successful as his earlier Broadway efforts. They included *Take My Advice* (1927), *Mirrors* (1928), a revival of *Sherlock Holmes* (1928), *Say When* (1928), *The War Song* (1928), and *Jonesy* (1929). Like Jeanette, he usually toured in the plays as well. He also was involved in some publicity stunts to promote the shows, like competing with *Jonesy* co-star Nydia Westman, with both working in the box office on alternate days to see who could sell the most tickets. In Hollywood, Gene worked with several of his Broadway co-stars, including Ralph Morgan of *Take My Advice*, Sylvia Sidney of *Mirrors*, and Shirley Booth and William Gargan of *The War Song* in movies, radio, and television.

In 1929, Gene signed a contract with the Shuberts. His first and only role was that of Gene Gibson in the hit play *Young Sinners*. Gibson was a spoiled young playboy whose father hired a man to reform him so that he could take over the family business. When Gibson's underage girlfriend smuggled herself in to visit him, the changed young man refused her advances, preferring to wait until she was of age and they could marry. It ran for almost three hundred performances on Broadway and toured for another season.

Gene and Dorothy Appleby in a promotional flyer for the 1929 play *Young Sinners*.

On September 28, 1930, while Gene was in Chicago with *Young Sinners*, he first saw Jeanette on screen in *Monte Carlo*. He recalled feeling low on the day that his play was to open and said that attending a matinee of the film lifted his spirits. Later, he said that, while he was in Chicago, he saw the movie twelve times. In a foreword for Jeanette's unpublished autobiography, he wrote, "She was all a young man could envision as <u>his girl</u>. I am sure there were many other young fellows with that [sic] same dreams as I had of Jeanette MacDonald. But, you see, my dreams played themselves out and I 'got the girl'!"[114]

According to *Variety*, in the fall of 1930, during the tour of *Young Sinners*, Gene wrote a book, *Notes on the Experimental Theatre*, published by McCaulay Co. In February 1931, the stunts in the show caused him to wrench his back and he left the play to recover. Checks auctioned on eBay showed Gene getting treatment and an X-ray from two New York doctors in February 1931.

Gene's success in *Young Sinners* led to a string of movie offers, including one from MGM for $800 per week, now over $13,000 per week. In May 1931, he chose to sign with Paramount. Like Jeanette, he was under contract to the Shuberts and, for months, he paid them $250 a week of his $1,000-a-week salary. Today, that's about $4,100 of $16,500. In December, he went to New York to buy out the remainder of his contract from the theater producers and, in March 1932, they settled for an undisclosed amount.

Paramount requested that Gene change his name from the hard-to-pronounce Raymond Guion to Gene Raymond, combining his *Young Sinners* character's first name with his real first name. He adopted it right away, but waited until March 7, 1934 to go to court in New York, where, on April 18, he legally became Gene Raymond. "Changing an established name is looked upon with horror by professional people," he said. "But after having suffered with a difficult handle for so long, I appreciated the chance of getting rid of it. I've spent hours trying to have people understand it over the telephone. I once worked for a producer for two years—and at the end of that time he'd call me 'Ginion.'"[115] According to a 1936 article, his name was pronounced Geón.

Gene planned to go to Hollywood in September 1931 to begin his film contract. However, in June, he received a call from Paramount, requesting that he make a movie at their Astoria, Queens, New York studio: *Personal Maid* (1931) with Nancy Carroll and Pat O'Brien. It was the same place that Jeanette filmed her Paramount screen test. Gene felt more relaxed before the cameras when he learned that Mary Boland, his *Cradle Snatchers* co-star, and Donald Meek, who played his father in *The Potters* and *Jonesy*, also were in the movie. The plot concerned a woman (Carroll) who fell for her employer's son (Gene), while she was working as a maid. Although some of Gene's friends warned him that Carroll was bossy, he appreciated her teaching him how to act before the camera, which was very different from acting on stage. They remained friends and, in 1946, he considered suggesting her for a role in *That's for Remembrance*, the Jane Cowl play that he planned to do on Broadway; however, after meeting with Carroll, he decided that she looked too Irish for the part.

When *Personal Maid* was completed, Gene and Bob drove to California, while their mother headed west by train. The brothers stopped in Chicago to visit some friends and had a narrow escape when a tire burst and their new Ford spun around three times. In order to make up time, they drove over nine hundred miles in thirty-six hours, only to find that, when they arrived in Hollywood, Gene wasn't put to work for two months. Having lived in hotels while he was touring in plays, Gene was anxious to settle down in a real home with a large garden. He rented a house on the corner of Hillside and North La Brea Avenues that was the former home of his Paramount boss, Jesse Lasky. Gene spent much of his spare time horseback riding and walking, two pastimes that Jeanette also enjoyed.

Gene was very athletic and enjoyed the outdoors. When he was twelve, he began to learn every acrobatic and physical exercise he could, thinking that they may help his career. As a teen, after a show, he often went roller skating with fellow actors in Central Park at night. In July 1926, during the run of *Cradle Snatchers*, Gene won a 100-yard dash at an event sponsored by the Lambs Club, America's oldest theatrical organization. At age seventeen, he learned to fence, thinking the skill someday may be needed for a swashbuckling stage role. While he was doing a play in Chicago, he became the champion at a prominent athletic club and even gave exhibition fencing matches with his instructor. In 1935, Gene was an honored guest at the Olympic fencing tryout at Los Angeles' Hungarian Athletic Club.

From the time Gene was young, he liked baseball and, in Hollywood, he played in several charity games featuring teams made up of actors versus comedians. He liked to golf and, in 1934, he joined the Bel-Air Country Club. In addition to being proficient in tennis and swimming, he was an excellent gymnast who often did tricks on the diving board. While vacationing in Florida, he studied aquaplaning, similar to water skiing on a board, until he could ride standing on his head.

Gene won awards for his equestrian skills on jumpers.

Gene enjoyed riding horses, both for pleasure and in competition. During the Chicago run of *Young Sinners,* which played 150 performances, he spent two and a half months learning to clear jumps. One of his proudest moments was winning a blue ribbon for the four-foot jump. When he first went to Hollywood, he played polo with humorist Will Rogers, actor Will Rogers, Jr., and director John Cromwell, until he was injured during a game and Paramount forbade him from playing. Gene explained, "In attempting to make a difficult shot, I was struck by the horse's head. They took several stitches in my face and the picture in which I was working was delayed for three weeks. So I quit polo. I like the game, but I also work for a living."[116] Later, when he and Jeanette began dating, they often attended polo matches at the Riviera Country Club.

Gene also liked to hunt and fish. During a 1936 trip to Florida, he caught a ninety-pound marlin, which he had mounted. Prior to his marriage, it hung in his dining room. Afterwards, it hung above the fireplace in the old English-themed tap room, which Jeanette and Gene used for casual entertaining. He belonged to the "Pin-Tail Duck Club," a group of celebrity duck-hunters who met in Bakersfield, California to hunt and play gin rummy. Other members of the club, which they jokingly referred to as the "Tin-Pail Duck Club," included actors Clark Gable, Robert Taylor, Fred MacMurray, and Frank Morgan. In the 1940s, Gene sometimes went hunting with David Tannenbaum, law partner of Louis Swarts.

In Hollywood, Gene appeared in *Ladies of the Big House* (1931) with Sylvia Sidney, *The Night of June 13* (1932) with Frances Dee, *Forgotten Commandments* (1932) with Marguerite Churchill, and *If I Had a Million* (1932) with Frances Dee. Paramount also loaned Gene to MGM for *Red Dust* (1932), a romantic drama about infidelity on a rubber plantation in French Indochina, with Jean Harlow, Clark Gable, and Mary Astor. Gene played Astor's cuckolded husband; it was his first major hit on screen. In 2006, *Red Dust* was added to the National Film Registry for preservation in the Library of Congress. To date, it is the only one of Gene's movies to be included. In 1932, he earned over $39,000, now equivalent to over $716,000.

Jeanette and Gene posed in the tap room in their home with the ninety-pound marlin that Gene caught in Florida in 1936.

After a year with Paramount, Gene was tired of being typecast, often as men unjustly accused, and decided that he wanted to free-lance. He hoped to get stronger roles on his own and, in October 1932, asked for his release from the studio. He initially planned to head back to New York and resume his stage work; however, he changed his mind when he received movie offers. He kept busy, working for MGM, Fox, Warner Bros., Columbia Pictures, United Artists, and RKO in dramas, comedies, and musicals. In 1933 alone, he appeared in seven movies. During this period, his films included *Ex-Lady* (1933) with Bette Davis, *Zoo in Budapest* (1933) with Loretta Young, *Brief Moment* (1933) with Carole Lombard, *The House on 56th Street* (1933) with Kay Francis, *Ann Carver's Profession* (1933) with Fay Wray, *I Am Suzanne!* (1933) with Lilian Harvey, *Coming Out Party* (1934) with Frances

Dee, *Transatlantic Merry-Go-Round* (1934) with Nancy Carroll, Jack Benny, and Ralph Morgan, *Behold My Wife!* (1934) with Sylvia Sidney and Ann Sheridan, *The Woman in Red* (1935) with Barbara Stanwyck, and *Transient Lady* (1935) with Frances Drake. He starred opposite Dolores del Rio in *Flying Down to Rio* (1933), a musical best known for introducing dancers Fred Astaire and Ginger Rogers as a screen team. In *Sadie McKee* (1934), Gene's singing of "All I Do Is Dream of You" to Joan Crawford helped popularize the song.

Gene's main memory of working with Bette Davis involved her inviting him for what Davis called a New England Christmas dinner with her and her mother, as his family was in New York during the holidays. He was surprised to learn a New England Christmas dinner was baked beans.

A 1995 overview of Gene's career noted that he was much more serious about his work than many of his contemporaries. It claimed, "In order to pick up bits of characterization for his roles, he would pass time studying people at the Los Angeles Railroad Station. In *I Am Suzanne[!]*, with Lillian [sic] Harvey, he played the part of a puppeteer and studied real marionette operators in preparation for his role."[117]

Gene disliked many of the parts that he was offered, which was one of the reasons that, throughout his career, he often free-lanced, rather than staying under contract to one studio. In 1934, he observed, "One poor picture can do more to ruin an actor than ten stage plays."[118] He also found that many of the directors that he worked with gave little direction and, unlike the theater, the movies had very little rehearsal time. In a 1932 interview, he said, "There is no chance to better a performance. In the theatre one has time to build up a certain quality. In the films we work so hastily that good 'takes' seem like acts of God. For the bad ones there is nothing to do but writhe around in your seat knowing 'There it is—and I can't improve on it, ever.'"[119]

Later, in several interviews, Gene recalled his shock at seeing crowds lined up to see *Flying Down to Rio* at Radio City Music Hall. He talked about working without a script for much of the filming and the disorganization of the production, claiming that Fred Astaire and Ginger Rogers were the only ones who knew what they were doing because they had plenty of rehearsal time for their dances.

In 1934, Gene aspired to appear in swashbuckling pictures, which, at that time, seldom were being produced on screen. He said, "I can be independent and walk out of the roles that I don't like—but I can't walk into the roles that I like if they aren't written!"[120]

Gene appreciated the experience he received on the stage and, through the mid-1960s, he continued to work in the theater. In a 1933 interview, which ran in early 1934, he suggested that the studios invest in theaters in New York and allow their players to spend half the year making movies and half acting on stage. He explained how Hollywood gave actors financial stability. "But no creative artist can afford to do altogether without the theatre," he insisted. "It is disconcerting to work one's feelings and emotions up for a big scene in a picture and then to hear 'Cut' intercepted into one's mood." Gene said that actors in Hollywood were "apt to become too full of our own importance," adding that he felt his work deteriorated when he was miscast by Paramount and he was forced into stories that he didn't like. In the same 1933 interview, Gene extolled the virtues of New York. "If one lives in New York, there are devotees of all the Arts [sic] to mix with. In New York, as in London, film stars leave the studios after their day's work and become ordinary human beings with other interests. In Hollywood, they are always film stars. Hollywood takes itself too seriously."[121]

Early in Gene's career, he became active in causes that affected his profession. On July 12, 1933, the Screen Actors Guild (SAG) was formed to keep studios from forcing actors to work long hours and holding actors to oppressive multi-year contracts. Prior to the union, actors weren't allowed to accept offers from rival studios when their contracts expired. The initial meeting was held at the home of character actor Frank Morgan, best known as the Wizard in *The Wizard of Oz*, and who later appeared in four movies with Jeanette. SAG's first President was Morgan's brother, Ralph, who worked with Gene on Broadway in *Take My Advice* and in the movie *Transatlantic Merry-Go-Round*. Both Jeanette and Gene were founding members of the union. In June 1993, Gene was one of sixteen founding members honored at a sixtieth anniversary tribute.

On October 15, 1933, Gene was among a group of actors and screenwriters who protested the enforcement of the Production Code at a meeting in Hollywood. They sent letters to President Franklin D. Roosevelt; however, they did no good since the Code was not established by any government entity, but the studios themselves. It's interesting to note that, in the 1930s, Gene was against censorship, but, in the 1950s and 1960s, when censorship became more lax, both he and Jeanette complained about the sordid content of movies.

Like Jeanette, Gene took his mother on a European vacation. On December 29, 1933, they sailed on the S.S. Bremen and, en route, met soprano Amelita Galli-Curci and her husband, accompanist Homer Samuels. Coincidentally, young Jeanette sang along to Galli-Curci's records on the Victrola and considered the singer to be one of her idols. Gene and his mother traveled to England, France, Germany, Hungary, Austria, and the Kingdom of Yugoslavia, before returning to New York on the S.S. Europa on January 25, 1934.

On June 7, 1934, Gene was named defendant in a lawsuit for a freak accident that happened on the previous Fourth of July at a Santa Monica, California beach club. According to the suit, four-year-old

Jacqueline Clark was hit in the face when Gene set off a skyrocket that misdirected and set off other skyrockets, which caused a projectile to hit the little girl and permanently disfigure her. Her father asked for $30,000 in damages, currently equivalent to almost $564,000. On June 27, 1935, the judge ruled in favor of the plaintiff, but awarded her $500 (currently about $9,400) and her father $217.45 (currently equivalent to about $4,100), rather than the $30,000 they requested. Barbara Biorkman, almost fifteen at the time of the accident, also asked for compensation for her injuries. On June 28, 1935, the court awarded her $82.55, currently equivalent to around $1,550. Given the rulings, it is assumed that both girls' injuries were minor and the judge thought that the Clarks were trying to take advantage of a celebrity by filing a $30,000 suit.

In 1935, Gene starred in RKO's *Hooray for Love*, his first screen pairing with Ann Sothern, filmed in March and April, and released in June. The plot was a backstage story about a producer of college shows (Gene) who had a crush on a singer (Ann) and invested in a Broadway production that starred her. Like Gene, Ann had worked on Broadway under another name, Harriette Lake, and adopted a new moniker in Hollywood. As a result of the film's success, in July 1935, RKO signed Gene to a long-term contract. He told reporter Lenore Samuels, "You know, I've been free-lancing for several years. I think I've gone as far as I can that way. So I'm trying my luck with 'a termer' again." He elaborated on why he decided to accept a contract: "I felt that I'd reached rock bottom so far as good free-lancing parts were concerned. . . . I decided that the big companies put their featured players in the roles that were sure to shine out—for this reason—if they clicked, and clicked big, the company would reap the reward with the success of the player's succeeding role. . . . Whereas, if a free lance player clicked, his roving assignments would take him right off the lot where he'd made a hit, to another one which would cash in on his previous performance."[122]

Before Gene's marriage, RKO reteamed Gene and Ann Sothern in a series of light romantic comedies: *Walking on Air* (1936), *Smartest Girl in Town* (1936), and *There Goes My Girl* (1937); they appeared in one more after his marriage, *She's Got Everything* (1937), his last film under his RKO contract. Their characters often bickered, but, by the end of the pictures, they were in love. *Walking on Air* cast Ann as a stubborn woman who hired a struggling singer (Gene) to pretend to be her obnoxious boyfriend, in an effort to get her parents to approve of the man that she really wanted to marry. Naturally, in the end, she fell for Gene. On August 14, 1936, Gene and Ann recreated their roles on Louella Parsons' radio program, *Hollywood Hotel*. In *Smartest Girl in Town*, a model (Ann) longed for a rich husband, but fell for a poor model (Gene), unaware that he really was wealthy and only pretending to be poor. *There Goes My Girl* was about rival newspaper reporters (Ann and Gene) whose employers tried to break them up after they became engaged.

In *Smartest Girl in Town*, Gene introduced "Will You?," a song he also wrote, which was copyrighted on December 15, 1935. In 1937, when Jeanette sang it on her radio show, *Vicks Open House*, she mentioned that he wrote it for her. On November 19, 1936, Gene recorded the song for Brunswick Records, backed with "Twinkle, Twinkle, Little Star" from the movie *Hats Off* (1936). Gene laughed about "Will You?" and his experience dealing with composer Irving Berlin's publishing company. "When the number first came out, I received a $500 check from the music company. And was I stunned! So much money for one little song! I saw a whole new field open up to me. Then came the clinker. Another letter from Berlin's company. This one said that my song had been over-printed by 30,000 copies, which the company couldn't sell and that I had to return $350 out of the $500 I had received."[123] The current equivalent of $350 is about $6,300, and $500 is about $9,000. According to a 1940 article in *Variety*, the amounts were $149 and $49, now about $2,700 and $887. In Gene's wartime letters, he continued to joke about his paltry song royalties.

In between Gene's films with Ann Sothern, he made other movies for RKO: *Seven Keys to Baldpate* (1935) with Margaret Callahan, *Love on a Bet* (1936) with Wendy Barrie, *The Bride Walks Out* (1936) with Barbara Stanwyck, *That Girl from Paris* (1937) with Lily Pons, and *The Life of the Party* (1937) with Harriet Hilliard. Although many of Gene's RKO movies were low-budget B pictures, they usually made money for the studio.

Despite Gene's dissatisfaction with the lightweight parts that he was given, in the 1930s, he was very popular, especially with female audiences. He regularly was seen in movie magazines, and his personal appearance tours broke records. Crowds of women waited outside his hotels, as well as the theaters, hoping to catch a glimpse of him or get an autograph. He also had his share of obsessed fans. During a 1935 tour, a group broke into his dressing room and one fan admitted that she contemplated stealing his cigarette case. On May 16, 1935, eighteen-year-old stenographer Helen Zeh of San Francisco announced that she and Gene would be married on June 2. When reporters quizzed Gene about the engagement, he asked who she was because he never met her. During a 1936 personal appearance tour, a group of over-enthusiastic autograph-seekers knocked him to the ground. That same year, co-eds at the University of Southern California (USC) voted him their favorite screen romancer.

At RKO, Gene often was paired with Ann Sothern. Prior to her 1936 marriage to actor Roger Pryor, the studio sometimes sent Gene on dates with her. Here they attended a performance of the play *Tobacco Road* in early 1935. Coincidentally, Pryor's father, Arthur, was conductor of the Capitol Orchestra when Jeanette appeared in *Ned Wayburn's Demi Tasse Revue*. Nat Finston succeeded him as the Capitol's conductor.

While Jeanette was called The Lingerie Queen, Gene could have been dubbed The Shirtless King, as the scripts often called for him to show off his muscular form by wearing only boxer shorts and an undershirt, swimming trunks, or even a towel. The movie magazines took advantage of this and frequently ran photos of him without a shirt. Later in life, he still received fan letters, commenting on his physique. In 1990, after a woman saw a TV airing of *Love on a Bet* (1936), which she wrongly identified as *Cross-Country Romance* (1940), she noted, "No one looks as good in his underwear as you do. . . . I still think you quite a hunk, – today, yesterday, tomorrow and always."[124]

One of Gene's pet peeves was the way that reporters and fans focused on his hair. Blonde and naturally curly, it photographed platinum, especially after he spent time in the sun. He became frustrated when people teased him about it and found that casting directors seldom took him seriously because brunette leading men were more in vogue for dramatic roles.

Unlike Jeanette, whose fans thought that she was involved romantically with her screen partners, Gene was rumored to feud with Ann Sothern, although, before her 1936 marriage to actor Roger Pryor, she and Gene occasionally went on studio-arranged dates. Instead, Gene's name was linked with actresses Marian Nixon (whom Jeanette had known in New York), Mary Brian, Frances Dee, Carole Lombard, and Janet Gaynor, all of whom he claimed were just friends.

In a 1934 interview, Gene discussed his love life. "The trouble with this business is that nobody takes it seriously but the actors," he said. "If you're an actor, automatically you must be married or you must be in the middle of a love life or you must be a playboy of the western world. You can't just take a girl out once in awhile for an evening, unless you're expected to marry her." He continued, "I like women and I like to be with them—but I don't want to marry one until I've got a lot of money saved up. I'm a solitary dog; I like to be by myself—and when I come home at night, I don't want to be agreeable. I want to get into an old bathrobe or smoking jacket and rest. Selfish, I admit—but when I marry I want to devote my life to my wife—and not to my career!"[125] Less than two months after the interview ran, he met the woman who made him want to give up being "a solitary dog."[126]

Chapter Four

Through the years, numerous times, Jeanette and Gene told the story of their first meeting in late 1934; however, actually, they casually knew each other much earlier. An article in *The New Movie Magazine* described a 1932 Halloween barbecue hosted by Gene's *Red Dust* co-star, Mary Astor, and her husband, Dr. Franklyn Thorpe, where the guests included Jeanette and Gene. He arrived alone, but paid attention to starlet Dorothy Wilson, who, coincidentally, was later one of the unbilled Maxim's girls in *The Merry Widow* with Jeanette. When reporter Grace Kingsley arrived, Jeanette, Gene, Dorothy Wilson, and actresses Fay Wray and Jobyna Ralston were playing the word game ghosts on one side of the bonfire. Jeanette won. It probably was very casual; however, if five people were playing a game, they had to be acquainted. Interestingly, five years later, Fay Wray was one of the bridesmaids in the Raymonds' wedding.

Paramount founder Jesse Lasky also claimed that he introduced Jeanette and Gene during a weekend party at Lasky's Santa Monica beach house. Given the number of stars that Jeanette and Gene each encountered at parties, it's possible that they both forgot about these meetings or found them to be inconsequential.

On October 27, 1934, almost two years after the Thorpes' Halloween barbecue, department store heir Irving Netcher gave a belated birthday party for his wife, Rozsika "Rosie" Dolly, one of the internationally famous entertainers known as the Dolly Sisters, whose birthday was October 25. Both Jeanette and Gene were among the 150 attendees. Gene arrived late at the Netchers' house and encountered another guest on the doorstep: the always-tardy Jeanette, who also came alone. They introduced themselves and, when Rosie opened the door, she assumed that they came together. As Jeanette later recalled, director Howard Hughes was pursuing her that night, and Gene was more interested in his *Zoo in Budapest* co-star, Loretta Young. According to DeWitt Bodeen, Gene saw Hughes send Jeanette a note, and Gene sought her out afterwards to tell her that he hoped that she wasn't going to date Hughes, a notorious playboy. Coincidentally, Irving Netcher's father founded the Boston Store in Chicago, unrelated to the store of the same name where Jeanette's ex-boyfriend, Irving Stone, worked in Milwaukee.

Sources disagree on the timing of Jeanette and Gene's next meeting at the home of Louis and Emma Swarts, ranging from a few days to two weeks to several months later. Through the years, when the Raymonds retold the story, even *they* were inconsistent on the details of the length of time between the Netchers' party and their second encounter. Because of the inconsistencies, some sources claimed that they met in June 1935, shortly before their first official date. Jeanette never was good at remembering exact dates or details, which accounts for some of the confusion over the sequence of events in her autobiography.

From January 16 to March 10, 1935, Gene was far from Hollywood, vacationing in Palm Beach, Florida, and New York City, and making personal appearances in Detroit, Michigan, and Chicago, Illinois to promote *Transient Lady*. Early in the year, the Netchers sailed to Europe and didn't return until April, proving that their party had to have been held months before Jeanette and Gene's second meeting. Also, given the timing between their second and third encounters, the second had to have happened after Gene's March return to California.

In the meantime, in December 1934, Jeanette began filming *Naughty Marietta*, her first screen pairing with Nelson Eddy. The movie changed the story and eliminated some songs and characters from Victor Herbert and Rida Johnson Young's 1910 operetta. The film plot concerned a French princess (Jeanette) who, in order to avoid an arranged marriage, switched places with her maid and escaped to New Orleans, Louisiana. There, she fell in love with a mercenary soldier (Nelson), and together, they headed west to make a life together.

Jeanette worried a bit about working with Nelson, concerned that, if the movie flopped, she would be blamed, since she was the star and it was his first large film role. Previously, he had appeared in specialties on screen, singing but not acting. Nelson praised her generosity: sharing tips for acting before the camera, insisting that he sing "Neath the Southern Moon," originally intended for her, and giving him equal billing. No one expected the movie to be anything special. At the beginning of filming, Jeanette joked to Woody Van Dyke, "What's naughty about her? It seems to me that she's just crazy to throw over a castle in Spain for a swamp in Louisiana. Let's call it 'Nutty Marietta.'"[127]

Jeanette found Van Dyke's style of directing was very different from that of Ernst Lubitsch, although each began their careers as actors. While Lubitsch often acted out scenes and wanted the actors to copy his performance, Van Dyke believed in spontaneity and encouraged his actors to improvise. Jeanette appreciated the freedom and said it allowed more of her own personality to shine through in her performance. She particularly enjoyed the comic bits and tried to inject a bit of humor into each role, like eating on the ship while she was in disguise in *Naughty Marietta*.

During filming, Van Dyke, a notorious playboy, invited Jeanette out for dinner and dancing. At the end of the evening, on Jeanette's doorstep, he tried to take her in his arms, but she stiffened. He politely kissed her cheek and left. The next day, a bouquet of yellow roses was delivered to her dressing room, along with a note reading, "To Naughty Marietta. P.S. Not so naughty." Jeanette observed, "That established our relationship. Good friends, but no nonsense."[128]

The movie was an enormous hit, surprising MGM, as well as its stars, and ushering in an era of screen operettas. *Etude music magazine* said that *Naughty Marietta* showed the possibilities of filming operettas and enlivening them for a new generation. On stage, the songs stopped the action when the leads stepped to the footlights to sing; in the movie, the songs were sung while the action proceeded, with each reinforcing the other. *Naughty Marietta* was nominated for an Academy Award for Best Picture and won for Best Sound (Douglas Shearer). The film made a profit of $407,000, currently equivalent to almost $7.5 million, more money than any musical up to that time, and launched the screen team of MacDonald and Eddy. Many film historians said that "Ah! Sweet Mystery of Life" was a grand and defining moment in musical history. It, along with "Indian Love Call" from *Rose-Marie* and "Will You Remember" from *Maytime*, became Jeanette and Nelson's most recognizable duets. *Naughty Marietta* also included what would become one of Jeanette's most requested recital pieces, "Italian Street Song." She liked to challenge herself, seeing how long she could hold a note near the end of the song. Jeanette and Nelson recreated their roles on radio adaptations of *Naughty Marietta* on *Vicks Open House* on December 20, 1936 and *Lux Radio Theatre* on June 12, 1944.

In 2003, *Naughty Marietta* was named to the National Film Registry for preservation in the Library of Congress, the only MacDonald/Eddy pairing included, as of this writing. A 2004 article in *The New York Times* noted that the film was added after years of impassioned pleas from fans.

Around March 24, 1935, about the same time that *Naughty Marietta* was released nationally, Jeanette and Gene met for the second time, when they each arrived late for brunch at the home of attorney Louis Swarts and his wife, Emma. Jeanette was standing on the doorstep when Gene whistled from behind her. She turned and he teased her, asking if she always looked when men whistled. This time, they seemed more interested in each other, making eye contact across the table. Through the years, Louis Swarts remained a loyal friend to Jeanette and Gene and often advised them on their careers, as well as legal matters. Jeanette considered him a surrogate father. Both the Netchers and the Swarts were mentioned in Jeanette and Gene's wartime correspondence.

A few days later, on Friday, March 29, Jeanette and Gene's third encounter happened at a preview of *Les Miserables* at Grauman's Chinese Theatre. Jeanette was with Anna; sources disagree over whether Gene was with his mother or his attorney, Neil McCarthy. Both Jeanette and Gene arrived late and ran into each other while picking up their tickets. They decided to sit together and, afterwards, walked down the block on Hollywood Boulevard to C.C. Brown's for sodas, accompanied by Anna and whoever was with Gene. Given Jeanette and Gene's mutual love of ice cream, and Gene's love of chocolate, it's surprising that they didn't have sundaes, since, in 1906, the restaurant's founder was said to have created the hot fudge sundae.

Gene invited Jeanette to go out dancing the next night, saying that there already were rumors in Hollywood that they were dating and they should make it official. Instead, she insisted that it would be more proper if he had dinner the following evening at the home that she shared with Anna at 912 North Rexford Drive. There were two stories that came out of that dinner. 1) In the beginning, Jeanette and Gene each were nervous and Anna had to carry most of the conversation. Eventually they relaxed and told each other their life stories, finding that they had a great deal in common, having both begun working on the stage as children, being under contract to the Shuberts on Broadway, and launching their screen careers at Paramount. Gene insisted that he was too talkative because of nerves. 2) Jeanette served eggplant, which Gene detested, but he politely ate it anyway.

Later, after Jeanette learned that Gene disliked eggplant, when he was on a trip, she routinely sent him the vegetable as a joke. During a 1936 personal appearance tour to promote *Love on a Bet*, she had Blossom paint "Good luck" in gold on an eggplant, which she sent to his New York hotel. While Gene was vacationing in Florida during that same trip, he wrote Jeanette a silly letter to tease her about the eggplant that she sent him.

> I smelled an eggplant on my doorstep this morning with your card attached. I don't quite know how to thank you, though I'm getting an idea or two. They have lovely scorpions here, guaranteed to bite. Or would you prefer something in tarantulas as a house pet? I esteem you so highly that on second thought I'd be willing to stretch a point and send you both. Don't thank me. It's nothing really. Just varmints to a varmint.
>
> I'll keep the eggplant always—in the garbage can. As to what I think of you, remind me to tell you some time.
>
> I'll be back next week. Will you keep Friday night for me?[129]

In 1938, when Gene did a personal appearance in Chicago, reporters noted that he had a good luck eggplant on his dressing table from Jeanette. In 1940, when he was in San Francisco for a personal appearance for *Cross-Country Romance,* Jeanette had a fan carve "hello" on an eggplant and present it to Gene backstage in an elaborately wrapped box. Gene also got in on the gag by sending Jeanette an entire case of eggplant on the first day of filming *San Francisco.*

Gene described that first dinner as "a flopperoo" [sic]. He recalled, "Jeanette has since told me that she'd heard I was rather quiet. She rather likes quiet, reserved men so it was certainly not putting my best foot forward when I was so talkative no one else could insert a syllable into my verbal syllabus. What is more, I went to positive lengths to impress her mother. Mrs. MacDonald played up to me and the two of us practically excluded Jeanette from the conversation. When I left, so in love by this time that I was wacky, I turned to Mrs. MacDonald and said, 'I'll call you tomorrow!' then to Jeanette I added, carelessly, 'See you soon.'"[130]

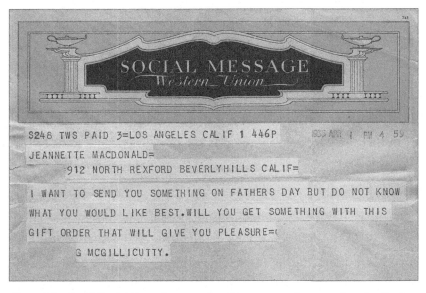

One of the April Fools' Day telegrams that Gene sent to Jeanette shortly after he dined at her house in 1935. The telegraph operator misspelled her name.

Despite the stories about Jeanette and Gene being nervous during that first dinner, they must have hit it off enough for him to tease her. Two days later, he sent her at least four joke telegrams on April Fools' Day, all signed G. McGillicutty. Through the years, McGillicutty was one of the silly nicknames that Jeanette and Gene used in their correspondence. Later, Gene named one of his Irish Setters Mike McGillicutty. It isn't known whether he sent these initial telegrams with a fake name to keep nosy Western Union operators from spreading gossip or, if during that initial dinner, he and Jeanette really had a closer rapport than they claimed. Sentimental Jeanette saved the wires.

On April 5, Jeanette and Anna sailed to Honolulu on the S.S. Lurline for a month-long vacation. Gene sent a bale of newspapers to the ship, joking that it would give Jeanette something to do in her spare time. Fredda Dudley Balling, one of the ghostwriters who collaborated with Jeanette on her unpublished autobiography, said that Gene also sent Jeanette a wire in Honolulu, asking why she hadn't sent him a postcard. In her autobiography, Jeanette mentioned a wire from Gene, asking when she was coming back. This was from someone who had yet to go on a real date with her.

It was during this trip that Jeanette met Dr. Francis "Pete" Halford and his wife, Marge, who became lifelong friends. According to their oldest daughter, Joan Halford Rohlfing, Jeanette had to visit a doctor during the trip, but Rohlfing didn't know why. "She went to my dad and I guess they got to talking and he probably invited her to our home. My mother had been a music major in college and played the piano, so he thought they might enjoy one another. They became good friends."[131] Although some fans erroneously claimed that Jeanette had a heart attack during the trip, it is more likely that Jeanette saw Dr. Halford because of her allergies, since the floral leis aggravated them during other trips to Hawaii. The Halfords frequently were mentioned in the Raymonds' wartime correspondence and, in 1942, several times Marge and the Halford children stayed with Jeanette at the Raymonds' home while they were evacuated from Honolulu.

Some twenty-first century fans criticized Jeanette for not promoting *Naughty Marietta*, trying to read something suspicious into her trip and even erroneously suggesting that she went to Hawaii to annul a marriage to Bob Ritchie. While Jeanette didn't attend a screening of the film in Washington, D.C. with Nelson Eddy and Woody Van Dyke, according to *Film Daily*, the premiere scheduled for New Orleans was cancelled. In February and March, Jeanette attended three previews of the film in California, including a star-studded preview in lieu of a premiere, held at Grauman's Chinese Theatre on February 16, and a party afterward at the Trocadero. During her vacation, on April 18, she attended a private screening for MGM officials in Hawaii, doing more than her share of promoting the film.

When Jeanette and Anna returned to California, Gene was away on another personal appearance tour, which he combined with a vacation in New York. Around June 10, he arrived back in California. A week later, on June 17, Jeanette and Gene had their first official date at the Cocoanut Grove, a nightclub in the Ambassador Hotel. During dinner, Jeanette kept looking at her watch, and Gene worried that she was bored. However, when the clock struck 12:00, she delightedly announced that it was her birthday. To celebrate, Gene ordered champagne and a cake with candles, relieved that the date wasn't a disaster. Some sources, including Jeanette's autobiography, erroneously said that the Raymonds' first official date was at Ciro's; however, the nightclub didn't open until January 30, 1940. Presumably, with all of the nightclubs that Jeanette and Gene visited through the years, Jeanette confused them.

In an outline for Jeanette's autobiography, she wrote about her first impressions of Gene: "He was handsome, clean cut and good fun—meeting the standards nature had set for me in looking at a man. I felt the thrill that marked every great romance."[132] Despite Jeanette's two engagements, she was adamant about staying single, even after she met Gene. Before getting engaged, they dated for a year and, even then, she wanted time to prepare for a wedding and not elope like many Hollywood couples. "Marriage must wait," she said. "When I marry, it will be forever and there will be nothing to interfere with it. Marriage is a career in itself, and I intend to give it my full time."[133] It's interesting to note that she and Gene dated for only two years before their wedding, while her other engagements were much longer.

When Gene met Jeanette, he was somewhat wary of women, mostly because of the female fans who chased him. During his 1935 personal appearance tour, over a thousand women lined up in front of his Chicago hotel to get a glimpse of him. Gene was realistic about his fame. In 1935, he told a reporter from *Modern Screen*, "Listen, I know I'm not anything wonderful. I know it isn't really I that they admire, it's the men I portray on the screen. It's the lines I say and the makeup and lighting and background and all the other artificialities. I could be the same person and drive a truck for a living and I'd go about unnoticed. So when women, as you say, 'make a fuss' over me, I feel exactly as though I'm being lied to. I wonder what I have that they want—certainly not myself [sic] and I want to get away as fast as I can." Conversely, he continued, "If a woman meets me and doesn't 'make a fuss' over me I'm forced to think she's being cagey, using reverse strategy. . . . I want to do my own pursuing. I want to go about under normal circumstances and be able to tell when a girl likes me for myself and nothing else."[134]

It's interesting to note that both Jeanette and Gene's professional lives underwent a major change around the time that they started dating. Jeanette had made one movie with Nelson Eddy, *Naughty Marietta*, which was released shortly after she and Gene attended the Swarts' brunch. That summer, she was cast in *Rose-Marie*, leading to Jeanette and Nelson officially being labeled a screen team. Gene's first movie with Ann Sothern, *Hooray for Love*, was released on June 14, three days before his first official date with Jeanette. In July, he signed a contract with RKO, and in February 1936, Sothern signed with the studio, which led to their screen pairing in four additional films.

During Jeanette and Gene's courtship, they spent time at Ocean Park Pier, often posing for silly pictures like any other couple.

During the summer of 1935, Jeanette and Gene dated steadily. They spent many evenings at Ocean Park Pier in Santa Monica, riding the roller coaster and the serpentine slide, often posing for silly pictures to commemorate the occasion. Sometimes, they went dancing at the Miramar Hotel in Santa Monica. Jeanette recalled, "We had investigated every little hideaway dine & dance spot up and down the coast, hoping to find a place where we could be merely a dating couple instead of a pair who—whenever we appeared at Ciro's [sic] or The [sic] Grove—were announced by the orchestra's striking up, 'All I Do Is Dream of You,' followed by 'The Merry Widow Waltz,' or 'Ah, Sweet Mystery of Life.'"[135] They frequently went to the theater to see movies and plays. One of their favorite games was to eat at a drive-in restaurant and the first one to be recognized had to pay the check.

Initially, Jeanette and Gene were casual about their relationship. They were having a good time, but had no expectations about the future. In her autobiography, Jeanette wrote, "He was so downright gentlemanly I was convinced he didn't love me and never would."[136] Despite that, as early as August 1935, two months after Jeanette and Gene's first official date, the Hollywood press was sure that they were going to run off to Yuma, Arizona, a popular elopement spot for celebrities, because they had been seen together so often.

In addition to going out, Jeanette and Gene also spent time swimming and sunning by the pool at Jeanette's Brentwood home at 193 North Carmelina Drive, where she and Anna moved in June 1935. The couple perfected a duet stroke, which, as evidenced in their home movies, rivaled anything that Esther Williams did in the water with her screen partners. Although Jeanette loved to swim, she seldom dove because the sudden rush of water into the sinus area could have produced severe complications. She always wore a bathing cap, not only to protect her hair from the chlorine in the pool, but to protect her ears. Her motion sickness also was related to inner ear problems. Since childhood, she suffered from ear trouble and, one year, she even went deaf because of colds or undiagnosed allergies that affected her ears. In an outline for her autobiography, Jeanette called herself "a half-well child" because of the childhood colds and allergy attacks.[137]

While Jeanette and Gene were dating, they spent a great deal of time swimming at Jeanette's home on North Carmelina Drive. She always protected her ears in the water.

In notes for Jeanette's autobiography, she recalled her home on North Carmelina Drive: "It was an awfully attractive house—I re-member it vividly now. It had a swimming pool and a tennis court and when I started *Rose-Marie* I had been taking some tennis lessons—and primarily, because Gene played an awfully good game of tennis and it seemed to be a good idea—so that I could play with him. And then the picture started and all these things are interruptions that stopped any hope for a brilliant atheletic [sic] career."[138] Jeanette described that summer as "some of the most wonderful, carefree days of our lives."[139]

Jeanette took tennis lessons from Eleanor "Teach" Tennant, the first female tennis player to turn professional and known as the greatest tennis coach in the world. Her pupils included tennis cham-pions Alice Marble and Bobby Riggs, as well as many Hollywood stars. An excerpt from Nancy Spain's 1953 biography, *"Teach" : The Story of Eleanor "Teach" Tennant*, ran in *The Magazine Of The Jeanette MacDonald British Fan Club.*

> Jeanette Macdonald [sic] had lernt [sic] tennis from her for many hours before Teach discovered who she was. "I am not particularly a musical picture fan, so I didn't recognise [sic] her," says Teach, remarking to her well-known pupil "Why don't you get off the dime and shake your stumps and get those shots over?" To which Jeanette, with angelic control, retorted "Would you mind singing the E in Alt.?" "I'd sure love to," said Teach, "but I can only sing six different keys like a horse."
>
> Fortunately Jeanette was amused by all this and continued to play tennis, but Alice Marble was horrified by Teach's wide-eyed innocence.
>
> "Haven't you ever heard of Jeanette Macdonald [sic] and Nelson Eddy?" she cried. No, Teach hadn't, but she liked Jeanette as a person and that was good enough for her. "I don't know what Jeanette's philosophy was," says Teach, "but I was always quite sure that she was thinking in something of a metaphysical family. She is very attractive and very well-made and a most dependable person."[140]

During this time, the public thought that Jeanette was still engaged to Bob Ritchie, who, in early 1934, was sent to Europe to scout talent for MGM, partly because the studio thought that his presence in Hollywood was a liability to Jeanette's reputation. Through the years, during his travels, he helped the studio sign actresses Luise Rainer, Hedy Lamarr, and Greer Garson; he also assisted MGM in acquiring rights to several unnamed properties, which they planned to film.

In Jeanette's autobiography, she wrote, "By all outward appearances, I was still Bob Ritchie's girl. He often stayed with Mother and me on his journeyings [sic] East and West, I still wore the 'engagement' ring, and we still kissed, though more like old friends than lovers now."[141] Jeanette put engagement in quotes because she said that she was the one who purchased the ring. While there is no doubt that she discussed marriage with Bob, she also claimed that she bought the ring to make other men think that she was taken. A 1931 letter to Irving Stone implied that Bob gave her the ring; however, she may have kept the fact that she paid for it a secret from Irving to make Bob appear more prosperous. It's also possible that she wanted her relationship with Bob to sound less serious in her autobiography so she emphasized that she bought the ring. In any case, the ring sent up a red flag to Gene, who asked her about her relationship with Bob, as he did not want to cut in on another man's girl. She insisted that she was no longer serious about Bob, confiding, "I don't tell it usually—and the only reason I told him was because I liked him better than I should. I didn't want him not to keep coming to see me."[142]

Despite Jeanette's correspondence to Bob and Irving Stone to the contrary, Jack Ohmeis' brother, Herbert, said that Jeanette told their mother that her engagement to Bob was a matter of convenience, that she was not in love with him, and that she never planned to marry him. In a 1993 interview, Gene said that Jeanette also told him that she never intended to marry Bob. Whether or not she really felt that way, it's obvious that she had doubts or she wouldn't have had such a lengthy engagement.

On September 11, 1935, Jeanette went on location to Lake Tahoe, on the California and Nevada border, to film *Rose-Marie* with Nelson Eddy. Upon her arrival, Gene sent her roses. During the month that she was gone, they carried on a flirtatious correspondence, with numerous letters and telegrams, as well as nightly telephone calls. Jeanette called Gene pet names like "cutie,"[143] "princey [sic],"[144] and "cutest man in the world."[145] In between flirting, she reported on the *Rose-Marie* filming, which often was delayed because of the weather; her allergies, which were aggravated by the outdoor shooting; and the visitors to Lake Tahoe, who included the mothers of Woody Van Dyke and Nelson Eddy. Jeanette's long distance and telegram bills were so large that she joked that she bought the lodge where she stayed. After one lengthy call, she wrote "32.65 wasn't bad for last nite [sic] – no indeedy [sic]. Think of the pretty hats I could buy with that to charm you with when I return."[146] Currently, $32.65 is almost $600. She also corresponded with Bob Ritchie and, in September, after he returned from another business trip to England, she frequently talked to him too.

Being on location gave Jeanette time to think about both beaus, as well as the future, and she was very open with each of them. According to her autobiography, when Bob visited her in Lake Tahoe to deliver a Bedlington Terrier that she asked him to bring from England, she compared their relationship to a college romance, where both parties grew apart. What Jeanette didn't say was that he actually visited her twice and, presumably, he brought Sunny Days (named after the show that Jeanette was doing when they met) the first time and, about ten days later, she broke up with him during the second trip. It's possible that Jeanette forgot that he was there twice or that her book collaborators combined the trips to simplify matters.

When Sunny began affecting Jeanette's allergies, she offered him to Gilbert Adrian (known professionally as Adrian), who designed many of her MGM costumes; however, the dog bothered his allergies as well. Eventually, Sunny went to live with Blossom; he died in 1949.

When Bob was in California, he continued to occasionally escort Jeanette, causing much gossip, with the columnists speculating about which man Jeanette really loved. In February 1936, Jeanette wrote to Bob, asking him to make it clear that they broke up some time ago so it didn't look like Gene cut him out while Bob was working in Europe. Although Bob remained a bachelor after he and Jeanette split, he dated many famous women in the years that followed, including actresses Hedy Lamarr, Dorothy Lamour, Greer Garson, Eva and Zsa Zsa Gabor, and Nanette Fabray. After World War II, he worked in film and television distribution and as a sales executive with Stephen Leedom Carpet Company in New York. In 1960, Jeanette was last in touch with him to get permission to use his name in her autobiography. Always affable, he offered to help in any way that he could and advised her not to rush with it.

Jeanette, Bob Ritchie, and Sunny in Lake Tahoe during the filming of *Rose-Marie* in the fall of 1935.

Bob spent his last years in and out of hospitals. In 1972, when he died of cancer at age seventy-six, he was broke and had considerable debts. An article in *Variety* said that, after his death, fifty to sixty keys, many of which appeared to go to safety deposit boxes, were found in his apartment. His brother and sister never were able to find out if he had hidden money in any of them, as it was impossible to match the keys to the unknown banks. Because he left no will, the state took his few possessions.

In Jeanette's unpublished autobiography and preparatory notes, she answered those who thought that she belonged with Nelson Eddy instead of Gene. She said that Nelson's mother was sure that they would make a "happy twosome."[147] Jeanette admitted that she dated Nelson and could have been interested in him, if she hadn't met Gene. "The truth of the matter was that whatever attraction Nelson and I might have felt for each other was interrupted before it ever got started."[148] She succinctly summed up her feelings for Gene, Nelson, and Bob Ritchie in an outline for her book: "Gene it was! No doubt about it."[149]

In a 1966 interview, Nelson discussed his feelings for Jeanette: "Many people thought Miss MacDonald and I were married. Actually, our relationship was cordial but formal. We each had our own private lives, and refused to let the studio publicity department create an artificial romance for us. But with each new picture the image grew."[150] He was amused by the ignorance of some admirers and even saved a letter from an outraged fan who wrote to "break the terrible news to you that your wife, Jeanette MacDonald, was seen publicly holding hands with an actor named Gene Raymond."[151] In the 1960s, Dick Van Dyke and Mary Tyler Moore had similar experiences when they played husband and wife on *The Dick Van Dyke Show* (1961–1966).

MGM Publicity Director Howard Strickling said that Jeanette dated Nelson, as well as actors James Stewart and Henry Fonda, "but it was all for publicity sake. It was already a strong thing between her and Gene Raymond. It was one of the most unaffected love stories I ever came across."[152]

When the cast and crew of *Rose-Marie* returned from Lake Tahoe, they finished filming at MGM. Although some of the promotional materials for the movie spelled the title without the hyphen, on screen it was hyphenated. The film *Rose-Marie* changed the plot and dropped most of the songs from the 1924 Broadway musical of the same name. The new story concerned an opera singer (Jeanette) who went in search of her brother (James Stewart), who escaped from prison and killed a Mountie. During her travels in the Canadian wilderness, she met and fell in love with another Mountie (Nelson), who was sent to capture her brother. In addition to the classic duet "Indian Love Call" with Nelson, Jeanette sang excerpts from Charles Gounod's *Romeo et Juliette* and Giacomo Puccini's *Tosca* with Allan Jones, and soloed with the charming "Pardon Me, Madame" and "Three Blind Mice."

James Stewart, who previously appeared in one short and one feature, spoke kindly about Woody Van Dyke, who helped him tremendously. "And Jeanette MacDonald helped me a lot too," Stewart recalled. "A wonderful lady. When we got to do our scenes together, she told Woody to make sure I had all the best coverage with the camera. Most actresses, I learned, liked to hog the best angles for themselves. But Jeanette knew the audience had to get to know my character in a short space of screen time."[153]

The film earned $1,695,000 domestically and $1,820,000 overseas, now about $30.7 million and almost $33 million. *Rose-Marie* became Jeanette and Nelson's best known—and most parodied—film, and "Indian Love Call" became their signature song. On June 23, 1947, Jeanette and Nelson reprised their roles in a radio adaptation on *Screen Guild Theater*.

While Jeanette was on location, Gene filmed *Seven Keys to Baldpate*, based on the 1913 novel by Earl Derr Biggers and the 1913 play by George M. Cohan. The plot concerned a novelist (Gene) who bet his friend that he could write a book within twenty-four hours. He went to a remote inn to work, where the caretakers assured him that he had the only key. After numerous visitors arrived at the inn, the novelist became involved in a mystery; he lost the bet, but fell in love with a reporter (Margaret Callahan) that he met during his stay.

In October, after Jeanette returned from Lake Tahoe, she and Gene saw each other almost every day. They often went to premieres and restaurants, as well as the racetrack and polo matches. They spent much of their courtship horseback riding, a sport they both loved, renting horses at the Riviera Country Club or the Bel-Air Stables, owned by actors Allan Jones and Robert Young. Jeanette was one of the few women in Hollywood who rode sidesaddle. When her hay fever flared up, she took pills and shots, never telling Gene that all the riding was affecting her allergies. In addition to horses, hay fever attacks were brought on by household dust, feathers, wet paint, fragrant flowers, and heavily scented perfumes. Despite being allergic to animal fur, Jeanette refused to get rid of her dogs. In 1946, columnist Erskine Johnson remarked, "We've never met a gal with more allergies than Jeanette."[154]

Between films, Jeanette and Gene frequently went to the B-Bar-H Ranch in Palm Springs, California, usually with Anna or publicist Helen Ferguson and her husband, Richard Hargreaves, acting as chaperones so the press wouldn't report on an unmarried couple traveling together, since it was standard for actors to have morals clauses in their contracts. Helen, a former actress, opened her publicity office in 1933. Gene was one of her first clients, and she and Jeanette were very close friends. After Jeanette and Gene's marriage, the B-Bar-H

Ranch remained one of their favorite getaways. Before and after their marriage, they also occasionally visited Lake Arrowhead (including June 1936, August 1939, and September 1940) and Lake Tahoe (including July 1936, September 1948, and August 1957). Additionally, Jeanette and Gene shared a love of dogs, walking, reading, dancing, music, and travel. And, had they both not had a penchant for being late, they wouldn't have met on the Netchers' or the Swarts' doorsteps or at the *Les Miserables* preview.

Jeanette was one of the few women in Hollywood who rode sidesaddle. As movies proved, she also could ride astride.

Gene possessed many of the characteristics that Jeanette described for her ideal man: athletic, good sense of humor, good sportsmanship, and Old World courtesy. She told reporter Jerry Lane, "I don't believe any romance can really mature into something worthwhile and lasting if it's handled casually. There has to be something *special* about it. And that requires a sense of appreciation and understanding on the man's part as well as on the girl's. He has to be fine, tolerant. He has to have decent instincts and live by them. I suppose more than anything else, I want my husband to be a loving partner. *Someone to share laughter with.* Someone who hasn't lost his enthusiasm and never will!"[155] Gene described his dream girl as being "a girl you feel completely comfortable with, and yet who embodies Romance with a capital R. A girl with the gallant and feminine charm of the old days, and yet with a strictly modern outlook."[156] Jeanette was touched when he sent roses for the three-month anniversary of their meeting. Presumably, this was the Grauman's meeting, since they were not that impressed with each other at the Netchers' party.

Initially, Jeanette and Gene were nonchalant about their relationship, insisting that they didn't want to marry anyone because of their careers. However, as time passed, they each realized that they had been in love for a long time. In 1993, Gene said, "Jeanette was just right for me, everything I wanted."[157] In an outline for her autobiography, Jeanette described it as "a sense of two halves of a coin being joined together." Just one thing bothered her. "But it took forever to get him to kiss me," she complained. "When he did, I almost swooned."[158]

Gene felt it necessary to warn Jeanette about his mother, usually referred to as Mrs. Kipling, even by her family. "I don't think she ever will give you a chance to let herself [sic] know you the way I'd like her to," he said. "You know how I feel about you, but you're going to have to accept this situation."[159] After Jeanette prayed, and discussed Mrs. Kipling with Anna, Jeanette decided that her feelings for Gene were stronger than her concern over any future problems with his mother.

Mrs. Kipling split her time between New York and California, spending six months a year in each place. Usually, she stayed in California from May to September, making sure to spend Mother's Day with her sons; then she returned again for Thanksgiving and Christmas.

In 1935, Gene bought his mother an eleven-room house in Beverly Hills at 919 Benedict Canyon Drive, furnishing it lavishly. He added a playroom, tennis court, and swimming pool. Initially, Gene and his brother lived there with her. Gene also bought his mother a Packard limousine. When Mrs. Kipling said that she didn't like the car, he wrote her a check for a new one. Despite Gene's generosity, Mrs. Kipling never was satisfied. Through the years, she continued to demand more from her son, usually with a feeling of entitlement.

In the beginning, Gene's mother was friendly toward Jeanette; however, when Mrs. Kipling realized that Gene was more serious about Jeanette than the other women he dated, she became jealous and vindictive. In the fall of 1935, after Jeanette returned from Lake Tahoe, Gene hosted a housewarming party. Jeanette gave him a silver service for twelve and presented Mrs. Kipling with a ceramic good luck black cat for the hearth. Although the silver was similar in cost to what other friends gave him, Mrs. Kipling scolded Jeanette for buying Gene such an elaborate and expensive gift. Jeanette was bothered by Gene's mother's hostility, after she seemed friendly on earlier occasions. It was a hint that Mrs. Kipling didn't want Jeanette getting too close to her son. In Jeanette's autobiography, she described another party where Mrs. Kipling invited Jeanette upstairs on the pretense of seeing her doll collection. Once Jeanette was in the room, Mrs. Kipling locked the door and threatened her, demanding that she marry Bob Ritchie and leave Gene alone.

Mrs. Kipling's behavior completely baffled Jeanette, as she never had problems with the mothers of her beaus. Although Jack Ohmeis' mother initially suspected that Jeanette was a gold digger, Mrs. Ohmeis soon thought of Jeanette as a daughter. Mrs. Ohmeis even allowed Jeanette to use her charge account to buy her first mink coat, letting Jeanette pay her back in whatever weekly installments that she could afford. Jeanette was very friendly with Irving Stone's entire family and corresponded with his parents and socialized with his cousins long after she stopped dating Irving. Bob Ritchie's mother adored Jeanette; after Jeanette and Bob broke up, his mother continued to keep in touch with her. Similarly, Anna was very fond of Gene, although she worried about how his relationship with his mother would affect his relationship with Jeanette.

As Jeanette and Gene became closer, he told her about his unhappy childhood and his alienation from his father. When he spoke lovingly of dogs, Jeanette bought him a nine-month-old Irish Setter for Christmas, which infuriated his mother, who thought that the dog would tear up the house. Before Christmas, Jeanette took his mother into her confidence because she wanted Mrs. Kipling to hide the dog house when it was delivered. Mrs. Kipling spoiled Jeanette's surprise by telling Gene about the dog ahead of time and insisting that he refuse it. Undaunted, Gene fell in love with the Irish Setter as soon as he saw him, naming him Smilin' Tray o' Hearts, Tray for short, after composer Stephen Foster's "Old Dog Tray." Through the years, Jeanette and Gene had many dogs, but Tray remained Gene's favorite, partly because he reminded Gene of his first Christmas with Jeanette.

In February 1936, while Gene was on a personal appearance tour, he asked Jeanette to visit Tray at the kennel, adding, "I'm really anxious to see him again! But only if you go to see him with me!"[160] Tray died September 12, 1948. When Sunny died a few months later, Jeanette said, "I hope they have a happy reunion in dog heaven."[161] Through the years, Jeanette gave dogs to several of her friends and colleagues, including Nelson Eddy, producer Hunt Stromberg, cinematographer Oliver Marsh, Technicolor cameraman Allan Davey, and producer/director Robert Z. Leonard. Although Jeanette also liked cats, she was very allergic to them. When a fan left one on her doorstep, she gave it to her *Naughty Marietta* co-star, Elsa Lanchester.

For Christmas 1935, Gene gave Jeanette a gold and jade charm bracelet, along with a card that read "For no particular reason, except to say 'Merry Christmas!'" Jeanette explained the significance in her autobiography. "That phrase 'for no particular reason' has become a shibboleth between us, because we knew even then that it meant a good deal more than it said."[162] The charms on the bracelet represented each of their dates. A dancing couple signified their first official date at the Cocoanut Grove. A couple on horseback represented the Riviera Country Club riding trail, where they often rented horses and rode. A camera recalled the preview at Grauman's Chinese Theatre, where they initially were photographed by the press. It was the first of many charm bracelets that Gene gave her through the years, with charms depicting personal and professional milestones or memorable occasions that they shared.

Not long after Christmas, Mrs. Kipling tried to cause trouble for the couple. She booked a table for ten at the annual Mayfair Ball, held on January 25, 1936, with Gene to act as escort for her and Janet Gaynor, purposely excluding Jeanette. Undaunted, Jeanette booked another table for ten and took her neighbors, James Stewart and Henry Fonda, as her dates. Mrs. Kipling's stunt backfired and the evening's separation only made Jeanette and Gene closer.

In February, Mrs. Kipling hired numerologist Ariel Yvon Taylor to prepare charts for Jeanette and Gene. Although Taylor predicted a long friendship and a successful working relationship, she wrote, "But when it comes to marriage, here and now—the weather shows more difficult sailing, in that each has his own definite cycle of progress to follow—which neither heart nor head can offset."[163]

Around the same time, Jeanette began shooting *San Francisco*, which remains one of her most respected films. Unlike many of her other movies, *San Francisco* was a drama with music, focusing on the relationship between a preacher's daughter (Jeanette), who aspired to sing opera, and the rough-and-tumble owner of a nightclub on the Barbary Coast (Clark Gable), shortly before the 1906 earthquake that leveled San Francisco. Spencer Tracy played Gable's childhood friend, now a priest. Critics praised the special effects, which hold up well today. Jeanette said that some of the earthquake scenes were done with miniatures.

San Francisco gave Jeanette the chance to sing excerpts from Giuseppe Verdi's La Traviata and Charles Gounod's Faust, including "The Jewel Song." She sang the waltz "Would You," hymns "Jerusalem" and "Nearer My God to Thee," and joined the cast for the inspiring "Battle Hymn of the Republic." She also introduced the title song, which became one of the city's two official anthems, along with Tony Bennett's "I Left My Heart in San Francisco." The film was nominated for six Academy Awards: Best Picture, Best Director (Woody Van Dyke), Best Assistant Director (Joseph M. Newman), Best Actor (Spencer Tracy), and Best Original Story (Robert "Hoppy" Hopkins), winning only for Best Sound Recording (Douglas Shearer). At the time, there was no annual award for visual effects. In 1936, it was the top grossing film worldwide, earning over $6 million, equivalent to over $108 million today. In 1965, at the time of Jeanette's death, San Francisco remained in the top twenty moneymakers of all time.

Sadly, many accounts of the film's history leave out Jeanette's role in getting it produced, convincing the front office that Hoppy Hopkins had a sound idea. Clark Gable was against making a movie with Jeanette because he was afraid that he'd have to stand around while she sang. However, he was impressed that she not only was willing to wait for him to do the film and lose thousands of dollars while she was between pictures, but also that she was willing to take second billing to work with him. Jeanette said, "Better to be a co-star in a hit than to take all the bows in one not so good."[164]

During production, Hoppy Hopkins nicknamed Jeanette The Iron Butterfly, contrasting her delicate beauty with her shrewd business acumen. Although many people around the lot didn't call her the name to her face, Jeanette was secretly proud of it. However, over time, she tired of it and, when the sobriquet was suggested as the title for her autobiography, she bristled.

Although Jeanette fought with the studio to get the film produced, and to co-star with Gable, making *San Francisco* was not an entirely pleasant experience for her. Most of the time, Gable ignored her on set, making it clear that he disliked her. His agent, Phil Berg, claimed that Gable was angry that Jeanette, like Irene Dunne, and later, Elizabeth Taylor, had a clause in her contract that gave her time off during her menstrual cycle. In Jeanette's autobiography, she talked about how she didn't get along with Gable, and how his garlic and hangover breath repulsed her. Although there is speculation that, in the 1950s, Gable apologized to Jeanette for his behavior, it is unlikely, or she surely would have mentioned it in her book, which was written a few months before his death.

During the making of *San Francisco*, Jeanette also was worried about her relationship with Gene. While she was filming, he went on a personal appearance tour to promote *Love on a Bet*, a romantic comedy that cast him as a producer who bet his wealthy uncle that he could recreate the plot of a play, which involved traveling across country with no clothes or money and falling in love within ten days. If Gene won, the uncle would back his show; if he lost, he'd join his uncle's meat packing business. Gene's personal appearance tour broke house records at the RKO Theatre in Boston, Massachusetts, with over ten thousand people attending the three shows on opening day. In Philadelphia, he did better than entertainer Eddie Cantor, who played the same theater the previous week. On February 23, 1936,

Gene recreated a scene from the movie on the radio program *The Magic Key*, broadcast from New York.

During the filming of *San Francisco*, Jeanette asked co-star Spencer Tracy for advice about Gene. Here, they checked out the buffet at a party at Woody Van Dyke's house.

After the tour, Gene spent a week vacationing in Florida with his mother. The previous fall, while Jeanette was on location in Lake Tahoe, Mrs. Kipling made it clear that she did not appreciate how much time Gene spent writing and calling Jeanette so, while Gene was in Florida, he told Jeanette not to write to him and that *he* would contact *her*. Jeanette was so concerned about his feelings for her that she lost a tremendous amount of weight, making her face look emaciated. The studio ordered her to drink a quart of milk a day to get her weight back to normal. She confided in her co-star, Spencer Tracy, wondering if Gene was serious about their relationship or making a fool of her. Tracy told her that Gene was testing himself even more than he was testing Jeanette and, that when he figured out his feelings, she would find out too. Her worries disappeared when Gene sent her a one-word telegram from Florida: "Bored."[165] Neither of them realized that the real trouble with Gene's mother was about to begin.

Chapter Five

Gene's Florida vacation with his mother was a turning point in his relationship with Jeanette and led to an emotional tug-of-war that lasted for most of their married life. During the trip, Mrs. Kipling discovered that, a few months earlier, Jeanette gave him one of her favorite books, Kahlil Gibran's *The Prophet* (1923). The book's teachings, as well as its nude drawings, incensed Mrs. Kipling. She called Jeanette "sophisticated"[166] and accused her of trying to corrupt Gene with an "indecent book."[167] She also was furious that Jeanette had underlined passages about passion and independence, encouraging Gene to stand on his own. Mrs. Kipling refused to return to California until Gene broke up with Jeanette.

When Gene came home from his vacation, he tried to explain to Jeanette about his mother's disapproval. In Jeanette's autobiography, she described the conversation.

> He said, "Being a positive, opinionated and determined
> woman, she is pretty voluble in expressing herself. Let's face
> it; I've inherited a certain amount of determination myself,
> and I've formed some rather positive opinions of my own

about you. The opinions, mine and Mother's, don't jibe, so between us we raised the roof every night for weeks before we went east. She'd be waiting up for me when I came home from a date with you, and the argument would begin. I took her to Florida to try to help her find a way to adjust. I gave it a good try, but I think I succeeded only in making things worse."

He took my hand as he went on, "I hope she'll be different when she gets back, but—to be honest—I don't expect an improvement. I think her attitude is going to be more hostile than ever. If it is, I'm going to move out."

It was obvious that he had to force himself to go on. . . . "I'll continue to do what I can to cope with the situation, but if she gets mean, ill-mannered, and generally cantankerous, as well as childish and unreasonable, I can only reason with her, trying to persuade her to see my position. I can't clamp her in irons and toss her into the hold; I can't spank her and send her upstairs to bed. Happily or not, she's my mother."

He ended with a wry grin, "I'm telling you these things, because you're going to have to make a decision. To understate it: My mother could get to be one great, big, ridiculous nuisance, and the only reason for you to put up with that sort of situation is … … .me!"[168]

On April 29, Gene sent his mother a letter, trying to make peace.

Because I try to find my own happiness, is no reason to term me an unworthy son. I have never shirked my responsibilities. My first goal has always been to see you financially independent, and I'm very happy to have attained that goal. It is a very comfortable feeling to know that whatever might happen to me, you are independent. However, my feelings do not end there. My first thought has always been for your happiness, and it makes me feel badly to see you adopt this attitude. But you have apparently made up your mind to put your feelings on one basis: "I won't come home unless you stop seeing Jeanette!"

As you know, I like Jeanette very much. I'm proud to be the recipient of her friendship. She is the finest girl I have ever known. And you agreed with me when you said: "I think she is a fine high[-]class girl, and if she were'nt [sic] interested in you I could like her very much." Now you know, Mother, That's [sic] a hopeless attitude for me to cope with, especially when you told me that you doubted if you'd be satisfied with any girl I chose. If you won't like anyone I pick out, then to what could I look forward? If I did as you ask me now, and [I] later became interested in someone else, you would again feel the same way. So we might just as well face the issue now, as later. That is only common sense.[169]

In June, Gene moved out of the Benedict Canyon house and into The Town House, a luxury apartment hotel on Wilshire Boulevard, causing Mrs. Kipling to write a vitriolic five-page letter to Jeanette, accusing her of coming between mother and son.

What you so shamelessly & deliberately started out to do last winter, undermine Gene's love & affection for me – seems to have borne fruit, for the time being, at least. He left home this morning, & he said he wouldn't be back. I wonder how proud you really can be, to know, that in only 6 mos. you have undone the work of 27 years! That's what you <u>really</u> wanted, it seems, when you shoved a book upon Gene, which was filled with pictures of naked men & women, written by a sex-crazed Hindu, checking off all passages referring to "passion," "desire" & "ecstasy" (!) but you knew of his great love & affection for me so you had to set about undermining that love & affection.... You knew that to arouse his sex emotion was <u>not</u> enough; you must break down his love for his mother to <u>hold</u> him in that condition. And yet, you dare to pose as so very <u>proper</u> & <u>respectable</u> & you go about spreading your poison, in a most systematic way; with a most gracious manner, & a most charming & disarming smile! ...

You had better use your <u>wits</u> & see that Gene gets back to normal. <u>You</u> made a shameless mess of everything that should be decent. Now, try to <u>undo</u> the harm that you did, last winter, with that <u>disgusting</u> book. I <u>will not</u> allow Gene to go the way of Wally Reid, even if I have to "go down" fighting for him.[170]

In 1923, silent film actor Wallace Reid died of morphine addiction, causing a great scandal.

Mrs. Kipling also wrote to Bob Ritchie with threats: "Will you kindly inform Jeanette that if Gene does not return within a week, I will take it up with several organizations, & if she dares to inveigle him into marriage, I will still brand her publicly as a cheap common temptress, showing how she went about it, to enslave him & to deliberately separate him from his mother. Public opinion will do the rest & no doubt separate <u>her</u> from her thousands a week she now collects, <u>thanks to you</u>."[171]

Jeanette and Gene tried to ignore his mother and her letters, keeping busy with work and dates. In April and May, Gene filmed *The Bride Walks Out*, a romantic comedy with Barbara Stanwyck and Robert Young. The plot concerned an aspiring engineer (Gene) who tried to convince his fiancée, a fashion model (Stanwyck), that love was more important than money. She gave up her career for marriage; however, when she found that she couldn't live on her husband's meager salary, she secretly returned to her job, which eventually caused marital problems. An alcoholic department store scion (Young) helped the couple reunite. On June 5, 1936, Gene and Stanwyck reprised their roles on Louella Parsons' radio program, *Hollywood Hotel*.

Thirteen days later, on June 18, Gene hosted a birthday party for Jeanette with a *Rose-Marie* theme. The guests, who included her film co-stars Nelson Eddy and James Stewart, as well as longtime friends, like Helen Ferguson and Richard Hargreaves, actor Johnny Mack Brown and his wife, Connie, and actresses Anita Louise, Inez Courtney, and Shirley Ross, were asked to dress as one of the characters from the movie; some cooperated and some didn't. The elaborate cake depicted Rose-Marie in the mountains with "Happy Birthday Jeanette" spelled out across the lake. Gene gave her a platinum dinner ring of baguette sapphires and diamonds.

In many interviews, Gene talked about marriage and the future. In 1935, he said, "I want a lot of things. I want all the things money can buy—I want the perfect love, certainly—I want the international fame that comes with being a star. But I've got to have this *first*: I've got to fight discouragement, and I've got to have success with myself." He continued, "Even if I never get any of those other things—if I have nothing left but the knowledge that I've lived up to my convictions—then I shall have succeeded in life."[172] He insisted that he could not be serious with a woman when his career kept him so busy. In 1936, he told a reporter, "I hope to marry when I have reached the point in my career where I can be sure of making no more than two or three pictures a year. When I can dictate my own terms and my own time. Then and only then will I qualify as a husband. I can 'keep company' with my wife. We can travel and entertain and be together as a man and wife should be. But I must reach that place before I can feel decent about asking any girl to share my life with me. For I must be able to share too."[173] By the summer of 1936, he felt that he was ready.

Despite Mrs. Kipling's disapproval, in July, Gene proposed to Jeanette after they had been riding in the hills of Santa Monica. She recalled the details, which began with Gene suggesting that they stop to rest and look at the view. "We dismounted and sat on a huge, flat boulder, watching the sea in silence. Finally Gene took my hand and said lightly, 'I've been waiting a long time for you to propose to me. Since you can't seem to get up your nerve, I guess I'll have to.' I leaned over to be kissed. 'In all seriousness,' he added, 'You must have known I wanted you to marry me.' 'In all seriousness,' I answered, 'You must have known I'd say yes.'"[174] A week later, he gave her a nine-and-a-half carat sapphire engagement ring in a platinum setting, which matched the dinner ring that he gave her for her birthday. Gene designed the engagement ring and had it executed by jeweler William Ruser, who, over the years, made many other pieces for the Raymonds. Sapphires were among Jeanette's favorite stones. Later, she said, "We're sentimental souls, you know, and sapphires mean faith and simplicity."[175] Gene said he chose it for two reasons: they both loved sapphires and the stone had the age-old meaning "faithful forever."[176]

Jeanette recalled how Gene gave her the ring: "Gene gave a party 'for no particular reason' at the Ambassador Hotel, taking a suite in which to hold a cocktail party, then reserving a table in The [sic] Grove for dinner and dancing. He and I were in the midst of our first dance of the evening when he said, 'Slide your hand into my right-hand coat pocket.' Lying loose in the pocket was a ring. 'Let's go back to the suite so I can slip it on your finger with proper ceremony,' he suggested. It was one of the loveliest rings I have ever seen: a square-cut sapphire, darker than the blue of mid-ocean, set in platinum."[177] Later, Jeanette asked how he knew that she would accept his proposal. Gene answered, "Whenever you entered a room I was the first person you looked at—and the last you spoke to."[178]

Meanwhile, Mrs. Kipling returned to California and hired famed attorney Jerry Giesler to work out a financial agreement with Gene and his attorney. Through the years, Giesler's celebrity clients included actor Rudolph Valentino, director Busby Berkeley, actor/filmmaker Charles Chaplin, actor Errol Flynn, gangster Bugsy Siegel, and actress Marilyn Monroe.

On August 11, Mrs. Kipling wrote to Jeanette and her mother, who, after their lease ended on the North Carmelina Drive house, were living at the Beverly Wilshire Hotel while they looked for another house to rent. Mrs. Kipling invited them to her home for dinner the next evening and to a birthday party that she was giving for Gene at the Cocoanut Grove on August 13. She told Jeanette, "I realize that our association in the past has not been exactly a pleasant one, but it does not have to remain that way. Gene and I are trying to compose our differences, and I think we are succeeding very well. Suppose you and I try to do the same. Many things are said and done when one is angry or emotional, that lead to misunderstanding; things that in calmer moments, we can attribute only to emotion. Therefore, I suggest that you give this matter as much consideration as I have, to the extent, that <u>we</u> can compose <u>our</u> differences."[179] It is not known whether Jeanette and Anna accepted Mrs. Kipling's dinner invitation; however, on Gene's birthday, Jeanette went to the Hollywood Bowl to see a ballet choreographed by Adolph Bolm. Jeanette's birthday gift to Gene was a horse that he admired at a horse show, which he named Black Knight.

On August 20, 1936, Anna announced Jeanette and Gene's engagement at a tea at the Beverly Wilshire Hotel, marking the last time their families were together. Left to right: Bob, Mrs. Kipling, Gene, Jeanette, and Anna. Photo from the Dale Kuntz collection.

On August 20, Anna hosted a tea at the Beverly Wilshire Hotel to formally announce Jeanette and Gene's engagement. Among the guests were Gene's brother, Bob; Connie and Johnny Mack Brown; Nelson Eddy; Grace Newell; comedian Harold Lloyd and his wife, silent film actress Mildred Davis; director Mervyn LeRoy and his wife, actress Doris Warner, daughter of Warner Bros. founder Harry Warner; Fay Wray and her husband, writer/director John Monk Saunders; Ernst Lubitsch; Anita Louise; Helen Ferguson and Richard Hargreaves; Woody Van Dyke's mother, Laura Van Dyke; and Louis

B. Mayer's executive secretary, Ida "Kay" Koverman. Nelson kidded Gene, "You may be the best man, but I'm still the leading man!"[180] Jeanette's sisters were unable to attend the tea, as Blossom was appearing in the Broadway play *Dead End* (1935) and Elsie was teaching in Pennsylvania. Gene's mother arrived late, missing Anna's speech to the couple and toting a book that was too large to be *The Prophet*. It was the last time the families were together.

Shortly after the engagement announcement, Mrs. Kipling returned to New York. Before she left, she gave an interview about her sons to Alma Whitaker of the *Los Angeles Times*. "I don't like basking in reflected glory and just being somebody's mother," Mrs. Kipling insisted. "I tried to guide them in the development of their own talents, rather than shape them in a mold." She bragged about how Gene's salary had increased through the years: "Gene was earning $50 a week at 14, $75 a week at 15, $125 at 17, and $400 at 22. Now, at 27, Gene earns more in a week than he used to earn in a year."[181] Today, those amounts would be about $749, $1,100, $1,798, and $6,029. There was no mention of Gene's engagement. It was obvious from her words, as well as her subsequent actions, that money was more important to her than her son's happiness. Before Mrs. Kipling left, she threw a farewell party for herself. The guests included her son, Bob, Connie and Johnny Mack Brown, Nydia Westman, who worked with Gene on Broadway in *Jonesy*, and Nelson Eddy's mother, Isabel. Jeanette and Gene did not attend.

Just as Mrs. Kipling threatened Bob Ritchie in June, in New York, she launched a campaign to defame Jeanette, sending vitriolic letters to columnists, Jeanette and Gene's studios, the Catholic Legion of Decency, and even Motion Picture Producers and Distributors of America President Will Hays. Joseph Breen, head of the Production Code Administration, called Gene in for a conference, which Jeanette described in her autobiography. "Gene, humiliated and helpless, explained the situation and asked, 'What can I do? Deprive her of pen, paper, and stamps? How?'"[182]

Mrs. Kipling called Jeanette a cradle snatcher, pointing out that she was five years older than Gene. (Like many actresses, for career reasons, Jeanette publicly shaved four years off her age. The erroneous date was on her passport, driver's license, and even her crypt. Coincidentally, Mrs. Kipling also was five years older than her ex-husband and lied about her age on her marriage license.) She accused Jeanette of indecent conduct, hinting at things from Jeanette's past and her relationship with Bob Ritchie, and suggesting that she seduced Gene. Mrs. Kipling also continued to focus on *The Prophet* and its nude drawings. She even threatened to destroy her son's career if he followed through with the marriage.

Finally, Gene had enough. On October 18, he wrote his mother a letter, promising to financially support her if she returned to California, but politely telling her that he had chosen a bride and it was none of her business. In the letter, he accused her of staying in New York "for the purpose of maligning my fiance [sic] and me 'to teach me a lesson' and to 'ruin my career, if necessary.'" At her insistence, while she was in New York, he moved back into the Benedict Canyon house. He wrote that he and Bob were moving out on November 1. "It will await your occupancy – or you can rent it for a very substantial sum. . . . I cannot continue what amounts to the financing of a campaign designed to wreck my happiness."[183]

In November, Mrs. Kipling wrote to Gene's attorney, Neil McCarthy, accusing Jeanette of dictating Gene's October 18 letter and insisting that Gene was punishing her for refusing to give him back *The Prophet*. She wrote, "If Gene claims that not to be true, let him prove it by allowing me the inalienable right to live my own life in my own way, where I please – not where Jeanette MacDonald decides I should live."[184] She demanded 10% of Gene's earnings, asserting it was her right for her role in launching his career. Mrs. Kipling hired another attorney and threatened to sue Jeanette and Gene, claiming that Gene agreed to pay her a certain amount and that Jeanette had induced him to break the contract. Neil McCarthy contacted Will Hays, asking for his help. McCarthy explained that Gene not only gave his mother a furnished home, worth $85,000 (currently equivalent to over $1.5 million), but an allowance of $1,000 a month (currently over $18,000 a month), plus $30,000 in cash (currently over $543,000). McCarthy added that Gene had been willing to sign a contract about supporting his mother, but when he found that it didn't change her mind about Jeanette, he decided against it. McCarthy asked Hays to contact Mrs. Kipling's attorney to tell him the facts and prevent a lawsuit, which would bring negative publicity to Jeanette and Gene, as well as their studios. Hays contacted Carl Milliken, former Governor of Maine and Chief Spokesman for the Motion Picture Producers and Distributors of America, who, in turn, spoke to Mrs. Kipling's attorney.

In December, Mrs. Kipling complained about Jeanette to her friend, Lillian Garrick Malmsten, comparing Jeanette's influence over Gene to England's constitutional crisis caused by Wallis Simpson, the American divorcee for whom King Edward VIII abdicated the British throne. Mrs. Kipling wrote, "ONE WOMAN was able to accomplish what Nations [sic] have never been able to accomplish and so it goes in the lesser stations of life. That MacDonald woman has been able to change Gene from the lovely character as you knew him and as he remained until about a year ago, to what you see now. She has taken full charge of our affairs; she has made Gene move out of our lovely home, leaving it unprotected and forcing me to sell it."[185]

The trouble continued into 1937. In January, Gene wrote to Neil

McCarthy, reiterating all that he had done for his mother. Despite his financial support, he said that Mrs. Kipling was spreading malicious gossip about him, as well as Jeanette, leading to comments in the New York newspapers. "Also, she deliberately wrote untruths about Miss MacDonald and myself and had them transmitted on Western Union and Postal Telegraph wires, knowing such actions would cause gossip and reportorial comment," Gene said. "There could have been no other reason for her using telegraph as she had already stated the very same things by letter."[186]

In February, Neil McCarthy contacted Mrs. Kipling's attorney again, explaining that Gene planned to support his mother because he wanted to, not because of a contract. He also addressed Mrs. Kipling's offer to give her blessing—for a fee. "You cannot buy the blessing of anyone," he wrote. "A person's good will is either voluntary or not at all. Mr. Raymond has no desire to pay his mother money for her blessing. If she gives her blessing, he will be pleased of course. If she does not, that is her concern."[187]

Putting up with Mrs. Kipling's abuse proved just how much Jeanette and Gene wanted to be together. They were embarrassed by the situation, but relieved that Mrs. Kipling's virtual blackmail didn't cause a public scandal or harm their careers. Once again, it was clear from her actions that she was more concerned over losing her meal ticket than about her son's happiness. It also said a lot about the power of the studios and how much the press liked Jeanette and Gene, since most newspapers only hinted that Mrs. Kipling disapproved of the marriage.

One positive thing came out of Mrs. Kipling's poison pen letters: Jeanette and columnist Louella Parsons became friends. When Jeanette went to Hollywood, she was unimpressed with the celebrities that she met, mostly because she had been busy working in the theater and didn't recognize their names. Parsons was offended when

Jeanette went to a 1929 party at Ernst Lubitsch's house and remained in one room talking, while actress Carmel Myers was singing in another. The relationship between Parsons and Jeanette became icier when Jeanette insisted on being paid to appear on the columnist's radio program, *Hollywood Hotel,* though celebrities were expected to do it gratis. Jeanette reasoned that if she sang on Parsons' program for free, other shows would expect not to pay her. Parsons made many digs about Jeanette in her column and, at Ginger Rogers and Lew Ayres' 1934 wedding, the two women exchanged hostile words.

In the fall of 1936, Mrs. Kipling sent Parsons a nasty letter about Jeanette. The columnist immediately called Helen Ferguson, Jeanette's publicist, to tell her that she was burning it. Parsons said, "This could really wipe up the ground with Jeanette MacDonald, but I think it's below the belt."[188] It is assumed that, like in other letters, Mrs. Kipling accused Jeanette of seducing Gene and alienating him from his mother. Given Jeanette's virginal, family-friendly image in MGM's operettas, this could have caused great harm to her career. Jeanette was so grateful to Parsons that she invited the columnist to lunch and offered to appear on her radio show. Parsons explained that she didn't destroy the letter for that reason. In turn, Jeanette said that she would do the show, not because Parsons destroyed the letter, but "because you're a good, decent woman, and I like you very much."[189] On November 13, 1936 and, again on April 2, 1937, Jeanette appeared on *Hollywood Hotel,* gratis; she remained friends with Parsons for the rest of her life.

Friends were happy about Jeanette and Gene's impending marriage and commented on their compatibility. "They're both idealists," a friend told reporter Ida Zeitlin. "Half measures hold no attraction for them. . . . That's why Jeanette found the right man in Gene—because she could love him without reservation, with respect as well as with tenderness. Gene will never let her down. He's good to the core. .

. . He's loyal and kind and generous and strong. . . . Jeanette recognized this quality and loved him for it. They have the same sense of genuine values, the same distaste for shoddiness."[190] Reporter Harry Lang noted that Jeanette and Gene's story was amazing, not because two of the biggest stars in Hollywood were marrying, but because neither had been married before.

Many of Jeanette's fans wondered why she was marrying Gene, instead of her frequent co-star, Nelson Eddy. *Screenland* even ran an article with Nelson's byline titled "Gene Raymond Is a Lucky Guy." In it, Nelson complained about the fans who assumed that he and Jeanette were a real-life couple off-screen. "She had her friends; I had mine; and almost never did the twain of us meet, away from the cameras," he explained. "We have gone out together about twice, and I have been at her house a few times, on party occasions. That's all."[191] He went on to say that they got along fine and enjoyed each other's company or they wouldn't keep working together. He said that Gene was lucky because Jeanette had so many positive traits, including unselfishness, lack of egotism, and a penchant for being gracefully frank. Nelson also described how much Jeanette and Gene had in common: music, wit, and a love of games.

After the Raymonds' marriage, a reporter observed, "It is very doubtful that anyone would ever have seen this mood of cooperation around the house if, by chance, Jeanette had married Nelson Eddy. Charming though Nelson is, he has only one love, his own voice, and despite the thousands of maidens who pine for him, Nelson himself is perfectly content in the company of his mother." The reporter continued, "All that red-hot glow Nelson and Jeanette get into their love scenes together is a tribute to their acting alone. They have never had so much as one romantic twinge about each other in private life. Probably matching high 'C's' on a sound track [sic] isn't conducive to it."[192]

Meanwhile, at the end of July 1936, Jeanette began work on *Maytime*, her third picture with Nelson. The original film was produced by Irving Thalberg and directed by Edmund Goulding, with Paul Lukas, Frank Morgan, and Julie Haydon in the cast. The melodramatic plot concerned two singers (Jeanette and Nelson) who fell in love while working in a second-rate touring company headed by Morgan. Although they married others out of spite, they reunited years later, only to be parted again when the woman's jealous husband (Lukas) tried to shoot the male singer, wounding his wife (Haydon) instead. It included excerpts from Giacomo Puccini's *Tosca* and Giuseppe Verdi's *Il trovatore*, as well as the song "Farewell to Dreams."

For years, it was rumored that *Maytime* was to be MGM's first full-length Technicolor movie; however, film historian Yannek Cansino examined studio records and proved that the now-lost footage was shot in "Platinum Tone" Sepia, a process that gave an almost 3-D quality. It also was used for the original releases of *The Firefly* (1937), *The Girl of the Golden West* (1938), and *Broadway Serenade* (1939). Jeanette delayed production twice, first postponing the prerecording of "Will You Remember" for two days, due to an intestinal virus, then losing days of filming, following a Labor Day weekend yacht trip to Santa Catalina Island, California with Gene, Helen Ferguson and Richard Hargreaves, and Connie and Johnny Mack Brown, where Jeanette was severely sunburned.

On September 14, after suffering from a longtime heart condition, Irving Thalberg died of pneumonia. Out of respect, MGM shut down production on all of its films. Through the years, Jeanette sang at the funerals of many friends and colleagues, including Louis B. Mayer, directors Woody Van Dyke, George Fitzmaurice, and Ernst Lubitsch, cinematographer Oliver Marsh, and actresses Marie Dressler, Charlotte Learn Garrity, and Jean Harlow. However, when

Norma Shearer asked Jeanette to sing at Thalberg's funeral, Jeanette refused her request because she said that she couldn't bear the ordeal. It is not known if she was particularly affected by Thalberg's death because he helped bring her to MGM, if she was upset by the fact that he had a wife and two young children, or if the heart problem reminded her of her own father. On September 16, Jeanette attended the service at B'nai B'rith Temple, where Grace Moore sang The Psalm of David, "The Lord Is My Shepherd: I Shall Not Want."

When work resumed at MGM, *Maytime* underwent serious changes. Louis B. Mayer never liked the story, which involved infidelity and unsympathetic characters; he ordered the footage to be scrapped. In late September, production shut down to rewrite and reorganize the film. Hunt Stromberg was assigned as producer of the new version; Robert Z. Leonard took over as director; and an entirely different script was written. Although MGM newcomer Noel Langley received sole writing credit on screen, he built upon Stromberg's directives, as well as previous drafts and revisions by Alice Duer Miller, Claudine West, Jane Murfin, and Frances Marion. Film historians and fans alike hope that someday footage from the first *Maytime*, which reportedly was half-finished, will be found and released. Thankfully, many stills survived.

With Jeanette still recovering from her sunburn, and production on *Maytime* shut down, on September 17, 19, and 21, Jeanette and Nelson had time to record five songs for RCA Victor at Hollywood Recording Studio: "Will You Remember," "Song of Love," "Ah! Sweet Mystery of Life," "Indian Love Call," and "Farewell to Dreams." In early 1937, two 78s were released, featuring four of the duets. Inexplicably, "Song of Love" was held back; its first issue was on the LP *Jeanette MacDonald and Nelson Eddy*, released after Jeanette's 1965 death. In 1938, Nelson signed an exclusive contract with Columbia Records, where he recorded from 1939 through 1952. Therefore, until 1957, when Jeanette and Nelson reunited in the recording studio for a 1959 LP, these four songs were the only commercially released duets by the screen team who came to be known as America's Singing Sweethearts.

During Jeanette's break, she introduced Gene to her friends, Pete and Marge Halford, who visited from Hawaii. Jeanette recalled how Gene broke the ice: "Filming went on at his studio later than expected the night of our dinner date. Arriving out of breath, he said, 'Jeanette has told me a lot about you, and I want you to know that I'm sorry to be late for INSPECTION.' That did it. Everyone laughed, and Gene became an instant member in good standing of the Halford–MacDonald league."[193] Through the years, the Halfords and Raymonds shared many happy times in Hawaii and California.

On September 30, while the new *Maytime* was being prepared, Jeanette and her mother left for a vacation in New York. They saw some shows, including Blossom's play, *Dead End*; visited Elsie, as well as Bob Ritchie's mother; and had dinner with Bob's best friend, Steve Kroeger. Back at Jeanette and Anna's hotel suite, after Anna retired for the evening, Kroeger made Jeanette cry when he begged her to give Bob another chance. However, she insisted that she was in love with Gene and planned to marry him. On October 14, she returned to California to begin work on the revised *Maytime*.

The new *Maytime* script borrowed from Noel Coward's operetta *Bitter Sweet* (1929), opening with Jeanette's character as an old woman relating her story to a younger one, with the movie then flashing back to tell the story of her life, which included the murder of the man she loved. In 1940, when MGM filmed Coward's operetta, they shot the flashback device, but cut it before the movie's release because it was too similar to *Maytime*.

The plot of the new *Maytime* centered on a young opera singer

(Jeanette) who accepted the proposal of her mentor, shortly before she met and fell in love with another young singer (Nelson). Years later, the two lovers were reunited in an opera production and decided to level with the singer's husband about their relationship. However, in a jealous rage, the husband killed his rival, ending any of the characters' chances for happiness. On October 23, when production resumed, Paul Lukas, Frank Morgan, and Julie Haydon were no longer in the cast; instead, John Barrymore and Herman Bing took over, respectively, as the Svengali and the male singer's confidante, and Haydon's role was eliminated. The *Tosca* and *Il trovatore* excerpts were replaced by "Nobles seigneur, salut" from Giacomo Meyerbeer's *Les Huguenots* and an original opera, *Czaritza*, written by Herbert Stothart, Robert Wright, and Chet Forrest, and based on themes from Pyotr Ilyich Tchaikovsky's *Fifth Symphony*, which mirrored the plot of the movie. They wrote an original opera because the film's plot called for a fictitious composer to write an opera for Jeanette's character. In 2018, a section of the *Fifth Symphony* that was used in *Czaritza* was played before Senator John McCain's funeral. Jeanette also sang "Les filles de Cadix," which became one of her favorite recital pieces; "Le Regement de Sambre;" a montage of brief opera selections; and, with Nelson, "Carry Me Back to Old Virginny." The only music used in both versions of *Maytime* was the duet "Will You Remember," which many called "Sweetheart" from the lyrics "Sweetheart, sweetheart, sweetheart."

Jeanette enjoyed working with Robert Z. "Pop" Leonard, who became one of her favorite directors. Like Ernst Lubitsch and Woody Van Dyke, he began his career as an actor so he could relate to filming from that perspective. Early in his career, he also sang on stage so he understood the musical aspects of movies more than some of her other directors. In her autobiography, Jeanette said that Van Dyke loathed music, as well as horses.

The press tried to stir up trouble between the co-stars, with the London *Daily Express* claiming that Jeanette was displeased that Nelson had more musical numbers than she did, which was not true. Jeanette vehemently denied the rumor and MGM executive Bob Vogel sent the newspaper a wire, quoting her: "IF NELSON DID HAVE MORE SONGS THAN I I WOULD NOT OBJECT AS WE AND OUR MOTHERS ARE ALL CLOSE FRIENDS."[194] The movie was nominated for Academy Awards for Best Music Score (Nat Finston) and Best Sound (Douglas Shearer). Its initial domestic gross was about $4.5 million (currently over $78.6 million) and it was one of the biggest worldwide moneymakers of 1937. Sources disagree over whether *Maytime* or *Snow White and the Seven Dwarfs* (1937) took the top spot. The prologue, epilogue, and May Day scenes originally were released in a pink tint.

On April 2, 1937, Jeanette and baritone Igor Gorin performed highlights from *Maytime* on Louella Parsons' radio program, *Hollywood Hotel*. According to a note on the back of a photo, Nelson did not appear on the show because he was not allowed to sing on the radio for free for anyone, as it was prohibited by his radio contract with CBS and *Vicks Open House*, the program he hosted. On September 12, 1944, Jeanette and Nelson reprised their roles in a radio adaptation on *Lux Radio Theatre*.

After critics praised Jeanette's beauty in *Maytime*, she sent cinematographer Oliver Marsh a telegram, giving him all of the credit for her appearance. It repeated all of the usual credit lines: Miss MacDonald's gowns by Adrian, Miss MacDonald's hats by Daré, etc., adding her own credit, "Miss MacDonald's beauty by Oliver Marsh."[195] At Jeanette's insistence, he worked on all of her movies until 1941, when he suffered a heart attack while filming tests of her for *Smilin' Through*. He died shortly after arriving at the hospital; two days later, on May 7, 1941, she sang at his funeral.

Many fans and film historians feel that *Maytime* is an underrated gem and contains Jeanette and Nelson's best work. During a 1971 revival, a critic noted how well the film held up thirty-four years after its release, acknowledging the success of another sentimental movie, *Love Story* (1970). He wrote, "But the Ali MacGraw fans might learn a thing or two by dropping in for a look–see at 'Maytime' to see how a real star made tear ducts function at a time when 'sentiment' was not just the newest fad in making box-office [sic] dollars."[196]

Through the years, Jeanette always called *Maytime* her favorite film, with *San Francisco* and *Smilin' Through* alternating for second place. All three offered her the chance to show off her acting talents and prove that she was not just a singer. It's noteworthy that she didn't mention the music in *Maytime* or *Smilin' Through,* only the acting challenges they presented. In census records, Jeanette always listed her occupation as actress, not singer. In a 1992 documentary about Jeanette and Nelson, host Jane Powell noted, "Jeanette . . . took her film roles very seriously and put her all into them. She thought of herself as an entertainer who could act well, sing better than most, and dance a little."[197]

A press release from RCA Victor quoted Jeanette on why *Maytime* was her favorite: "It had a dramatic range such as is seldom offered an actress. The story took Marsha [sic] Mornay from the time she was an ingenuous romantic girl of twenty until she was a magnificent grande dame of eighty. . . . Marsha's [sic] character underwent development and a maturing process . . . a kind of part which gives an actress use of her powers in the characterization."[198] Robert Z. Leonard observed, "Few stars would care to undertake this task without having to worry about singing in addition. Jeanette worked hard for weeks on that characterization. She studied makeup, voice change, and how to affect the walk of an aged woman before we started work."[199] During filming, studio workers didn't recognize Jeanette, made up as the older Marcia, known as Miss Morrison, as she walked to the soundstage with lead in her shoes to slow her gait, nor did some moviegoers when she first appeared on the screen as the elderly woman, despite the opening credits listing that Jeanette played Marcia *and* Miss Morrison.

Many columnists remarked that Jeanette looked particularly radiant in *Maytime*, noting that it was filmed during the height of her romance with Gene. When critics later commented that her voice was warmer and her acting had much more fire and depth because of her feelings for him, Jeanette was quick to dismiss them. "Pooh! It's not so much a matter of love as of work and training and growth. I thought I was in love before. And while I know now that was only a shadow of the substance, the emotional experience I went through was real. I'd like very much to give my husband the credit, but I don't see how my voice and acting could have changed overnight."[200] In 1959, when Jeanette was asked which film she most enjoyed making, she told her fan club, "'Maytime' was the one that I enjoyed making. It was such a gratifying role—old lady, young girl, mature woman—besides which Gene and I were engaged at that time and I was happy in my personal life as well."[201]

Jeanette considered *San Francisco* a favorite because it was a drama with music, rather than a standard operetta. It gave her the chance to sing opera, a waltz, three hymns, and a rousing rendition of the title song. She had to do love scenes with a leading man that she didn't get along with off-screen, which also was an acting challenge. In several scenes, her eyes convinced audiences that she was in love with Clark Gable's character as much as the dialogue.

In *Smilin' Through*, Jeanette played two characters who lived in different centuries and she had to make them two distinct personalities. She also said that she enjoyed working with her real-life husband:

"I never realized how much fun filming could be, acting with someone you really love, instead of just pretending to be in love because the script says so."[202] In 1959, Jeanette admitted to her fan club that the dual roles were difficult, but worth the work. "The complete change of make-up [sic], wig, etc., changing the voice—both singing and speaking and serious mannerisms which had to be carefully watched and avoided made it a very exacting role—but a very gratifying one and the critics were most kind."[203]

Meanwhile, in the fall of 1936, Gene made *That Girl from Paris*, a musical romance that starred Jeanette's longtime friend, French soprano Lily Pons. Gene played a musician/band leader who met a runaway bride (Pons) while he and his band were in France. She stowed away in their cabin on the ship and wreaked havoc after they arrived back in the United States. However, as the band's vocalist, she helped them gain fame, and she and the band leader fell in love. The film received an Academy Award nomination for Best Sound (John O. Aalberg).

While Jeanette was filming *Maytime*, she began making wedding plans. She best summed up her feelings to reporter Jerry Lane: "I want a beautiful start to what I hope to make my most beautiful adventure."[204]

Chapter Six

Although elopements were popular in Hollywood, Jeanette wanted to do everything the old fashioned way, with a proper lengthy engagement, a trousseau, bridal showers, and a traditional church wedding in June. Shortly after her engagement, she told reporter Dorothy Manners, "I want all of it. The squeals of girls opening linen shower gifts, and all the fuss of planning the bridesmaids' dresses, and a church wedding with reception, and a honeymoon, and rice and old shoes, and a veil and a brand new house of our own to live in. I even want them to leave the old-fashioned words like 'honor and obey' in the ceremony and to wear 'something old, something new, something borrowed, something blue.'"[205]

Jeanette told columnist Reine Davies why the couple didn't elope: "I am just old-fashioned enough to believe that marriage should only be undertaken after much time and consideration. So there will be nothing hurried about our wedding. A happy marriage is a progressive and growing thing. Its full significance can not [sic] be discerned in a moment. Hence the necessity of time, contemplation and spiritual preparation. And if it is to last it must not be treated casually as though it were just another step like passing from one school grade to another." She continued, "We selected June because it is more romantic. . . . It's really going to last 'until death do us part.' There isn't going to be 'another time.' And that is why we consider it as the most momentous event of our lives."[206]

On January 25, 1937, Jeanette and Melvyn Douglas starred in the romantic drama "Tonight or Never" on *Lux Radio Theatre*. Two weeks later, Gene appeared on the same program in "Graustark," the tale of a reporter romancing a European princess. Before he and Jeanette each started another picture, in February, they went on a skiing trip to Yosemite National Park with Gene's brother, Bob, and some friends. When their bobsled tipped over, all three were shaken up and received lacerations. Bob's injuries were most serious, as he sprained his wrist. Although Gene skied later in life, from then on, Jeanette stuck to horseback riding, swimming, and summer sports.

On March 27, actor Basil Rathbone and his wife, Ouida, hosted a costume party at the popular restaurant Victor Hugo to celebrate their eleventh anniversary. Each woman received a nosegay in paper lace and an artificial diamond ring; the men were given boutonnieres. The Rathbones asked their celebrity guests to dress as famous pairs. Gene and Jeanette came as Romeo and Juliet, with Jeanette borrowing a costume from MGM that Norma Shearer wore in the 1936 film version of the William Shakespeare play. Some fans said that Gene's donning tights proved just how much he loved his fiancée.

In March, Jeanette and Allan Jones began work on *The Firefly*, a spy story set during the time of Emperor Napoleon I. It is best remembered for introducing Jones' signature song, "The Donkey Serenade." Through the years, he praised Jeanette for her generosity in their scenes and for treating him as an equal, although she had star billing. In 1982, he called her his favorite leading lady. On screen, they shared the charming duet "Sympathy." Jeanette often sang "The

Donkey Serenade" and "Giannina Mia" from *The Firefly* as encores in her recitals.

On March 27, 1937, Gene and Jeanette shared a laugh at Basil and Ouida Rathbone's anniversary costume party, where they dressed as Romeo and Juliet. Later, Gene would play Mercutio on stage and Jeanette would sing the role of Juliet in Charles Gounod's opera. Photo from the Dale Kuntz collection.

The Firefly was a particularly taxing picture because of the amount of dancing involved. Choreographer Albertina Rasch, who had worked with Jeanette in her Broadway days, as well as on *The Merry Widow*, trained her for the role. "And she practically stands over me with a club," Jeanette joked.[207] For a month before filming began, Jeanette rehearsed four to five hours every day, using muscles that she'd forgotten existed. She was too much of a perfectionist to ever use a double. "I have never slaved so hard in my life," Jeanette lamented. "And in those Spanish dances you exercise your whole body, not just your feet."[208] Rasch was impressed with her work ethic, saying, "Jeanette owes her success to the fact that she works twice as hard as any other star."[209] In 1989, Gene echoed Rasch's sentiments, describing Jeanette's "infinite capacity for hard work."[210] He recalled how she rehearsed with Rasch in the morning, filmed all day then went for a vocal lesson with Grace Newell. In a 1951 appearance on *The Carmel Myers Show,* Jeanette said that the dancing was doubly difficult because of the elaborately beaded costume. She rehearsed in a muslin copy and, when she initially tried to dance in the finished gown, she barely could lift her legs because of its weight. Although *The Firefly's* combined domestic and foreign grosses were higher than its costs, domestically, it lost $251,000, now almost $4.4 million.

Meanwhile, Gene filmed *There Goes My Girl* with Ann Sothern and *The Life of the Party* (1937) with Harriet Hilliard, who later gained fame on radio (1944–1954) and television (1952–1966) in *The Adventures of Ozzie and Harriet.* The plot of *The Life of the Party* concerned an aspiring singer (Hilliard) who became involved with an heir (Gene) who would lose his inheritance if he married before he was thirty. Like most of Gene's movies of this era, it was a B comedy that did little to advance his career.

When Jeanette and Gene became engaged, each told their studios that they wanted at least a month for their honeymoon, giving them plenty of advance warning. Jeanette loved Hawaii and wanted to share its beauty with Gene. They also talked of visiting the Orient, if they had time. In 1989, Gene recalled their wedding and how they talked to their studios in advance. "It was very important to us that it came off the way we planned," he insisted.[211]

Friends were anxious to celebrate the upcoming nuptials. One star-studded shower was given at the home of Mildred and Harold Lloyd. Guests included Irene Dunne, Anita Louise, and Irene

Hervey, as well as Jeanette's *San Francisco* co-star, Shirley Ross. Helen Ferguson's mother, Emelie, gave another shower, with members of Anna's celebrity mothers club attending. Jeanette's old friends in Philadelphia also hosted a shower for her, although Jeanette was too busy with work on *The Firefly* to attend. During the party, she called and talked to all fifteen guests, spending two hours on the long distance line. She handwrote thank you notes for each gift. In early June, Harold Lloyd hosted a stag party for Gene and his ushers.

On June 5, 1937, Allan Jones and his wife, Irene Hervey, hosted a Hawaiian-themed pre-nuptial party for Jeanette and Gene. Here they chatted with Connie and Johnny Mack Brown. In Jeanette's will, she left Connie the sterling silver fruit compote that the Browns gave the Raymonds as a wedding gift.

In addition to showers, Jeanette and Gene were busy with other pre-nuptial celebrations. On May 16, they hosted a dinner party for their attendants at Jeanette's home. On June 5, close friends Allan Jones and Irene Hervey threw a Hawaiian-themed party in honor of

Jeanette and Gene. The women were given leis and bridal veils, and their escorts were given silk top hats to wear as they strode into the dining room to the wedding march. The table centerpiece represented a miniature sea, with a replica of the S.S. Lurline, the ship that the couple was taking to their Hawaiian honeymoon. On one side of the water was a tiny bridal party and on the other, a reproduction of Waikiki Beach. In October, Jeanette reciprocated by hosting a star-studded baby shower for Hervey, who was expecting her son, singer Jack Jones. Although Jeanette was rumored to be his Godmother, in 2014, when Jones was asked if it was true, he said, "No, but a good friend, as well as her husband, Gene Raymond."[212] On June 12, Jeanette hosted a dinner for her bridal attendants. The cast and crew of *The Firefly* also threw a party for Jeanette and Gene on the set. Anna, Blossom, her husband, Rocky, and Irene Hervey were included as well. The cast and crew gave Jeanette and Gene a silver flower basket and a silk-bound book containing all of their names.

As the wedding approached, gifts poured in from fans around the world. One article noted that they came from every country except Persia (now Iran) and Iceland. They included dishes, glassware, handmade Afghans, lampshades, magazine and newspaper subscriptions, and even lingerie. Jeanette's favorite present was a tea set for two from Hong Kong. Gene liked a set of six original prints of horse racing scenes from Epsom Downs, a gift from a London fan. Perhaps the most bizarre present was a huge rolling pin from an Irish fan, who had penciled on it "So if Gene tries staying out late o' nights!"[213] Many fans wrote to Jeanette, requesting a wedding invitation as a souvenir, but she had to refuse because of the cost.

Meanwhile, Mrs. Kipling continued to stir up trouble. She wrote to Louis B. Mayer, asking him to intercede and have Gene live up to his financial agreement. She threatened to sue Gene, writing to Mayer,

"I cannot and will not stoop so low as to beg for what is rightfully mine, so long as there remains to me an opportunity to fight for it."[214] Mayer contacted Gene and offered to help. Embarrassed, Gene wrote to him, explaining his mother's jealousy of Jeanette, what he had given Mrs. Kipling, and that no financial contract existed. He said:

> I am deeply mindful of the distressing embarrassment imposed on Jeanette, and it has been and will be my intention to fully protect her against these untrue accusations. I feel that the happiness we hope to find in marriage will be great enough to completely overshadow such troublesome and annoying vindictiveness. Needless to say, I am completely willing to dedicate myself to that end.
>
> Both Jeanette and myself [sic] are greatly appreciative of your kindness in offering your assistance. I know that if anyone could help the situation you could but I honestly believe there is nothing anyone can do. Several of my friends have told me that they went through the same difficulties on the occasion of their marriage, so I suppose a certain disapproval is natural in Mothers in general, though I cannot understand why this should be so.[215]

According to Mayer's grandson, Daniel Mayer Selznick, Mayer "adored Jeanette and her husband."[216] Mayer, his two daughters, and their husbands, all attended the Raymonds' wedding.

In November 1936, Jeanette and Gene announced that they planned to marry on Thursday, June 17, 1937, the second anniversary of their first official date. Months later, they selected a church. Although Gene was raised Catholic and Jeanette Presbyterian, they chose to hold the ceremony at the Wilshire Methodist Episcopal Church. It not only was less than two miles from the house that

Jeanette and Anna were renting at 401 North June Street, but its minister, Dr. Wilsie Martin, was the father-in-law of John Woolfenden, the publicist that MGM assigned to the wedding. On May 17, Jeanette and Gene learned that the church was booked for June 17, so they moved the ceremony a day earlier to June 16, as it was supposed to be bad luck to postpone a wedding. It said a great deal about their character that they did not use their clout as celebrities to force the other couple to change their wedding date.

Due to Jeanette and Gene's shooting schedules and the fear of being mobbed at the Hall of Records during business hours, it was impossible for them to obtain a marriage license the normal way. Instead, on the evening of May 27, they went to the home of Rosamond Rice, clerk in the County Marriage License Bureau, and asked her to file their application. Rice, who was preparing for bed, was startled but thrilled to see the celebrity visitors. She eagerly took their information and arranged for the license, which was dated June 4, 1937. Jeanette gave her address as 401 North June Street; Gene gave his as 325 Bel Air Road, a house he leased in the fall of 1936, after he and his brother moved from the home that Gene bought for their mother. It became standard procedure for celebrities to go to Rice's home; in 1945, singer/actress Judy Garland and director Vincente Minnelli also obtained their marriage license that way.

On June 7, the world was shocked when Jean Harlow died of kidney disease at the age of twenty-six. In addition to starring in *Red Dust* with Gene, she had been an extra in *The Love Parade* and her dressing room was next to Jeanette's at MGM. According to most reports, she and Jeanette knew each other casually, but they were not close friends. Publicist John Woolfenden accompanied Jeanette to the funeral, which was held on June 9 at Wee Kirk o' the Heather Church at Forest Lawn in Glendale, California. MGM closed for the day and the other studios observed a moment of silence at 9:00 that morning in memory of the star. To add to Jeanette's pre-wedding stress, Harlow's mother asked her to sing one of Harlow's favorite songs, "Indian Love Call," at the beginning of the service. At the end of the funeral, Nelson Eddy sang "Ah! Sweet Mystery of Life." Contrary to some reports, according to 1937 newspaper articles, Jeanette and Nelson did *not* sing a duet.

Through the years, Jeanette spoke kindly of Harlow, insisting that she was nothing like her sexy screen image and would have been happier with a home and children than as a movie star. Jeanette recalled an incident at a party where Harlow kissed her hand, as if she was in awe of her, which greatly embarrassed the singer. Years later, when Gene was asked if Harlow and her mother had been invited to the Raymonds' wedding, he thought that they were, since both Jeanette and Gene worked with her, and since many of Jeanette's MGM colleagues attended.

A few days before the wedding, Jeanette and Gene exchanged gifts. He gave her a diamond necklace; she gave him a pair of platinum and diamond cufflinks, along with a note on a "Miss Jeanette MacDonald" calling card. She underlined the Miss and wrote:

My dearest one –

This is the last time I'll send one of these. With this gift goes my devotion my love and my complete faith in you –

I hope I will make you happy. Anyhow – you won't hate me for trying will you.[217]

They each wore their gifts on their wedding day. Through the years, Jeanette often wore the necklace with a sapphire and diamond brooch that Gene gave her in 1936, which could attach to a necklace or be worn separately as a pin. During a 1944 recital, the brooch fell off her dress and she remarked that it was part of her wedding gift from Gene.

Despite MGM's offer to help with arrangements, Jeanette was

determined to handle everything herself. That included choosing her attendants, the flowers, the music, and the singer. In a 1985 interview, Gene recalled, "It was really a marvelous wedding, all arranged by Jeanette. She always wanted a church wedding, and she had it."[218] Jeanette said, "This is my wedding and it means a lot to me. If the studio handles it, people will think I'm using it for publicity."[219] However, the day before the ceremony, after the police department called to ask about directing traffic and controlling the expected crowd around the church, she gave in and let the studio assist with security. Because of superstition, she refused to give any details to the press ahead of time, although she did a magazine spread of fashions from her trousseau and revealed the names of her attendants. "Everybody says it's unlucky to talk about your wedding," she explained, "and I don't want to be unlucky about this."[220] The attendants also were sworn to secrecy. Gene blamed nerves for his silence. "I'm sorry," he told reporters, "but I'm so nervous I can't even talk to myself."[221] On her wedding day, in order to ease her nerves, Jeanette visited her dogs at the kennel.

Meanwhile, in May, Mrs. Kipling returned to California to put her house on the market as a sign of protest. When she showed up at MGM, the guards refused to let her in the front gate. Gene tried to make peace. In Jeanette's autobiography, she recalled the conversation between mother and son: "[Gene] telephoned her to say, 'It would make Jeanette and me very happy if you'd occupy the traditional front pew on the right.' She snapped, 'I have no intention of attending your goddamned wedding,' and hung up."[222]

Despite Mrs. Kipling's hostility, on the evening of the wedding, Jeanette and Gene held up the 9:00 p.m. ceremony for half an hour, waiting for her. When the car that Gene sent for her arrived at her hotel, she already was en route to San Francisco. Just in case Mrs. Kipling showed up and caused trouble, plain-clothes policemen were stationed in the church. Although Gene was estranged from his father, he sent Roy a wedding announcement, and Roy sent the newlyweds a congratulatory telegram in care of the church.

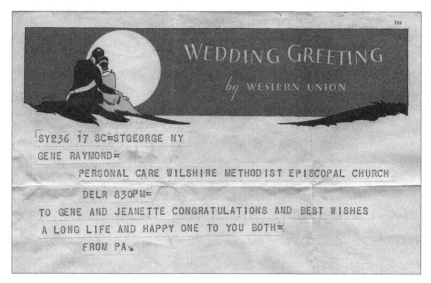

Gene's father's telegram to the newlyweds.

An estimated crowd of fifteen thousand lined the streets to get a glimpse of the bride and groom and the celebrity guests. "No parking" signs were put up on surrounding blocks. Police had to turn off the traffic signal at Wilshire and Plymouth Boulevards so they could keep traffic under control.

Guests had to show their invitations at the door; an alphabetical list was handy in case anyone forgot to bring them. Those closest to the couple sat in the front of the church in an area marked with pink silk ribbons. Presumably, they were the guests who also were invited to the reception for 250 that was held at the home that Jeanette had shared with Anna. Some newspaper reports compared the wedding to a movie premiere. One caustic reporter called it "America's Answer [sic] to the Coronation."[223]

The list of attendees read like *Who's Who in Hollywood*. The guests, numbering between 750 and 800, included friends, like Irene Dunne, Loretta Young, Ernst Lubitsch, Mary Pickford and Charles "Buddy" Rogers, Norma Shearer, Grace Moore, Marian Nixon and William Seiter, Carmel Myers, Doris and Mervyn LeRoy, and Ben Lyon and Bebe Daniels, as well as celebrities, like Eddie Cantor, Al Jolson and Ruby Keeler, Maureen O'Sullivan and John Farrow, Theda Bara, and Dick Powell and Joan Blondell. Many of Jeanette and Gene's co-stars and colleagues also were guests, like Ann Sothern, Eleanor Powell, Ann Sheridan, Fred Astaire, Mary Boland, James Stewart, Robert Taylor, and Barbara Stanwyck. Executives from practically every studio in town attended, including Louis B. Mayer, Jack Warner, Carl Laemmle, Jr., Samuel Goldwyn, David O. Selznick, and William Goetz. Even Will Hays and Joseph Breen and their wives were invited.

However, not everyone was famous. Many behind-the-scenes workers from Jeanette and Gene's studios attended—from directors and writers to electricians and hairdressers—as did Peg Watson, Jeanette's childhood friend from Philadelphia, Emily Wentz and her mother, whom Jeanette befriended during her Broadway days, and Rose and Henri Coen, Jeanette's maid and chauffeur/hairdresser. One movie magazine noted that, besides Gene's mother, among the missing were Clark Gable, Myrna Loy, and Joan Crawford, although Crawford's mother did attend.

The attendants also were celebrated. Blossom, who changed her name to Marie Blake and soon would do bit parts in movies at MGM, was Jeanette's matron of honor, donning a blue gown. Ginger Rogers, Fay Wray, Connie Brown, and Helen Ferguson were bridesmaids in pink. Gene's brother, Bob, was his best man. Allan Jones, Johnny Mack Brown, Harold Lloyd, Basil Rathbone, Helen Ferguson's husband, Richard Hargreaves, and Blossom's husband, Rocky, were ushers. For years afterward, on the Raymonds' anniversary, Jeanette sent hand-written thank you notes to her attendants.

After the ceremony, the Raymonds' wedding party posed at Anna's house. Left to right: Nelson Eddy, Allan Jones, Helen Ferguson, Richard Hargreaves, Blossom Rock, Robert Marlow, Jeanette, Gene, Fay Wray, Harold Lloyd, Ginger Rogers, Clarence Warren "Rocky" Rock, Connie Brown, Johnny Mack Brown, and Basil Rathbone.

In April, Jeanette wrote to Nelson Eddy, then on a recital tour, asking him to sing at the wedding. Always the joker, he replied:

> Sure I'll sing at the wedding. Kindly select numbers from the following:
>
> 1. Ciri Biri bin [sic] [soprano Grace Moore's signature song]
>
> 2. One Night of Love [another song associated with Moore, who was considered Jeanette's rival]
>
> 3. Oft in the Stilly Night [a musical version of Thomas Moore's poem about death]
>
> 4. Vive l'opera! [Nelson's *Maytime* song that poked fun at sopranos]

5. All I do [sic] the Whole Night Through [Gene's theme song from *Sadie McKee,* which actually was titled "All I Do Is Dream of You"]

Love,

Nelson[224]

Jeanette and Gene chose the hymn "O Perfect Love," which Nelson sang while the couple was kneeling at the altar. Jeanette asked Lily Pons to sing "I Love You Truly," with pianist Andre Kostelanetz accompanying her; however, Pons was working in New York so she asked CBS to pipe her voice into the church for the ceremony. When Jeanette learned that it also would be broadcast, both she and the minister thought that the idea was too commercial and banned the network, leaving Nelson to sing both songs at the last minute.

The church was decorated with thousands of Jeanette's favorite Joanna Hill roses. Floral web sites describe them as various shades of yellow fading to cream on the outer petals; however, Jeanette said that they were peach and many reporters called them pink. The hybrid tea roses are thornless or nearly thornless.

Jeanette wore a flesh-pink mousseline gown over pink taffeta, and a shell-shaped lace cap with a pink tulle veil. Louella Parsons noted that it was probably the longest train ever seen in Hollywood, even on screen. Adrian, who had dressed Jeanette in many of her MGM movies, designed the gown, the first that he made for a real wedding. He also designed the attendants' dresses. Jeanette carried a single Joanna Hill rose and an ivory silk prayer book with a cross and the initials "G" and "J" embroidered in gold.

Columnist Dorothy Manners, then Louella Parsons' assistant, recalled, "Jeanette was one of the first brides ever to break from the traditional white. Profusions of pink roses decorated the church, pink satin ribbons adorned the pews of the center aisle and 750 guests turned up to gasp at the beauty of the red-haired bride, in all pink, as she walked down the aisle to meet Gene at the alter [sic]. Even the wedding cake and champagne was [sic] pink."[225]

Prior to the wedding, Jeanette was quoted that she wanted to use the old-fashioned vows; however, the single-ring ceremony did not include the word "obey." For luck, she followed the tradition of having something old, something new, something borrowed, and something blue, as well as having a sixpence in each shoe. The something old was a lace handkerchief that she carried that had been in her family for many years. Something new was her bridal ensemble. Something borrowed were her shoes, on loan from MGM. Something blue was her sapphire engagement ring, worn on her right hand. The sixpence came from Fay Wray and Richard Hargreaves. Jeanette walked to the altar alone to Richard Wagner's "Wedding March" from *Lohengrin*. Newspaper reports said that all the way down the aisle, her eyes never left her bridegroom.

Gene had a message inscribed inside Jeanette's size 2 ¼ platinum wedding band. He told her what it said and it remained a secret between them. She took her vows very seriously; she never removed her ring so she never saw the inscription. When she was playing an unmarried character, she wore another ring over her wedding band or covered it with makeup or court plaster, a plaster made of silk or cloth with an adhesive. Later, Gene gave her a larger gold band to wear over the platinum one when she wore other gold accessories, as Jeanette was very fastidious when it came to matching jewelry. She laughed about how the slipcover ring fit so snugly that Gene often had to use a bobby pin to remove it.

Newspapers reported that the Raymonds had a medium-long kiss. No photographs were allowed during the ceremony. Walter Winchell, who once claimed that Jeanette was married to Bob Ritchie, tried to sneak in a camera, but the candlelight was too dark for his film. Other newspaper columnists and movie magazine writers were on the guest list, including Harrison Carroll, Jimmie Fidler, Erskine Johnson, Edwin and Elza Schallert, Ella and Billy Wickersham, Elizabeth Wilson, Grace Kingsley, Kay Mulvey, and Ruth Waterbury. The only member of the press invited to the reception was Louella Parsons, who smuggled in a portable typewriter so that she could meet her deadline. When Jeanette caught her writing her column in the upstairs guest bath, she led Parsons to a small table with a glass of champagne, a slice of wedding cake, and a telephone so she could call in her column in comfort. Hedda Hopper, who would become Parsons' biggest rival, did not begin her *Los Angeles Times* column until 1938.

After *Life* magazine estimated that the wedding cost $25,000 (currently about $437,000), frugal Jeanette wrote a letter to the editor to argue about it. She insisted that neither the wedding, nor her trousseau, cost anywhere near that, estimating the costs closer to $5,000 (currently over $87,000). What she didn't say was that some things, like the ninety-pound cake from Freihofer's Bakery in Philadelphia, had been donated, and that she took the cost of the bridal party's dresses and her trousseau as tax deductions, noting that photos of them ran in publications all over the world and that the bridal party's gowns could not be salvaged. While some may question Jeanette taking the deductions, it isn't that different than current celebrities selling exclusive rights to their wedding photos to publications. The Raymonds were particularly popular in England, where their wedding picture appeared on the cover of the December 18, 1937 issue of *Picture Show* and in Belgium they were depicted on the song sheet for "The Lovers Lullaby."

Jeanette and Gene on the happiest day of their lives. Jeanette was interred with the ivory prayer book that she carried at the wedding. Her sapphire engagement ring—worn on her right hand—was her "something blue." Photo from the Dale Kuntz collection.

After the ceremony, Jeanette and Gene had to run to their limousine to avoid the mob of photographers and fans outside the church. When Jeanette saw the size of the crowd, she audibly gasped. Police held back the onlookers, while six motorcycle officers escorted the Raymonds to the reception. As Jeanette got out of the car, a photographer stepped on her veil, tearing it in half. She wore it that way to receive her guests and in the wedding pictures, before changing into her going away ensemble, a white dress with white orchids on her shoulder. It took the attendants over an hour to get through the crowd and join the newlyweds at Anna's house to pose for pictures. Jeanette and Gene drank their champagne wedding toast from gold chalice cups, a gift from Helen Ferguson and Richard Hargreaves. Gene reminded everyone to refer to his bride as Mrs. Raymond, then forgot and introduced her as Miss MacDonald himself.

Following the reception, the newlyweds headed off for a brief honeymoon, as, on June 21, Jeanette had to be back at work for retakes on *The Firefly*. Sources disagree over whether Gene told Jeanette that they were driving to Santa Barbara or to the Mission Inn in Riverside, California. However, unbeknownst to his bride, he secretly had purchased and furnished an English Tudor-style house at 783 Bel Air Road, with the help of Helen Ferguson, Richard Hargreaves, Rose Coen, and Sylvia Grogg. Helen, who was in charge of the project, referred to Gene as Michael Rasmussen to keep nosy workers and neighbors in the dark. At the time, the neighborhood was called West Los Angeles, but later, it became known as Bel Air. Gene decorated the house to Jeanette's tastes and had all of her things in place, including their wedding gifts. During their engagement, Jeanette thought that he was getting cold feet about the wedding when he found fault with every house they toured.

Shortly before the wedding, Louella Parsons found out about the house, which Gene had Helen Ferguson purchase under her married name so the press wouldn't spoil the surprise. Parsons agreed to keep Gene's secret until after he revealed it to Jeanette.

When Gene drove up and announced that it was their home, Jeanette didn't believe him. It was only after she asked how much he paid for it—and he refused to tell her—that she realized that he was serious. Jeanette recalled, "My mouth sagged open. My dresses, shoes, books, records, keepsakes, wedding presents, all were in place as though we'd been living there for months. . . . I dreamed all my life of a place I'd call home. I found it that night."[226]

The two-story house had a thatched roof, and stucco and stone exterior. The front door was decorated in a fleur-de-lis pattern. The paneled mahogany foyer reached to the second floor and had two long staircases. One led to an expansive sunken living room, the other to the second floor. The Raymonds used the living room for formal entertaining and numerous photo shoots. John Phillips of the rock group the Mamas and the Papas, who owned the estate in the 1960s, described the living room as feeling "large as a basketball court."[227]

For informal entertaining, there was Ye Old English Pub, an English-style tap room, complete with carved gargoyles above the entrance, a bar, oak paneling, two bearskin rugs on the flagstone floor, rustic barrel-shaped tables and chairs, and the marlin that Gene caught in 1936, hanging above the fireplace. The library had leaded windows, a fireplace, comfortable furniture, and plenty of personal photos hanging on the walls.

Jeanette's collection of Czechoslovakian cobalt blue crystal stemware was displayed in an enormous breakfront in the dining room. Attending to every detail, Gene had the rug dyed to match her crystal. The table had many leaves to accommodate large dinner parties. When the Raymonds were alone, they often ate at a small table for two by the enormous bay window. Later, Jeanette's nephew, Earle Wallace, painted a pastel mural in the dining room.

The first floor also included a kitchen, a breakfast room, a powder room, and maid's quarters. In addition to eleven steps up to the second floor and eight down to the living room from the foyer, many of the rooms were a few steps up or down from adjoining rooms so the Raymonds got their exercise. There were even stairs leading from the lawn to the driveway and garage.

There was a blue flagstone terrace off the living room with blue and gold cushioned patio chairs. A striped canopy covered the area, in case of inclement weather. The Raymonds often hosted Sunday brunches for friends and family, with Jeanette cooking her famous homemade waffles. They said that they liked hosting brunches because it reminded them of their second meeting at a brunch at the Swarts' home.

The second floor featured three bedrooms, two dressing rooms (both off the master bedroom), three baths, and a sitting room. The Raymonds had separate bedrooms, bathrooms, and dressing rooms so one wouldn't disturb the other when one had an early studio call and the other didn't. But, as Gene noted in one of his wartime letters, the fact that they had separate bedrooms didn't mean that they always used them. Given the sexual innuendo in the Raymonds' correspondence, both during and after the war, it's clear that they had an active love life. In a 1947 letter, he wrote to Jeanette, who planned to meet him in Detroit for the opening of his play, *The Greatest of These*, "I'll see you a week from tonight, and I promise I won't be too tired! So you'd better get rested on the train!!"[228]

The master bedroom, sometimes referred to as Jeanette's room, was decorated in her favorite color, peachy pink, which she described as the color of the center of Joanna Hill roses. Later, it was redecorated in coral. One wall had an enormous mirror that framed a tiled fireplace. There was a small table where the Raymonds sometimes ate breakfast. A glass cabinet in one corner held many of Jeanette's treasures, including contralto Ernestine Schumann-Heink's coral rosary, soprano Adelina Patti's snuff box, the pair of gold chalice cups given to the Raymonds by Helen Ferguson and Richard Hargreaves for their wedding toast, and the prayer book that Jeanette carried at their wedding. Although some reports on the Raymonds' wedding erroneously described the book as pink, reporter Mayme Ober Peak, who, in 1939, saw it displayed in the bedroom, called it white, and a 1954 inventory of Twin Gables said it was ivory. Presumably, the candlelight at the church distorted the color and reporters assumed that it matched Jeanette's wedding gown. Following Jeanette's funeral, there was confusion over the book, which was in Jeanette's casket, as reports described it as white, making some think that it was different from the one that Jeanette carried at her wedding.

The master bedroom, often referred to as Jeanette's room, included some of her fan collection. The glass cabinet in the left corner held many of her treasures, including the prayer book that she carried at her wedding and the gold chalice cups used for the Raymonds' first toast. They were engraved "God bless you, Jeanette" and "God bless you, Michael," the alias Gene used when he and Helen Ferguson were remodeling the house to surprise Jeanette.[643] In 1957, Helen still called him Michael when she signed Jeanette's guest book.

The bedroom that the Raymonds referred to as Gene's room was more masculine, with beige and burgundy décor. It included a desk for his typewriter, his gun collection hanging on one wall, a comfortable window seat for studying scripts, and plenty of framed photos of Jeanette on display.

Both Raymonds frequently suffered from insomnia so, when they were working, it was better that they slept apart. Jeanette rated her sleepless nights, with a particularly bad one being a "dilly."[229] She often slept only two hours a night, but was able to catnap during the day. In 1940, she told reporters, "I can drop down to sleep any time and come right out of it. I do it all the time at the studio, when I'm making pictures. . . . Some people can't sleep in the daytime, I know Gene can't. He says it takes him half the afternoon to wake up."[230] Gene sometimes called himself "Whirling Willie" because he tossed and turned so much.

Gene's dresser was loaded with photos of Jeanette through the years.

After V-E Day, anticipating Gene's return from service, Jeanette collected estimates for a custom-made bed, box spring, and mattress for the master bedroom, but decided that it was too expensive, with estimates currently equivalent to about $6,000. In the 1950s, when neither Raymond had an active movie career, the bedroom that they referred to as Gene's room had a couch that converted to a bed since no one slept there on a regular basis.

The house had two attics and, beneath the first floor, there was a walk-in vault that had been converted into a wine cellar. The two-acre property included stables for their horses, Black Knight (a birthday gift from Jeanette to Gene in 1936) and White Lady (a gift from Gene to Jeanette for her upcoming birthday, two days after the wedding), and a small corral. After the horses won ribbons, the Raymonds proudly hung them in the tack room in their stables. Eventually, the Raymonds found that it was too difficult to deliver hay to the stables, as it took two men and a dolly to transport it down the hill from the driveway. They moved the horses to the Riviera Country Club, where they often rode before their marriage.

Next to the stables was a kennel for Jeanette and Gene's six dogs and a fenced-in play area. In 1987, Gene recalled how, every morning at 6:30 a.m., he would go down to feed and walk them. Six little faces always were lined up waiting and he couldn't figure out how they knew the time.

The five levels of terraced gardens included a grape arbor, a rose arbor, fruit trees, and a small fountain. At one time, there were 152 varieties of roses growing on the property. There was a fenced private area for Jeanette that Gene called "Le Jardin de la Princesse" (the Garden of the Princess), where Jeanette grew old-fashioned perennials. In 1939, Jeanette told Mayme Ober Peak, "I love pansies. I have a little donkey cart Ida Koverman gave me last Christmas which I take down to the garden and fill with pansies. I can sit and look at these pansies and see faces of people I'm fond of."[231] Stormy, and later Misty, Jeanette's Skye Terriers, were the only canine members of the Raymond family to have complete run of the gardens; the other dogs usually played in the fenced-in area. The property was so attractive that Helen Ferguson sometimes brought other clients, like Barbara Stanwyck, there for photo shoots. In 1952, the Raymonds hosted the *Modern Screen* Fashion Board luncheon and fashion show at their estate.

The Raymonds gathering fruit in their orchard at Twin Gables in the late 1930s. They grew grapes, peaches, limes, tangerines, figs, cherries, plums, apricots, persimmons, and avocados on the property.

Above the three-car garage were two servants' rooms and a bath. Down the hill, five levels below the main house, was a small building that the Raymonds called the playhouse. It had a huge room, decorated in MacDonald plaid, with a large fireplace, a bar, a small kitchen, and two dressing rooms and baths. Additionally, there was another small building that the Raymonds used as an office and additional storage. Behind the house was a bridal path that led to the Bel-Air

Stables, which, in 1946, were converted into the Hotel Bel-Air. On a clear day, Jeanette and Gene could see the Pacific Ocean, about ten miles away from their hilltop home.

Marion Smith Glendening gave the Raymonds Twin Gables coasters based on a sketch by Jeanette's nephew, Earle Wallace.

The estate became known as Twin Gables because of the pair of peaks above the doorway. Gene often referred to it as "the garden spot of the world" because of the rows of terraced flower gardens and fruit trees on the property. In correspondence, Jeanette usually called it "783" after the address. Blossom sometimes called it "Gables." Jeanette loved her home so much that she had stationery made, using a sketch that her nephew did of Twin Gables. In 1939, her childhood friend, Marion Smith Glendening, gave the Raymonds disposable coasters to match. Even the mailbox was a wooden replica of the house with a metal container inside to hold the mail.

Jeanette was as proud of her new initials as she was of her home. She always was greatly pleased that her initials J.A.M. spelled a word, which was supposed to be lucky. "I retained my good luck when I married," she said, "as I went out of the J.A.M. into the J.A.R."[232] She had many monogrammed accessories, including clothing, purses, luggage, belts, a compact, earrings, and a bracelet. After her marriage, her letterhead, envelopes, calling cards, and address labels usually used Jeanette Raymond, Mrs. Gene Raymond, or the initials J.A.R. unless it was the "Jeanette MacDonald at the Studio" stationery that she used for answering fan mail at MGM.

One of Gene's wedding gifts to his bride was a blue leather book with "Milestones" embossed in gold, containing photos of their courtship. Through the years, the Raymonds added to it with pictures chronicling their marriage.

Jeanette and Gene became known as "the MacRaymonds" to their friends, the press, and themselves. Jeanette had a variety of other nicknames that different people gave her. Sometimes her family, in addition to many of her childhood friends, referred to her as "Jimmee" (also spelled Jimmie) and she signed correspondence to them that way. When she was young, she also was called "Jessie," "Jennie," and "Jammie." In correspondence, Blossom sometimes referred to Jeanette as "J." To Charlotte Learn and Jack Garrity, Jeanette was known as "Pickles" because of her affinity for the vegetable that went back to childhood. In a 1936 article about Jeanette, Anna recalled how her youngest daughter enjoyed munching on a fat sour pickle en route to school the way other children ate candy. Bob Ritchie called Jeanette "Shorty" because he towered over her; even in 1960, when Jeanette contacted him about her autobiography, he still referred to her that way. In correspondence, Helen Ferguson and Jeanette often called each other "Nellie" and "Nettie." Helen referred to Gene as "Michael" or "Mike" after the alias he used while they were working on Twin Gables as a surprise for Jeanette. He named one of his Irish Setters Mike too. Publicist Constance Hope referred to Jeanette as "Janine" and Jeanette sometimes signed letters to her that way. The Raymonds even had "Janine and Gene" stationery.

Gene called his wife "Bunky," "Bunko," or "Bunk," the origins of which neither could remember. The earliest appearance seen by this author was from June 1938, shortly after the Raymonds traveled by train from Arizona to New York. At the time, most compartments had upper and lower bunks and it's probable that's where the nickname originated. Adding an O was a term of affection, as Gene also occasionally referred to Jeanette's dog Stormy as "Stormo." Jeanette often called Gene "Pappie" (sometimes spelled Pappy), both in person and in letters. She even referred to him that way on *This Is Your Life* (1952), just as he called her "Bunk" on the show. The Raymonds also had a series of names that they frequently used in correspondence, including "Flora MacIntosh" (sometimes spelled McIntosh)/"Jake McGillicutty," "Mrs. Crispee" (sometimes spelled Crispy), and "Old Lady Raymond"/"Old Man Raymond" (abbreviated as O.L.R. and O.M.R.). In one letter that Gene signed "Pappie," he jokingly addressed Jeanette as "Nappie"[233] and, in another, he called her "Ma goo."[234]

The Raymonds enjoyed each other's company and, before the war, their life was full of contentment. Jeanette said, "Marriage is not only that deep sense of rightness you get in belonging together, it's a hundred little things that make up your days. And life is made up of days."[235] One reporter noted how well matched the Raymonds were. "[Gene's] absolutely nonsensical sense of humor matches Jeanette's and, what is more important, his great love for her makes him think

constantly of her welfare and happiness. . . . When you see them together, you see a dozen little ways in which Jeanette is consciously
playing wife, deferring to Gene, giving in to him to make his happiness greater. That is the sort of give and take you see going on in
happy marriages in other places, but it is just about the rarest of all
sights in Hollywood."[236] James Stewart observed, "Gene has the right
idea about the way to treat a girl. He never forgets the little attentions.
He does everything right, like surprising Jeanette with the house, all
furnished and everything. . . . He always remembers flowers for little
anniversaries. Always says nice things. The right things."[237] Reporter
Eunice Field noted, "People who saw them together at home or in
public had no doubts about their profound love for each other. One
observer was quoted as saying, 'Doggone them, they're not only the
happiest pair I ever saw . . . they look happy!'"[238] In 1989, fan club
President Clara Rhoades said, "They both thought the other was
'more talented.' I guess this is one of the reasons their marriage was
so strong and so devoted in a business that can wreck marriages. They
were very much alike in their ethics and morals & left show business
at the front door in private."[239]

To show their affection for one another, the Raymonds often left
each other notes around the house. One of the earliest came from
Gene on June 23, 1937, a few days before they left for their real honeymoon, accompanying a volume written by Jeanette's favorite classical author, Victor Hugo. The brief message read: "A whole week and
I love you twice as much!"[240] It was written on a Mr. Gene Raymond
calling card, with the name crossed out, and signed McGillicutty, the
same silly nickname that Gene used in his April Fools' Day telegrams
in 1935. For the first year of their marriage, each week, Gene gave
Jeanette another gift to celebrate the anniversary of their wedding.
In addition to books, they included a gold key to Twin Gables and

a replica of their wedding cake, complete with bride and groom. In 1963, when the Raymonds moved from Twin Gables, Jeanette gave the twenty-volume set of Victor Hugo books to longtime fan Mary Dunphy, who was a teacher.

One of the many things that Jeanette and Gene had in common was their love of music. Long before he met Jeanette, in a 1932 interview, Gene said that one of his favorite pieces was Franz Liszt's "Liebestraum," which Jeanette sang in *The Girl of the Golden West*, her first film after their wedding. A 1954 inventory of Twin Gables included a homemade record of Gene playing the piece. Before and after their marriage, the Raymonds often attended concerts at the Hollywood Bowl and Philharmonic Auditorium. Sometimes they arranged to be in New York for the opening of the Metropolitan Opera. The music room at Twin Gables, located in the playhouse, had two pianos so they could play duets. For Gene's first birthday after their marriage, Jeanette gave him an electric organ. He also played the accordion and ukulele. In 1940, they had a Baldwin grand piano custom made for the living room, and Jeanette had friends autograph the lid. She was modest about her piano skills, but DeWitt Bodeen and several other friends said that she could transpose music on sight. In late 1944, a fan gave Jeanette an antique harpsichord, which Gene had restored for her next birthday. She treasured the rare instrument and kept it in a place of honor in her bedroom and, later, in the upstairs sitting room. In Gene's wartime letters, he mentioned how much he missed the piano and how he relished any time spent playing.

The Raymonds also were avid game players. Among their favorites were tennis, ping-pong, croquet, backgammon, canasta, and gin rummy. Emily said that, although Jeanette was a terrible gin rummy player, she always won. When the Raymonds entertained, they often played charades, as well as cartoons, a drawing version of charades similar to Pictionary. In a 1938 interview, Jeanette laughed about their enthusiasm for games: "Our Christmas tree resembled a six-year-old's idea of what Santa would do in a generous mood. Every game in the toy departments was there."[241] Perhaps the most bizarre game that they played was sardines, which Jeanette described in a 1939 article in *The Family Circle*. One guest was chosen to be the sardine, then the lights were turned off and the others hunted for him or her. When found, each guest remained with the sardine, often squeezing into a tight spot. "And it's not unusual to find the sardine perched atop a mantelpiece, under a ping-pong table or behind a couch," Jeanette said. "You can imagine what the scene looks like when the lights go on."[242] Pictures from a 1949 party showed the Raymonds playing musical chairs, with Jeanette gleefully removing a chair from her guests while Gene played piano.

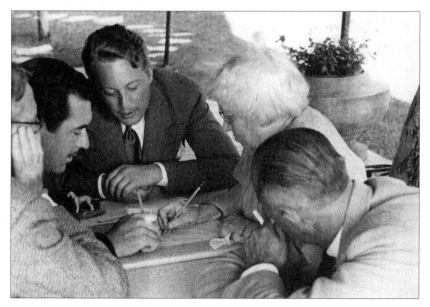

One of the Raymonds' favorite games was cartoons, a drawing version of charades. Here, Gene played with brother-in-law Rocky, Ida "Kay" Koverman, and two unidentified friends.

Jeanette and Gene both loved to walk. When they were filming, after dinner, they routinely took a half-hour stroll together. Usually, the dogs joined them, turning it into a run and romp. When the dogs were with them, the Raymonds kept to the open, uncultivated spots of their property. Jeanette dressed casually in slacks and loved to roll around on the lawn with her canine family. After the dogs were worn out, Jeanette and Gene explored their gardens.

Many remarked that Twin Gables was not just a house, but a home, as the Raymonds furnished it with things that they loved. Jeanette collected fans that belonged to famous women, like Marie Antoinette, Queen Victoria, and Swedish soprano Jenny Lind. Many were framed and hung on the walls in the master bedroom. Coincidentally, it was Rosie Dolly's twin sister, Jenny, who started Jeanette's collection when Jenny gave her a fan that belonged to Empress Josephine, after Jeanette admired it during her 1931 trip to France. Gene sometimes added to his wife's fan collection on special days. In 1958, when the Raymonds were interviewed by Edward R. Murrow on *Person to Person*, Gene joked about looking for Lady Windermere's fan, alluding to the Oscar Wilde play. Jeanette also collected miniature figures of musicians—until the dust they accumulated began to bother her allergies. Eventually, she donated them to the Los Angeles Orthopaedic Hospital.

The library was filled with books on music, philosophy, dogs, and various other subjects, as well as some of Gene's collection of Abraham Lincoln memorabilia. Many of the shelves and tables were lined with dog items, including ashtrays, cigarette boxes, figurines, and bookends. The Raymonds' dogs' trophies and ribbons were displayed beside Jeanette and Gene's awards. Framed photos of friends and family decorated many rooms. Some of the furniture and accessories were purchased at antique shops that the Raymonds visited during their travels. Jeanette also shopped when she was on the road performing, causing Emily to tell a reporter, "We always have more parcels going home than we have baggage!"[243] DeWitt Bodeen recalled attending a dinner party where Jeanette rattled off who gave the Raymonds various pieces of china, silver, and crystal. "I love using our wedding gifts," she said, "because then I think of the friends who gave them."[244]

In this 1949 photo, Jeanette, Gene, and their Skye Terrier, Misty, relaxed in the library. During and after the war, many of Gene's Army Air Force photos adorned the walls. The picture next to the trophies was of Helen Ferguson and Richard Hargreaves. In a 1954 inventory of Twin Gables, it was referred to as a photo of Nellie and Dick.

Artist Henrique Medina posed with his portrait of Jeanette, known as "The Pink Lady." He also did the young painting of Hurd Hatfield that was used in the movie *The Portrait of Dorian Gray* (1945).

In 1940, Jeanette had her portrait painted by Portuguese artist Henrique Medina. In it, she was seated, holding a single Joanna Hill rose. Known as "The Pink Lady" after the color of Jeanette's evening gown, the painting was displayed prominently in the living room. The dress, which she sometimes wore in her recitals, was Gene's favorite. Around this time, Jeanette wanted to redecorate the living room, but Gene was against the idea. She didn't argue or press the matter; however, after she gave him her portrait for Christmas, he realized that the colors used in it clashed with the décor so he acquiesced to Jeanette. A painting of Gene by Polish artist Stan Poray hung above the fireplace in the library. In 1935, Gene had it painted as a Christmas gift for his mother, but, after their falling out, she didn't want it. In 1953,

Gene had another portrait done by American artist Keith Martin and it hung in the upstairs foyer, although Jeanette told Marjorie Merriweather Post that they weren't satisfied with it.

Gene was an enthusiastic amateur photographer, with a still camera, as well as a movie camera, and Jeanette was his favorite subject. He told a reporter, "Now that I've discovered color, I'm so excited about it that the black-and-whites seem tame, and I'm always making her wear this or that for a color shot. . . . I find the best way to get pictures of Jeanette is to put her where I want her, start kidding until she laughs, then when she can hold still enough to shoot, grab the picture! Once, though, the horse began to laugh too and that ruined the shot!"[245] Jeanette also took pictures, but said that Gene often had to help her focus and frame them. Although Gene admired artistic shots, he said that he and Jeanette took pictures "for the sake of keeping happy memories."[246] During the war, Gene frequently encouraged Jeanette to send pictures of herself or the crowds at her performances.

Unlike many celebrities, the Raymonds didn't have a projection room, but had a screen hidden behind drapes in the living room. They occasionally borrowed films from the studios or watched their own home movies. In the 1950s, Jeanette tried to purchase copies of her pictures from Paramount and MGM, but the studios refused. She said that Norma Shearer also tried in vain to get copies of her movies from MGM. In 1959, Ken Richards gave Jeanette a lead on a man who was willing to copy some of her films on 16 millimeter. At the time, owning them was considered illegal, since the studios themselves did not sell them, so Jeanette never pursued the matter. In the early 1960s, Jeanette complained to her fan club about not being able to own copies, as well as the fact that she received no royalties when they were re-released or televised. After Jeanette's death, when ownership laws became less stringent, Gene had one of her fan club Presidents purchase some copies of both Raymonds' movies for him. He was delighted when they became available on videotape so everyone could watch them at their leisure. When he saw new releases advertised, he often sent the ads to her fan club to make sure members knew that the tapes were available.

Jeanette enjoyed making ice cream almost as much as she liked eating it. Photo from the Fay La Galle collection.

Jeanette never had to worry about her weight; she usually had problems gaining. Gene also ate almost anything in order to put on weight. One of their indulgences was ice cream. Jeanette lovingly reminisced about making ice cream with her father, and she continued the tradition with Gene, often using fruit from their orchards. Her favorite flavor was peach; his: chocolate. She said, "That's one of the reasons why we married—because we feel the same way about peach ice cream. And a lot of other nice things."[247] She insisted that the best ice cream came from Philadelphia and, when she visited her home city, she always had to have some. In 1988, Gene recalled how Jeanette claimed that the best ice cream in Philadelphia came from Schilling's

Ice Cream Parlor and how she tried to recreate it. "Jeanette initiated me into the vagaries and idiosyncracies of making this sweet product on a home basis," he said. "I was never able to find out whether this recipe of hers had anything to do with Mr. and Mrs. Schilling of Arch Street. But I can tell you that many a Sunday morning, I spent cranking out this marvelous ice cream—this MacDonald delicacy. And it was a delicacy—I can tell you it was a Philadelphia delicacy!"[248]

While on the road, wherever Jeanette went, she managed to find the best ice cream parlors. On several occasions, she took a group of fans out for a dish or cone. According to longtime fan Irene Daligga, whenever Jeanette visited Detroit, she went to Sanders Chocolates for a hot fudge sundae. The Michigan firm is still famous for its hot fudge and caramel dessert toppings. During the war, while Gene was stationed in England, Jeanette sent him powdered ingredients to make ice cream sundaes.

Aside from ice cream, Jeanette's appetite was quirky. She liked apple pie, but never ate the crust, reasoning that she just liked the way apples were cooked in pie. She often ordered oyster stew, but told the waiter to hold the oysters. She even autographed a photo to her Philadelphia classmate Rose Landesberg Devon, "Yours for oysterless [sic] stews."[249] Jeanette frequently carried a thermos of applesauce and milk. In 1963, she told a reporter that the concoction kept her young. In a 1952 interview, Jeanette claimed that she was allergic to fruit juice, "But that's my solo food problem," she erroneously stated.[250] A wartime letter referred to her allergy to white bread; later, she discovered that she had many food allergies, including chocolate. She disliked fried foods, as well as Mexican, Hawaiian, Chinese, and Japanese food. She didn't like peanut butter because, as a child, she ate too much of it in one sitting. In 1952, she admitted, "I've been known to eat everything from vegetable soup to apple pie for breakfast! It's always seemed such a dull meal, limited to toast, eggs, and cereal. Besides, I like my eggs boiled just one and a half minutes and my toast burned. It's so difficult to convince room service of this when I'm traveling, so I simply order baked beans or some other foolproof dish and avoid trouble!"[251] She once fooled Anna and Blossom by serving them horsemeat, telling them it was beef. Gene knew her tricks and recognized it when she tried to pass off rabbit as chicken.

Both Raymonds loved to eat, although Gene's appetite was much less finicky than that of his wife. He had the same breakfast every day: half a grapefruit, a soft boiled egg, and coffee. He was an avid lover of snacks and Jeanette indulged him. A fan recalled running into Jeanette in a New York candy store, buying Cocoa Almonds for her husband. After Marion and Frank Glendening sent the Raymonds nuts and Bachman pretzels for Christmas, Gene raved about them and noted how many he ate. When Jeanette was in the hospital during Christmas 1963, there was a box of Nabisco pretzels under her table-top tree for him. In 1964, Jeanette called Gene "a bit of a lustful eater."[252] After fan club President Clara Rhoades sent the Raymonds some honey and jellies, Jeanette said, "I'll get around to trying them out & sharing with Old Man Raymond – who usually partakes generously of such on his biscuits or muffins in true male fashion."[253] He kept his weight down by exercising and participating in sports. In addition to the Bel-Air Country Club, he was a longtime member of the New York Athletic Club. He also occasionally worked out at the Hollywood Athletic Club, practicing on the horizontal bar.

After the height of Jeanette's movie career, when she did not get as much exercise, she always took off weight if she noticed that she gained a few pounds. In several letters, she mentioned that she and Gene "ate themselves out of shape" during vacations and that she would be attending Elizabeth Arden, a beauty spa, until she was back to her normal size.

In a 1947 letter to Elsie, Jeanette made it clear that the Raymonds didn't keep chocolate on hand, but relished it when they received it as a gift. She wrote, "Thank you for the lovely Easter eggs, which (forgive us) we have already started on. We have been craving candy for so long, that when they arrived we simply decided not to save them for Easter – they are delicious."[254] In 1949, Emily Wentz said, "Miss MacDonald is looking and feeling very well—has gained several pounds, and I think she looks wonderful with the added pounds. However, she won't be satisfied until she takes them off. She is always after me to take off a <u>few</u> (!?!) pounds but I think she has given it up as a bad job. I just haven't the will-power [sic] when it comes to food. Miss MacDonald, however, is a marvel—she says she is going to stop eating this or that, and she does! I last for about one day—or maybe two! But I <u>did</u> stop smoking five years ago, and haven't had a cigarette since—(I must blow my own horn just a little.)"[255]

Jeanette admitted that she was not a stellar cook, but bragged about her eggplant parmesan, and her baked beans, a recipe that she learned from her mother, which Jeanette served with steamed brown bread. Although the beans sometimes gave her indigestion, she said that occasionally she had to splurge and eat them. She also liked to make waffles and homemade soups. Gene loved to barbecue and was a master with steaks and chicken.

In 1940, to celebrate the Raymonds' third anniversary, Jeanette redecorated the playhouse for Gene and he had a sixty-foot free-form flagstone-bordered swimming pool built for her. The pool was five levels below the house so, when they finished swimming, they had quite a hike. In one of Gene's wartime letters, he teased about pushing her back up the hill to the house. In later years, the climb became too taxing on Jeanette's heart.

The living room in the main house originally had a vaulted cathedral ceiling, but the Raymonds found that the heat collected at the top so they had a lower ceiling built, which also eliminated an interior balcony. Through the years, they did other renovations on Twin Gables, including turning part of the lower attic into an elaborate climate-controlled trio of closets for Jeanette to store her gowns, furs, and accessories. Although the construction was expensive, it saved always-frugal Jeanette a fortune in storage bills. Singer/actress Michelle Phillips, who owned Twin Gables after the Raymonds moved out, described it in her autobiography.

[Jeanette] had taken a side of one wing of the house and converted it into drawers of different sizes to house her lingerie and accessories. There were great stretches of drawers in layered rows, one above the other. Each glove drawer, so slim and smooth, would contain a different pair of gloves: 'rose lace, black leather, white silk,' and so on. Each drawer was labeled with hand-inscribed tape. There seemed to be some sort of code; everything was very organized. She must have been a very orderly woman. She certainly had an extravagant wardrobe. . . . This woman had drawers for her ball gowns, deep king-size drawers so the ball gowns could be fully stretched out, without folds or squashing. You could have gotten a person in each drawer inside the gown. These drawers were labeled with the name of the designer and the color of the gown. Such a lot of money must have been invested in there. They obviously socialized a *lot*. The cedar closet itself was magnificent. On the left-hand side there was a hanging space and more drawers. These closets were also built to take her furs. There was a secret door from the main part of the house; it was her place, and the aroma in there, the cedar, was overwhelming.[256]

Phillips later regretted destroying the closets to build a sitting room for Honest John's Studio, the recording studio that she and husband John Phillips of the Mamas and the Papas installed behind it. In 1967, John Phillips wrote another famous song about San Francisco, "San Francisco (Be Sure to Wear Flowers in Your Hair)," which was recorded by Scott McKenzie in the studio at Twin Gables. The cover of the Mamas and the Papas' 1968 LP *Deliver* was shot in the pool on the estate.

Helen Ferguson was one of the well-wishers who saw the Raymonds off on their honeymoon. Jeanette fingered her favorite sapphire and diamond brooch, which she often wore with the diamond necklace that Gene gave her before their wedding. The brooch, which could be worn as a pin or necklace, matched Jeanette's engagement ring and the dinner ring that Gene gave her for her birthday in 1936.

On June 22, 1937, Jeanette finished retakes for *The Firefly*. Four days later, the Raymonds sailed to Honolulu on the S.S. Lurline. Their wedding party chartered a bus to see them off on their honeymoon. Also on the ship were newlywed actors Mary Pickford and Buddy Rogers, both of whom Jeanette knew since the early 1930s. According to a newspaper report, the Raymonds and the Rogers dined together twice during the trip, with the Raymonds being guests of the Rogers one evening and the Rogers being guests of the Raymonds another night.

On July 1, the Lurline arrived in Honolulu. Crowds of fans and press mobbed the newlyweds. It was estimated that the Raymonds and the Rogers attracted a larger crowd than Shirley Temple, who vacationed in Honolulu two years earlier. When Gene was asked what he thought of Nelson Eddy, Gene replied, "He's a swell fellow, but I'll never be able to sing like he does."[257] Another reporter wondered if the newlyweds would continue their careers. Gene answered in the affirmative. "I have no desire to cut in on Mr. Eddy's pictures with Mrs. Raymond. I can't sing too well. Anyway, I heartily approve."[258]

After the Raymonds finished dealing with the press, their friend, Pete Halford, herded them through the crowd to an awaiting car. Through the years, whenever Jeanette and Gene visited Hawaii, the Halfords always met them, even when they arrived in the pre-dawn hours.

Upon the Raymonds' arrival in Honolulu, they were draped in leis, from chins to thighs. When they reached their honeymoon cottage, they removed them, playfully spelling out "Aloha nui" with the floral necklaces on the lawn. "Aloha nui loa" means "all my love." Although the climate in Honolulu didn't bother Jeanette's allergies, the floral leis did. However, she didn't want to insult the Hawaiians who greeted her by refusing them. "Never let it be said that I am not a good trouper," she smiled. "I have been wrapped up in leis ever since I got off of the boat and have nearly sneezed my head off."[259] Newsreel footage and some photos showed a lei-clad Jeanette with puffy eyes. She also kept quiet about her dislike of Hawaiian food.

When the Raymonds departed Honolulu, they were covered in leis again. After they boarded the ship, they tossed their leis overboard, believing the tradition that, if the leis floated toward land, the Raymonds would return to the island someday. The superstition proved true, as they visited Hawaii twice more together during their marriage.

The Raymonds held hands as they debarked in Honolulu and were smothered in leis. During their honeymoon, the floral leis wreaked havoc with Jeanette's allergies, making her face and eyes puffy, but she was too polite to tell anyone and risk hurting their feelings.

**The Halfords loaned the Raymonds their
Lanikai Beach cottage for their honeymoon.**

Jeanette and Gene spent most of their honeymoon at the Halfords'
Oahu cottage at Lanikai Beach, hoping to have some privacy from the
press and fans. They noted that every time they went to the beach at
Waikiki, they were besieged by autograph seekers. The Raymonds also
visited Jeanette's friends, Philip and Flora Rice, on their ranch at Kipu
Kai and the Rices' mountain home at Kokee, both on Kauai. Jeanette
said, "It was the most perfect honeymoon a couple could possibly

have. It is my dearest memory."[260] They spent almost six weeks in the Hawaiian Islands, and their home movies showed them seeing sights, having fun with Jeanette's friends, riding, sunning, playing ping-pong, and attending a luau and pig roast. They also went to a Hawaiian fishing festival. In order to take care of some social obligations, they spent a weekend at the Royal Hawaiian Hotel.

To promote *The Firefly, Los Angeles Times* Drama Editor Edwin Schallert and his assistant, Alma Whitaker, interviewed the Raymonds by telephone, along with Robert Z. Leonard, who arrived with his wife on July 22, three weeks after the Raymonds, for a Hawaiian vacation. When the reporters asked if Gene was proving a manageable husband, Jeanette answered, "Don't be silly. He's quite perfect."[261] Later, she said, "I'd always heard that a good son made a good husband, and it certainly seems true in Gene's case."[262] After the Raymonds returned to Twin Gables, Jeanette reminisced about their trip. "[Staying at the hotel] was fun too, but not exactly our idea of a honeymoon. We were grateful to get back to our house again. . . . It was all lovely, and, loveliest of all was the knowledge that we were going back home again, together."[263]

Chapter Seven

The newlyweds had to cut short their honeymoon to return to California for the August 6 premiere of *The Firefly*. On July 31, the Halfords saw Jeanette and Gene off on the S.S. Lurline. Since the ship wasn't due to arrive in Los Angeles until August 7, they debarked in San Francisco on August 5 and flew to Los Angeles, where Anna, Blossom, and Elsie met them at the airport. Press photographers chronicled the Raymonds' every move, even snapping them while they had a snack at the airport diner.

The next few weeks were busy with social engagements. On August 13, Jeanette hosted a birthday dinner for Gene. The sixteen guests included Grace Newell, Helen Ferguson and Richard Hargreaves, Fay Wray and John Monk Saunders, Harold and Mildred Lloyd, Allan Jones and Irene Hervey, Blossom and Rocky, and Janet Gaynor. On August 18, Jeanette hosted a tea for a writer from *Picture Play*. On August 24, the Raymonds threw their first family party. Jeanette made waffles and blew a fuse. Three days later, Jeanette hosted a luncheon for some of her female friends, including Mildred Lloyd, Charlotte Learn Garrity, Sari LeMaire (wife of MGM casting director Rufus

LeMaire, who knew Jeanette in her Broadway days and suggested her for *Irene*), and actresses Inez Courtney and Eleanor Masters.

On August 28, Basil and Ouida Rathbone hosted a party to celebrate the Raymonds' marriage, as well as that of Mary Pickford and Buddy Rogers. Guests included Blossom and Rocky, Allan Jones and Irene Hervey, Harold and Mildred Lloyd, Fay Wray and John Monk Saunders, and opera singers Lily Pons, John McCormack, Rosa Ponselle, Grace Moore, and Gladys Swarthout, most with their spouses.

On August 28, 1937, Basil and Ouida Rathbone hosted a party for newlyweds Mary Pickford and Buddy Rogers, and Jeanette and Gene. Coincidentally, Gene and Buddy Rogers also shared a birthday.

In between parties, the Raymonds spent their weekends fishing in California. Columnist Harrison Carroll noted "It must be love" for Jeanette to go fishing, since she was very seasick off San Diego.[264]

That fall, the Raymonds each went back to work at their respective studios. Jeanette made *The Girl of the Golden West* with Nelson Eddy, Walter Pidgeon, and Buddy Ebsen, adapted from the David Belasco play about a woman running a saloon in a California mining town and

falling in love with a bandit. It was best remembered for Jeanette's sing-
ing of "Liebestraum" and Charles Gounod's "Ave Maria." Jeanette and
Nelson prerecorded a duet of "Who Are We to Say" (also known as
"Obey Your Heart"), but it was not used. Jeanette rode her own horse,
White Lady, in the movie. *The Girl of the Golden West* earned $2,882,000,
a profit of $243,000, now over $51.4 million and $4.3 million.

In September, Gene owed RKO one more movie when they let his
option lapse. That fall, he filmed *She's Got Everything* (1937) with Ann
Sothern, his last picture under his contract. *She's Got Everything* was
a romantic comedy about two people caught up in the matchmaking
schemes of their friends. It marked Gene's fifth and final screen pairing with Ann Sothern. On December 31, 1937, they recreated their
roles on Louella Parsons' radio show, *Hollywood Hotel.*

Hoping to get stronger roles, Gene returned to free-lancing. In
December, he began filming *Stolen Heaven* (1938) with Olympe
Bradna at Paramount. *Stolen Heaven* was a drama about jewel thieves
posing as musicians to avoid the law. Gene had a dance number, and
Jeanette arranged for director Andrew L. Stone to present him with
a bronze dance trophy on the set. She recalled, "Gene all but died of
embarrassment and I nearly died of laughter when he came home that
night and told me about it!"[265] It wasn't the first time that she arranged
for him to receive a dance trophy. A few months after they started
dating, at his 1935 birthday dinner, she had orchestra leader Orville
Knapp present Gene with a silver loving cup at the Beverly Wilshire
Hotel to tease him about how many times they'd been dancing.

Gene spoiled Jeanette, sending her flowers on the first day of shooting, as well as adding to her collection of charm bracelets by giving
her charms to commemorate each film and personal milestone. She
had charms representing every movie, including *The Love Parade.* One
bracelet had charms designed like the music of her favorite songs, with

gold musical notes making up the chain. The movie charms included a film strip engraved with *Maytime* and individual letter charms spelling out "sweet" next to a charm of two hearts, a nod to *Maytime's* "Will You Remember;" a pair of guns and an upright piano from *The Girl of the Golden West*; a miniature gold album of photos from *Broadway Serenade*; and an angel, complete with wings and halo, representing *I Married an Angel*. Jeanette was superstitious about wearing the movie bracelets. "I wear each one throughout the picture," she claimed. "I wouldn't shoot a single foot of film without wearing it, even if I have to put it in my shoe. I've always been superstitious about anything like that."[266] In interviews, she often mentioned the bracelet that Gene gave her for Christmas in 1935, with charms representing their dates. Her favorite charm was a miniature spectacle case that opened to disclose a tiny pair of dark glasses. Jeanette had so many charm bracelets that she often wore them hooked together as a necklace.

Joanna Hill roses, the flowers used at the Raymonds' wedding, had a special meaning for the couple and were sent on many occasions. When they were unavailable, Gene usually sent pink or yellow roses, as Jeanette said that red roses died so quickly. In later years, she expressed a preference for sterling silver roses.

In addition to Jeanette's charm bracelet superstition and needing Louis B. Mayer to wish her luck on the first day of each new picture, she had several other superstitions related to her work. She thought it was lucky to wear her plaid coat on the first day of filming. There are photos of her wearing it on set, from *Naughty Marietta* (1935) through *The Sun Comes Up* (1949). She considered green her lucky color because, when she was in school, she claimed that she passed tests whenever she wore a green serge dress. She usually wore green at least once in each of her movies, even when they were filmed in black and white. After the success of *Naughty Marietta*, she began thinking M's were lucky and, from then on, most of her characters had a first or last name beginning with that letter. Often, the names began with MAR. She also said that dropping a comb signified disappointment—unless, before picking it up, the person stepped on it.

Gene said that his only superstition was that, like many actors, he didn't like to be wished "good luck." However, a 1936 column claimed that he still wore a tattered, ill-fitting dressing gown on set. Allegedly, he wore it in his first successful stage production and was afraid to give it up, thinking that his luck might change.

Shortly before Jeanette's marriage, she signed a contract to star on the radio show *Vicks Open House* for the 1937/1938 season, replacing the previous host, Nelson Eddy. Every Sunday, from September 26, 1937 to March 20, 1938, Jeanette hosted the musical program, with time off while she was filming *The Girl of the Golden West*, as MGM usually didn't allow outside broadcasts during production. She was paid $5,000 per episode, now over $87,000. *Vicks Open House* aired opposite the top-rated comedy program *The Jack Benny Show*.

Always wanting to include her fans, before the show's debut, Jeanette asked them to send in suggestions for a theme song. "Will You Remember" from *Maytime* narrowly beat "Indian Love Call" from *Rose-Marie* so she opened the show with the love call, the Master of Ceremonies announced the show's title, and she sang a snippet of "Will You Remember." *Vicks Open House* gave Jeanette the opportunity to sing a wide variety of music, from popular to classical, as well as songs from her movies. She sang Gene's composition, "Will You?," on two different broadcasts and Daniel MacDonald's favorite song, "Daddy's Sweetheart," on another.

Jeanette surrounded herself with friendly faces, like longtime friend Emily Wentz, who sang in the chorus, and MGM recording engineer Mike McLaughlin, who not only handled technical aspects of the program, but walked Jeanette around the block before each broadcast to ease her nerves. In 1963, Jeanette called him "my favorite-of-all working companions."[267] Gene was a guest on the second show, an adaptation of Sigmund Romberg's operetta *The Student Prince* (1924), which had Gene acting the title role and baritone Wilbur Evans singing it. Woody Van Dyke appeared on the fourth episode, which featured songs from *San Francisco*. Jeanette had the Vicks shows recorded so she could critique her performances; some were released on CD and for downloading.

Jeanette with MGM recording engineer Mike McLaughlin, who also worked on *Vicks Open House* during the 1937/1938 season.

The tagline on the program was "Good night and don't catch cold." Unfortunately, in December 1937, Jeanette did just that, causing her to miss the Christmas broadcast and appear only briefly in a remote from Palm Springs on the first show of the new year. Since the sponsor made products to combat colds, press reports said that Jeanette had ptomaine. However, Louella Parsons reported that Jeanette actually had bronchial pneumonia. She often caught colds after intense activity and when she was overtired, like when she was traveling or filming, which lowered her immune system.

Always proud of her Scottish heritage, in a running gag on *Vicks Open House*, Jeanette talked about playing the bagpipes and, on the final broadcast, they pretended that she did. The last show also included some of her favorite songs from previous programs, including "Will You?" Live radio broadcasts always made Jeanette nervous so, after one season, she gave up the series and made occasional guest appearances on other programs.

Although Jeanette was a bigger star than Gene and earned a larger salary, at home she made it clear that he was boss. She said, "I feel that *respect* is one of the most essential and lasting qualities to the success of wedded life and Gene commands my respect as a *man and a husband. He is the head of our home, not I!* Our home was his purchase, and furthermore, he has always paid for the running of it."[268] For tax reasons, they had separate bank accounts for various things, like business and household expenses. During the years that Jeanette gave recitals, there was a separate concert account, which not only was used for expenses on the road, but to pay for a rehearsal pianist and masseuse before she departed.

Jeanette and Gene tried to stick to two rules to maintain a happy marriage. When they were together, they vowed to always kiss before going to bed, no matter how tense the situation was. When they were apart, they promised never to believe anything said or written about the other until they could talk about it. Gene said that Jeanette was adamant that they never go to bed angry. Both admitted that they did their share of bickering and had private spats like any couple. They were prepared for problems. "We started our marriage with the knowledge that it would not be easy, that we'd have to work for its success," she said. "We knew the chances we were taking. We knew that it was up to us alone. But we had the advantage. We were two people in love. And we were determined to make our marriage a wedding of people, not of careers."[269] In 1989, Gene summed up the Raymonds' years at Twin Gables: "We did have a very happy life in that house. And we had our fights and we had our arguments and we had our make ups, and it was a lot of livin' in that house—which is the way it's supposed to be."[270]

In a 1939 *Movie Mirror* article, Jeanette and Gene recalled how two trips led to one-word reminders to quell an argument. As noted previously, in late February 1937, they went to Yosemite with a group of friends. One afternoon, while Jeanette was changing at the hotel, the men decided to go skiing. Gene left a note with a maid, but she forgot to give it to Jeanette. When Jeanette arrived in the lobby, she was furious to find herself stood up by Gene. After waiting for over an hour, she tacked a note to his door and drove home in the dark. The next day, he tried to make up, but Jeanette refused. In early March, Helen Ferguson suggested that Jeanette go to Palm Springs with her. Gene called Helen, asking for advice on how to reconcile. When Helen mentioned the trip, Gene asked her to make sure their car stopped in Azusa, California. After Helen made an excuse for stopping, Gene kidnapped Jeanette and put her in his car. En route to Palm Springs, Jeanette and Gene reconciled, with Helen following them in her car. The article concluded, "Wheretofore [sic], since that time, whenever healthy young temper flares in the Raymond household, one of the two pauses to remark: 'Yosemite.' And the other, relaxing, replies, 'Oh, all right. Azuza.'"[271] Although some may claim that the reporter concocted the story, notes in Jeanette's wardrobe and entertainment schedules for her 1937 income tax verified that she was in Yosemite on February 23, and Palm Springs at the B-Bar-H Ranch on March 2, when she paid for Helen Ferguson's dinner, presumably for her role in helping with the reunion.

Rumors plagued the couple from the beginning. In 1940, Jeanette told a reporter, "I have two obsessions—my husband and my career. Everything else in my life is secondary. I am riled quickest by reading untrue statements about myself and my marriage."[272] The Raymonds tried not to pay attention to the columnists, who played up the disparity in their fame and salaries and predicted divorce. "The public even seems to disbelieve denials," Jeanette lamented. "Every time a star or stars marry there's as much speculation on the marriage's success as if it were a football game. I wonder if the fans realize that Hollywood marriages are deeply sacred to most of the couples. They want their marriages to succeed. But because from the moment you marry here there are predictions of divorce, it seems to the world that our marriages are a trivial matter."[273] Gene once joked, "I think we should get divorced and marry someone else and then remarry each other, just so people would stop talking about how long we are married."[274]

In 1966, Gene said, "Jeanette and I made a point of ignoring the many items about us through the years, never bothering to deny, but preferring to laugh about them. Else one can be in a perpetual stew."[275] However, occasionally the rumors upset them. One Sunday, while Gene was in the shower, Jeanette sat on the bed, listening to the radio. Walter Winchell announced that she was on her way to Reno for "you know what." An incensed Gene stormed out of the shower, saying that he wanted to bust the columnist in the jaw. Later, Jeanette said, "I will not play that 'look how happy we are' game. What Gene and I do in private is private."[276]

Jeanette was not one to take things for granted. In 1940, when a reporter told her that she had everything—a loving husband and family, a successful career, and financial security—Jeanette was quick to clarify what she appreciated most. Given her last years, her words were prophetic: "You have forgotten the most important thing, the thing for which I am most grateful—wonderful health and the energy of 10 women. Without health, everything else turns to dust and ashes, even the sunshine becomes painful and sinister. . . . Nothing in life is so priceless as health, yet we are inclined to take it lightly when we have it. Until we lose it, we never appreciate it."[277]

Jeanette was a perfectionist who was very critical of her work. In 1939, when asked if she liked watching herself onscreen, she answered, "It's like a nightmare. All you can think of is the mistakes you are making—the things you should have done or left undone. Every time I see myself in a picture, I look around at the audience and wonder if they are seeing the same mistakes I see."[278]

Jeanette was particularly critical of her earlier films: "I made 28 [sic] pictures, of which I think there were four bad ones. . . . *The Vagabond King* with Dennis King and three humdingers at Fox: 'Oh, for a Man!,' 'Don't Bet on Women' and 'Annabelle's Affairs.' . . . I didn't hit my stride till I went from Paramount to Metro."[279] When asked if she had seen all of her films, she answered, "Yes, tho [sic] a few of them only once!"[280] In 1939, a reporter mentioned *Monte Carlo* to Jeanette, who, after seeing a revival two years earlier, was very negative about the movie and her appearance. "Don't ever see it again," Jeanette warned. "They revived it in Hollywood not long ago and I gathered some of my friends together and we went to see it. Honestly, it was atrocious—the costumes were simply horrible. I don't see how

I ever could have looked like that. I looked so big and fat."[281] A fan recalled sitting in front of Jeanette and Gene during the revival and hearing Jeanette's laughter and a startled "Oh no"[282] when she yawned, scratched her head, and went looking for the key. When longtime fan William Corcoran wrote that he had seen *The Lottery Bride* twice, Jeanette replied, "Good God! You saw that thing twice?"[283] Longtime fan Annabelle Alling had a similar experience when she met Jeanette, who recalled *Annabelle's Affairs*. "I once made a picture with your name in the title," Jeanette told her. "If you ever get a chance to see it, don't."[284] Of her MGM films, she most disliked *Broadway Serenade* (1939), *I Married an Angel* (1942), and *Cairo* (1942).

Similarly, Gene was critical of his movies. In one of his wartime letters, he remarked that he probably would never like watching himself on screen. When *Cross-Country Romance* played near his base in England, he joked about taking a group to see it and organizing a booing party. When pressed for a favorite, he always named *Zoo in Budapest*, as it gave him the chance to show off his athletic abilities, as well as his acting. In the film, Gene played the son of a zookeeper, who grew up in the zoo and hated the outside world. His character was against people killing animals and using their fur. Although Gene fished and hunted, he also was a lifelong animal lover, particularly dogs and horses.

The Raymonds shared other traits. In 1940, a reporter described Jeanette as "blessed with a gorgeous wit and an amusing slant on practically everything, she glides over the pitfalls as if they were a ribbon of mist."[285] Gene also had a fine wit and a sharp sense of humor, although problems with his career frequently depressed him and affected his demeanor, another trait that Jeanette shared. "I am by nature, tremendously moody and subject to appalling fits of depression," she admitted. "When I am depressed I sleep badly. And the next morning I am more depressed because I have slept badly. But that old practical side of my nature comes to the fore. I finally decided that moodiness is terrifically unfair to the other people with whom one comes in contact and even more unfair to Gene, who is, himself inclined to moods."[286] They also both admitted that they had tempers. Jeanette said, "Maybe I do have a temper, but I'm not temperamental, and I can't see why people say I am. The only angel in the family is Gene, who has to be one to put up with me."[287]

As Jeanette came to know her husband better, she realized that, although they had a great deal in common, their personalities were very different, partially due to their family backgrounds. In 1945, she told a reporter, "...I'm instinctively a happy person. I've had a happy life, with the usual disappointments but no major tragedies. I like people. I'm not shy, I have idiosyncrasies, but I don't think I have inhibitions."[288] While Jeanette was very open and sometimes too forthright, she described Gene as "self-sufficient, self-disciplined and self-contained, with a kind of secrecy inside which he'd developed as a boy."[289] She explained, "Gene's childhood had left deep scars. I had to guard every word I said so that he wouldn't retreat into his shell again. I had to deny myself any form of 'mothering' him, all tears and anything else that would bring back the least echo of his unhappy years as a boy."[290] Over time, Gene began to let down his guard; however, even in the 1960s, when he needed to think, he still went for long drives by himself, without telling Jeanette where he was going or when he would return.

The Raymonds also had different ways of memorizing their scripts. Although Jeanette learned music quickly, when it came to dialogue, she was a slow study and repeatedly wrote out her lines to memorize them. Gene had a photographic memory and only had to look at a page once to remember it, an ability that frustrated and eluded his wife. Emily said, "It used to make Jeanette so mad."[291] Jeanette often relied on Gene to help her with details, as his memory was much better than hers. In joint interviews, he sometimes corrected her when she recalled facts. On the back of one of their wedding photos, now in the collection of Kayla Sturm, Jeanette wrote that they wed on June 17, with Gene correcting it underneath her caption. In 1960, she had him sit in on a meeting with James Brough, one of the collaborators on her autobiography, and type up notes about it for her attorney since she didn't trust herself to remember everything.

After the wedding, Gene's mother continued to stir up trouble. Mrs. Kipling wrote to Gene, "She married you for two reasons, neither of which has anything to do with love. First to spite me and show her power over you ... and the second reason was so she could get a house and property settlement out of you if and when she is through with you, while she socks her money away. I refuse to allow sex to disrupt our relations."[292] In 1938, she accused Jeanette of forcing Gene to grow a moustache so he would look older, despite the fact that he also wore one in *Walking on Air* the year before he was married. Mrs. Kipling harassed Louis Swarts, saying that he encouraged a rift with her son, and made anti-Semitic remarks about him. She sent Gene her bills, insisting that she could not live on the allowance that he gave her and demanding that he buy her a home in New York. When Mrs. Kipling was in the East, the Raymonds' friends often warned them about her activities, including condoning Adolf Hitler and getting into a physical altercation with her German maid. Jeanette and Gene were relieved that none of it ever ended up in the newspapers. All they reported was that Mrs. Kipling gave lectures on vocational training and guidance.

Around March 26, 1938, after the conclusion of Jeanette's job on *Vicks Open House*, the Raymonds set out on an extended seven-week vacation, spending time in Flagstaff and Mesa, Arizona; New York City; and Philadelphia. In Flagstaff, they encountered snow, and Jeanette had fun teasing Gene because he refused to bring a topcoat on the trip. They spent almost two weeks at El Rancho Grande, a Mesa guest ranch, before heading East on April 7. Jeanette wrote to Marion Smith Glendening, "Gene and I enjoyed our trip so. We started out to get some sunshine in Arizona but stepped off the train into a snow bank instead – imagine! It didn't take us long to get out of there. We finally located the 'sunshine' and had a grand rest before starting for New York."[293]

The Raymonds' train was delayed by more snow in western Kansas. When they finally arrived in Kansas City, nine hours late, they strolled around the station in dark glasses, refusing to pose for the press because of their bad mood over the delay. A newspaper photographer snapped a picture of them anyway, causing Gene to shout, "There are times when I'd like to sock you photographers in the eye."[294] Jeanette kept quiet and disappeared into the train station before reporters could ask her opinion. On April 9, the Raymonds were in better humor when they switched trains in Chicago and posed for a photographer from the *Chicago Tribune*. When they finally arrived in New York on April 11, Jeanette suggested that they register under assumed names to get some privacy so they checked into their hotel as Mr. and Mrs. George Randall, retaining their same initials because of their monogrammed luggage. Unfortunately, their identities, as well as the name of their hotel, soon were revealed in the press. Twenty-five years later, when Jeanette was hospitalized for arterial transplant surgery, she used the Jeanette Randall alias again to keep her condition secret from the public and press.

Despite the lack of privacy, during the spring of 1938, Jeanette and Gene enjoyed their first real vacation in New York. Throughout their marriage, they returned there many times, for work and pleasure. Photo from the Dale Kuntz collection.

During the 1938 New York trip, the Raymonds saw shows, shopped, and "kept shocking hours,"[295] doing the town with Irene Dunne and her husband, Dr. Francis Griffin, who happened to be vacationing in the city at the same time. They all had fun teasing Gene when he dragged them to Childs restaurant for a late-night meal of chicken croquettes with white sauce, and peas, which didn't turn out the way he planned because the restaurant said that it was too late in the evening for white sauce, and peas were out of season. During the Raymonds' stay, actress Helen Menken gave a cocktail party for them. She was best remembered by some as being Humphrey Bogart's first wife; they married in 1926, while Bogart and Gene were appearing in *Cradle Snatchers* on Broadway. Fans mobbed the Raymonds when they saw their friend, Allan Jones, performing at Loew's State Theatre and visited him backstage between shows. They also were mobbed at Radio City Music Hall and when they took a romantic carriage ride through Central Park. They laughed because the fans walked faster than the horse.

In mid-April, Jeanette and Gene posed for a *Sunday News* cover, which ran on July 10. They told reporters that they were "so happy we're afraid to talk about it without knocking on wood first."[296] On April17, the Raymonds attended Easter service at St. Thomas Church. Five days later, they were guests at the wedding of Francis Warren Pershing, son of General John "Black Jack" Pershing, who led the American Army into France during World War I.

In late April, Jeanette showed her husband her childhood home on Arch Street and introduced him to the joys of Philadelphia ice cream. Jeanette said that she was disappointed how small and run down her birthplace looked. Gene claimed that she was more intent on having ice cream than seeing the house or any of her relatives, as she insisted on eating it every day. He gave her a charm shaped like an old-fashioned ice cream container, along with bus and thermometer charms, to commemorate the trip.

While the Raymonds were in New York, Gene also reconciled with his father. Jeanette's happy stories about her childhood made Gene wonder if Roy were as evil as Mrs. Kipling had depicted him. During the trip, Gene received a letter from family friend E.A. Mariam, who urged him, "Ray/Gene; I'm praying that you contact your Dad and arrange to have him meet your adorable wife. He loves you both. 'To err tis [sic] but human. To forgive most divine.'"[297] Gene visited his father's modest upholstery shop in Great Kills, Staten Island, where Roy had living quarters in the back. Gene also took him to the hotel to meet Jeanette. She quickly warmed to Roy and called him "Dad Guyon." Sensing Roy's loneliness, in early May, while the Raymonds were still in New York, they bought him a six-month-old Smooth Fox Terrier named Foxy Jack of Wissaboo, known as Foxy, from prize-winning breeder James Austin of Catawba Farm in Old Westbury, Long Island. Jeanette and Gene each began corresponding with Roy. In December 1938, Gene even wrote a note to Foxy, sending him some treats and signing it "Merry Xmas – from the son of your old man!"[298]

During the Raymonds' stay in New York, they shopped at Saks Fifth Avenue, Bonwit Teller, De Gez, Inc., and F.R. Tripler & Co., and Jeanette bought two daytime gowns, a suit, and a hat from actress/couturier Grace Menken Lytell, sister of Helen Menken. Grace was one of Jeanette's favorite designers, and she and her husband, actor Bert Lytell, were close friends of Jeanette and Gene. On May 5, Jeanette had a press luncheon at the Colony with Regina Crewe of *The New York American*.

In mid-May, Jeanette had to return to California to begin work on MGM's first full-length Technicolor film, *Sweethearts*, her fifth picture with Nelson Eddy. Gene remained East for two weeks of personal appearances in New York and Chicago to promote *Stolen Heaven*. Before Jeanette left New York, she attended his May 9 opening at the Paramount Theatre. Prior to the appearance, she told a reporter, "He's going to do three of his own songs in the act, and I think they'll catch on. They're 'swing' and that's what the public wants—though I don't at all. I think my husband is extremely talented—but I don't have to listen to his music if I don't want to; I like his ballads, but I can't take 'swing.'"[299] Despite Jeanette's adamant dislike of swing, she sang it well in portions of "Pretty as a Picture" in *Sweethearts* and "For Ev'ry Lonely Heart" and "High Flyin'" in *Broadway Serenade*.

On May 10, Jeanette's girlfriends gave her a goodbye luncheon at 21 while Gene had a press luncheon at the Tavern Club to promote his personal appearances. Two days later, Jeanette left for California by train.

Sweethearts was the only movie in which Jeanette and Nelson's characters were married throughout the picture. The script, written by poet/satirist/critic Dorothy Parker and her husband, Alan Campbell, was a backstage story about a pair of actors in a long-running Broadway show, whose producer schemed to break up their marriage so they wouldn't go to Hollywood. The show within the movie used songs from Victor Herbert's operetta *Sweethearts* (1913), including "For Every Lover Must Meet His Fate," "Pretty as a Picture," "Sweethearts" (also known as "Sweetheart Waltz"), and "Wooden Shoes." "Badinage" (also known as "Summer Serenade") and "Little Grey Home in the West" were interpolated in the off-stage section. The film was nominated for Oscars for Best Sound (Douglas Shearer) and Best Musical Scoring (Herbert Stothart). It received a special Academy Award for its Color Cinematography (Oliver Marsh and Allen M. Davey). The realistic three-strip process allowed fans to see that Jeanette's peaches and cream complexion, sea-green eyes, and stunning red hair were made for Technicolor. The film's domestic gross was $2,017,000, now over $36 million. On March 25, 1946 and December 15, 1947, Jeanette and Nelson reprised their roles on *Screen Guild Theater*.

Gene's personal appearance tour did fair business in New York, but was a big success in Chicago. *Motion Picture Daily* noted that it was the best business Chicago's Oriental Theatre had done in months, grossing $21,600, $3,600 above average; today, these figures are about $385,600 and $64,300. *Variety* said, "This zoom-up is due primarily to Gene Raymond's presence on the stage."[300]

On May 29, Gene returned to California. Frustrated with the parts that he was offered and disappointed that the lead in *Golden Boy* (1939), for which he was in the running, went to newcomer William Holden, Gene decided to take a leave of absence from his film career and concentrate on music. He already had written several songs, including "Will You?," "Alligator Swing," "It Can't Be True," "You Are Mine," "You Little Devil," and "I Would Slumber." In a 1939 interview, Gene said that Jeanette disliked his songs because they weren't serious music. "Some of my compositions are like the currently popular 'Mad Dogs and Englishmen,' hardly a ballad and certainly not a love song. [Jeanette] thinks they are awful, but I think they are swell."[301] With his wife's blessing, Gene began studying musical harmony and theory with Jean Howard. "I am right behind him, even if it takes him 10 years to hit his stride," Jeanette insisted, angry with reporters who called Gene "jobless." "As long as he works at something he really loves, so long as he's improving himself for the future and makes his wife happy and proud, you could hardly call Gene Raymond jobless."[302]

Although Nelson Eddy advised Gene not to study singing because he sang so naturally, during Gene's film hiatus, he also took lessons from Jeanette's vocal teacher, Grace Newell. During his sabbatical, he received many offers, including two movies, several stage shows, and a chance to do personal appearances at $4,500 a week, currently over $80,000. In 1939, there were unfounded rumors that he would collaborate with composer/arranger David Guion, whose arrangement of "Home on the Range" popularized the cowboy song. Despite the similar last names, he was not related to Gene. Ultimately, he hoped to write a symphony and do piano recitals.

In 1938 and 1939, Gene took a sabbatical from movies to work on his music.

On June 11, 1938, Blossom hosted a "Fifty Years Hence" costume party in honor of her husband, Rocky, and to celebrate the start of *Sweethearts*. Guests, who included columnists Billy and Ella Wickersham, character actor George Zucco, Helen Ferguson and Richard Hargreaves, and Emily Wentz, were asked to dress as how they would look in fifty years. Many came as angels, devils, and skeletons. Blossom dressed as the perennial ingénue, with one foot in the grave. Jeanette and Gene had MGM makeup artists make them up as elderly versions of themselves. When they knocked on the door, Blossom didn't recognize them and thought they were friends of Anna's. They won first prize for their costumes. Sadly, by 1988, Gene and Emily were among the few guests who were still alive.

On June 16, Gene wrote a letter to Jeanette, expressing his happiness after one year of marriage.

Happy Anniversary!

And since this is our <u>first</u> one, this letter serves a two-fold purpose! First: it's your paper anniversary present, and second: an official notification that the contract drawn up, and agreed to by us on June 16, 1937 is hereby renewed and extended for a period of forty-nine (49) years. After that, of course, the customary six month leases (on life) will be in order!

Have I told you that I am tremendously appreciative of your every kindness and thoughtfulness, and that I'm mighty proud of you and the grace with which you've accepted a most difficult in-law attitude? Well, I am! Perhaps other brides have borne the same kind of cross – but none so admirably!

I love you more each day! I'm happy for the first time

in my life! And I'm enjoying the prospect of your sharing a
lifetime of work and play and I hope, success and the love
and respect of everyone, with –

Your Old Man![303]

Although Gene was kidding about the paper gift, through the years, he
often gave Jeanette anniversary gifts based on the traditional themes,
like silk (fourth), steel (eleventh), and silver (twenty-fifth).

Over the Fourth of July weekend, the Raymonds went to
Coronado, California. Recalling what happened two years earlier during the filming of *Maytime*, the studio ordered Jeanette to stay out of
the sun because sunburn didn't look pretty in Technicolor. Jeanette
and Gene spent Labor Day weekend at the Malibu, California beach
house of Robert Z. Leonard and his wife, silent film actress Gertrude
Olmstead. Other guests were Allan Jones and Irene Hervey; actor
Robert Young and his wife, Elizabeth; director Tod Browning and his
wife, silent film actress Alice Wilson; and producer/director Edwin
Marin and his wife, actress Ann Morriss.

After Jeanette finished filming *Sweethearts*, on September 18, she
hosted a tea at MGM for 250 Gold Star Mothers who were attending
the American Legion convention in Los Angeles. All of them had lost
sons in the First World War, and ten were over ninety years of age. One
woman said to Jeanette, "My husband told me I needn't come home
without the shake of your hand—you're his favorite." Jeanette kissed
her on the cheek and said, "Take him that."[304] The tea was held on a
Viennese garden set from *The Great Waltz* (1938). Anna MacDonald
and the mothers of Woody Van Dyke, Nelson Eddy, actors Jack Oakie,
Joan Crawford, and William Powell, and Twentieth Century–Fox
founder Darryl F. Zanuck were on hand to converse with the Gold
Star Mothers. Gene was Master of Ceremonies for a program, which

included songs by fifteen-year-old contralto Leni Lynn, who had just been signed by MGM, and Jeanette's *Sweethearts* co-stars, Douglas MacPhail and Betty Jaynes, who were said to be Jeanette's protégés. Anna beamed with pride and told columnist Hedda Hopper, "Am I not lucky having him for a son-in-law?"[305] Jeanette closed the program with "The Star Spangled Banner" and the Gold Star Mothers sang with her.

Two days later, on the evening of September 20, Jeanette entered Good Samaritan Hospital for an ear operation, scheduled for the next morning. In July, she had been hospitalized with an abscess in her right ear, following a cold. She told Marion Smith Glendening, "I had been having some trouble with my ear so hied myself to a hospital and had it lanced."[306] In those days, doctors lanced ear drums and drained the middle ear to ease painful pressure when bacteria from a cold or sinus infection invaded the middle ear. Today, doctors treat ear infections with antibiotics. Dr. Herbert Anderson, who performed Jeanette's ear lancing, treated Gene in 1936. Newspaper reports said that Jeanette's September 1938 operation was a follow-up to the July ear lancing. Unlike current conditions, where patients seldom stay more than one night after surgery, Jeanette expected to be hospitalized two weeks, but ended up being there three weeks and four days. She read, knitted, and made out her Christmas list. Displaying the Raymonds' mutual and self-described "screwy"[307] sense of humor, Gene sent her roses and forget-me-nots in a planter shaped like an ear. After Jeanette's October 15 release, she and Gene went to Palm Springs for a few days so she could rest and recuperate, before beginning work on *Broadway Serenade* with Lew Ayres.

Broadway Serenade was the tale of a struggling singer (Jeanette) and her composer husband (Lew Ayres), whose marriage collapsed when she became a Broadway star. Like *San Francisco*, it was more of a drama with music than a musical or operetta, as most of the songs took place onstage or at a rehearsal. Jeanette sang "Un bel di vedremo" from Giacomo Puccini's *Madama Butterfly*, which she repeated ten years later in her last film, *The Sun Comes Up*. She showed off her dancing skills in the production number "High Flyin'" (also known as "Flyin' High"). Fans loved a scene in a dime store when a salesgirl recognized Jeanette's character and asked her to sing; it reminded them of something Jeanette would do in real life. They were less impressed with the surrealistic finale, directed by Busby Berkeley. *Broadway Serenade's* combined domestic and foreign grosses were $1,234,000, with a loss of $50,000, now over $23.3 million and $905,000. It was one of Jeanette's least favorite MGM movies.

Around this time, Jeanette discussed her marriage and film career with the press. She said that she had divided her life into two separate careers since her marriage: show business and running a home. She split her time between her work and planning menus for the cook, making shopping lists, and other household duties. "When you are successful and encouraged in one venture, it gives you more confidence to attack another," she said. "My husband is my only audience, and my most important one for my career as a homemaker. When I succeed in that role it is easier to please my other audiences with performances on the screen. I'm absolutely convinced that happiness is the key to success."[308]

On December 24, Jeanette and Gene went Christmas caroling. They spent Christmas day at Anna's, before hosting dinner for family and friends at Twin Gables, a tradition that they continued for most of their marriage. Their guests included Helen Ferguson and Richard Hargreaves; actress Barbara Kent and her husband, producer/agent Harry Edington; Anna, and Blossom. On New Year's Day, the Raymonds attended the Rose Bowl game with Anna; Blossom; Irene

Dunne and Dr. Francis Griffin; Connie and Johnny Mack Brown; Vitagraph Studios founder Albert Smith and his wife, Lucile, who acted under the name Jean Paige; and former USC football and track star Herschel Bonham. USC beat Duke University, 7 to 3.

Jeanette received a guest book for Christmas, which was signed by many of the famous and not-so-famous guests that visited Twin Gables. She first used it at Christmas dinner, where Blossom wrote the most memorable inscription: "'Blood is thicker than water'—May your own happiness be equal to that which you've extended always to me. Welcome Gene again & you are taking such nice care of my little sister!"[309]

Chapter Eight

In the spring of 1939, Jeanette went on her first recital tour, performing in twenty-two small cities in the Midwest, South, and Pacific Northwest. The tour allowed her to mingle with fans in small-town America who attended her movies and bought her records. She knew their support was the foundation of her success. She chose to avoid New York, Los Angeles, and Chicago so the critics who looked at her as a movie star, not a serious singer, would not crucify her. She explained, "I believe in building a career slowly. When one is not sure, one wants to find out whether people are ready to accept you. And so I went first before the real understanding people, the home folks, the backbone of the nation."[310] She compared singing in small towns to stage productions trying out in other cities before opening on Broadway. She said, "I want to prepare myself completely before I attempt an appearance in New York or Los Angeles."[311] Later, she recalled, "I knew that only persistence, patient perseverance, could alter the opinion of the music world skeptics. They had not been impressed by the fact that I had repeatedly refused $25,000 a week for personal appearances in movie houses in order to do two or three concerts a week for less than half that figure."[312] Today, $25,000 is equivalent to almost $453,000. The difference in salary proved how much Jeanette wanted to be taken seriously as a singer and not thought of as just a movie star.

Despite Jeanette's lack of recital experience, her screen reputation led to sold-out houses. In Pittsburg, Kansas, the box office had to turn down five thousand applications for tickets. A visiting couple from Oklahoma City, Oklahoma offered $100 per seat, now equivalent to over $1,800. The 3,500-seat auditorium in Peoria, Illinois sold out so quickly that Jeanette agreed to sing a second program. In Selma, Alabama, there were 2,013 attendees in an auditorium meant for 1,600. Because of the crowd, the venue couldn't have a traditional intermission so everyone just stood at their seats. Today, fire laws would prevent this kind of over-selling of tickets.

Jeanette was surprised that she caused a stir wherever she went, whether she was traveling by train or car. In several cities, fans caused a mob scene at the station or camped on the side of the road to get a glimpse of her as her car passed. In Stillwater, Oklahoma, state troopers had to be called to control traffic. A Columbus, Georgia furniture store furnished her hotel suite with the best of their line. After she left, they put the bed and other furniture on display in their showroom's enormous picture window. Historian Clason Kyle reported, "Nearly everybody in Columbus wanted to see where she had slept."[313] In Peoria, fans almost tipped over a police car that came to escort her from the train. In Selma, fans stole the tableware, napkin, and tablecloth as soon as Jeanette finished eating in a restaurant. It was the same type of adoration that Elvis Presley, the Beatles, and other rock stars would see years later, with fans clamoring for anything she touched. In Bloomington, Indiana, a recital attendee remarked, "Even if Jeanette couldn't sing a note, it would be worth the price of admission just to see her smile."[314]

But Jeanette found that not everyone knew her. In Oklahoma

City, she ordered a large cake to be served to reporters at a press conference. When it arrived, her name was misspelled McDonnald. She asked how it happened and the baker apologized, insisting that he had no way of knowing because he never heard of her. Nonplussed, Jeanette laughed about it to a reporter, saying, "He didn't know who I was, but I didn't know him either so that makes us even."[315]

During Jeanette's first tour, her entourage included secretary Sylvia Grogg Wright, maid Rose Coen, concert manager Charles Wagner, and Wagner's assistant, Edward Snowden. Jeanette received 70% of the box office receipts and the sponsor received 30%. Expenses and salaries for her entourage came out of Jeanette's share. Wagner praised Jeanette's work ethic: "I've never managed an artist who is more conscientious about her concerts and her public than Miss MacDonald. She never does anything until she is fully prepared. For three years before she went on her first tour . . . she was working for that goal."[316] In addition to months of planning her program and rehearsing, for over a year before she began touring, Jeanette studied the programs of the artists that she and Gene saw perform, considering each concert as research—and therefore, tax deductible. A 1938 entertainment schedule from the Raymonds' community account noted, "Miss MacDonald attended Opera [sic] and Concert [sic] series to secure ideas for operatic arias, concert numbers, the musical arrangements, orchestral accompaniment and delivery of songs all as part of her preparatory work on her own concert program which she is to sing on tour during the Spring Season 1939."[317] Despite Jeanette's aversion to math, when it came to taxes, few people were as savvy as she was about deductions. Through the years, she continued to study other artists' repertoire and costumes. In the 1940s, while she was on tour, Gene reported on seeing contralto Marian Anderson and soprano Grace Moore, detailing their programs and appearance for his wife.

While Jeanette traveled, she found that she had time to catch up on her reading. She laughingly told reporters the title of one of the books she carried with her, *Demon Daughters*, a gift from Anna. The inscription illustrated the playful relationship between them: "To my daughter, Jeanette, by no means a demon, but has her moments."[318]

One of the things that Jeanette liked best about the tour was meeting her fans. "Audiences I faced became suddenly live friends," she said, "and I hope I made loads of new friends."[319] She was startled by how many people came to see her. "Such large crowds gather at the stage doors that my manager whisked me through to a waiting car, but it was grand to see their smiling faces. It was one of the most enjoyable parts of the tour and I felt very grateful to them for their eager interest and excited acclaim. It was really heart warming [sic] and gave me a feeling of knowing the fans much better after such close contact."[320] In Stillwater, Oklahoma, one of the patrolmen who escorted her through the crowds observed, "She certainly is a charming person. I know she was pretty much used up, but she laughed and looked like she was having the time of her life."[321]

Jeanette's patience was stretched when fans peeked in the window of a restaurant, watching her eat or, worse yet, snapped her picture during her meal. She signed so many autographs—sometimes as many as a thousand in one day—that her arm hurt. "In the next world I'm going to pick out the shortest name there is," she told reporters, making reference to her eighteen-letter name, one of the longest in Hollywood.[322] Despite the strain, Jeanette remained cheerful. Sylvia Grogg Wright told a reporter, "She never seems to tire of meeting the fans, of laughing and talking and engaging in pleasant talk with the people she meets. She enjoys thoroughly such meetings as this one. I have never heard her say she was bored or displeased because of the tremendous interest taken in her."[323]

A student reporter sent Jeanette a copy of the article the young woman wrote for her college newspaper and told Jeanette how much she enjoyed the recital. Her feelings were typical of the way people reacted to Jeanette's graciousness onstage. "During your program at Norman, Oklahoma, I said over and over, 'please sing "Indian Love Call"'—and when you did, I pretended it was because I had wished so hard. I also liked to pretend that you smiled just to me. Everyone else thought the same thing, so we all were happy."[324]

In Evansville, Indiana, Jeanette visited the Hillcrest Home for Girls, a residence for young female wards of the court, taking them candy, flowers, and colored eggs for Easter. On future tours, Jeanette made sure that she spent even more time with her fans.

Although Jeanette sang professionally since childhood, surprisingly, she was bothered by stage fright, which first appeared when she was eleven and the principal intimidated her during a school performance of "The Jewel Song" from *Faust*. Prior to the 1939 tour, Jeanette consulted a psychiatrist about the problem. He suggested that she imagine that the audience was filled with heads of lettuce. In Pittsburg, Kansas, she told the story to her initial audience, endearing her to them with her honesty, as well as her voice. In 1940, she recalled her debut: "I was never so frightened before or since: all the time I was singing my knees were trembling and I couldn't stop them. I had given some concerts in Europe that were very successful, but that was no help at all: here I was in my own country, and no European press notices were going to do me any good if I didn't please that audience."[325]

Through the years, stage fright continued to plague Jeanette. In their wartime correspondence, Gene encouraged her, insisting that if she came to love singing, her nerves would be eased. While it's clear that Jeanette *liked* to sing, she was a perfectionist who often put so much pressure on herself, worrying about every detail before a live performance, that he thought that she needed to just relax and enjoy her music. Unlike the movies, there were no retakes in recitals, on the radio, or later on television, all of which made Jeanette extremely nervous. In the 1940s and 1950s, to ease Jeanette's pre-recital nerves, Emily said that she and Jeanette used to try to read each others' minds in a darkened dressing room.

In a 1950 interview, Jeanette said, "I'm still scared to death and nervous every time." She explained that her fear was two-fold. "First, you know everybody has paid an admission to see you. They've paid perfectly good money for an illusion and you're worried whether you can live up to it. Your other fear is that you won't be able to sing as well as you know you can."[326] She said that a singer could tell by the way an audience acted whether or not they liked a song. "When they start coughing during ['Indian Love Call'], that's when I'll have to start thinking about retiring," she laughed.[327]

According to a 1978 article in *American Classic Screen*, Jeanette was the first classical singer to appear on the concert stage who did not use the traditional stance: one foot forward, hands together at the chest, and usually holding a chiffon scarf. Instead, she sang naturally, sometimes with one hand on the piano, or providing gestures when she sang songs like "Nicolette" and "Summertime." Pianist Giuseppe Bamboschek, a former conductor for the Metropolitan Opera, accompanied her.

Attending to every detail, Jeanette brought her own tinted pink slides for the spotlights. She preferred the lights to cast no shadow under her nose and plenty under her chin. During her performances, she laughed and talked, endearing her to fans. Her program consisted of traditional classical pieces; then she sang songs from her films as encores, usually taking requests from the audience. Often, "Italian Street Song" was her cue that it was her final song. Many fans had no interest in the classical pieces, but waited patiently for the encores that they knew. A 1950 article noted that, at one recital, when Jeanette announced that she would sing "Indian Love Call," a little old man leaped to his feet, clapping and shouting, "Goody, goody, goody."[328]

Jeanette's range ran from low A to high E flat. Although some criticized her choice of songs and said her voice was small, many reviews commented on her perfect diction and that she could be heard anywhere in the auditoriums, long before modern amplification systems. They also praised her stage presence, charm, and graciousness. Jeanette learned not to read reviews until the tour was over, a practice that she continued later in her career when she did stage musicals. She found that critics often disagreed and it was futile to try to please them. All that really mattered to her was making the audiences happy.

Jeanette compared recital work to singing for the movies: "When I told friends at the studio that I often sang 25 numbers in an evening they all exclaimed what hard work that must have been in comparison with the ease of recording a song for pictures, which is so much nonsense. For there's nothing more wearing than singing the same song from 11 in the morning until nightfall when recording. It's so much easier to stand in front of a friendly audience and sing your heart out. At least you get variety from the diversified selections and you aren't nearly as tired as a result."[329]

During Jeanette's first tour, she had a few strange experiences. In Columbus, Georgia, after she attended the Georgia Chick Show, she was given a crate of baby chicks and ducks. She cooed over them and won the hearts of the crowds by giving them to two children as pets. A photo of Jeanette with her feathered friends appeared on the front of *Poultry Item*, probably the only time that a movie star graced the magazine's cover. In Evansville, Indiana, a load of lumber, intended for the theater to fasten extra seats together, mistakenly was delivered to her hotel. When she left Bloomington, Indiana, a Davenport, Iowa furniture salesman reserved her suite, insisting that nothing be changed, including the sheets, as he wanted the rooms just as Jeanette left them. In Salina, Kansas, the elevator dropped a floor and a half while Jeanette was riding it. The elevator operator seemed nonplussed, like it was a regular occurrence; Jeanette was not as calm.

In Oklahoma, en route to engagements in Stillwater and Norman, Jeanette's taxi stopped in Tulsa. She spent an hour walking with Sylvia Grogg Wright and Rose Coen, thrilled that no one recognized her. During their walk, the trio became hungry, and Jeanette said that they should knock on a door and ask for a piece of toast and a cup of tea. Sylvia dared her to try it, but Jeanette couldn't get up her nerve. She told the press, "I knew, if we told them who we were, they'd either think we were crazy or they'd say, 'Now isn't that just like a movie star, wandering around, knocking at strangers' front doors.'"[330] In Norman, Jeanette stayed overnight in the housemother's suite at the Kappa Kappa Gamma sorority house at the University of Oklahoma, hoping that it would be quieter than a hotel. When she left for her recital, she signed the book that the coeds signed when they went on dates. In the space labeled "When will you be home?" Jeanette wrote, "I shan't be very late—honestly!"[331] When she returned after her performance, she had crackers and milk with the girls and showed them her evening gowns.

In Selma, Alabama, Jeanette drove out in the country, changed into an old pair of shoes in the car, and climbed a barbed wire fence to take a walk in a field. She sat down on a log and sang to a cardinal, laughing, "But he would have none of me and flew away."[332] In Indiana, when her entourage drove from Evansville to Bloomington, they stopped for lunch in French Lick, where Jeanette insisted on feeding the squirrels.

Because Jeanette came in contact with many flowers during her spring tour, she had to have allergy shots every ten days, which she usually prearranged with doctors on the road. During her 1940 tour, she became concerned when one doctor used a different size needle than she was used to, and she had Gene check with her regular physician to make sure that it wasn't a problem.

During the 1939 tour, Gene attended Jeanette's first recital in Pittsburg, Kansas, as well as several others. He never followed her on her entire tour, afraid critics would call him Mr. MacDonald. At Jeanette's debut, Gene helped adjust the lights and proudly sat in the audience, joining his wife backstage during each break. *The Pittsburg Sun* reported, "His beaming face and hearty applause attested to his interest in Miss MacDonald's concert and his pleasure at the results."[333] The day after her Lexington, Kentucky performance, the horse-loving Raymonds visited Faraway Farm and saw the legendary Thoroughbred Man o' War. Jeanette joked that Gene was more interested in seeing Man o' War than her recital.

During Holy Week, notorious for being the slowest in show business, the Raymonds took a brief vacation in New Orleans. Before they arrived, they requested "a dignified hotel, not in the business district, where we won't be disturbed."[334] Although the Raymonds were granted a few hours' privacy, eventually, they consented to hold a press conference to keep reporters from hounding the hotel staff. When asked why they chose New Orleans, they said that neither had been to the city. "I see so little of her," Gene told reporters. "We're just going to spend a few days."[335] Another reporter asked if they ever were called Mr. Sothern or Mrs. Eddy because of their screen partners, causing the Raymonds to laugh. "Mr. Sothern," sneered Gene. "I should say not." "Mrs. Eddy," said Jeanette with scorn. "I should say not." Then they laughed again.[336]

During the trip, Jeanette wanted to see the Ursuline convent where the Casquette girls, who were depicted in *Naughty Marietta*, stayed before marrying colonists. The Raymonds also visited several antique shops, hoping to find some additions for Twin Gables. Gene told the press, "We want to poke in patios, and eat all the things we've heard about, and just be lazy and play around without any definite plan at all, but maybe we should have come here for Mardi Gras, so we wouldn't be so noticed."[337] Columnist Penelope Penn reported that the New Orleans citizens, who spotted the couple while they were sightseeing, mistook Gene for Nelson Eddy. Penn was impressed with the Raymonds' behavior. "They wrote personal notes after every attention, left behind no criticism as to their manners. Their keynote was kindness, consideration, thoughtfulness. I hope they stay married, for they are in every instance meticulously good form. They certainly seemed loverly [sic] and, as for the ecstatic greetings of the populace, accepted it all with calm and modesty."[338]

A few weeks after Penn's column ran, the Raymonds received a typed letter quoting from it, postmarked from Indianapolis, Indiana, and signed only "One of your many friends." It said:

> So do we all hope you stay married, for you are the two people in all the tinseled population of the world's most tinseled city, the two people that everybody hoped and believed had enough decency, backbone and good sense to build your lives on the rock of permanence and stability, rather than on the shifting sands of selfishness, stupidity and lack of understanding, which seems to be the regular basis of Hollywood marriages.
>
> If two people who reflect breeding in everything they say and do, sensitivity in every expression on their faces,

can't make a go of marriage in the new Babylon, nothing good can come out of Hollywood.

Don't let each other down, and so let all the world down. It isn't worth it, not for you nor anyone else in Hollywood. And too many of us believe in you as a sort of guarantee that decency still does exist, even in Babylon.[339]

Jeanette was so touched by the letter that she pasted it in her scrapbook.

At the end of the Raymonds' New Orleans vacation, when Gene put Jeanette on a train for her next recital, he said, "Whoever told you we didn't have a good time, told you wrong. It's been swell."[340] Jeanette confided to reporters, "We just loafed. Saw the town and each other. We were hemmed in at the hotel, I guess, but oh, well. You get used to it."[341]

While Jeanette was on tour, Gene wrote a classical piece for her called "Let Me Always Sing." When he sent it to her, he modestly told her that she could throw it away if she didn't like it. On April 17, 1939, she introduced the song in Peoria, and, through the years, made it a part of her repertoire. At her Peoria recital, she announced a change in the program, explaining that the song was written "especially for me by someone specially [sic] fond of me, my husband." After it received hearty applause, Jeanette said, "I'll tell him he was the hit of the evening."[342] When she reported to Gene about the response on the phone, she said he was "as pleased as a little boy."[343] On April 24, Gene heard her perform his song for the first time at her Salina, Kansas recital.

On September 11, 1939, Jeanette recorded "Let Me Always Sing," with Gene at the piano. Later, he gave her a record-shaped pin with the title spelled out in gold. In 1940, he wrote "Release," the second in his seasonal song cycle, which Jeanette also performed in her recitals and on the radio, although she never recorded it. In 1947, he composed "At Last" and "I Can't Recall," which Jeanette often sang in veterans' hospitals, with Gene accompanying her on piano.

On April 19, 1939, while Jeanette was in Rochester, Minnesota, she had a routine checkup at the Mayo Clinic. Her endocrinologist, Dr. E. Kost Shelton, sent her complete case history to Dr. Edward Rynerson of the Mayo Clinic to expedite the examination and cut through any red tape. Endocrinologists deal with hormone imbalances, which could have affected Jeanette's inability to gain weight or get pregnant, as well as her insomnia, irregularity, and sensitivity to cold. That evening, she was the first to sing at the Mayo Civic Auditorium, which opened on March 9.

Jeanette and Gene loved their canine family. When they married, they had six dogs between them. In 1938, Jeanette said, "A MacDonald home without dogs is like ham without eggs."[344] In a magazine interview that ran in 1940, she told a reporter, "I am adult about everything but my dogs. We speak a language of our own, and at the drop of a hat I hurry them in and brag."[345] Jeanette thought of taking her Skye Terrier, Stormy, on her 1939 tour, but said, "I was afraid people would say, 'There's the prima donna, dog and all.'"[346] While she was on the road, she missed Stormy so much that, when Anna and Blossom drove to see her perform in Salt Lake City, Utah, they brought the dog along with them. He finished the tour with Jeanette, often stealing the limelight at her press conferences, much to Jeanette's delight. The Raymonds' wartime correspondence occasionally mentioned Stormy, Gene's Irish Setter, Tray, and Jeanette's Newfoundland, Nick, a Christmas gift from Gene in 1936.

Gene, Helen Ferguson, and Grace Newell also were in the audience for Jeanette's performance at the Mormon Tabernacle in Salt Lake City. After Jeanette sang "Let Me Always Sing," her husband blew her a kiss from his seat. During the recital, Jeanette acknowledged her mother, saying that some of the songs that she performed were

Anna's favorites. After the recital, Jeanette told reporters, "Without her I would never have been here tonight."[347]

On April 28, 1939, Jeanette and Gene faced the crowds as they left their hotel to go to her recital at the Mormon Tabernacle in Salt Lake City.

On May 11, Gene met Jeanette again in Tacoma, Washington, the last date on her tour. From there, they went on a three-week fishing vacation in Washington and British Columbia, which included a thirty-mile canoe trip on the Lower Quinault River with a Native American guide. Gene caught a nineteen-inch cutthroat trout and Jeanette caught a fourteen-inch salmon, the largest of the season. On their way home, they drove through California's Redwood forest. She reported to her fan club, "We caught some trout and salmon and would have stayed longer but the Northwest rains set in, so we wended our way home."[348] Through the years, during each of Jeanette's tours, Gene continued to attend several performances, often concluding with a vacation. In 1949, when Jeanette was asked about the nicest incident that ever happened during her recital tours, she answered, "When Gene surprises me with a visit."[349]

Jeanette's first American recital tour was a tremendous success. She was named the third largest female draw of 1939, behind established concert artists Lily Pons and Marian Anderson. The largest male draw was Nelson Eddy. For the next twenty years, Jeanette continued to sing on stage, in recitals and in concerts with symphony orchestras.

During Jeanette's 1939 tour, she repeatedly told reporters that she thought her next picture would be *New Moon*, although she wanted to do *Smilin' Through*. When asked with whom she wanted to work, besides Nelson Eddy, she mentioned Robert Taylor, Tyrone Power, and Gene. She said that the studio didn't think that it was a good idea to pair a married couple on screen. In answer to questions about their marriage, she said, "Ours is not the customary Hollywood romance. Our private life has nothing to do with box-office values. We are really in love."[350]

Meanwhile, in April 1939, Jeanette's contract with MGM was up for renewal. She took her time re-signing, admitting in a letter to MGM Publicity Director Howard Strickling that her first tour had been good for her ego. "You know, after you have been around a studio long enough, you just can't help absorbing some of that 'all actors have bad judgement' propoganda [sic], and of course I don't need to tell you, one also gets a feeling that he should be awfully pleased to even have a job! But all this changed on a tour like this. Looks like I am going to be difficult if I ever come back, doesn't it? But I shan't be. However, I do think I have found a real value on myself."[351]

Jeanette wanted a guarantee of two pictures per year, with a salary of $10,000 a week, and fifteen weeks scheduled per picture, the current equivalent of almost $5.4 million per year. Her other demands included sole above-the-title billing, that all her movies be filmed in Technicolor, veto power over the studio's choice of co-star, and script approval. She also wanted to work with directors Woody Van Dyke or Robert Z. Leonard, cinematographer Oliver Marsh, recording engineer Mike McLaughlin, musical director Herbert Stothart, and couturier Adrian. She received most of her demands; however, only two of her movies were filmed in Technicolor (*Bitter Sweet* and *Smilin' Through*), *Smilin' Through* was directed by Frank Borzage, and Nelson Eddy also was billed above the title in their pictures, as were Brian Aherne in *Smilin' Through* and Robert Young in *Cairo*. In 1941, Adrian left MGM to open his own fashion house so Jeanette's post-*Smilin' Through* costumes were designed by others. As noted previously, Oliver Marsh died in 1941.

In July 1939, Jeanette settled with the studio, with the help of Eddie Mannix, Louis Swarts, and Bob Ritchie. Louis B. Mayer found her attitude ungrateful. Jeanette noted in her autobiography, "I could feel the temperature falling. L.B. still gave me his good wishes when I went in to see him on the first day's shooting, but something had gone wrong between us."[352]

Jeanette's major demands were script approval, prompted by her dislike of *Broadway Serenade*, and to make only two movies a year, giving her time for recital tours and to spend with Gene. After her first tour, she said, "All Summer [sic] I really owed it to my husband to be a wife."[353]

On July 6, Jeanette and Gene hosted a birthday party for Anna at Twin Gables. The guests included Blossom; Elsie; Elsie's son, Earle Wallace; Gene's brother, Bob; Charlotte Learn and Jack Garrity; Helen Ferguson and Richard Hargreaves; Helen's mother, Emelie; Woody Van Dyke's mother, Laura; actor Walter Baldwin and his wife, Geraldine; and Emily Wentz. Jeanette gave her mother a season box at the Hollywood Bowl. In addition to being active with the Hollywood mothers club, Anna often played cards and socialized with another group of women. With the box, she could invite her friends to join her at concerts.

Gene had a longtime interest in flying. In 1932, he met aviatrix Amelia Earhart when she visited Paramount.

Later that summer, the Raymonds spent a month at Lake Arrowhead. During their vacation, they frequently went swimming and Gene taught Jeanette how to sail and how to drive a motorboat. On September 1, when the Nazis invaded Poland, officially beginning what would become World War II, Connie and Johnny Mack Brown, and Irene Dunne and Dr. Francis Griffin were visiting the Raymonds for Labor Day weekend. Two days later, Britain and France declared war on Nazi Germany. Always interested in aviation, Gene told Brown that he wanted to learn to fly because he was certain that the United States would enter the war and he wanted to be prepared to serve. He explained to Jeanette, only half in jest, "I want to be up in the air, dishing it out, not down below getting it."[354] Long before the war began, Gene kept up with current events and made his patriotism known. In 1934, he told a reporter, "I like to read and study. . . . If my country goes to war, little Gene will be just right for the front lines. Before anything like that happens, I intend to know what I am going for—and for whom!"[355]

In mid-October 1939, the Raymonds spent several days at Marshallia, a dude ranch in Casmalia in Santa Barbara County, California. Always protective of Jeanette, Gene wrote to his father, "Jeanette had an attack of hay fever which, in turn, brought on insomnia. She got no sleep for about a week, so I packed her up and brought her up here, for a change. This ranch is near the ocean, as I thought the salt air would be beneficial. So we piled in the car and left about two in the morning. After about an hour of driving Jeanette fell asleep and stayed asleep for two hours – the first sleep she'd had in almost a week! We arrived here about five-thirty [sic] A.M., went to bed and slept like babies until twelve noon! When Jeanette woke up she felt like a youngster again. Her hay fever is better today so I think she'll be alright now."[356] Through the years, Gene continued to be sensitive to Jeanette's allergies, accompanying her to other parts of California, like Palm Springs, Santa Barbara, and La Jolla, when the West Los Angeles smog got to be too much for her. He could relate to her suffering, since he had allergies and hay fever himself, though not as severe.

In the fall of 1939, the Raymonds rented a Malibu beach house that had belonged to Jeanette's *Don't Bet on Women!* co-star, Edmund Lowe, and his late wife, actress Lilyan Tashman. Around this time, Jeanette complained about the temperature in West Los Angeles to Marion Smith Glendening: "For the past week we've been in the throes of an unusual heat wave – 106 – and even our place perched atop a hill as it is – has been unbearable – We've not been able to sleep nites [sic] for the heat. The weatherman promises no relief!!"[357] In Malibu, Jeanette prepared for *New Moon*, her sixth film with Nelson Eddy. That fall, she also did some recording for RCA Victor and appeared on several radio shows. She told the press that Gene was writing an operetta, "which he modestly says may be done when we are both too old to enjoy it."[358] He still was working on it during her spring 1940 recital tour, the last time she mentioned it in the press. He became too busy with flying lessons and a return to his movie career to finish the score.

The Raymonds celebrated Christmas at the B-Bar-H Ranch in Palm Springs. In January and February 1940, they also spent several weekends there. In between, in January, Gene had his tonsils removed. He shared a room with Jeanette's nephew, Earle Wallace, who was hospitalized for a minor nasal operation. In a letter dated January 19, 1940, Gene joked to Marion Smith Glendening and her husband, Frank, "The Tonsil [sic] twins were laid quietly to rest over a week ago. Since they were so criminally inclined, I'm sure the nation will not mourn their loss – although I must admit there is an aching void in the vicinity of Detroit!"[359] Gene was less amused when, during his hospitalization, an anonymous practical joking friend sent him a florist's box filled with goldenrod, the flowers which most irritated his hay fever. When he realized that he couldn't holler for a nurse to remove it, he dove under the sheets to hide, unaware that the flowers were artificial. He didn't think the joke was very funny. Given the way the Raymonds liked to tease each other, it wouldn't be surprising if Jeanette sent the phony flowers.

In April, Gene resumed his film career, re-signing with RKO for a three-picture deal. He appeared in *Cross-Country Romance,* a romantic comedy that cast him as a doctor who drove across the United States with a runaway bride (Wendy Barrie). Many thought that the film would have been better with a different leading lady. Gene darkened his hair for the role, reportedly rubbing the color from an eyebrow pencil into his blonde locks. He hoped the color change would lead to more serious roles. In May, he had a sinus operation at Good Samaritan Hospital.

While Gene was re-launching his film career, Jeanette was continuing hers at MGM. In 1940, she made two movies with Nelson Eddy: *New Moon* and *Bitter Sweet.* The plots of both films were compared to earlier MacDonald/Eddy movies, *Naughty Marietta* (class differences and location) and *Maytime* (lovers parted by death); neither was as popular with fans or critics as the earlier films.

New Moon utilized part of the music and plot from the Sigmund Romberg/Oscar Hammerstein II/Frank Mandel/Laurence Schwab operetta *The New Moon* (1927), but eliminated some characters. In the movie, a French noblewoman (Jeanette) locked horns with a Duke (Nelson), masquerading as a bond servant, in order to lead a revolt in eighteenth century New Orleans. After they were stranded on an island, the noblewoman realized the pettiness of her class prejudices and married the Duke. Jeanette's songs included "One Kiss," "Lover, Come Back to Me," and the sensuous duet "Wanting You." When she sang "One Kiss," she held a fan from her collection that originally belonged to Marie Antoinette. *New Moon* grossed $2,527,000 in domestic and foreign markets, now over $45 million.

In between pictures, in the spring and fall of 1940 and the winter of 1941, Jeanette did recital tours. Before she left, she planned Gene's meals for the cook, often attaching recipe cards to the menus.

Although she was thousands of miles away, she knew what he was eating, and he knew that she cared enough to plan for him. On February 12, 1940, he attended her opening in El Paso, Texas. So many seats were sold that, in order to see his wife sing, he had to stand on a table in the back of the auditorium.

Wherever Jeanette went, crowds continued to besiege her. In Montgomery, Alabama, the squeal of fans made her shrink back on the train because she thought someone had fallen on the tracks. In Raleigh, North Carolina, the mob crushed her shoe and tore her stocking.

Jeanette was humbled by the hospitality that she received throughout her tour. Alabama Governor Frank Dixon held a tea in her honor at the executive mansion and left a car at her disposal. In Washington, D.C., attorney Mabel Walker Willebrandt hosted a tea for Jeanette and took her and her entourage to see the Philadelphia Orchestra play at Constitution Hall. At Jeanette's request, Gene typed up a speech for her and sent it to her Airmail for the Washington reception. John Stewart Bryan, President of William and Mary College in Williamsburg, Virginia, also held a tea for her.

During Jeanette's spring 1940 tour, she fulfilled a lifelong dream of singing at the Philadelphia Academy of Music, thrilled that she could share the experience with relatives and childhood friends. In the fall, she recalled the recital and how she was inspired after seeing soprano Geraldine Farrar at Boston's Symphony Hall in the 1920s. "It seemed to me then that to sing in a place like that, all by yourself, in front of a great audience, with no scenery or properties or actors to help you, would be the most wonderful thing imaginable. So you can understand how it was, when I gave a recital at the Academy of Music in Philadelphia last season that I felt I had made the most important step in my career. Philadelphia is, of course, my home and to come back there, not as a musical comedy actress nor as a screen star but as a concert singer was both exciting and a little terrifying. If they hadn't liked me, it would have been pretty bad."[360]

After the recital, Marion Smith Glendening hosted a party for Jeanette, with many of her former classmates and teachers in attendance. Through the years, Marion and her husband, Frank, saw all of Jeanette's Philadelphia performances and often socialized with her during her stay there. During the tour of *The Guardsman*, Jeanette and Gene went to the Glendenings' home for a post-performance visit. The Glendenings also saw some of Gene's plays and visited the Raymonds at Twin Gables.

Because of train connections, Jeanette frequently took a circuitous route to get from city to city. When she complained, Gene teased her. She told reporters, "Gene is the flyer in the family. He goes everywhere by air. And that makes it a little awkward for me, because I can't write him when I've had a particularly tiresome trip. He's sure to write back 'Well, if you'd flown, it wouldn't have taken you so long.'"[361]

On March 20, Gene met his wife in Springfield, Illinois and attended her recital there. After she sang "Let Me Always Sing," the audience insisted that he join Jeanette on stage. From Springfield, they went to Chicago for a brief vacation over Easter weekend, seeing Raymond Massey in the play *Abe Lincoln in Illinois*. Jeanette laughed that she spent much of the play leaning into the aisle because her hat blocked the view for the patron sitting behind her. Jeanette refused to remove the hat because she spent a long time styling her hair around it. On Easter, Gene flew to New York to discuss a return to Broadway and a possible radio show, as well as meet with Schirmer Bros. about publishing his songs "Release" and "I Would Slumber." Before Jeanette headed to Grand Rapids, Michigan for her next recital, she attended Easter service at the First Presbyterian Church of Chicago.

During Jeanette's recital tours, Gene liked to tease Jeanette about how much time she spent riding and waiting for trains. Here she sat with some of her luggage, including her makeup case, monogrammed J.A.R.

While Jeanette was on tour, Gene routinely wired silly limericks to wish her luck and relax her before her performances. He sometimes signed famous or fictitious names, including Henry Wadsworth Longfellow, Lord Byron, Wendell L. Ramie, Kernel Custer, Busy Brandon, Mr. Penny Pincher, and B.C.R. (Budding Composer Raymond). The poets were to kid about his rhyming skills. In his correspondence, both before and during the war, he often told Jeanette to "be my girl" and they each frequently said, "You're the best." A telegram from April 8, 1940 described the construction going on at Twin Gables.

I'm starting to work on the pool,

So when you return you'll be cool.

It'll be nice and sunny,

All rustic and funny,

And we'll swim like two fish in a school.[362]

Sometimes, he was more sentimental, observing, "WITH YOU AWAY THE HOUSE SEEMS EMPTIER IF THATS [sic] POSSIBLE."[363]

Jeanette always ate light before her performances, usually fruit with cottage cheese or yogurt; after the show, she had a more substantial meal. Columnist Jack Sheridan recalled attending a post-show reception with Jeanette and Emily in 1956, where the cuisine was limited to finger sandwiches. Afterwards, Jeanette confessed that she was starving so he took them to a diner at 1:00 a.m. "We wound up in the corner circular booth at a local drive-in where the eager red-head [sic] attacked a huge platter of ham and eggs and fried potatoes and toast with a vigor that would have put a longshoreman to shame!" he said.[364]

Jeanette loved to explore fruit markets wherever she went. While she was on tour, her regimen also included getting out in the fresh air and walking a mile and a half. If she wore a scarf on her hair and little makeup, often, she could go unrecognized. In Milwaukee, Wisconsin, Jeanette drove out of town for her walk then ended up with a flat tire. She knocked on a door and asked to use the phone. While she waited for someone to pick her up, she sunbathed in the woman's backyard, chatting and watching her hang laundry.

In Texas, Jeanette called the house detective when she found a flying cockroach in her hotel room. Although she admitted that she liked to kill the normal kind, the flying one apparently was too much for her; she laughed that she didn't know who else to call. In Grand Rapids, Michigan, Jeanette was resting before her recital when someone knocked on the door and asked her to autograph her "Do Not Disturb" sign. Through the years, this was repeated many times in other cities. Her funniest experience came when a woman in Toledo, Ohio met Jeanette's train at 6:00 a.m. After giving Jeanette the once over, the woman exclaimed, "Good heavens! I've got to hand it to you. I wouldn't believe anyone could look so pretty at this ungodly hour."[365]

A reporter in Milwaukee asked if Gene was Jeanette's favorite composer. She answered, "Gene is my favorite actor, my favorite friend, and my favorite husband. If I said he was my favorite composer, somebody might think I was prejudiced."[366] She told the press that "Ah! Sweet Mystery of Life" was her audiences' favorite song. "I don't know just why," she insisted. "Perhaps, because it is romantic, and today, when life is so full of sordidness, people like to be lifted above it all—hence they turn to romance. And so I sing this song in my concerts feeling that if I can lift my hearers above it all, for just a little while, it will all be worth while [sic]."[367]

Before cell phones and flat rate telephone plans, long distance calls were expensive. Although Jeanette often joked about her frugality, she said that her one extravagance was the telephone. "It's a positive phobia with me," she explained. "When I was in New York the autumn before Gene and I were married, well, I had a phone bill and it was a honey! When I was in Tahoe on location, ditto. I never think of waiting for the lower rate hours. I talk and talk and talk, for hours."[368] When she was on tour, the Raymonds frequently called each other— usually every day that Jeanette wasn't on a train—and sent numerous telegrams. On Thanksgiving 1940, Jeanette called Gene at Anna's house and talked to each member of the family, causing him to remark, "I'll bet that bill was a humdinger!!!"[369] During a 1941 press conference, Jeanette told reporters about their lengthy phone calls, which usually ended with one of them saying, "My Heavens, I wonder how much this is costing us!"[370] In one wartime letter, Gene talked about pumping $25 worth of quarters, currently about $348, into a pay phone after one of their calls. During a May 1962 visit to Twin Gables, Ken Richards said that Gene called, and Jeanette excused herself to talk to him. When she returned about twenty minutes later, she said that they had a deal not to talk long when they called long distance, but "they just always can't help it."[371]

During Jeanette's spring 1940 tour, she continued to campaign for MGM to cast Gene in a movie with her. She was happy that many of the student reporters at her press conferences agreed with her. "Youngsters are the pulse of the public," she said. "You can talk to them and really find out what audiences likes and dislikes are. That's why I'm going to take up with the studio the question of doing a picture with Gene. I believe to the youngsters, we represent honest romance and this is what inspires the question."[372]

Jeanette always was appreciative of her fans. She said that she received her first fan letter when she had her first singing part in a show. Although she did not identify the musical, her first non-chorus role was in *Irene*. She said the letter made her feel like a star and she was grateful to fans ever since. In 1934, she told a reporter, "Fans have helped me tremendously to be the girl I am today. I have received a lot of honest criticism and advice from them. I corrected a number of bad habits of speech and ugly little mannerisms through their help. . . . I pay a lot of attention to my fan letters."[373]

Jeanette had many famous admirers, including her peers, Academy Award winners Vivien Leigh and Bette Davis. In 1964, when Leigh was filming *Ship of Fools* (1965), she contacted Jeanette and wanted to meet her because Leigh was a fan of Jeanette's movies. By then, Jeanette was too ill to go out, but she sent Leigh an autographed picture, inscribed, "My dear Vivien – I couldn't be more flattered and pleased by your admiration – Believe me – It's Mutual [sic]!! Sincerely, Jeanette."[374] In the 1970s, Davis called Jeanette "a damned good actress."[375] On the January 2, 1975 episode of *The Merv Griffin Show*, dancer Ann Miller said that Jeanette was the greatest and there would never be another like her. Character actor Reginald Owen, who worked with Jeanette in *Rose-Marie*, *I Married an Angel*, and *Cairo*, said that she was his favorite co-star. Character actor Douglass (sometimes spelled Douglas) Dumbrille, who worked with Jeanette in *Naughty Marietta*, *The Firefly*, and *I Married an Angel*, once remarked that there were only good stories about working with her and that he always looked forward to the films that he made with her. He added, "There was always an air of kindness and friendship on Miss MacDonald's sets. . . . [I had] such pleasure working with that dear lady."[376] In 2006, when Turner Classic Movies (TCM) aired a month-long tribute to Jeanette and Nelson as Stars of the Month, showing their movies every Monday in March, host Robert Osborne recalled how actress Lauren Bacall came up to him at the Academy Awards and said, "I've got to see Jeanette MacDonald and Nelson Eddy on Monday night."[377]

Other celebrities grew up watching Jeanette on screen and dreamed of performing like her. Among her more celebrated fans were singers Kathryn Grayson, Jane Powell, Marni Nixon, Shirley Jones, and Susanna Foster, entertainer Sammy Davis, Jr., writer/actor/director/comedian Carl Reiner, and actress Joanne Woodward. In their autobiographies, some of them wrote about seeing Jeanette. Opera singer Beverly Sills, a fan since childhood, recorded several songs that Jeanette made famous. When asked how she acquired her enthusiasm for classical music, Sills answered, "I was raised on it! Was there anything in the world more beautiful than Jeanette MacDonald and Nelson Eddy?"[378] As a child, singer/actress Edie Adams had a picture of Jeanette on her bedroom wall. Adams later impersonated her on TV and in her nightclub act. Broadway actress/singer Barbara Cook admired Jeanette so much that she convinced herself that she met her idol, despite the fact that she didn't. Lawrence Welk's Champagne Lady Norma Zimmer was a longtime fan who met Jeanette when Zimmer worked in the chorus on Nelson Eddy's radio show, *The Electric Hour*. Zimmer expressed her admiration for Jeanette on *The Lawrence Welk Show* and occasionally sang songs that Jeanette made famous. In actress/comedienne Carol Burnett's 2015 acceptance speech for her Screen Actors Guild Lifetime Achievement Award, she mentioned being a Jeanette MacDonald and Nelson Eddy fan. Burnett often told reporters how she and her cousin reenacted the team's movies as children, something that Burnett later did on her TV series. When she was young, she always had to be Nelson, but on TV, she was Jeanette. Even *Playboy* magazine publisher Hugh Hefner was a fan.

In TV interviews, actress Betty White frequently mentioned her childhood adoration of Jeanette and Nelson, saying that it made her angry when people made fun of them. In her autobiography, she recalled seeing *Naughty Marietta, Rose-Marie,* and *Maytime* multiple times during their initial runs. She said, "I went to every one of their concerts, and I cut their pictures out of magazines until I had boxloads [sic]. In all truth, the reason I am in the entertainment business today is due, for the most part, to my feeling for them."[379] In a 2018 PBS documentary, *Betty White: First Lady of Television*, she called Jeanette her idol and said that Jeanette and Nelson were almost as important to her as her parents. In 1959, the week after Jeanette was in *Bittersweet* in Warren, Ohio, White starred in *The King and I* and, after Jeanette's final performance, they met backstage. "She could not have been warmer or more gracious . . . and you can't imagine the thrill it was to receive a beautiful bouquet in my dressing room the next evening . . . TO BETTY, LOVE, JEANETTE MACDONALD!" White continued, "Later, back in California, our paths crossed again on several occasions, and she always treated me like a dear friend."[380] One can't help wondering if they ever discussed their mutual love of dogs.

When actress Dina Merrill was young, she saw *Naughty Marietta* forty times. She claimed that she was seven; however, given that she was born December 29, 1923, she was eleven when the movie was released. In a memorial brochure sent to Jeanette's fan clubs, Merrill recalled how Jeanette inspired her acting ambitions. "The nourishment for my ambition was—your example," she wrote. "Obstacles overcome—ceaseless study of your craft, always-higher goals set for yourself, in your world of lovely music. I was not beguiled by copycat aspirations—Jeanette MacDonald's accomplishments would not be equalled in our day—or ever. But, within my heart, within my ambition to act, was one alikeness [sic]. I could—and I did—share the quality of your determination." Merrill remembered meeting Jeanette through her mother, socialite and General Foods, Inc. owner Marjorie Merriweather Post. Jeanette's graciousness, beauty, and vivacity left a lasting impression, leading Merrill to conclude, "The Jeanette MacDonald 'magic'—was real."[381]

Royalty and politicians around the world also admired Jeanette. King Albert of Belgium attended a screening of *The Love Parade* because he was a fan of Maurice Chevalier; however, after seeing the picture, Jeanette became his favorite star. Coincidentally, King Albert was the father of Princess Marie-Jose, whose husband was rumored to be involved with Jeanette in the scandal that led to Jeanette's 1931 tour in Paris and London.

A 1935 item in *The Hollywood Reporter* noted that the Sultan of Johor, Ibrahim al-Masyhur, sent Jeanette a lot of fancy trinkets and gold knickknacks for Christmas. In a 1938 *James A. FitzPatrick Traveltalk* on Singapore and Johor, FitzPatrick said that the Sultan asked FitzPatrick to give his regards to Jeanette MacDonald, his favorite star. In 1943, Jeanette sent an autographed photo to the wife of Chiang Kai-Shek, leader of the Republic of China, when she heard Madame Chiang was ill. Jeanette also was a favorite of the British Royal Family, and Prince Felix Yusupov and his wife, Princess Irina, the only niece of Czar Nicholas II, the last Czar of Russia.

In 1937, President Franklin D. Roosevelt invited Jeanette to his birthday celebration. Often, Presidents Harry Truman and Dwight Eisenhower attended Jeanette's recitals and, reportedly, she was President Eisenhower's favorite singer.

Even Adolf Hitler named Jeanette, along with Greta Garbo and Shirley Temple, as his favorite actresses, running their movies over and over. Throughout the war, Hitler endlessly listened to his favorite operetta, Franz Lehar's *The Merry Widow*, often referring to himself as Danilo and quoting the character. He even asked Lehar to divorce his wife because she was Jewish. Given Hitler's obsession with the stage version of *The Merry Widow*, one would think it also was his favorite of Jeanette's movies. However, in 1934, after he became Chancellor of Germany, he banned all films made by Jews, including *The Merry Widow*, directed by Ernst Lubitsch.

Through the years, Jeanette had numerous fan clubs. During her lifetime, the three most active were the Original Jeanette MacDonald Fan Club, the Jeanette MacDonald International Fan Club (JMIFC), and the Jeanette MacDonald Club.

In 1930, Pearl Katzman formed the first club as the Chevalier–MacDonald Club, honoring Jeanette and her frequent co-star, Maurice Chevalier, and produced a journal called *Chevalier–MacDonald News*.

Eva White succeeded Katzman as President. In 1932, Glenna Riley took over and remained President until the club disbanded in 1965 after Jeanette's death. In 1940, Chevalier was dropped and, eventually, the name was changed to the Original Jeanette MacDonald Fan Club, sometimes known as the *Musical Echoes* Club, after its re-named journal, or Glenna Riley's Club, because she was President for so long.

In 1937, Canadian fan Mary Miller organized the JMIFC, which, from 1938 to 2003, produced a journal called *The Golden Comet* and, from 1965 to 2006, issued a newsletter *La Petite Comet* (known as *The Junior Comet* for two issues). In 1941, after Miller's health forced her to resign, the Presidents were Marie Waddy (later known as Marie Waddy Gerdes), Martha Farrington, Margaret Cloghessy, Clara Rhoades, and Tessa Williams. By the 1940s, the club had over eighteen hundred members.

In 1939, the Jeanette MacDonald Club was founded by California fan Alma Calligan. During its brief run, it produced a quarterly journal called *The Skylark* and had over three hundred members. In 1942, when Calligan's health failed, the club merged with the JMIFC.

Jeanette often wrote letters to the clubs and answered fans' questions. Some clubs had local chapters that met monthly and attended Jeanette's recitals and movies as a group. Occasionally, Jeanette invited her fan club Presidents to MGM to watch her filming. She also had clubs overseas, including one in England that produced a quarterly journal called *The Magazine Of The Jeanette MacDonald British Fan Club*; in 1954, it merged with the JMIFC.

Before the war, Gene had fan clubs as well. In 1937, his American club, run by Richard Carroll, had over three hundred members and published *The Gene Raymond Fan Club News*. Gene had another club in Great Britain.

Unlike male singers, who only attracted female admirers, or screen sex symbols, who appealed solely to male audiences, Jeanette attracted fans of both sexes. Although her romantic movies often brought more women into the theaters, especially during the Depression, when they needed an escape from everyday drudgeries, her recitals drew men, women, and children. Some already were patrons of classical concerts. Others knew her from the screen and were introduced to classical music through her films, records, and recitals.

Always appreciative of her fans' loyalty, during the spring 1940 tour, Jeanette began inviting members of her fan clubs to visit her backstage after the performances. All they had to do was show their membership cards. The practice became a life-long tradition. Betty Bradley recalled how Jeanette always tried to include everyone in the backstage conversations, not just talk to her friends or certain fans. When the fans sent her candy or flowers, in her dressing room after the performance, she usually encouraged each one to take a chocolate or gave them a rose as a souvenir. Often, Jeanette also obtained tickets for her radio and TV broadcasts for club members and allowed them to come backstage after the programs.

Sometimes, Jeanette arranged for fan club members to attend press conferences and rehearsals, even when the management objected. During one tour, she invited members to her hotel suite for a visit. On another, she took two members to an inn outside of town so they could dine with her and her secretary and accompanist. On the evening before the opening of her summer stock run of *The King and I*, she hosted a dinner for twelve fan club members who were in Kansas City, Missouri for the premiere. On the way back to her room, one fan fainted from the excitement; Jeanette paid for a doctor to check her and sent her flowers. Several fans attended the entire two-week run.

Like the fans known as Deadheads who followed the Grateful Dead, many fans attended Jeanette's recitals in multiple cities and got to know her on a first-name basis. She sometimes joked that she should change a few songs, just for those who followed her on her tours. Backstage, she told fan club members, "You know who I sing 'I'll See You Again' for? You members!"[382]

Emily recalled, "Many times the stage doorman would tell Jeanette she could slip out another way to avoid the crowds, but she never would. She said if they waited so long to see her personally she wouldn't disappoint them."[383] When Jeanette had to leave immediately after a 1944 Boston performance to travel to Lowell for her next date, she sent individual letters of apology to Massachusetts fan club members for being unable to meet with them backstage. In 1948, when Jeanette had to cancel several recitals because of a cold, she had Emily send telegrams to fan club members so they wouldn't travel in vain. In 1951, after years of corresponding, Jeanette scolded longtime fan Elsie Pyette because she didn't go backstage to introduce herself after she saw *The Guardsman*. "I was very annoyed with you for not coming Backstage [sic] after the Performance [sic] of 'The Guardsman,' and so was Gene," Jeanette said. "I never want my friends to think that I am 'Too [sic] Important [sic]' to approach. Shame on you. I shall however arrange a meeting with you at some later date."[384]

The rule about only allowing fan club members backstage sometimes encouraged audience members to join one of the clubs; occasionally, it also scared off Jeanette's friends. In 1956, after she performed *The King and I* in Kansas City, Missouri, she received a letter from former First Lady Bess Truman, explaining why she and President Truman didn't congratulate Jeanette after the show. Mrs. Truman wrote, "And I must tell you that we and our guests expected to ask if we might go backstage to speak to you until they announced there were two thousand [sic] MacDonald Club 'fans' coming backstage after the show! We were fans but did not belong to the Club and felt it would be an imposition to add one more handshake."[385]

Just as Jeanette fought for fans to be allowed backstage and to attend private rehearsals, her fans were quick to defend her when anyone criticized her. After the editor of *Film Weekly* said that she preferred pre-Code Jeanette to the Jeanette of 1937, Lesley Lindsay wrote an irate letter, praising the improvement in Jeanette's voice since her days under the direction of Ernst Lubitsch. "Her trill is a delight, her diction excellent and unaffected, her breath control is phenomenal and, however shrill her top notes, they are less so than Lily Pons' bird-like coloratura," Lindsay insisted. "Besides, her voice has a warmth and individuality unequalled by any other Hollywood prima donna, which seems to me to be the logical development of that very personal metallic note which was first heard in THE LOVE PARADE."[386] Movie magazines frequently ran letters from angry fans who felt Jeanette was criticized or slighted.

When Jeanette was on the road, fans often asked if they could do anything to help her. The day after a 1940s concert with the Cincinnati Symphony Orchestra, she had a pair of fans deliver her bouquet of roses to conductor Eugene Goosens. She had worked with him at a previous concert and heard that he was in the hospital. The fans were thrilled to help, despite the fact that they had to put the flowers in the bathtub in their hotel room to keep them fresh overnight. During the 1951 tour of *The Guardsman*, Jeanette sent a fan to buy yogurt and cottage cheese, and another walked Misty. In 1954, when Jeanette played St. Charles, Illinois in *Bittersweet*, she asked fans to pick up a cake for the cast party and some pecan rolls for her snack. The next year, when she did *Bittersweet* in Dallas, a fan heard that Jeanette couldn't get her favorite Yanni yogurt so the fan made yogurt for her. After Jeanette borrowed some furs for a 1950s New York TV appearance, Ken Richards recalled taking the subway to return them because Jeanette didn't offer to pay for a cab.

In July 1961, the Raymonds hosted a party at Twin Gables for longtime fan Mary Dunphy. Above: Fans posed with Jeanette, Mary Dunphy (left of Jeanette), Rosemary Sullivan (behind Jeanette), and Emily Wentz (behind Dunphy). Below: Jeanette and Gene clowned for their guests.

Both Jeanette and Gene liked to tease the fans who followed her from city to city, but the Raymonds were grateful for their support. Gene had great fun ribbing Mary Dunphy, who traveled across the country to see Jeanette the same week that Gene was appearing in a play in Dunphy's home state of Massachusetts. When Dunphy attended a February performance of *The Guardsman*, Jeanette joked, "We don't know if Easter vacations have started early in the East or if the teacher's playing hookey [sic]."[387] Dunphy had a reputation for laughing so hard that she cried and, during one of the tours, the fans chipped in and gave her a crying towel, which led to more teasing from Jeanette. While Dunphy was in Washington, D.C. to see Gene in the pre-Broadway tour of *A Shadow of My Enemy* (1957), she learned about Jeanette's appendicitis before he did, since he was rehearsing. Dunphy almost got stranded in New York because of snow when she attended the show's Broadway opening and worried how she would explain to the principal of her school if she didn't go to work the next day. The Raymonds were so fond of Dunphy that, during her July 1961 California vacation, they hosted a party for her at Twin Gables. After Jeanette's death, Dunphy continued to keep in touch with Gene. When he learned that she had cancer, he offered her financial help.

Gene also liked to kid Pauline "Sarge" Moore, a WAC (Women's Army Corps) who always managed to get leave to attend Jeanette's performances. However, the joke was on the Raymonds when, during the 1949/1950 holiday season, she just happened to be stationed in Heidelberg, Germany while they were there to entertain the troops and their families.

At the 1962 JMIFC banquet, Gene saluted Pauline "Sarge" Moore, one of his favorite fans to tease.

Jeanette remained modest about her appeal. She wrote to Elsie Pyette, "We have been writing to each other now for Twenty [sic] years. Sometimes I wonder what I ever said or did to deserve 'such Loyalty [sic].'"[388]

Jeanette made her fans feel like they were friends. For years, she corresponded with many of them, sending birthday, Christmas, and get well cards, encouraging notes, and even wedding presents. In 1952 or 1953, she had ornaments made by the New York firm Christmas Ornament Decorators Service, with snowflakes and "Merry Christmas" on one side and her autograph on a gift tag on the other; she mailed them to special fans. When former JMIFC President Marie Waddy Gerdes named her daughter after the singer, Jeanette gave the baby a pearl bracelet that she had as a child. Another fan wrote that she hoped to have a daughter and name the baby after

Jeanette. However, when she had a son instead, she wrote that she named him "for the person you love best—Gene."[389] Jeanette sent her a congratulatory note and gift. Although Jeanette's health was declining in December 1964, she handwrote a brief personal note on a Christmas card to Australian fan Fay La Galle. The international mail took several weeks and it arrived on the day before Jeanette died.

Jeanette took special interest in fans who were going through difficult times, like Elsie Pyette, who was bed-ridden for three years, and Edgar Bradley, who underwent multiple amputations. In a 1962 issue of *The Golden Comet*, Bradley recalled Jeanette's kindness, thoughtfulness, and encouraging letters. "A great many friends (?) deserted me after I lost my legs," he wrote, "but a famous lady like Jeanette could find the necessary time to drop me a line while these close friends found it an impossible task. 'Beauty is as beauty does!!!!'"[390] During the war, Jeanette sent a food parcel to the President of her British fan club, and inspirational material and gifts to a fan imprisoned in a Japanese internment camp.

For years, Jeanette suggested that fans donate to charity, rather than send gifts for her anniversary, birthday, and Christmas. The Original Jeanette MacDonald Fan Club, the JMIFC, and the Jeanette MacDonald British Fan Club supported several charities, mostly involving disabled or underprivileged children, or troubled youths. During the war, the JMIFC donated to patriotic causes and proudly listed the names of members who were serving, whether it was in the Armed Forces or as Red Cross blood donors.

In 1962, at Jeanette's suggestion, the JMIFC established the Therapy Fund. Members contributed to a kitty that was used to send flowers and gifts to ill members or financial help to those who needed it. Jeanette chose the recipients herself and kept their identities secret, unless they publicly thanked the club. Her family knew how much the fund meant to her. In 1964, Jeanette said that the only thing that she wanted for Christmas was her health back; instead of buying her a gift, Blossom sent a check to the Therapy Fund.

After Jeanette's death, the Therapy Fund continued, with Gene offering suggestions about who should receive checks and often contributing himself. The club paid for a motorized wheelchair for Edgar Bradley, as well as hand controls for his car.

Jeanette often went above and beyond the call of duty to please her fans. In the 1940s, she performed at the Robin Hood Dell, an outdoor theater in Philadelphia. As she finished her brief rehearsal, she noticed six nuns sitting in the back of the theater. The lighting man explained that they traveled thirty miles from their convent to hear her rehearse, as they weren't allowed to attend public gatherings at night. Jeanette ended up running through her entire program for them. When she finished, they approached the edge of the stage to thank her. Jeanette was stunned when she learned that, before one nun entered the convent, she had been in the chorus of *Naughty Marietta*.

Jeanette also encouraged young singers. She received so many letters asking for career advice that, in 1940, she had a pamphlet printed titled "No Royal Road to Song" to serve as a standard reply. Within nine months of publication, her secretary estimated that eighty thousand copies had been sent. One of those encouraged by Jeanette was Tessa Williams, then known as Tessa Piper, who had a successful singing career and was the last President of the JMIFC.

Jeanette stressed the importance of being prepared. She said, "It has been my experience that stage fright, mike fright, all the frights of appearance before an audience are the result of fear of making an error." She fought her own self-consciousness with study and experience, striving for perfection. "To be letter perfect in every word and note one utters before an audience is the only solution," she insisted.[391]

Jeanette and Gene with her protégé, Ann Torri, at the Waldorf Astoria in the 1950s. Ann took the Raymonds out to thank them for all that they had done for her. When a cigarette girl snapped their photo, they each inscribed it to Grace Newell. Jeanette: "To Gracee [sic], See! I am vitalizing, Love Jeanette." Gene: "Hello Gracie---Having fine time---on Annie, Love, Gene." Ann: "Love you lotsy [sic], lotsy [sic], Love, Annie." Photo from the Eleanor Knowles Dugan collection, with special thanks to Ken Richards.

In 1944, an Ohio couple wrote to Jeanette about their daughter, Ann Cannata, a nineteen-year-old member of her fan club. Jeanette called the aspiring singer to offer encouragement. Later, Ann changed her name to Ann Torri, a shortened version of Torriani, in honor of Ferdinand Torriani, Jeanette's late voice teacher and originator of the technique that Grace Newell taught. In the 1950s, Ann became Jeanette's protégé, studying with Grace, who she affectionately called "Miss Noodle." When the Raymonds played Columbus, Ohio in *The Guardsman*, the Cannatas hosted an after-performance party for them. Ann even briefly lived with the Raymonds in New York. In Jeanette's will, she left Ann a silver dessert plate depicting a sketch of her in costume for *Naughty Marietta*. Similar plates from other movies went to longtime friends, like Mike McLaughlin (*The Merry Widow*), Nelson Eddy (*Rose-Marie*), Allan Jones (*The Firefly*), and newspaper Entertainment Editor Lily May Caldwell (*Maytime*).

Although Jeanette treated everyone the same, from fans to celebrities, there were some people who impressed her enough to keep their correspondence. She saved a thank you letter from President Franklin D. Roosevelt, Christmas cards from California Governor/ Supreme Court Chief Justice Earl Warren, a funny get well card from actress Greer Garson, notes from actresses Mary Martin and Mary Pickford, and a program from her own Washington recital, signed by President Harry Truman. Although Jeanette considered many of them friends, the envelope she kept the letters in was labeled "personal Correspondence [sic] from Famous [sic] people."[392] Staunch Republican Jeanette didn't vote for President Roosevelt, but she was so in awe of him that she declined an invitation to his 1937 birthday celebration because she was afraid to meet him. She said, "And if he asked me to sing for him, my voice would just die in my throat and I'd stand there, dumb!"[393] Gene was less nervous and attended President Roosevelt's 1942 Birthday Ball.

Jeanette was a great believer in the old adage that the show must go on. She never wanted to disappoint her audience, knowing that many people traveled hundreds of miles to see her. For that reason, the only time that Jeanette cancelled performances was when a cold threatened to harm her voice, or an illness, like food poisoning, made her too sick to sing. She had a sensitive stomach, as well as numerous allergies, therefore food and water from certain areas often affected her health. In the 1950s, after several bad experiences, she began carrying bottled water when she visited other countries.

Jeanette often complained about the dressing rooms on tour, like this one in Albany, New York in 1950 that had makeshift walls.

When Jeanette was on tour, the long hours traveling on cold trains, lack of rest, and drafty theaters and dressing rooms made her particularly susceptible to colds. She took precautions, traveling in long underwear in the winter, sometimes wearing a hood backstage to protect her ears and throat, and occasionally donning a fur coat onstage. Trains didn't always connect to her destinations; in many cities, she took a train part of the way then completed her trip by car. This not only exposed her to more cold temperatures, but tired her and lowered her immune system. During her press conferences, when reporters coughed or mentioned that they recently had a cold or the flu, she tried to keep her distance. In 1937, her ear, nose, and throat specialist said, "I have, a great many times, forbid Miss MacDonald to use her voice because of danger to her larynx which I could see might arise, and again at other times, my sole advice has been that it would be perfectly safe for her to sing in spite of some pathological difficulty. I have always felt with singers that my particular job was to preserve their voice as much as it was to treat any acute difficulty."[394] During a November 6, 1945 recital in Columbus, Ohio, a fan reported that Jeanette wasn't feeling well and a doctor treated her during intermission. She not only finished the show, but afterwards, she was charming to fans in her dressing room. During several performances of the 1951 tour of *The Guardsman*, Jeanette left the stage to throw up in the wings, but continued the show.

As the end of Jeanette's 1940 spring tour approached, she grew tired of trains. She said that she greatly looked forward to "a bed that doesn't wiggle" and "a bathroom big enough to turn around in."[395] Her tour concluded in California, with recitals in Pasadena (April 22) and Los Angeles (April 25), where she sang before a celebrity audience that included tenor Tito Schipa, soprano Marion Talley, and director Alfred Hitchcock, as well as many of her friends, like Connie and Johnny Mack Brown, Marian Nixon and William Seiter, Robert Z. Leonard, Ida Koverman, Eddie Mannix, Woody Van Dyke, and Louis B. Mayer. Gene, Anna, Blossom, and Irene Dunne attended both performances. Before returning to MGM for retakes on *New Moon*, Jeanette spent a week resting at the Desert Inn in Palm Springs, unaware of how the rumblings of war in Europe would soon affect her world.

Chapter Nine

While Jeanette was on her 1940 spring recital tour, Gene secretly took flying lessons at Santa Monica Airport. Upon her return, he presented her with his solo flight pin. Jeanette was more upset that he kept it a secret than about the dangers of flying. After Gene explained that he didn't want to worry her while she was on tour, Jeanette replied, "Pooh! What's the difference if I'm worried three months ago or now?"[396] Despite her concern whenever he went up, Jeanette, who hated airplanes, realized that she never could ask him to give up flying. She didn't want to ruin the pleasure it gave him or force him to deceive her. In 1938, when Gene was just a passenger and an aspiring pilot, she told the press, "If he has the will and courage to fly, if that's part of his man's life, I have no right to let my fears make a ninny or a liar out of him. . . . So when he flies, he flies with my blessing."[397]

Jeanette's fear of flying traced back to March 17, 1929, after fourteen passengers were killed in Newark, New Jersey, when a sightseeing plane, heading for a tour of Manhattan, crashed into a freight train. Two of the craft's three motors malfunctioned and authorities thought that the pilot was trying to land the plane when it crashed into the train. As of 2017, the crash remained in the top ten deadliest aviation accidents in New Jersey. Jeanette was one of the passengers on the plane's previous trip over Manhattan. She and others reported that the plane flew jerkily and made them airsick. Jeanette was so grateful to get back safely that she vowed never to fly again; naturally, she didn't keep that promise, since her work sometimes necessitated traveling by air. After Dramamine was introduced in 1949, she often chose to travel by plane rather than ship for long destinations, like Europe and Hawaii. In 1949, she told Marion Smith Glendening, "You will love flying over [to Hawaii] – I, frankly, think it is the only way."[398] Nevertheless, Jeanette remained a nervous flyer for the rest of her life. She said that flying was better when Gene was with her.

In later years, Jeanette and Gene often flew to see each other perform, causing friends to laugh that the Raymonds used planes like other people used taxis. One of Jeanette's many superstitions was that she thought that it was bad luck to be photographed boarding a plane, although she had no qualms about having her picture taken after a trip.

Jeanette's fear of flying didn't stop her from taking advantage of a wise business investment. In the early 1930s, a group of celebrities realized how long it took to get from Los Angeles to Reno, Nevada and the area around Lake Tahoe: twenty-four hours by train, fifteen hours by car, or five hours by plane. Jeanette formed a partnership with her *Oh, for a Man!* co-star Reginald Denny, actress Ann Harding, and others, and started the Los Angeles to Reno Air Service, which offered three faster and more convenient flights each day.

In 1940, before the United States entered the war, the Raymonds showed their patriotism by participating in many charitable events to support the European war effort. On January 17, while Gene was recovering from his tonsillectomy, Jeanette attended a dinner at the Cocoanut Grove to benefit Franco–British War Relief. On February

16, while Jeanette was in Shreveport, Louisiana during her spring recital tour, she made a personal appearance at an auction to benefit
the Finnish Relief Fund, which was started after the Soviet Union attacked Finland the previous fall. In May, when Jeanette heard about
the German invasion of Belgium and France, her first thought was
"Those poor little refugee children! They must have milk."[399] She arranged to send 425 pounds of powdered milk to Europe every year
until conditions were back to normal. Both Raymonds served on
the International Committee for Refugees in France, which not only
raised money and collected staples, like medical supplies, dried fruit,
powdered milk, and unrefined brown sugar, but also provided bicy-
cles, refrigerators, knitting needles, and gasoline.

On July 15, Jeanette sang "The Star Spangled Banner" on a radio
broadcast for the Red Cross and Allied Relief Funds. A week later,
the Raymonds attended a Red Cross benefit party at the estate of
Tom May, Executive Vice President of the May Company stores. At
the party, Jeanette, along with fellow actresses Irene Dunne, Myrna
Loy, and Claudette Colbert, collected funds for the charity. During
the war, when Jeanette heard that movie magazines were difficult to
obtain in the United Kingdom, she organized a committee of stars
to collect and ship them to fans there. In the fall of 1940, Jeanette
donated a wedding gown from one of her films for an exhibit of celebrity fashions at the Beverly Hills Hotel to benefit the British War
Relief Fund. Jeanette was touched when a British ambulance driver
wrote about how she took her gramophone to an air raid shelter and
Jeanette's records calmed the crowd.

One of Jeanette and Gene's favorite charities was the Los Angeles
Orthopaedic Hospital. Although Gene often was quoted that he
was not a great lover of children, a 1940 article called the hospital

Gene's pet charity, noting that he brought gifts to the young patients at Christmas, Easter, and Halloween, as well as between holidays. Every Christmas, Jeanette and Gene went to the hospital at 7:00 a.m. to sing carols to the children. It was only after Gene went overseas that their generosity was revealed. Through the years, Jeanette often supported charities involving disabled children, promoting fundraising campaigns for Easter Seals and The March of Dimes. The JMIFC contributed to rehabilitation facilities for children in Alabama and Kansas. On May 1, 1950, Jeanette participated in a radio program, broadcast on five Albany, New York stations, to help raise funds to establish headquarters for the Cerebral Palsy Foundation in Albany. On April 5, 1952, Jeanette appeared in an NBC radio drama, *Lesson in Love*, to help the Easter Seals campaign. On March 10, 1955, she sang two songs on *The 1955 Easter Seals Parade of Stars*.

In May 1940, after corresponding for two years, Gene convinced Roy to move to California to be near his sons. Gene bought him a Packard, and Roy drove across the country, shipping his Smooth Fox Terrier, Foxy, and his dog house to the Raymonds. Gene reported, "I guess Foxy has never seen so many dogs since he left the kennels in Long Island – because he seemed more concerned about playing with the other dogs than greeting Jeanette, Bob and me – he paid no attention whatsoever to us!"[400] Jeanette and Gene invited Roy to move in with them, but he refused, settling instead with Bob in a house at 9630 Yoakum Drive in Beverly Hills. Gene leased a Shell gas station at 4420 Riverside Drive in Burbank, setting up Roy as manager; Bob also worked there until he enlisted in the Army on March 11, 1941. Initially, Bob was stationed at Camp Roberts, near Paso Robles, California. Mrs. Kipling was furious when her sons became close to their father, but Jeanette's family eagerly accepted Roy.

When Roy moved to California in 1940, Jeanette's family warmly embraced him. Gene took this snapshot of Anna, Elsie's daughter-in-law, Patricia Wallace, Jeanette, Roy, Blossom, and Rocky.

Gene and Bob frequently went fishing with their father and took him to the racetrack. While Jeanette was on tour, Roy had Thanksgiving dinner at Anna's house with Anna, Blossom, and his sons; he spent Christmas at Twin Gables with the Raymonds.

During the summer of 1940, Jeanette filmed *Bitter Sweet*, her seventh movie with Nelson Eddy. *Bitter Sweet* was the tale of a struggling Viennese composer (Nelson) and his wife (Jeanette), a British singer from a wealthy family, who found success after the composer was killed in a duel. Noel Coward's score included "What Is Love," "Zigeuner," and the haunting duet "I'll See You Again." Jeanette prerecorded "If Love Were All," one of Coward's more popular songs, but it was cut from the movie before its release. The film was nominated for Academy Awards for Best Color Cinematography (Oliver Marsh and

Allen M. Davey) and Best Art Direction (Cedric Gibbons and John S. Detlie). It cost $1.1 million and grossed $2.2 million, now almost $20 million and over $39.5 million.

Gene and Roy deep sea fishing in 1940.

On August 13, Jeanette hosted a surprise birthday party for Gene at Anna's house. Eight days later, she surprised Blossom and Gene's brother, Bob, with a joint birthday party. Jeanette loved surprising others, but didn't like people surprising her. The Raymonds spent Labor Day weekend in Lake Arrowhead at the home of oil executive Hoke Woodward.

In 1940, the Raymonds paid Blossom $100, now almost $1,800, for secretarial work on a play synopsis. It is not known if it was a project that they planned to do together or one that they were considering as an investment.

On October 16, 1940, Gene registered for the draft. His hair was dark for *Mr. and Mrs. Smith* (1941).

On October 16, 1940, Gene was one of the first actors in Hollywood to register for the draft. His brother registered at the same time. Later in October, the Raymonds went to a ranch near Victorville, California for a brief vacation before Jeanette embarked on her fall recital tour, which began on November 11, 1940 in Little Rock, Arkansas. She sang in eleven cities, while Gene supervised remodeling and repairs at Twin Gables and filmed *Mr. and Mrs. Smith* (1941).

Prior to 1939, Thanksgiving was celebrated on the last Thursday in November, rather than the fourth Thursday, as it is today. From 1939 to 1941, President Franklin D. Roosevelt moved the holiday to the second-to-last Thursday to bolster retail sales since, at that time, it was considered improper to have Christmas sales before Thanksgiving. Many Republicans, including Jeanette, dubbed it Franksgiving. On Thanksgiving 1940, Jeanette sang in Cincinnati, Ohio. Since she couldn't eat heavily before a performance, she and her entourage celebrated a week later on the traditional date. Although she was away from her family for Thanksgiving, she told reporters that she would be home for Christmas, partly because she was slightly jealous when Gene worked with a pretty co-star, like Carole Lombard, even though Lombard was married to Clark Gable. "I'm accustomed to the girls admiring him, but I know I've got him," Jeanette said. "I'm a poor loser. But you see, I've won him and that's what counts."[401]

Jeanette continued to shatter attendance records wherever she went, breaking the records set by humorist Will Rogers in El Paso, Texas, and tenor Enrico Caruso in Springfield, Massachusetts. Although Jeanette later was very vocal about her politics, during her 1940 fall tour, she refused to endorse a Presidential candidate. "I don't believe it is an actress' place to discuss politics publicly," she said, "and, after all, I sing before Republicans and Democrats."[402] She spoke sadly of the war in Europe and the May 1940 German invasion of France: "France, at least the France we knew, will have to be just a fond memory. England, too. I don't think they will ever be the same, at least not in our lifetime."[403] Although Adolf Hitler banned many musical compositions, Jeanette continued to sing German songs in her recitals, insisting, "Many things German are too fine to give up in spite of the way we feel about Hitler."[404]

When Jeanette was in Nelson Eddy's native Rhode Island, she addressed their relationship. "We have had clashes," she admitted, "but they were the petty quarrels that come with long hours of rehearsals and strain of studio work. But we are lasting friends."[405] In Providence, she saw her first singing teacher, Wassili Leps, whom she studied with in Philadelphia and New York, as well as Nelson Eddy's father, whom she met three years earlier when he visited the set of *The Girl of the Golden West*.

While Jeanette was gone, Gene filmed *Mr. and Mrs. Smith*, a screwball comedy about a couple (Carole Lombard and Robert Montgomery) who found out that their marriage wasn't legal. Gene played Montgomery's law partner and friend, who pursued Lombard. He welcomed working with esteemed director Alfred Hitchcock, who asked Gene to darken his blonde hair a couple of shades because it photographed platinum. Sources disagree over whether it turned blue or purple after the initial dying, much to Jeanette's amusement. Gene ended up coloring his hair brown for the movie, but it photographed even darker in black and white. Neither fans, nor Jeanette, liked him as a brunette and, in future roles, Gene went back to his natural blonde hair. Jeanette complained to reporters, "Imagine ruining those beautiful platinum locks like that. Of course, I don't blame him for getting tired of being kidded about having a permanent wave and of peroxided [sic] hair. But that wave is natural and so is the platinum. And I love it."[406] After the premiere, Gene wired Jeanette on her recital tour: "PICTURE WENT VERY WELL ALL SCENES SEEMED TO CLICK HITCH WAS PLEASED ITS [sic] AN IMPORTANT PICTURE AND BESIDES THAT I LOVE YOU."[407]

On December 1, Gene attended Jeanette's recital in Hartford,

Connecticut and, after her afternoon performance, they took a train to New York City so they could see the opening of the Metropolitan Opera the next day. Gene also joined her for her recital in White Plains, New York, which concluded her tour. Afterwards, they returned to New York City, where they saw shows and shopped. Jeanette told reporters, "I love to shop in New York and just walking up and down Fifth Avenue looking in the windows is such fun, especially at this time of year when everything is so gay."[408] Near the end of their vacation, Jeanette wrote to her secretary, Grace Smyth, "We're exhausted but happy!"[409]

Due to the Raymonds' busy work schedules, much of Jeanette and Gene's life involved saying hello and goodbye in train stations. Here, they kissed at Grand Central Station during Jeanette's 1940 tour. Notice Jeanette's monogrammed handbag.

There were rumors that Jean Arthur wanted Gene to star opposite her in *The Devil and Miss Jones* (1941), but Robert Cummings replaced him. Gene also was announced for *Three Girls and a Gob* with Maureen O'Hara, produced by the Raymonds' old friend, Harold Lloyd. However, by the time the film came to the screen in 1941, it was known as *A Girl, a Guy and a Gob*, and Lucille Ball and George Murphy had the leads.

After the holidays, Jeanette went back on the road. On January 14, 1941, she opened the second half of her tour in Memphis, Tennessee. At her first recital, just as she inhaled to sing, a train whistle blew. It was just off pitch and caused Jeanette and the audience to burst into laughter. Columbus, Ohio proclaimed the day of her recital "Jeanette MacDonald Day" and Mayor Floyd Green gave Jeanette a flowery proclamation. In Huntington, West Virginia, she drew a bigger crowd than 1940 Republican Presidential candidate Wendell Willkie. In Columbia, South Carolina, chartered buses brought fans from sixty-seven cities in four states to Jeanette's recital. After she heard that several women fainted when Nelson Eddy performed in Pittsburgh, Pennsylvania, she kidded reporters, "I'll be downright disappointed if a couple of men don't swoon for me!"[410]

Due to the flu, initially reported as a cold, Jeanette had to postpone her Pittsburgh recital, as well as her performance in Asheville, North Carolina. The Pittsburgh doctor described her throat as badly inflamed. In between the dates, she thought that she recovered enough to sing in Roanoke, Virginia. Because there was no direct train from Pittsburgh to Roanoke, she had to transfer in Washington, D.C. Her Pittsburgh train was late and she missed her connection, forcing her to spend the night in Washington. She further irritated her throat when she inhaled tear gas in the Roanoke auditorium. The gas came from moving National Guard equipment in the venue earlier in the day; it not only affected Jeanette, but the audience as well. The Roanoke doctor ordered her to cancel her Asheville recital and rest in Florida for a few days before her next scheduled performance in Orlando.

Some twenty-first century fans erroneously claimed that Jeanette really wasn't sick, but cancelled recitals to have a rendezvous with Nelson Eddy, who was in Washington, D.C. for President Franklin D. Roosevelt's inauguration on January 20. They were unaware that Nelson returned to California on January 23, the day before Jeanette arrived in Washington. Additionally, Jeanette took her marriage seriously and would not have been unfaithful to Gene.

There is a tremendous amount of evidence that Jeanette really was sick. Newspaper reports in Pittsburgh mentioned that she had a fluttery stomach on the train en route to the city and, that during a press conference in her hotel room, she sat by the radiator to keep warm. She also had to cancel an appearance at a reception in Pittsburgh because she wasn't feeling well. Tax information for Jeanette's 1941 tour noted medical expenses in many cities. Most were a few dollars, presumably for routine prescriptions or a masseuse. The highest were from hotel doctors in Pittsburgh for $40.02, Washington for $16.48, Roanoke for $19.65, and New Orleans for $27.24, and a private physician in Orlando for $60. Currently, these are about $685, $282, $336, $466, and $1,027. In a wire to Gene, sent from Roanoke, she mentioned eating pineapple sherbet to soothe her throat. Jeanette was much too professional to cancel a performance unless she was really sick and could harm her voice by singing.

The 1941 tour also included Jeanette's first Latin American engagement, a recital in Havana, Cuba. She joked to reporters about Cuban politics: "I'm afraid the revolution down there wasn't over me, although I rather wish it had been."[411]

When reporters asked about Jeanette's absence from Gene, she insisted that occasional periods apart were good for their marriage. "Then when we get together again we have fresh things to talk about and we appreciate each other ever so much more," she said.[412] "Gene's just wonderful about it," she told another correspondent. "I guess I dislike it more than he—but no matter where I am we talk by telephone three or four times weekly." She added, "In spite of myself, I get lonesome for that certain someone."[413] At one press conference, she excitedly waved two letters in the air, saying, "One from my husband and one from my mother, what could be nicer than that!"[414]

Gene met Jeanette in New York City, where, on February 21, they appeared on the radio show *Campbell Playhouse*, in an episode titled "The Wreck on Deliverance." Jeanette planned to perform "Let Me Always Sing," however NBC and CBS were in the midst of a boycott of American Society of Composers, Authors and Publishers (ASCAP) compositions. The boycott, due to licensing fees charged by ASCAP, lasted from January 1 to October 29, 1941. Instead, Jeanette sang "Songs My Mother Taught Me" and "Les filles de Cadix." After the broadcast, on February 24, Jeanette returned to Pittsburgh for her rescheduled recital. Then, on March 2, she went back to New York to appear on *The Pause That Refreshes on the Air*, a radio program starring the Raymonds' friend, conductor/pianist Andre Kostelanetz. Jeanette sang "The Merry Widow Waltz" (also known as "I Love You So") and "Believe Me if All Those Endearing Young Charms," along with the hymn "I Think When I Read That Sweet Story of Old," which Jeanette sang as a child to the same tune.

On March 4, Gene accompanied Jeanette to Asheville for her final recital, rescheduled from January 28. After she sang "Let Me Always Sing" to thunderous applause, she marched backstage and brought Gene out to join her. The next day, the Raymonds headed home to California. In April, they hosted a barbecue for Gene's brother, Bob, on leave from Camp Roberts for Easter.

Gene often met Jeanette when she was on tour. This shot was taken in Asheville in March 1941. Naturally, Jeanette found dogs wherever she went.

In the spring of 1941, Gene received his pilot's license, having scored 100% on both the government's navigation and meteorology tests. Days later, he was doing "lazy eights" above Malibu when the engine of his plane malfunctioned. He had to make a forced landing at Santa Monica Airport, his plane setting down with a series of thumps. A few months later, after leaving Monterey, California, where he was visiting his brother, Gene made another forced landing when he experienced motor trouble about eight miles from Paso Robles, California. Despite the fact that the motor died, he was able to land the plane on an Army airfield there. Army attendants questioned him, but, after he identified himself and explained that the motor swallowed a valve, they invited him to spend the night. Gene was nonplussed by both incidents, causing Jeanette to later dub him "my air fiend."[415]

After Jeanette returned from her spring tour, she and Gene finally got a chance to appear together on screen in *Smilin' Through*, with each playing dual roles. They were coached by Jane Cowl, who not only acted in the play on Broadway, but also co-wrote the script with Jane Murfin, using the pseudonym Allan Langdon Martin. The plot was a sentimental tale of lovers, who met in England during the First World War, only to discover that, years earlier, the man's father accidentally shot the woman's aunt during her wedding. The woman's uncle/guardian was bitter about the man's father killing his intended bride and refused to give the young couple his blessing. Jeanette and Gene played the young lovers, as well as their relatives, and Brian Aherne portrayed Jeanette's uncle/fiancé. On January 5, 1942, the Raymonds and Aherne reprised their roles on a *Lux Radio Theatre* broadcast. The Raymonds entertained one hundred soldiers who attended the radio show and, afterward, kept busy signing autographs.

The Raymonds chatted with Brian Aherne, *Lux Radio Theatre* host Cecil B. DeMille, and Ann E. Todd, who played Jeanette's character as a child in the radio version of *Smilin' Through*, broadcast January 5, 1942. Later, Todd was Jeanette's middle child in the movie *Three Daring Daughters* (1948).

Jeanette did all of the singing in *Smilin' Through*. In addition to the title song, she sang "The Kerry Dance" and "Ouvre ton Coeur," both of which she often performed in her recitals, "Drink to Me Only with Thine Eyes," "A Little Love, A Little Kiss," "There's a Long, Long Trail," and "Land of Hope and Glory." She also prerecorded "Smiles," but her part was cut before the movie's release.

Jeanette and Gene enjoyed working together, although, later, they both said that their love scenes were among the most difficult that they ever filmed. They did not elaborate why; however, given their other comments, it's possible that they had to remember to stay in character or that they were uncomfortable being romantic in front of a crew. Jeanette told a reporter, "When you do a love scene with a stranger—or, worse, with someone you don't particularly care to have near you (*and that can happen*) you are a little timid about putting your head here, or there, on his shoulder—you don't know just how you will fit into his arms. Well, *I know how I fit in Gene's arms*."[416] Gene described it more succinctly: "*We don't grope!*"[417] Jeanette didn't understand the studio's reluctance to pair a husband and wife on screen. "When a married couple are [sic] in love—and if they're not, they wouldn't want to work together—there is real romance. There is the genuine article," she insisted. "You can believe love scenes when you see a husband and wife who are in love, making love. The thrill is not manufactured. The glamour is not gelatin. The director does not have to resort to emotional hypodermics. The emotion is not merely in the script. There is something back of two people who are in love, making love. Something back of that kiss, that embrace, that look."[418]

Every day, the Raymonds had lunch in Jeanette's dressing room. They watched the rushes together and, if one was shooting later than the other, they waited to ride home together.

Jeanette was impressed with Gene's acting skills, bragging that he didn't need any phony stimuli for a crying scene. She also was pleased to learn that he was kind to the crew, just as she was. The most difficult scene for her was the death scene, which took thirty-five takes. Gene was exceptionally nervous filming the love scenes, as well as the scene in which his character shot Jeanette, worrying that something would go wrong with the prop pistol and somehow he really would shoot her. He was equally awed to see his wife working, noting how punctual and professional she was, as well as how much she loved her work. He told a reporter, "She is open-eyed and eager all the time. She has worked awfully hard, but she has loved doing it. Because she loves doing it, she is where she is."[419] During filming, Jeanette said, "When you and your husband work in separate studios, in separate pictures, you come home and listen to each other's stories, and you *want* to, *but*—you have your own story to tell. Now we have *our* story to tell. It's very nice."[420] They found some real-life habits creeping into their screen performances, like automatically kissing after an argument. Director Frank Borzage told Jeanette that it wasn't necessary for her to kiss Gene during the scene, but she insisted that they always kissed to make up in private life. When Jeanette was asked about working with Gene, she replied, "After having been married to him for four years, and now, having worked with him, I still like him best—as a husband and as an actor!"[421]

The Raymonds' fourth anniversary fell during the filming of *Smilin' Through*. Jeanette gave Gene horseshoe cufflinks studded with gold nails. Taking a tip from the traditional fourth anniversary gifts of linen or silk, Gene arranged for silk gifts to arrive each hour of the day. The carefully wrapped packages included panties, brassieres, nightgowns, and a beanie, all made of silk. He also gave her some corn silk, with a note that it wasn't good for smoking. A spool of silk was wrapped in a box inside a series of larger boxes to fool her. While they were filming, a package arrived, with a card reading, "Something you always want and never have enough of."[422] Inside were fifty pairs of extremely thin silk hose. Jeanette was so thrilled that she kissed him and it took twenty minutes to repair their smeared makeup.

After the preview, Gene was upset when Nicholas Schenck, head of MGM's parent company, Loew's, Inc., insisted that one of Gene's most dramatic scenes be cut because it left the audience in tears. It showed the returning soldier, whose legs were injured in World War I, struggling on crutches and falling head first on the church steps. Gene recalled that Schenck was afraid that it would be considered anti-war propaganda and dissuade men from enlisting when the United States inevitably entered the war in Europe. In October 1941, *Smilin' Through* was released and, as Schenck predicted, the United States' entry into the war in December affected the box office over the coming months, as many audiences did not want to see a film that depicted the results of war. Although foreign earnings of $1,536,000 exceeded the cost of filming, the domestic release lost $237,000. These figures are now about $26.3 million and $4 million. It was Jeanette and Gene's only movie together.

Jeanette observed, "Instead of bringing our working lives closer together, it made a wide gap in our thinking. We abandoned our hope of becoming a Lunt and Fontaine [sic] of the movies for the time being."[423] Alfred Lunt and Lynn Fontanne were considered the greatest husband and wife acting team in the American theater; Jeanette and Gene often said that they aspired to be like them. In 1951, the Raymonds toured in a stage version of *The Guardsman*, which the Lunts did on Broadway (1924) and on screen (1931).

Around the time that Jeanette was filming *Smilin' Through*, she appeared on three non-commercial radio broadcasts. On May 4, she was on a program for the Children's Home Society of Los Angeles, hosted by Walter White, Jr. She was among the celebrities interviewing orphans and discussing cases from the home. On May 28, Jeanette and Nelson Eddy sang songs from *Bitter Sweet* for a broadcast that aired in England. On July 18, Jeanette sang "On Wings of Song" on *Proudly We Hail*, a public service show for the U.S. Army and Air Forces that paid tribute to defense workers.

Despite Roy's apparent happiness near his sons, in May 1941, after a year in California, he went back to New York, debating about where he wanted to live. According to a list of papers that Gene gave Louis Swarts after Roy's death, Roy's chauffeur's license expired in May so, presumably, his driver's license did too. In New York, a chauffeur's license was required to deliver furniture, which Roy needed for his upholstery business. Prior to 1941, in New York, both types of licenses were only good for one year; beginning in 1941, they were good for three years.

In early June, Gene tried to convince his father to return to California. "You have probably found that the cost of living is infinitely higher back there than it is here," he wrote. "It seems to me you have to have almost twice as much money to start in a business there as here – and even then, you don't get the same value. I think the climate in California is much better for your head. All in all, it's a pretty nice State [sic] to live in!"[424]

After Gene finished filming *Smilin' Through*, he planned to take a fishing trip; he invited Roy to drive out and join him. Roy sold his New York upholstery business and returned to California, arriving around July 2, in time to celebrate the Fourth of July at Anna's house, as well as Anna's seventieth birthday on July 6. He stayed with Jeanette and Gene until he could find a permanent place to live. In mid-July, he and Gene went fishing near Santa Catalina Island.

Shortly after the fishing trip, on July 21, Roy had surgery to remove the hernia sac of a right inguinal hernia. An inguinal hernia is caused by fatty or intestinal tissue pushing through a weakness in the abdominal wall near the right inguinal canal, leading to a bulge around the groin. The day after the operation, Roy was diagnosed with cardiac dilatation, an increase in the size of the cavities of the heart, and pulmonary edema, fluid in the lungs. At 5:35 a.m. on July 25, he died at Good Samaritan Hospital at the age of fifty-four. Although Jeanette's autobiography and some newspaper reports claimed that he had a heart attack on the operating table, there is no mention of a heart attack on Roy's death certificate; heart disease and fluid in the lungs are listed as the primary causes of death. Jeanette, Gene, and Bob were at Roy's bedside when he died.

On July 26, the Reverend H.R. Shaffer of Grandview Community Presbyterian Church in Glendale conducted a private memorial service at a chapel at Forest Lawn, Glendale. Gene and Bob provided tributes to their father. Gene's hinted at the differences between his parents. He wrote:

> I believe Dad's greatest quality was kindness. To accomplish a kind act or to be the beneficiary of one constituted Life's [sic] greatest joy for him and his. Gratefulness was ingrained.
>
> And yet there were many unkindness [sic] directed toward him during his life, a fact which in his habitual kindness, he was never quite able to understand. Unkind, ungenerous or hurtful acts against him found him bewildered and incredible. He preferred to ignore them rather than defend himself. His generosity was a great virtue.
>
> Though not endowed greatly with material things in life, what he did have, he worked hard and honestly for,

and with his own hands, as he often remarked. Always he gave freely of what he had, and asked nothing in return. His reward was a grateful feeling in his heart that he had been <u>able</u> to give what was needed.

The last year of his life held the greatest joy for him. He is happy in the knowledge that those he loved most, and who held for him the kindest thoughts, were beside him, loving him.[425]

Following the service, Roy's body left for Staten Island by train. The next day, Jeanette and Gene took a train to New York for the funeral. On July 31, Reverend George Dow conducted the service at the Methodist Episcopal Church at Woodrow Cemetery in Staten Island. Roy's friend, Reverend Frank Nickel, eulogized him, noting, "His face was young and his smile inevitable. He loved to sing, joke and laugh." Nickel also discussed Roy's extreme kindness and generosity, echoing Gene's sentiments. "His material possessions were few and he gave of them freely. But his real generosity was measurable in the large amounts of himself which he gave to those who had need of him, receiving meant much less to him, than giving. This was the <u>Blessed</u> part of the man." Nickel concluded, "There had been much unhappiness in his life, but I believe his last years were his happiest. This is just as it should be. This is ideal."[426] Roy is buried in the Guyon family plot in Woodrow Cemetery in Grave 44, Section 2. His headstone reads, "LEROY D. GUYON, YOUNGEST SON OF CORNELIUS D. GUYON AND MARY BURGHER GUYON, BORN JAN. 4, 1887, DIED JULY 25, 1941."

Jeanette said that Gene relaxed and opened up while Roy was living in California; however, after Roy's death, Gene retreated back into his shell. She told her friend, Entertainment Editor Lily May

Caldwell, "It was very sudden and a great shock, as we were so terribly fond of him. It has been a very sad time for Gene."[427] The Raymonds sold Roy's dog, Foxy, presumably because of his pedigree and the fact that he would have been a sad reminder of Roy.

Jeanette and Gene spent the summer of 1941 at home, entertaining Elsie and Barney, and the Halfords. On August 14, Gene played in a celebrity softball game to benefit Mount Sinai Hospital (now Cedars–Sinai Medical Center); Jeanette sat in the stands, rooting for him. Six days later, the Raymonds attended a party for mezzo-soprano Risë Stevens and her husband, actor Walter Szuroby, hosted by real estate developer Harold Janss and his daughter, Betty. Gene played the ukulele, while their houseguests, Pete and Marge Halford, did the hula. On September 22, Jeanette recorded six songs from *Smilin' Through* for an album for RCA Victor. This and other 1940s albums usually were made up of three 78 RPM (revolutions per minute) records with single songs on each side.

On September 28, the Raymonds initiated what would come to be called Date Leaves. It all began when Jeanette read a letter from a soldier in a national magazine, wishing that he and his fellow servicemen could meet "nice" girls, prompting Jeanette and Gene to open their home. "Gene and I want to do something personal about the problem of entertaining the boys in the service," she told reporters. "Oh, it's fairly easy to contribute to various causes—in the way of donations and so on, but we've searched for, and think we have an idea, whereby we may do something more—something by which we contribute more of *ourselves*."[428] Jeanette said that she wanted a catchy, descriptive name, like the charity Bundles for Britain, hence, the visits to Twin Gables were christened Date Leaves.

Every other Sunday, the Raymonds invited ten soldiers and sailors from nearby camps and ten coeds from the University of Southern

California (USC) and University of California, Los Angeles (UCLA) to Twin Gables for an afternoon of relaxation. Jeanette worked with the United Service Organization (USO) and the Deans of Women from the universities to extend invitations. The couples could swim, dance, play cards and ping-pong, and sing around the piano, with Jeanette and Gene acting as hosts, pianists, and chaperones. The Raymonds supplied trunks for the servicemen, but the coeds brought their own swimsuits.

Before the 4:00 dinner, Jeanette and Gene offered popcorn, sandwiches, and cookies as snacks. Initially, Gene barbecued hamburgers, grilled sirloin, or cooked ham, and Jeanette served her famous baked beans and homemade ice cream. After meat rationing went into effect, Gene roasted chicken. At one Date Leave, Jeanette served scrapple— a fried loaf made of pork, corn flour, wheat flour, and spices, popular in Pennsylvania—only to discover that six of her sailor guests were from Philadelphia. One of them remarked, "Wow! This tastes like the real thing!" Jeanette responded, "If it isn't, I've been eating wrong all my life!"[429]

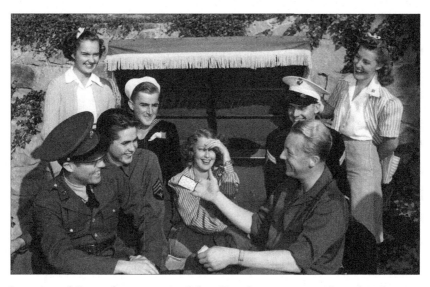

Jeanette and Gene often entertained their Date Leave guests with card tricks.

The Raymonds chatted with their guests, helping them relax and feel at home. Jeanette and Gene even entertained them with card tricks. Several soldiers told reporter Mayme Ober Peak, "Don't wake me up; I'm dreaming."[430] Jeanette said that she quickly learned two things: 1) don't serve baked beans and 2) keep the dogs in the kennel so the guests wouldn't get fleas. She told a reporter, "I'm still being kidded about my first faux pas in the menu line. Of all things, I served beans because I love them and have a wonderful recipe for a baked variety. You should have seen the men's faces!"[431] In addition to beans causing gas, when Gene entered Basic Training, he complained about all of the starch in military cuisine.

Occasionally, the Raymonds had amusing experiences at the Date Leaves. When a young soldier asked Jeanette to sing his mother's favorite song, she felt sentimental—until she learned that it was "Frankie and Johnnie," a popular song about a woman who shot her cheating boyfriend. Jeanette shocked the soldier by singing every verse and giving it her all. She also surprised her guests when she did the jitterbug and rumba with them, a contrast to her sedate screen roles. Sometimes the Raymonds held jitterbug contests, with the winners receiving a book of defense stamps.

One young soldier asked Jeanette to play gin rummy for money. When he won $1.56 (now about $27.00), he requested a check. "I didn't want the cash," he explained to a reporter. "I wanted a check with Jeanette MacDonald's name on it so I can show the boys back at camp that I beat her."[432] When some of the servicemen arrived, they were shy, in awe of being entertained by movie stars. However, one soldier told Mayme Ober Peak that he felt at home at Twin Gables. "I saw Miss MacDonald in 'Bittersweet' [sic]," he said. "I thought she'd be like this."[433]

Jeanette was particularly touched by a sing-along at one of the Date Leaves, which ended with everyone joining in on "The Star Spangled

Banner." "Those boys standing at attention, singing our national [sic] anthem [sic], looked so young, so vulnerable," she observed. "If I had needed anything to bolster my desire to do what little I can for them I'm sure that scene would have done it. We just can't half realize that these boys are preparing to protect us. As individuals we owe them something. It is so easy to think of the Army, the Navy, the Airforce [sic], the Marines, the Coast Guard. We have to learn, I guess to think of all those services as made up of individual human youngsters. Gene and I are learning, and it is giving us a deep personal happiness to know that we are spreading some joy among those boys. And at the same time, we're having the fun of our lives!"[434]

Occasionally, some of the servicemen were moved to tears, a combination of loneliness, homesickness, and gratitude for the Raymonds' hospitality. One G.I. told the Raymonds, "My parents never go to the movies. They won't know who Jeanette MacDonald and Gene Raymond are. But when they get my letter they will love you because of the joy you have given their son today."[435] After another serviceman left Twin Gables, he spent two hours composing a thank you letter to assure that the Raymonds would receive it the next day.

In 1959, Jeanette said that she still heard from some of the men who attended the Date Leaves, adding "It's very gratifying!"[436] Long after Jeanette's death, men who attended the Date Leaves continued to remember the Raymonds' hospitality. In 1992, JMIFC President Clara Rhoades received a letter from a soldier who was invited to a Date Leave. He wrote, "This was while I was in the Army Air Force during WW2, and I must say that she did not look like a movie star to me, but a beautiful red-headed girl. She was very nice to everybody there. . . . I will always remember Miss MacDonald as one of my favorite stars."[437]

The Raymonds were surprised when they received criticism for letting the servicemen dance and play cards on Sunday, at a time when it was thought of as a holy day of rest. "We have every respect for the opinions of these critics naturally," Jeanette insisted. "However, we feel just as much respect for the fact that the service of the boys, if our emergency becomes even more serious, will not be restricted to certain days of the week. So we shall not restrict them in their innocent enjoyment of our Sunday hospitality."[438]

Jeanette urged other celebrities to follow the Raymonds' example with Date Leaves, and it wasn't long before actress Constance Bennett and her husband, actor Gilbert Roland, and Mildred and Harold Lloyd also were opening their homes to servicemen. Even Anna participated, hosting two G.I.s and two women for badminton or croquet, along with a family dinner. Jeanette wrote an article on how to host a Date Leave so ordinary citizens could entertain G.I.s. The idea spread across the United States and Canada.

After Gene entered the service, when Jeanette wasn't traveling, she continued to hold Date Leaves at Twin Gables. Despite her admitted frugality, she let her military guests use her phone to call their families long distance. She also allowed servicemen to use the Twin Gables grounds and pool, whether she was home or not.

Sometimes the servicemen brought the Raymonds gifts. While Gene was in Basic Training, a group of sailors gave Jeanette a small heart-shaped locket with a Navy seal on the front, and Gene a Zippo lighter with the Navy insignia. Jeanette wrote to ask if he wanted her to save it until he returned home. Another group of sailors gave her a gold identification bracelet inscribed with "Cousin Jennie" and her blood type, which she still wore in 1944. She sent records to the servicemen and regularly corresponded with some of them.

Around the time of the first Date Leave, Jeanette began work on *I Married an Angel*, her eighth and final movie with Nelson Eddy. Coincidentally, in April 1933, shortly after Nelson signed with MGM, his first film was announced as *I Married an Angel,* with Jeanette as his leading lady. Rather than *The Merry Widow,* Jeanette's initial MGM contract called for her to make *The Cat and the Fiddle* and *I Married an Angel.* That production was cancelled because of censorship issues enforced by the Production Code Administration and, instead, in 1938, the Richard Rodgers and Lorenz Hart musical became a successful Broadway show, starring Vera Zorina, Dennis King, and Vivienne Segal, all of whom worked with Jeanette on screen. The score included the title song and "Spring Is Here," both of which became standards.

When *I Married an Angel* finally was filmed, the plot, which concerned a playboy marrying an angel, was changed to make the bulk of the story a dream. Both Jeanette and Nelson were concerned about the script and the censors, and both were vocal in their dislike for the finished product.

I Married an Angel was a troubled production on many levels. Initially, George Cukor was supposed to direct; however, when Cukor insisted on eight weeks of preparation, the studio replaced him with Roy Del Ruth. After several weeks of filming, Woody Van Dyke took over for Del Ruth. Van Dyke, who had a bad heart and was dying of cancer, was involved in recruiting for the Marines. Between his health and military obligations, he sometimes relied on help from others and, between multiple people contributing ideas and the censors insisting on cuts, it left some confusing scenes in the finished picture. Audiences disliked the film because it was a departure from the typical MacDonald/Eddy operetta. *I Married an Angel* lost $725,000, currently almost $11 million, and was MGM's least successful film of 1942. Modern audiences are much more appreciative of the movie's music and humor. Many twenty-first century fans especially like Jeanette's jitterbug with Binnie Barnes during "A Twinkle in Your Eye."

On September 18, 1941, Gene's brother, Bob, suffered facial lacerations when his car collided with a gasoline truck as he was driving from Monterey to Fort Ord, the Army post on California's Monterey Bay where he was stationed. His passenger, twenty-year-old Private Eugene Gibson, was killed in the accident. Two months later, the Raymonds hosted Thanksgiving dinner for Anna, the Halfords, Jeanette's childhood friend, Peg Watson, and Bob. One of the things for which Jeanette and Gene were most thankful was that Bob was not more seriously hurt, as initial reports said that he also suffered internal injuries. The Halfords, whose children remained in Hawaii because their two daughters were in school, returned to Honolulu on December 3. Four days later, the world changed forever.

Chapter Ten

In late 1941, to boost Army morale, Gene and his brother, Bob, wrote *Gold Brickers of 1941*, a servicemen's show to be staged at Fort Ord, with plans to take it to as many camps as possible. That fall, they rehearsed for six weeks; the final dress rehearsal was scheduled for the evening of December 7. However, that morning, the Japanese launched a surprise attack on Hawaii, sinking the USS Arizona, damaging seven other American battleships, destroying over three hundred airplanes, and killing 2,403 people. By late afternoon, the hundred-member cast of *Gold Brickers* was sent to guard the California coast against enemy airplanes, and the show was cancelled. Years later, Gene joked, "I have always thought that the only reason the Japs attacked Pearl Harbor was to prevent me from making *Gold Brickers of 1941* a reality!!"[439] On December 17, 1941, Gene copyrighted the show. In 1942, while Gene was serving in England, Bob successfully produced *Gold Brickers* alone.

Hours after Pearl Harbor, the Japanese attacked the Philippines, destroying dozens more American planes on the ground. Since only Congress can declare war, the next day, President Franklin D. Roosevelt asked for a declaration of war against the Empire of Japan.

It was unanimously approved, with the exception of lifelong paci-fist Jeannette Rankin, United States Representative from Montana. In President Roosevelt's famous speech that began, "Yesterday, December 7, 1941—a date which will live in infamy," he alerted the country that the United States was at war with Japan.[440] Later that day, diplomatic representatives of Nazi Germany and the Kingdom of Italy delivered their countries' declarations of war to Secretary of State Cordell Hull. In response, President Roosevelt asked Congress for a declaration of war against Germany and Italy; it also was approved almost unanimously, with only Representative Rankin withholding her vote. With the United States now part of the war, the Raymonds both immediately wanted to do all that they could for their country.

On December 10, Jeanette was one of the founding members of the Hollywood Victory Committee, along with the Committee's Chairmen, Clark Gable, James Cagney, George Murphy, and Hattie McDaniel, as well as many other stars. The organization's goal was to encourage entertainers who weren't in the military to contribute to the war effort by selling defense bonds and boosting the troops' morale. The Hollywood Victory Committee worked with USO Camp Shows, Inc. to provide entertainment for camps and military outposts, as well as with the Armed Forces Radio Service (AFRS), which pro-duced broadcasts for servicemen. Jeanette said, "I liked making the Armed Forces Radio transcriptions because I often wondered where and under what circumstances our men would listen to them."[441] The camp shows paid some performers, but the Hollywood stars donated their services, receiving only their expenses, which they often waived.

After Pearl Harbor, Gene was offered an important job in civilian defense work. Jeanette told him that she hoped that he would take it, but she didn't allow herself to interfere or pressure him. They always discussed the pros and cons of important matters and let the other make up his or her mind. Gene was hesitant to accept the offer, insisting, "If everybody takes defense jobs, there'll be no need for planes because there'll be nobody left to fly them."[442]

That Christmas, the Raymonds, who usually received about six thousand Christmas cards each year from fans, asked them to purchase defense stamps instead. Defense stamps cost 10¢ (now about $1.71) and, when enough were accumulated, citizens could purchase a defense bond, which, after ten years, increased in value. Following the attack on Pearl Harbor, the name was changed to war bond. American workers were asked to give 10% of their weekly salaries to buy bonds, which helped finance equipment needed to fight the war. Celebrities crisscrossed the country, selling bonds to an eager public that was as anxious to catch a glimpse of their favorite stars in person at the rallies, as they were to support the war effort. Credits at the end of movies urged audiences to buy bonds, which were sold in movie theater lobbies; if customers purchased a bond, they could see the film for free. During the four years that they were sold, Americans showed their patriotism by purchasing $190 billion in bonds, now over $2.6 trillion. Jeanette usually gave herself a piece of jewelry as a Christmas gift. In 1941, she cancelled the order and bought bonds instead.

A few days before Christmas, Jeanette and Gene had their traditional hanging of the greens ceremony, tying gifts for each expected guest on a tree decorated in red, white, and blue, which was set up in the playhouse near the pool. They hosted Christmas dinner at Twin Gables for Naval Officers stationed in Los Angeles, as well as Helen Ferguson (who had been widowed on November 12, when her husband had a heart attack at age fifty-two), Helen's two stepdaughters, Evelyn and Margaret Hargreaves, and some servicemen that they were entertaining for the holidays. Jeanette's secretary, Sylvia Grogg Wright, told Lily May Caldwell, "After dinner they played games and music and had a wonderful day. Mr. and Mrs. Raymond said it was one of the best Christmas Days they have ever spent together. They get so much fun out of entertaining the boys from camp that I never know who has the best time … [sic] the boys or their host and hostess!"[443]

At Gene's request, Jeanette gave him an identification tag for Christmas. She knew that it was his way of warning her that he was going to enlist. Later, she admitted that she knew that Gene would enlist long before Pearl Harbor, when, after visiting his brother at camp, he came home full of war talk. Jeanette had the stones removed from her engagement ring and from the sapphire and diamond dinner ring that Gene gave her for her birthday in 1936, and used the platinum for the tag. "Now he will always have something of *us* with him," she said. "Small comfort, but it is amazing what big comforts small ones can be, these days."[444] In Jeanette's autobiography, she confided, "I suspect that he was the only man in the U.S. Armed forces [sic] in World War II to wear platinum dog tags, a secret he kept as securely as if he had stolen the platinum."[445] After Christmas, Gene arranged for the stones to be put in a restyled ring as a New Year's gift. Jeanette often wore it with her favorite sapphire, diamond, and platinum brooch, which he gave her before their marriage. Both can be seen in the first scene in Jeanette's last film, *The Sun Comes Up*, and on the game show *The Name's the Same* (1952), which can be viewed on YouTube.

On December 28, Gene was on *Screen Guild Theater* in "Long Engagement" with George Murphy and Madeline Carroll. Stars appeared gratis on the program and the fees that they would have been paid went to the Motion Picture Relief Fund. The Fund, now called the Motion Picture & Television Relief Fund, was one the Raymonds' favorite charities. In 1980, Gene explained its importance: "The Fund was formed in 1921 for service people in the industry who had fallen on hard times. Working people contributed a percentage of their salaries. The original Board adopted the slogan 'We Take Care of Our Own.' This is still the slogan today."[446] The Raymonds often sent Christmas cards that benefited the fund, and Jeanette made a provision in her will to support it. The Motion Picture and Television Country House and Hospital, which, through the years, went through various name changes, remains one of its best-known projects.

In January 1942, Jeanette maintained her sense of humor when *The Harvard Lampoon* called her 1941's most unattractive actress. "That's marvelous," she remarked. "I've had such a hard time being called an actress, I've always been called a singer. Really, I think it was very nice of the children."[447] The university's humor magazine also named *Smilin' Through* as one of 1941's ten worst films and Nelson Eddy as one of the stars "fastest on the downward path."[448] In 1949, Jeanette wasn't as good natured when *The Harvard Lampoon* called her appearance in *The Sun Comes Up* the "worst reincarnation of the year."[449] Apparently, the Harvard University students didn't realize that Jeanette returned to the screen a year earlier in *Three Daring Daughters*.

On January 15, 1942, Carole Lombard, who appeared with Gene in *Brief Moment* and *Mr. and Mrs. Smith*, sold bonds in her home state of Indiana as part of the Hollywood Victory Committee, which was chaired by her husband, Clark Gable. Sometime after midnight, on her way back to California, she was killed when her plane crashed into a mountain near Las Vegas, Nevada. The *Chicago Tribune* quoted friends and co-workers, including Gene, who said, "I cannot express how shocked I feel."[450] Lombard was the first female casualty that the United States suffered during World War II, as well as the first casualty from Hollywood. Her death led to Gable enlisting in the Army Air Force later in 1942.

In addition to working with the Hollywood Victory Committee, Jeanette was a California State Director for the American Women's

Voluntary Services (AWVS) and regularly gave benefit concerts on their behalf. The group did everything they could to help with the war effort: delivering messages, driving ambulances, selling bonds, operating emergency kitchens, spotting aircraft, working in canteens, and even fighting fires. On January 27, 1942, she hosted a luncheon at Twin Gables for state and local AWVS leaders to discuss women's role in war work and defense activities.

On January 30, 1942, Gene attended President Franklin D. Roosevelt's Birthday Ball. Here, Gene chatted with Ilo Brown Wallace, wife of Vice President Henry A. Wallace.

The day before Jeanette's luncheon, Gene was one of a group of celebrities who took a special train to Washington to attend President Franklin D. Roosevelt's Birthday Ball, a charitable event to benefit the National Foundation for Infantile Paralysis, which helped polio patients. Jeanette had to remain in California for retakes on *I Married an Angel.* On January 30, Rosalind Russell, Betty Grable, Mickey Rooney, and Dorothy Lamour were among the celebrities attending a luncheon at the White House and the Birthday Ball that evening. According to a diagram sent with the luncheon invitation, Gene was seated a few seats away from the President; in 1993, Gene said that they were three seats apart.

On February 5, Gene wrote a letter to President Roosevelt, telling him how honored he was to be part of the birthday celebration. "Meeting you was an inspiration, sir! To know what tremendous accomplishments you have in back of you, and the stupendous task that lies before you, and to see the incredible balance you maintain as you go, is to make us grateful, indeed, that we have you in the White House! Good luck to you, sir. God goes with you!"[451]

Unbeknownst to his wife, while Gene was in Washington, he volunteered for the Army, the Navy, the Marine Corps, and the Army Air Force, hoping to be accepted by the latter. On February 13, Lieutenant Colonel Lauris Norstad, Assistant Chief of Staff for Intelligence of General Headquarters Air Force, wrote a memo, recommending Gene for an Officer's Commission in the Army Air Force.

On February 11, Jeanette appeared at the dedication of an open-air theater at the Marine Corps Base in San Diego. More than seven thousand servicemen stood in salute when she sang the National Anthem, honoring those killed by the Japanese at Wake Island on December 23, 1941. "I have never been so impressed with the force of America as I was last Wednesday night," she told the press. "Standing before those men and singing the greatest song in the World [sic]— the [sic] Star-Spangled [sic] Banner—I realized, as I looked out at the sea of faces before me, that our country was in safe hands."[452]

On February 15, the Raymonds were among the stars who attended the opening of the USO's hospitality center at the Beverly

Hills Hotel. For the duration of the war, the hotel donated part of the lobby and its swimming pool and athletic facilities to the military. At the opening, the Raymonds busily signed autographs and Jeanette danced with the servicemen.

A week later, on February 22, nearly six thousand people attended a memorial service for the victims of Pearl Harbor, as well as those killed in the Philippines and Dutch East Indies, at Long Beach Memorial Auditorium in Long Beach, California. At the request of Commander Bolton, Jeanette sang "Ave Maria" and "The Star Spangled Banner" with the Robert Mitchell Boys Choir. The next day, Bruno Walter led the Los Angeles Philharmonic Orchestra in a "Music for Victory" concert at Philharmonic Auditorium. In order to be admitted, attendees purchased defense stamps and war bonds in special victory music albums. During intermission, Jeanette made an appeal to the audience, and more than $250,000 in stamps and bonds were sold, currently equivalent to over $3.86 million.

In late February, Jeanette and Gene spent a few days in Indio, California, about twenty-three miles from Palm Springs, at a ranch that belonged to their friend, attorney Mabel Walker Willebrandt. Known as the First Lady of the Law, from 1921 to 1929, Willebrandt was U.S. Assistant Attorney General and, during Prohibition, she prosecuted many alcohol smugglers. In private practice, Willebrandt's client list included Clark Gable, Woody Van Dyke, Jean Harlow, and Louis B. Mayer. She also served as legal counsel to the Screen Directors Guild of America and MGM.

While the Raymonds were in Indio, a wire dated February 25 was relayed from Los Angeles, with Gene's orders to report to Bolling Field in Washington, D.C. on March 14. Gene couldn't keep his enlistment a secret any longer. He recalled that Jeanette looked at the wire and said, "So that's it! Well, that's what happens when you leave your husband alone—he comes back in the Army!"[453] Jeanette claimed that no woman needed to attend dramatic school if she was a serviceman's wife. "We learn to laugh when we want to cry; wisecrack when our blood is turning to ice; keep quiet when we long to break into a screaming tirade."[454] Later, she told reporters, "For Gene's sake I'm happy. He wants to serve his country. But I do get heartsick packing his things away."[455]

On March 2, Gene was sworn in, receiving a commission as First Lieutenant in the Army Air Force. Two days later, Jeanette accompanied him to Phoenix, Arizona, where he went to get extra flying hours. During the day, while he flew, she rehearsed songs for her upcoming movie, *Cairo*, and for several AWVS concerts, with pianist Margaret Hart. The Raymonds spent their evenings together, talking, playing the piano, and taking long walks, unsure of when they would see each other again after he left for Basic Training. He wrote to Marion and Frank Glendening, "I am looking forward to working hard and getting the thing over with as soon as possible. I have an idea that being 'just the old man' will seem like a mighty good prospect after while!"[456]

On March 12, the Raymonds returned to Twin Gables and, the next day, Gene left for Washington, D.C. Jeanette was upset when his Irish Setter, Tray, refused to pay attention to him. She had Rose hide a package in Gene's bag. It included a letter and a heart-shaped locket with Jeanette's picture on one side and Tray's on the other. In her letter, she told him to attach it to his key chain ". . . so that if 'going' ever gets difficult 'my heart' will be there to offer you whatever you need of me!"[457] According to JMIFC President Clara Rhoades, it was a Mizpah locket, named for the line in the book of Genesis "The Lord watch between me and thee, when we are absent from one another." Gene's parting words to Jeanette were "I'll keep 'em flying if you keep 'em singing."[458] Before he left, she gave him a four-leaf clover wrapped in cellophane. Throughout the war, he kept the clover with him. When he died fifty-six years later, it was still in his wallet.

From March 14 to April 1, Gene stayed at the Willard Hotel in Washington, while attending Officer's Indoctrination classes at Bolling Field. For the next eleven days, April 2 to April 12, he was stationed at Air Base Headquarters, Langley Field, in Hampton, Virginia, where he flew as an observer on B-17s on anti-submarine patrol off the Atlantic Coast.

On April 12, Gene reported to the newly organized Intelligence Officers School in Harrisburg, Pennsylvania, where he was assigned to the first graduating class. In his letters to Jeanette, he described the housing and his studies, as well as how his first two roommates quickly were sent overseas. During his training, he was on several committees, foreshadowing his post-war activities, serving on professional, military, and charitable boards. On May 19, 1942, he received orders to go to England; four days later, he graduated with his class then returned to California for a brief leave before he went overseas.

During this time, Jeanette was shooting *Cairo,* her last picture under her MGM contract, and was unable to be with Gene. As soon as the movie was completed, she planned to join him, wherever he was. Prior to filming, on March 20, she gave a recital in San Jose, California to benefit the British charity Bundles for Blue-Jackets and, on March 25 and 27, she gave concerts for the AWVS in San Francisco and Los Angeles. In San Francisco, seven hundred servicemen and Red Cross nurses sat in a phalanx behind her on stage. A critic from the *San Francisco Chronicle* wrote, "Miss MacDonald has all the assurance and breeze and cool nerve in the world, and one felt that if the Opera House had been bombed during her recital she would only have gotten up on top of the highest pile of rubble, sung another one of her Scotch songs and had us all singing too."[459] Before her Los Angeles concert, Gene sent her a wire, saying that he hoped the proceeds from her high C's would keep the Japanese off the high seas.

Cairo cast Jeanette as an American movie star, living in Egypt during the war, who mistook a newspaper reporter (Robert Young) for a Nazi spy. Similarly, the reporter suspected the movie star of being a spy and he convinced her to hire him as a butler so he could observe her. Singer Ethel Waters played the movie star's maid and confidante. The film gave Jeanette a chance to once again prove her comedic talents and show that, if given the chance, she easily could have played roles that went to Irene Dunne and Jean Arthur. Several scenes spoofed Jeanette's career or featured in jokes, like when Young asked if she'd ever been in San Francisco and she replied, "Yes, once with Gable and Tracy and the joint fell apart."[460] Jeanette sang "Les filles de Cadix" from *Maytime* in a movie clip and "A Heart That's Free" from *San Francisco* in the bathtub, reminding audiences of her roles as a prima donna, as well as a lingerie queen. Part of the "Les filles de Cadix" clip was filmed in 1942, showing how little Jeanette had aged in the five years since *Maytime*. Jeanette's character was named Marcia, just like her *Maytime* role, and the head of the spy ring was named Miss Morrison, like *Maytime* Marcia's alias. A large photo of Nelson Eddy was seen in the movie theater lobby.

On April 5, Jeanette appeared on *The Charlie McCarthy Show*, broadcast from Santa Ana, California, marking the dedication of the new West Coast Air Corps Replacement Center. A week later, she sang "Beyond the Blue Horizon" on *The Army Hour*. During the war, she changed the lyrics of the song, which she introduced in *Monte Carlo*, to "shining sun" instead of "rising sun," since the latter was the symbol on the Japanese flag. On April 15, Jeanette was one of many celebrities who attended the California State Guard Military Ball at the Hollywood Palladium. The event raised funds to buy much-needed medical and surgical equipment for Base Hospital No. 1 of the California State Guard.

On May 17, at the request of actor Ronald Reagan, then a Lieutenant in the 323rd Cavalry and, after Jeanette's death, President of the United States, Jeanette participated in "I Am an American Day" at Fort Mason, near San Francisco. In a 1965 letter to Clara Rhoades, Reagan explained, "The commanding [sic] general [sic] had asked if I could get someone to sing the National Anthem at ceremonies for I Am An [sic] American Day. Jeanette said yes without hesitation, but then said if she was coming all that way, couldn't she do something more to help. So on a Sunday afternoon she stood in one of the boxes at the old Dog Racing Track while 20,000 boys headed for the South Pacific, sat in the infield. She sang until there weren't any songs left and still they wanted more. Finally she told them she only knew one more song that was a great favorite of hers, and she started singing the Battle Hymn of the Republic. I will never forget her as she sang, those 20,000 boys came to their feet and finished singing the hymn with her."[461] According to a letter that Reagan wrote to Louella Parsons, Jeanette had a very busy schedule in San Francisco. She lunched with thirteen hundred servicemen, standing in line just like they did, then sang for a group of seven thousand men before the formal program for "I Am an American Day." Reagan said that Jeanette performed two programs at the Dog Racing Track, the first before seventeen thousand men and a second for another thirty-five hundred soldiers, all on her day off from filming *Cairo*.

Before Gene left for England, he had a five-day furlough in California. Jeanette recalled that she had days of violent indigestion, as well as heart murmurs. Her first reaction was "You can't DO this to me!," but she put on a brave face.[462] On May 29, Gene left California. Despite Jeanette's aversion to flying and frequent airsickness, she accompanied him on the plane to Washington, D.C. "That's the kind of girl she was," Gene said later.[463] From Washington, the Raymonds went to New York City, where they enjoyed their last moments together, doing ordinary things, like dining at the Waldorf Astoria and dancing at the Plaza Hotel. On June 2, Gene received his orders to go overseas and, the following day, Jeanette saw him off with other war wives.

On May 17, 1942, Jeanette posed with Brigadier General Frederick Gilbreath and Private First Class Solomon Crystal at "I Am an American Day" at Fort Mason. General Gilbreath conferred the Soldiers' Medal on Private Crystal for saving a fellow soldier from drowning.

According to a 1963 draft of Jeanette's autobiography, her indigestion was more than nerves; she was pregnant. She planned to write to Gene and tell him how happy she was that, even if something happened to him during the war, a piece of him would live on in their child. Sadly, she lost the baby "many weeks later."[464] It is not known whether or not she told him about the pregnancy or miscarriage at that time, as neither her letters, nor Gene's, have been found. In a 1976 letter to Clara Rhoades, Emily Wentz insisted, "She never was pregnant – much to her sorrow."[465] One can assume that Emily either didn't know about Jeanette's miscarriage, since it happened before she lived at Twin Gables, or, since she probably was the one who typed the 1963 draft, she didn't think that she should share Jeanette and Gene's private business. Interestingly, in April 1964, when Jeanette asked literary agent Russell Case for advice on her book, the miscarriage was one of the passages that he suggested that she eliminate or edit.

For the first time, the Raymonds were separated on their anniversary, as well as Jeanette's birthday. Before Gene left New York, he had a pair of Army Air Force wings customized and gold plated at Cartier, which he instructed the store to ship to Jeanette for her birthday. Instead of U.S.A., he had G.R. and J.R. engraved on them. Throughout the war, Jeanette proudly wore the wings.

To help ease her loneliness, Jeanette invited Marge Halford and her three children, who had been evacuated from their Honolulu home because of the war, to stay at Twin Gables. Jeanette recalled, "It was nice to have them there, laughing, making a lot of noise, filling that awfully empty house."[466] They arrived while Jeanette was in New York with Gene. Joan Halford Rohlfing remembered going to watch Jeanette shoot retakes for *Cairo*. Her observations were particularly interesting, since Woody Van Dyke's nickname was "one-take Woody." Rohlfing said, "Once we went to MGM when she was filming. It took so long to do one scene, until the director thought it was just right. We decided being in the movies was hard work."[467] Rohlfing recalled picking peaches with Jeanette, who made peach ice cream for her guests. It was the first time that the Halford children tasted that flavor. They also fell in love with Stormy, Jeanette's Skye Terrier, and later acquired a dog of that breed too. Rohlfing's eleventh birthday fell during their visit. Jeanette threw a joint birthday swimming party for her and character actor Guy Kibbee's daughter, Shirley Ann, at Twin Gables, with the children of her friends as guests.

When the Halfords left, Anna, Blossom, and Rocky moved in to help ease Jeanette's loneliness and occupy the house while Jeanette was on tour. Always frugal, while her family was at Twin Gables, Jeanette tried to rent Anna's house, but had no luck finding a tenant.

After the completion of *Cairo*, Jeanette left MGM. According to most sources, the studio did not renew her contract. Audiences' tastes were changing, and operettas had gone out of favor. Her last few films had not been profitable like her previous pictures. Also, at age thirty-nine, she found herself being replaced by younger actresses, whose films and salaries did not cost the studio as much money. Within a short period, MGM stalwarts Norma Shearer, Greta Garbo, and Joan Crawford also were gone from the studio whose reputation they helped to build. According to Jeanette's autobiography, Nicholas Schenck offered her a new seven-year contract, but she turned it down because she did not like her last movies. Gene's letters hinted that leaving the studio was her decision. In her book, Jeanette also claimed that she turned down offers from RKO and Twentieth Century–Fox. However, according to Gene's correspondence, the Fox offer "went cold" and he mistakenly wondered if the success of *Cairo* caused MGM to interfere.[468] Studio records state that *Cairo* lost $131,000 (currently over $2 million) so it was more likely that its box office *failure* caused Fox to lose interest. In any case, whether Jeanette's departure from MGM was her idea, the studio's, or a mutual decision, she decided to concentrate on doing recitals, concerts, and war work.

In July 1942, Nelson Eddy bought out the remainder of his MGM contract. He objected to the scripts that the studio gave him and said that he could make more in one recital than he earned per week making movies. He made three more films—*The Phantom of the Opera* (1943, Universal), *Knickerbocker Holiday* (1944, Producers Corporation of America), and *Northwest Outpost* (1947, Republic Pictures)—plus loaned his voice for "The Whale Who Wanted to Sing at the Met" segment of Walt Disney's *Make Mine Music* (1946, Walt Disney Studios). Despite being rumored for various screen projects, he never returned to MGM.

During World War II, entertainers were quick to donate their services to entertain the troops. Besides USO camp tours, there were numerous spots around the country where enlisted men could go for sandwiches, milk, and free entertainment. The most famous of these were the Stage Door Canteen and the Hollywood Canteen.

The Stage Door Canteen was located in the space below the 44th Street Theatre in New York City. Jeanette and Gene's former boss, producer Lee Shubert, leased the building from *The New York Times* and, when the American Theatre Wing approached him about running a canteen for servicemen in the basement, he donated it to the cause. On March 2, 1942, the Stage Door Canteen opened, with actress Selena Royle and the Raymonds' friend, Jane Cowl, as Co-chairs of the Canteen Committee. Broadway actors performed scenes from their shows, acted as waiters and hostesses, danced with the G.I.s, and washed dishes. Admission was free, as were the food and beverages, all of which were non-alcoholic. Neither officers nor civilians were allowed unless they were in the entertainment business and were volunteering. Each night, as many as three thousand servicemen came to the Stage Door Canteen. They were open seven days a week, even during the city's mandatory blackouts and curfews.

From July 30, 1942 to April 20, 1945, a weekly half-hour *Stage Door Canteen* radio show was broadcast from the Canteen on CBS. Well-known performers donated their services to entertain American and Allied servicemen, as well as civilians on the home front. The Raymonds' longtime friend, Bert Lytell, was Master of Ceremonies on the radio program. His sister-in-law, actress Helen Menken, was one of the founders of the American Theatre Wing and, during the war, she was Chairman of its Radio Division.

In 1943, United Artists distributed an all-star film about the Canteen, with 90% of the profits, about $1.5 million (almost $22 million today), going to the real Stage Door Canteen. Several of the Raymonds' friends made cameo appearances, including Jane Cowl, Bert Lytell, and Lanny Ross. The movie was directed by Frank Borzage, who directed Jeanette and Gene in *Smilin' Through*.

On June 30, 1945, which was after V-E Day but before V-J Day, the Canteen closed when Lee Shubert's lease expired; *The New York Times* tore down the building to construct a printing plant. A plaque remains on the former 44th Street printing plant to commemorate "the men and women of the entertainment world who brought cheer and comfort to the soldiers, sailors and marines [sic] of America and her Allies."[469]

Inspired by the success of the Stage Door Canteen, various movie guilds and unions banded together to renovate a building located at 1451 Cahuenga Boulevard, which became the Hollywood Canteen. Actors Bette Davis and John Garfield were the driving forces behind its creation; Davis served as its President. Jules Stein, President of Music Corporation of America (MCA), headed the finance committee. Just like the Broadway and entertainment communities in New York donated their services to the Stage Door Canteen, the movie, radio, and music communities in California united to make the Hollywood Canteen a success. The goal was to have a place for military personnel passing through Los Angeles to relax, mingle with their favorite stars, and feel appreciated for their sacrifice for their country. Everything was free of charge, including food, beverages, and cigarettes, all of which were donated. The only ticket needed was a uniform; all races were welcome.

Like the Stage Door Canteen, civilians and military officers weren't allowed unless they were connected with the entertainment industry and were there to volunteer. Officers and their guests were restricted to a second-story room with a window that looked out on the dance floor and stage. No matter how famous the volunteers were, all were finger-printed and photographed, as required by the FBI. From October 3, 1942 through November 22, 1945, the Canteen was open from 7:00 p.m. to midnight, Monday through Saturday, and 2:00 p.m. to 8:00 p.m. on Sunday. Each night, nearly two thousand G.I.s were served.

In 1944, Warner Bros. made a film about the Hollywood Canteen, with many of the stars who performed there playing themselves. The studio donated 40% of the movie's profits to the real Hollywood Canteen, about $1.68 million, equivalent to over $24 million today.

Thanks to Jules Stein's investments, after V-J Day, when the Canteen was no longer needed, $500,000 remained in its account in an irrevocable trust to benefit veterans. Currently, that would be almost $7 million. Stein established The Hollywood Canteen Foundation, which continues to help the Armed Forces by providing services for veterans, including health care, financial assistance, rehabilita-tion training, and counseling. It aids the American Legion, Paralyzed Veterans of America, the USO, and Angel Flight for Veterans, which provides free air transportation to medical centers around the world for veterans and active military personnel, as well as their families.

Jeanette loved entertaining the troops and, when she wasn't on tour, she tried to volunteer at the Hollywood Canteen every other Sunday. She didn't just sing; she served sandwiches, chatted with the G.I.s, and even had the servicemen lining up to jitterbug with her. Anna often volunteered in the kitchen.

Jeanette never knew what she would be doing at the Hollywood Canteen. Above: After her performances, she always signed autographs. Below: Sometimes Jeanette served sandwiches to hungry servicemen.

In 1943, longtime fan Roland Hammond met Jeanette at the Hollywood Canteen. He said that she was touched when he told her that, when he was a teen, her singing awakened his love of opera and operetta. She observed that he still looked young and asked his age. When he replied that he was only seventeen, she kissed his cheek and said, "Bless you."[470] Hammond recalled, "I could see a light dusting of freckles under her powder just like anyone we might know on our street or among family."[471] Jeanette sang for forty-five minutes without stopping, mostly taking requests from the servicemen. For her final song, she chose "Ave Maria." Hammond said, "The silence in that great room was amazing as hardened men thought of home and loved ones and buddies killed or wounded as she sang."[472] Louella Parsons was standing next to Hammond and, as Jeanette finished singing, Parsons remarked, "This moment should be bronzed."[473]

Chapter Eleven

On June 16, 1942, the Raymonds' fifth anniversary, Gene arrived in England. He was assigned as Intelligence Officer of the 97th Bombardment Group, the first heavy bomb group to raid France and Germany, and the first B-17 Group to initiate precision bombing. He was based in Polebrook, England, although, at the time, he wasn't allowed to tell Jeanette his location. It took a while for his mail to catch up to his unit, and his letters to Jeanette were equally slow to arrive, causing her great concern. When she finally heard from him, nearly six weeks after he left, Jeanette was full of relief. She wrote, "So glad to get your letter and to know you arrived safely after a good trip. Can't say I was worried; I refused to be. That's a joke for you. Me, a chronic worrier, giving up worry for the duration!"[474]

To celebrate Gene's first letter, Jeanette hosted a chicken dinner for the Hollywood War Wives. The group of celebrities and wives or sweethearts of actors met once a week to help each other through their loneliness. They spent another night entertaining servicemen, either at Date Leaves, or later, at the Hollywood Canteen. The group included actresses Jane Wyman (wife of actor Ronald Reagan), Brenda Marshall (wife of actor William Holden), Ann Sheridan (wife of actor George Brent), and Annabella (wife of actor Tyrone Power), columnist Louella Parsons (wife of Dr. Harry Martin), and Mary Ford (wife of director John Ford). Often, the women brought along their knitting. Jeanette, who claimed that she wasn't the knitting type, made several gifts for Gene while he was overseas.

Before Gene left for England, the Raymonds bought one hundred acres of land in Temecula, California, about 105 miles south of Bel Air, which Jeanette christened Ray's Ranch. Gene later said they bought it "just in case,"[475] which meant in case wartime shortages required them to grow their own food or in case they had to evacuate Twin Gables. There was a primitive house there, with no electricity or indoor plumbing. In their letters, they made plans to build a real home there when Gene returned. They also wrote of career plans, becoming a team on screen or stage.

Today, couples in the military can use email, Skype, and Face Time for instantaneous communication; however, during World War II, they had to depend on letters and telegrams, both of which often were delayed. Telephone calls to or from those serving overseas were forbidden, without special permission. Mail also had to pass through the censors so Gene not only had to withhold details about his military activities, but the Raymonds also had to limit any intimate thoughts that they had for one another, knowing that all correspondence would be read before they received it. While Gene was in England, both Raymonds sent letters with friends who were traveling to or from the United States, knowing that they would arrive faster than the mail and that they could speak more freely since the censors wouldn't be reading them.

Gene said, "Letters make all the difference between a good day and a bad day over there. Your first concern is, of course, your job. So far as your personal life is concerned, mail is all of it. Offer a fellow a meal or a letter and he'll take a letter every time."[476] His letters described conditions: the showers, the food, the incompetence he encountered, as well as the lack of toilet paper. He also talked about how much he missed Jeanette and the ordinary pleasures he took for granted, like walking the dogs and playing the piano, and their home, Twin Gables. At least twice a week, Jeanette tried to write to Gene and he tried to do the same. In her autobiography, she claimed that, while he was in England, she wrote to him every day, probably an exaggeration by Jeanette or her collaborator. She gave him the latest gossip from Hollywood and shared family news, trying to remain upbeat. She told reporters, "Our letters are full, not of unrest and disturbance, of the present, but of the planning for the peace of the future. All of us, I feel, must look up and outward. No matter what our religion, for these are times of deep spiritual revival, we must live that religion. We must learn to be calm and courageous, for it is going to take much courage to follow through."[477]

After *Cairo*, Jeanette asked Gene for career advice and whether she should go overseas to entertain the troops. Although he wanted to see her, he feared for her safety and discouraged her from leaving the United States. When she was lonely and depressed on the road, Gene tried to build her confidence and ego, reminding her how important her war work was and how proud he was of her. They found the Clipper, Boeing's flying boat that delivered mail overseas, to be faster and more reliable than telegrams.

"During the next three years Gene's and my relationship was not unlike a pen pal arrangement, particularly the early part of the correspondence when he first went to England," Jeanette recalled in her autobiography. "Knowing my own need for word from him, I sensed an equal urgency on his part—perhaps even more than mine, so I wrote every day. I'm sure intimate outpourings of devotion were duplicated by thousands of girls all over the world."[478] In her letters, she shared her busy schedule.

On June 23, Jeanette attended a Victory Rally meeting, headed by Kenneth Thomson, Executive Secretary of the Screen Actors Guild and one of the Chairmen of the Hollywood Victory Committee. In July, she was added to the Actors Sub-Committee of the Hollywood Victory Committee.

During the summer of 1942, Jeanette went on a twelve-city Army camp tour, entertaining the troops in the heat belt, the most undesirable route. She asked the Hollywood Victory Committee to poll the Commanding Officers to see where she would be most welcome. The answer was everywhere! According to a press release about her tour, in every poll, she was voted the favorite singing star of men in uniform. Since Jeanette's schedule didn't allow her to visit every camp, she asked the Hollywood Victory Committee to send her a list of camps where the soldiers had little, if any, entertainment. She was nonplussed when they ended up being in the heat belt, insisting, "If the men can train in blistering temperatures, I can sing and travel in it."[479] She left July 18 and returned August 11. In addition to her camp shows, in several cities, she sang at the post hospital.

Jeanette based her repertoire on requests that she received in letters from G.I.s, as well as titles shouted out during the performances and songs from her movies. Often, she sang as many as thirty-two songs in one show, more than in her paid recitals. "It was always awkward to break away, because I really loved to make the boys happy," she said later. "The officers, though, always came to my rescue. They felt sorry for me."[480]

As Jeanette travelled, she made it a point to get to know the servicemen on her trains. During the day, she rode in the coach, instead of her private compartment, meeting and talking with the G.I.s. Often, they didn't realize that they were chatting with Jeanette MacDonald.

When Jeanette learned that some of the G.I.s were turned away from her camp shows because there wasn't room in the recreational facilities, she wired Helen Ferguson to find out about a sound truck. "Just give me the sound truck and something to stand on and I'll sing in a field, if necessary," she said. "I don't want a big stage and fancy lighting effects. All I want to do is sing for as many of the boys as possible."[481] She was livid when civilians took up seats meant for servicemen. Gene offered advice on how to diplomatically handle the situation with the Commanding Officers. Later, Jeanette shared her thoughts on officers who brought their wives and children to the camp shows intended for G.I.s.: "When you go to sing to soldiers and see lots of women there, well, you feel the gesture is wasted." She said that the officers' wives could attend concerts on week nights when the enlisted men often could not get away from the base. "Speaking as an officer's wife— which I suppose I shouldn't—I feel that officers have the advantage of being able to have their wives with them, they get a little more money and they have certain privileges the soldiers don't have."[482]

Each stop on the tour was a new adventure. At Sheppard Field, Texas, Jeanette got off the train at 5:00 p.m. and sang at 8:00 p.m., giving her little time to rest or prepare for her performance. At O'Reilly General Hospital in Springfield, Missouri, Jeanette did a double take when a nurse asked if she'd like to meet Gene Raymond. Jeanette knew that her Gene was still in England because, the previous day, she received a cable from him. Private Gene Raymond was a stretcher case who also was in the Army Air Force. Jeanette recalled, "I couldn't think of what to say so I sort of blurted out, 'I see you have a mustache,' 'Yes,' he said with a grin, 'I grew mine when your husband grew his.' 'But I had Gene shave his off,' I said. 'Yes, I know,' he replied, 'but my friends like mine and won't let me shave it off.'" She continued, "We had a long talk about my Gene and the war. He was such a sweet boy.

His only complaint was that he was being held up in his war activities. 'I want to be over there with your Gene,' he said, and the way he said it almost broke my heart."[483] Jeanette began corresponding with the other Gene and, in 1944, she introduced Private Gene Raymond to Captain Gene Raymond at Twin Gables.

During Jeanette's 1942 camp tours, she met Private Gene Raymond, whose injuries forced him to be carried on a stretcher because he was unable to walk.

Jeanette was never afraid to laugh at herself. While entertaining patients at the same Springfield hospital, where many had been wounded at Pearl Harbor and the Bataan Peninsula in the Philippines, she couldn't understand why they requested so many Irish songs. "There must be a few Irishmen here," she commented, then giggled when they reminded her that she was at *O'Reilly* General Hospital. After she sang "Johnny Doughboy" for the third time, she said, "I hope my husband doesn't find a 'Wild Irish Rose in Ireland.'" Above the laughter, she heard one of the soldiers shout "He'll never find a rose like you, Jeanette."[484] At another camp show, she recalled how she was baffled by a soldier's request for "The Jersey Bounce." "I didn't know it was a song," she insisted. "I thought it was a ride or something."[485]

Jeanette dressed to the nines when she was performing for servicemen, just like she did in her paid recitals.

Jeanette always dressed to the nines for the soldiers, just like she did for her paid audiences. When an officer noticed her wearing white suede gloves in the heat, she explained, "I was raised in a white glove family. Hot or cold, I always wear white gloves. Isn't it awful!"[486] At Missouri's Fort Leonard Wood, nicknamed "Fort Lost-in-the-Woods," the temperature reached 110 degrees. Jeanette's accompanist, Margaret Hart, fainted, but Jeanette kept on singing, as she swatted flies and wiped her perspiration. Later, she said, "I never thought of myself as the perspiring kind, but after you've sung 25 songs, a chiffon dress is just a bundle of beads—of perspiration. I drip, honestly."[487] After the tour, she recalled, "I had perspiration dripping off my nose, my arms, my body for 24 hours a day—but what of it, those boys are perspiring month in and month out, surely I can take it for a few weeks."[488] Jeanette told another reporter, "Some days it was hotter than hot, but the boys seemed to like the songs and they asked for encores, quite a few of them."[489] Ironically, while Jeanette was suffering in the heat, Gene complained about how cold it was in England in the summer.

At Jefferson Barracks, near St. Louis, Missouri, Jeanette had her first jeep ride and swallowed a bug. She recalled, "There I was giving my all to 'My Hero' when the biggest bug I have ever seen flew right down my throat. There was nothing to do but keep on singing—and utter up a little prayer that it wasn't poisonous."[490] The jeep ride was almost as traumatic. "I rode in one once," Jeanette quipped, "and once was enough."[491]

The men at Scott Field Radio Communications School, near Belleville, Illinois, presented Jeanette with a corsage made out of radio tubes, and cleaned out an airplane hangar for her because there was a threat of rain. When the weather cleared, Jeanette admitted that she was a little disappointed that she missed the experience of singing in a hangar. At Camp Robinson in North Little Rock, Arkansas, she was told not to expect a crowd because it was payday. However, the stands were filled and Jeanette was touched. As a tribute to her, one Arkansas camp selected "March of the Grenadiers" from *The Love Parade* as their regimental march. At Fort Knox, Kentucky, she thrilled the four soldiers who were instructed to escort her to her train. When she found there wasn't a diner at the station, she invited them to a near-by joint with a jukebox and they joined her for sandwiches and music until her train arrived.

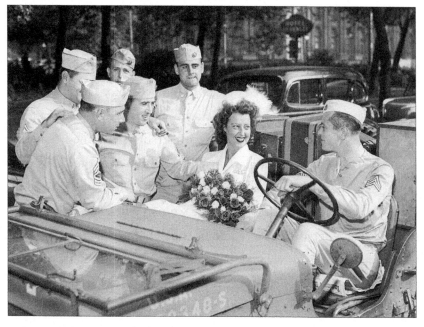

Jeanette said she rode in a jeep once and once was enough. In Gene's letters, he also complained about the discomfort.

Not every G.I. was glad to see Jeanette. Bob, a disgruntled Scott Field soldier, wrote a letter to the editor of *The Hutchinson News–Herald* in Hutchinson, Kansas, claiming that he and fellow service-men were ordered to attend Jeanette's performance, although they disliked classical music. He said that the post was restricted that night because press photographers were coming and the servicemen were ordered to pretend to be enthusiastic.

At William Beaumont General Hospital in El Paso, a photographer from near-by Fort Bliss asked if Jeanette would pose with the boys while singing a popular number. She was agreeable, but every time the photographer tried to take a picture, his flashbulb failed to go off. "I'm beginning to suspect that we are singing the wrong song," Jeanette laughed. "Let's try our luck with 'God Bless America.'"[492] The next flashbulb worked perfectly. At Camp Tyson, near Paris, Tennessee, a storm moved Jeanette's show into the barracks hall, where she sang to the servicemen in shifts. When the power went out, she shrugged, "If the Army can fight in the dark, I guess I can sing in the dark."[493]

Jeanette further endeared herself to the people of Paris when she visited the sweetheart of a soldier. Earlier in the year, while Jeanette was visiting an Army camp in California, she mentioned that she would be going to Camp Tyson. A soldier stationed at the California camp asked her to deliver a message to his sweetheart, who lived in Paris. Jeanette agreed to telephone the woman when she arrived, but decided that a personal visit would be much better. She inquired and found out that the serviceman's sweetheart worked in her brother's dental office so off Jeanette went. The woman was as thrilled to meet Jeanette MacDonald as she was to get the message from her boyfriend. From then on, Jeanette routinely called families and sweethearts of servicemen that she met in the hospitals, updating them on their loved ones and delivering messages. Often, she had to sing to convince the startled family members that it wasn't a joke when she identified herself as Jeanette MacDonald.

The large audiences touched Jeanette. She told reporters, "Singing before crowds of from 10,000 to 30,000 men in the outdoors, does something to you inside. I have heard the expression 'a lump in your throat,' but I never really experienced this sensation until I sang to these boys. This exaltation, the feeling that I was contributing just a small mite to their happiness, was compensation enough for the inconveniences of making these tours. It was a most moving experience."[494]

Jeanette's audiences numbered as many as thirty-five thousand. At Sheppard Field, Texas, soldiers climbed on the rooftops to get a better view. "It was a thrilling sensation to sing to such a tremendous crowd," she said. "It was inspiring, too, to have them always ask for serious songs. It makes one feel that they are drawing closer to God."[495] She was impressed that the most requested songs were "Ave Maria," "Battle Hymn of the Republic," and "Nearer My God to Thee." "When boys want religious songs, you don't have to worry about them," she insisted. "Americans have always prayed as they fought for their ideals. The fighting men of this war are proving no exception."[496]

In an article titled "I'm Proud I Believe in God," Jeanette shared her religious beliefs. Although the article most likely was written by Helen Ferguson, Jeanette's faith was very important to her.

I'm proud to say I believe in God, and I don't think any American today is a real DIS-believer. My husband is an officer in the Army Air Force Combat Command. He is overseas. I am sure he prays in his fashion as I pray in mine. We have never discussed our prayers. We have not needed the affirmations of our faith. We have had the evidence of it. . . .

It is not my habit to run here and there engaging in remarks of profoundly religious import. But it's my habit to pray to God in all humility. I believe in God and in prayer and I use prayer daily for guidance. With the conviction that our right prayers do not go unanswered. . . .

> Every man can't go to the front. Every woman can't participate in defense work. But every man, woman and child can pray without ceasing, as the men, women and children of our history prayed for Victory.[497]

Betty Grable may have been the servicemen's number one pin-up girl, but the soldiers voted Jeanette "The Army's Best Sweetheart" and dubbed her their "Star Spangled Singer." A 1944 article called Jeanette "America's finest home front soldier."[498] She was the only person licensed by the USO to perform an entire solo show. She later said that men in uniform "spoil you for any other audience."[499] She looked upon singing for servicemen as a privilege. She told reporters, "They're the best audience in the world. They don't care, just so you give."[500] After the war, she recalled, "Singing to a group of servicemen is the most satisfying experience, and of course, I never forgot that somewhere in Europe my husband might be listening to a singer under similar circumstances, so it gave me added heart."[501]

Despite the perspiration and uncomfortable conditions, Jeanette found the tour a positive experience. "I kept thinking to myself, 'Oh, God, I am thankful that I can do this.' Heat or no heat, I'm going to try and do it again real soon," she vowed.[502] Throughout the war, she entertained servicemen whenever she could and visited veterans' hospitals in California and on tour. She wrote a scenario about her experiences titled *Saints, Soldiers and Song*, but it was not produced.

Meanwhile, in England, it wasn't always easy for Gene in the service, fighting down the Hollywood stigma. One officer, who later befriended Gene, confessed to Jeanette that he was determined to put the celebrity in his place. Jeanette recalled, "So he called Gene up before him and said to him: 'I understand you're a movie star.' And Gene said to him: 'No, sir. I'm a lieutenant [sic] in the army [sic] air [sic] forces [sic], for the duration!' This commanding [sic] officer [sic] was so delighted by Gene's answer that he forgot all about how tough he was going to be."[503] On the whole, Gene said that he was lucky to have good Commanding Officers. Several times, he asked his wife to send autographed photos to members of his superiors' families because they were fans.

On August 17, 1942, twelve B-17Es of the 97th Bomb Group were escorted by Royal Air Force (RAF) Spitfires on one of the first U.S. Army Air Force raids over occupied Europe, bombing Hitler's arsenals. Two aircraft sustained minor damage, but the operation was a success, destroying rail yards at Rouen in northern France. As an Intelligence Officer, Gene's jobs included briefing pilots before their raids and questioning them after each mission. He gathered information from pilots, spies, and other units, acting as the Commanding Officer's closest adviser. Louella Parsons' column quoted a letter that has not been found by this author, which Gene began on August 17 and continued the next day. "Was interrupted yesterday but spent the rest of it and through to the morning hours in the midst of hectic activity. It was a great day and everyone went to bed late, tired and happy. By now, you know as much as I can tell you, if you read the papers or listen to the radio. Sufficient it is to say it was an historical day and I was mighty glad to be here in the midst of it."[504]

On September 16, Gene was promoted to Captain for his part in the raid. Five days later, he was assigned to the VIII Bomber Command in High Wycombe, England, serving first as an Intelligence Officer then as Assistant Operations Officer. The VIII Bomber Command planned and ordered bombing missions. Since Gene was considered an expert on identifying enemy aircraft, he spent some of his time traveling and giving lectures on the subject. On November 4, Gene received his wings and a Service Pilot's rating. As he explained to

Jeanette, this allowed him to fly practically any plane, except in combat. At that time, Service Pilots could fly overseas on cargo and utility transports with Air Transport, Ferry, or Troop Carrier Commands. Usually, a Service Pilot could obtain an unrestricted Pilot rating after one year of Army Air Force service, if he met certain flight experience requirements and passed an evaluation board. For Gene, it took longer because he didn't have enough flying hours. While he was in the service, he preferred remaining in the background, just doing his job, not trying to cash in on his celebrity status. When he was asked to appear on a radio broadcast because he was famous, he refused, saying, "I'm Capt. Raymond of the United States air [sic] force [sic]. If you want Gene Raymond, the actor, he's in mothballs for the duration."[505]

While Gene was serving, Jeanette tried to keep his name before the public. She mentioned him in interviews and reminded producers that, when he returned, he would be ready to work. When RKO Chief of Production Charles Koerner told her that he had a role that would be great for Gene, if he were home, Jeanette countered that she hoped that Koerner would remember her husband when the war was over.

That fall, Jeanette did a twelve-city recital tour to benefit Army Emergency Relief (AER), a nonprofit organization created to help soldiers and their families with rent, utilities, emergency travel, and other financial problems. Since 1942, AER aided over 3.7 million families and it continues to provide interest-free loans, grants, and scholarships to soldiers and their families. Jeanette explained, "There's no red tape to Army Relief. No nonsense. A woman whose husband is overseas gets her money immediately."[506]

The tour began on September 7 in Oklahoma City, Oklahoma, where several thousand fans waited at Union Station to greet Jeanette, despite the fact that her train was five hours late. Usually, she received a percentage of the box office on her tours, averaging between $3,500 to $4,000 per performance, equivalent to around $54,000 to $62,000 today. On the tour, she donated it all to Army Emergency Relief, paying her own travel expenses and auctioning off encores for the cause. She told audiences, "You give to the relief fund, and I'll sing as long as my throat holds out."[507] Although Jeanette and pianist Giuseppe Bamboschek remained friends and occasionally worked together on individual recitals or other projects, the AER tour was their last joint recital tour.

Jeanette with Oklahoma City Assistant Fire Chief Jacob "Jake" Amburg and an unidentified police officer on September 7, 1942. She always appreciated the security that she received on tour. She never traveled with a bodyguard.

During the AER tour, Jeanette had a few memorable experiences. When a patron in Tennessee asked her to sing "Chattanooga Choo Choo," she claimed that she didn't know the lyrics and substituted "San Francisco." In Columbus, Ohio, she forgot the words to "Little Grey Home in the West," confessing that she hadn't sung it in a long time and because someone was missing from *her* little grey home in the west. At another recital, a man requested "One Dozen Roses," but Jeanette was not familiar with the song. She brought forth her bouquet, saying there were two dozen roses and would she get $200? Today, the offer would be worth about $1,500 and $3,000. She encouraged audiences to whistle along when she sang "The Donkey Serenade." At almost every performance, she wore the wings that Gene gave her. A wartime press release quoted a typical review: "With her golden voice, shining spirit, moonglow [sic] personality, and titian hair, Miss MacDonald brings light into any auditorium, even in the darkness of a world war."[508]

Jeanette often had soldiers, sailors, Marines, and WACs seated behind her on stage. They always were admitted free to her recitals and, at each show, a few passed the hat to collect the money for her encores. When sales lagged, she asked the service people for their requests. As she announced the songs, she saluted them. When she sang facing the military audience, the paying customers never complained, grateful to those who were serving their country.

In Pittsburgh, one hundred soldiers of the 104th Cavalry Regiment sat onstage. The Regiment's band was in the orchestra pit, accompanying Jeanette when she sang "The Star Spangled Banner" and playing marches during the intermissions. In Birmingham, Alabama, Jeanette sold the first forget-me-not at the annual sale to benefit Disabled American Veterans. The group planned to use a large share of the proceeds from the 1942 drive to help Americans who were injured in World War II, rather than previous wars.

During Jeanette's tours, she often entertained at veterans' hospitals. After she sang Gene's composition "Will You?" at one hospital, a wounded soldier shouted out "Did you?" and she shot back "I did." Suddenly embarrassed, she hastily added, "I married the man who wrote that song."[509] The crowd roared with laughter and applause and it was several minutes before Jeanette could resume her performance.

Servicemen weren't the only ones who were thrilled to meet Jeanette. In Birmingham, Alabama, Jeanette had a private chat with a ten-year-old fan who was crippled by polio. The little girl was speechless when she met her idol, but left beaming, wearing Jeanette's orchids.

On September 13, 1942, Jeanette sang in Indianapolis for Army Emergency Relief.

The highlight of Jeanette's AER tour was hearing Gene on the radio. On August 28, he wrote that, on the following Thursday, he was going to record an appearance on *The Army Hour*, which aired on Sundays.

He didn't realize that the broadcast was really *American Eagle Club* and that the show would air a week later. On September 6, when Jeanette didn't hear his voice, she was deeply disappointed, as well as concerned. She told reporters, "I felt lower than at any time since he went away."[510] To her relief, the following week, on September 12, the show aired, the night before her recital in Indianapolis. Jeanette spent the evening at the home of pharmaceutical executive J.K. Lilly, listening to Gene's broadcast. She wrote her husband an effusive letter, clearly thrilled at hearing his voice for the first time in over three months. Helen Ferguson recorded Gene's part of the program and sent it to Jeanette while she was on the road. Jeanette told the press, "Whenever I want to hear Gene's voice now, all I have to do is to play over this little recording—and there he is!"[511] At her recital, Lilly, a collector of Stephen Foster memorabilia, donated $100 (now about $1,500) to Army Emergency Relief, requesting Foster's "My Old Kentucky Home." Will Hays and his wife were in Sullivan, Indiana, and made special arrangements to hear as much of Jeanette's Indianapolis recital as possible before they had to board a train for New York.

When Jeanette was asked how she found people on her tour, she spoke with conviction. "Something is changing inside of people's minds and heads. They realize that money isn't the only important thing in the world," she said. "They're in this nasty mess, and they know they've got to make sacrifices if they hope to get out of it."[512] She wasn't afraid to express her patriotism. "We must work harder than ever, today, that there may continue to be at least one country in this world with opportunities for all!" she insisted. "Our job is to work and give in our united effort to keep America free, prosperous and happy, glorying in her freedom."[513]

Always generous with autographs, during the war, Jeanette charged civilians for them, donating the money to Army Emergency

Relief. She carried a green suede box to hold the contributions and often brought it out at train stops to collect more money for the cause. Children had to contribute at least a nickel; adults were required to donate paper money. She never charged enlisted men or officers. She was surprised when one sailor wouldn't take her autograph, even for free. When she asked him why he didn't want it, he replied, "You're a married lady and I don't think it would look right for me to be carrying around your autograph in my pocket."[514]

Jeanette gave up answering fan mail for the duration because it was difficult to get photographic supplies for autographed pictures and there was a shortage of mail clerks. She told fans, "If you like me, please come to all my pictures. That will be showing your appreciation best until the war is over and normal conditions can be resumed. But don't expect answers to fan letters—not only from me but from other film stars who are trying to cooperate with the Government [sic]."[515] According to a 1944 article, one week she received four thousand letters. No wonder that she was concerned about tying up the post office.

Wartime travel wasn't easy. Servicemen rightfully were given priority. Sometimes weather conditions delayed the train's arrival and Jeanette missed her connection. A missed train often meant that she couldn't catch another one until the next day. During her AER tour, she told reporters in Springfield, Massachusetts, "Trains are very crowded these days and frequently late. They put us on the wrong train coming here so it is a wonder that we got here at all."[516] She sometimes carried extra suitcases of food, in case her party couldn't get in the dining car. In one city, fans loaded her up with food and, when the train broke down and she found that there was no dining car, she shared it with the other passengers. She also carried a small briefcase-sized suitcase that she called Operation Emergency. It included nylon pajamas that easily could be rinsed out, a white nylon-jersey dress that didn't require ironing, a sheer concert gown that didn't wrinkle, and two pairs of lace sandals. The emergency kit came in handy when her baggage occasionally was put on the wrong train when she transferred.

During one trip, Jeanette was seated in a coach full of G.I.s. She blended in with the other passengers and no one recognized her. When one of the soldiers began to sing, everyone joined him. After the singing was over, the soldier next to her remarked, "Your voice sounds just like Jeanette MacDonald's." Then he added, "Well, that's life for you! Look where she is—and look where you are!"[517] She didn't reveal her identity.

Jeanette's twelve-city tour contributed $94,681.87 to Army Emergency Relief, the largest cash amount to come from a single entertainer. Currently, it would be over $1.4 million. On October 4, she presented the loot, as she called it, to a representative of the AER at her final recital in Washington, D.C. She asked soldiers to bring out giant moneybags with the amount and the name of each city printed on the bags. Robert P. Patterson, Under Secretary of War, wrote to her, "Through your generous response to our request, your recent concert tour has made available approximately $80,000 for this worthy cause. Of this amount, over $15,000 was realized through your original idea of auctioning your encores. This was testimony both to your personal popularity and to the response which your own enthusiasm evoked. The tangible results of your tour can be measured, but the intangible benefits for the future success of these efforts to take care of dependents of Army personnel are immeasurable!"[518]

Following Jeanette's recital in Washington, Colonel Joseph F. Battley, Executive Officer Deputy Chief of Staff for Service Commands, wrote to Gene, congratulating him on his promotion to Captain and praising Jeanette's AER tour. Battley reported that over two thousand people were turned away at the door of Constitution

Hall. He told Gene, "When she sang 'One Kiss' I knew that she was thinking about you. . . . She is so proud of you and is still hoping that it is possible for you to come home for a short while, as an instructor or courier. However, she said that you would not be contented to stay here for the duration and she wanted you to do as you felt necessary. How about a leave?"[519]

Jeanette was modest when she received praise for her efforts for Army Emergency Relief. "It's for a good cause," she insisted. "And besides, EVERYBODY ought to be glad to work hard, nowadays."[520]

After the AER tour, Jeanette decided to do another brief recital tour. Within twenty-four hours of her announcement, seventy-five cities placed bids. In between tours, she went to New York City for a short rest. While she was there, she visited Jimmie Dwyer's Sawdust Trail, a rustic nightclub famous for its four white pianos. Jeanette managed to go unrecognized as she joined the community sing—until Dwyer asked if he could introduce an RAF pilot. Ironically, the pilot had never seen her on screen, but recognized her from a snapshot that Gene showed him a few weeks earlier in England.

On October 12, Jeanette launched her tour with pianist Stuart Ross in Portland, Maine, playing cities in the Northeast and Midwest. JMIFC President Marie Waddy noted that Jeanette had tears in her eyes when she sang "Do Not Go, My Love," sure that she was thinking of Gene during the song. While Jeanette was in Newark, New Jersey for a recital, she called an elderly fan who was too ill to attend. Jeanette surprised the woman by singing her favorite song over the telephone.

Jeanette often invited student reporters to her press conferences. In Youngstown, Ohio, one of them shocked her by asking, "Since you have sung in so many pictures with Nelson Eddy, have you had any outside romances besides the one with your husband?" Jeanette did a double take and answered, "I like Mr. Eddy, but I've been married five years and my courtship took up two more, so that rather covers the time I've been acting with Mr. Eddy."[521] Another student reporter was scolded for inquiring about her age.

Publicist John Springer recalled being one of those student reporters and how friendly and courteous Jeanette was to him. "Once in the room with the great lady, my courage deserted me but she smoothly helped me through the tongue-tied nervousness of a first interview with such a star. And when she found out that I couldn't see the concert—tickets were very expensive and I was, after all, a high school boy—she arranged for me to watch from the wings."[522]

When asked about future movie plans, Jeanette said that she was reading scripts, but had not found anything that she liked. "I didn't know there were so many bad scripts written. I'd like to try something dramatic. But I can't make plans. I stopped making plans when my husband left for England."[523]

Although some stars, like James Cagney, produced their own movies, Jeanette was hesitant to do so because of the heavy responsibilities involved and the criticism a woman would get for taking charge. DeWitt Bodeen said that she had the ability to see a project as a whole, not just in terms of her own role, an ideal quality for a film producer. During the war, Gene tried to convince her that she knew as much or more about production than any of the men in Hollywood. Finally convinced, after asking Gene's advice, in March 1944, she acquired the rights to Frances Parkinson Keyes' best-selling novel *Crescent Carnival* (1942), intending to produce a film version. The book was about three generations of two intertwined families whose pride, misfortune, and political and cultural differences kept prospective lovers from marrying, until two people broke the cycle. According to newspaper reports, Keyes thought Jeanette and Nelson Eddy should play leading roles, and, Paul Short, who owned the stage, screen, and radio rights to all of Keyes' work, told agents that it was for sale only as a co-starring musical for the pair. It is assumed that they would play multiple characters, like Jeanette did in *Smilin' Through*. In 1946, both Universal and Columbia Pictures were rumored to be producing the project; however, *Crescent Carnival* never was filmed. Before Jeanette acquired the rights, Gene compared the novel to *Gone with the Wind* (1936), remarking how expansive the story was and how much time and money would be required to prepare it for the screen. He thought only a studio like MGM or a producer like David O. Selznick could do it justice. It's possible that studio executives decided that it was too expensive to produce or they thought that post-war audiences, who preferred more serious fare to operettas, would not want to see it.

After Jeanette's fall 1942 recital tour, she returned to New York for some radio broadcasts and a brief vacation. She told a reporter that the wartime dim-outs in Manhattan made it difficult to window shop at night and scary to cross shadowed streets. On November 4, Jeanette attended a Metropolitan Opera Guild luncheon honoring soprano Marjorie Lawrence, marking Lawrence's first public appearance since being diagnosed with polio. Six years later, when Lawrence sang in Los Angeles, Jeanette and Gene hosted an after-concert party for her.

In New York, Jeanette held a press conference, discussing her films and MGM, as well as her AER tour. She made no secret of her dislike for her last pairing with Nelson Eddy, calling *I Married an Angel* "the most awful drivel." She told reporters, "For the first time I have been in 100 per cent [sic] accord with the critics. I turned down 'Angel' three times. I never should have made it. It was panned all over the country and with every justification." She criticized the studio and their choice of movies for her. "Good Lord, MGM made an enormous amount of money on my pictures. Some thing [sic] like 28 million dollars. Some of them were with Nelson so I don't know how much of that is credited to him, but they all made money. And I don't see why I should keep doing re-makes. They wanted Nelson and me to do 'Show Boat,' but I refused because I don't think anything would be accomplished by my doing it, when Irene Dunne did it so beautifully such a short time ago. Then I come along as much to say, 'here, ladies and gentlemen, I am going to show you how it should be done.' It would lay me open to criticism."[524] She was appalled that the studio even promised to make the Gaylord character less of a heel if she and Nelson did the picture. Today, $28 million is worth over $432 million. She questioned MGM's insistence in casting her in operettas, instead of a good story, with music as an added feature. "Sometimes I feel that a voice is a detriment," she said. "I don't know why they won't realize that I am a normal person, that I should not be difficult to cast, that I can fit into most stories. If I did not sing, then they would put me in stories that meant something in themselves. I wish they'd do that now—that they'd write a good script and then, only then, add the music."[525]

Jeanette also discussed the difficult accommodations that she encountered on her tour, the lack of food after her performances, and the four-hour layovers between trains. "But I'm not complaining," she insisted. "It's the least we women can do while our men are at the fighting front."[526] She told reporters that she could have gone with the first USO unit to England, but worried that people would say she only went to see Gene. She laughed about "doing a very feminine thing,"[527] paying $7.50 postage to send her husband $2 worth of chocolate, currently equal to about $116 and $31. The cost of the candy and postage varied in different interviews and Gene's thank you letter. However, given Jeanette's frugality, that was a truly romantic gesture.

On November 12, Jeanette appeared on the radio show *Stage Door Canteen*, singing "Home Sweet Home" and "Keep the Light Burning Bright in the Harbor," both of which were sung by her in *Cairo*. The patriotic song, written by Arthur Schwartz and Howard Dietz, was so popular with servicemen that the 148ᵗʰ Infantry Regiment adopted it as their song, adding special lyrics. On the broadcast, *Stage Door Canteen* Master of Ceremonies Bert Lytell told Jeanette that he had been talking to a man who saw Gene in England and that Gene sent something for her. After she guessed a letter or a charm for her bracelet, Lytell gave her a resounding kiss, causing Jeanette to quip, "What! Why, Bert Lytell! Only one!"[528]

After the program, Jeanette asked if it was the birthday of any of the G.I.s. A sailor and a Marine spoke up, and Jeanette and Emily treated them to a seven-course dinner at Sardi's. When Jeanette noticed the sailor becoming more and more nervous, he admitted that he stood up his girlfriend. Jeanette wrote her a note on the back of one of her recital programs: "So sorry to have detained your boy friend. It was all my fault, so please forgive him."[529] Later, the sailor said that his girl forgave him, but told him, "You sure are a dumb bunny, pulling out on a date with Jeanette MacDonald for one with me!"[530]

While Jeanette was in the East, she also attended several war benefits and went to Philadelphia to visit oldest sister Elsie and her third husband, Bernard "Barney" Scheiter, whom she married in 1939. On November 16, Jeanette and the Scheiters attended a performance of Giacomo Puccini's *La Boheme* in Allentown, Pennsylvania. It was sung by singers from the Metropolitan Opera and the Chicago Opera Company, conducted by Jeanette's former accompanist, Giuseppe Bamboschek, and produced by her concert manager, Charles Wagner.

On November 23, Jeanette attended the opening of the Metropolitan Opera with Andre Kostelanetz, where his wife, Lily Pons, sang Gaetano Donizetti's *The Daughter of the Regiment*. During the performance, the French-born Pons unfurled the Cross of Lorraine, flag of the Fighting French forces, instead of the traditional French tri-color flag. After the opera, Pons led the audience in singing "La Marseillaise," the French National Anthem, and "The Star Spangled Banner." Jeanette posed for photographers with one of the Lily Pons dolls that were sold at the performance to benefit the Fighting French. Two days later, Jeanette addressed a patriotic rally for a "Women at War Week" program in Pittsburgh.

On November 23, 1942, Jeanette posed backstage with Lily Pons and Andre Kostelanetz after Pons' performance of *The Daughter of the Regiment*.

Blossom joined Jeanette in New York for Thanksgiving and to accompany her back to California, as Jeanette disliked traveling alone. Actress Glenda Farrell and her husband, Major Henry Ross, hosted a dinner for the sisters.

On November 29, Jeanette appeared on *The Pause That Refreshes on the Air*, a program sponsored by Coca-Cola that starred Andre Kostelanetz. She sang a heartfelt rendition of "I'll See You Again," changing the lyrics from "Though my world may go awry" to "Though my world *has gone* awry," a message of significance to her husband stationed overseas. Her voice almost cracked on the line "When I'm recalling the hours we've had, why will the foolish tears tremble across the years?"[531] On the show, she explained that she chose the song because it was Gene's favorite. She also sang Gene's "Let Me Always Sing" and the touching "British Children's Prayer." Jeanette sent Gene multiple telegrams, reminding him of the show, clearly anxious for him to hear it. Although the program, which was broadcast on the eve of Prime Minister Winston Churchill's birthday, saluted the British people, and the announcer claimed that it was being transcribed for the troops, it was not broadcast in England. When Jeanette learned that Gene couldn't hear it, she sent him records of the show so that he could listen to the songs that she chose especially for him.

On November 30, Jeanette and Blossom left New York. Their train was over an hour late when it arrived in Chicago, where they had to transfer. Jeanette told her friend, publicist Constance Hope, "Fortunately, the conductor was most solicitous--and wired ahead and they held the 'City of Los Angeles' twenty minutes. You should have seen us (and various officials picking us up) going from one station to the other--if there was any press around, they got lost in the general rush."[532] On December 2, the sisters arrived in Los Angeles, with Jeanette having traveled over fifteen thousand miles on her camp and recital tours. As they got off the train, Jeanette was questioned about gas rationing, limiting most citizens to no more than four gallons per week. She said, "After all those miles, even gasoline rationing in Los Angeles holds no terrors for me."[533] She spoke effusively about the people she encountered on her tours: "Everywhere I've traveled there have been at least two carloads of soldiers on the train. It's certainly wonderful having a military escort constantly—even though they don't know they're that. And the people I've met—why I didn't know the Army had so many generals [sic] and colonels [sic]."[534]

Back in California, Jeanette kept busy, entertaining the troops at the Hollywood Canteen, military hospitals, and camps. On December 13, she planned to sing a few songs at the Canteen and ended up doing fifteen. Although today it's dangerous to pick up hitchhikers, during the war, like many patriotic Americans, Jeanette often gave rides to men in uniform. One Sunday, while she was driving to the Canteen, she saw two servicemen hitchhiking and she stopped to give them a ride. As she drove, one of them recognized her. Jeanette asked if they were going to the Canteen, but they said it was too crowded. When she offered to get them past the line, they readily accepted. Upon arrival at the Canteen, Jeanette took each of them by the arm and marched past the M.P. (Military Policeman) at the stage door, telling him that they were her cousins.

Jeanette did all she could to keep up morale, both for servicemen and on the home front. She told the press, "To work harder, to sacrifice more, to love more and to be more generous, these are the things we Americans must do to the utmost to win this war."[535] She welcomed a convoy of 250 Army men on short notice at Twin Gables after the USO asked the men the star that they most wanted to meet. It wasn't Betty Grable, Rita Hayworth, or any other pin-up, but Jeanette MacDonald. She gave each man a special greeting then they toured the gardens at Twin Gables. Before they departed, the soldiers named her "The Sweetheart of the Regiment."

In movie magazines, Jeanette offered advice to military wives, suggesting that they keep busy, doing their part for the war effort. She urged them to keep writing long, gossipy letters to their husbands to help keep up their spouses' morale. "Remember that this is the time for women to be partners, real partners. We can't fight beside our men, but we can stand by them. We can inspire them with our understanding and appreciation. And we can keep their minds free of any personal anxiety."[536]

On December 20, Jeanette received an early Christmas present: hearing Gene on the radio. During the war, American actors Ben Lyon and Bebe Daniels lived in London and hosted a program, *Stars and Stripes in Britain*, broadcast over the Mutual network in the United States. Gene appeared as guest, giving a special greeting to Jeanette and letting her know that two of her Christmas packages had arrived.

It was the Raymonds' first Christmas apart. The Lyons entertained Gene and some of his fellow officers, while Jeanette celebrated with Anna, Blossom, and the Halfords. Andre Kostelanetz and his friend from Chicago, Dr. Cutler, joined the family for Christmas dinner. Jeanette told Constance Hope, "I do not know whether they had a good time or not, although they seemed to enjoy it, but I do know they had a good dinner."[537] During the Halfords' stay, Jeanette made lime and tangerine sherbet with fruit from her orchards.

Jeanette knitted Gene a scarf and a union suit (one-piece long underwear) and sent him a roll of toilet paper, as he wrote an amusing letter about the lack of it when he was away from the base in England. He most treasured a card that read "This box contains more love than there's room for."[538] In addition to V-mail greetings, pictured in the Letters volume of this set of books, Gene arranged for Jeanette's favorite Joanna Hill roses to be delivered to her. He also sent her jewelry, causing the always-frugal Jeanette to balk at the $9 duty on the package, currently equivalent to around $139. She was even more distressed when, on Christmas day, her household servants quit before breakfast, leaving Jeanette and her maid, Rose, to do the cooking and housework for her guests. On January 5, Jeanette wrote to Elsie, "Have been unable to secure anybody as yet, so Rose and I have been doing the cooking ourselves, and, I might add, only fair. Besides, I hate to wash dishes."[539]

Jeanette spent New Year's Day singing at the San Diego Naval Hospital. After being in bed the two previous days with a cold, she defied doctor's orders and traveled four hours each way to put on a two-hour show for the wounded sailors. She also toured the wards for an hour and a half, talking to the men.

Jeanette further showed her patriotism by adopting pilot Joseph Francis Doyal through the American Flying Service Foundation, helping to pay his training expenses. She took him under her wing and was very proud when he graduated with honors. Unfortunately, shortly after graduation, he was killed at the age of twenty-two. On January 5, 1943, two Navy training planes collided in mid-air at the Naval Air Station at Los Alamitos, California. Doyal leaped clear of his plane, just before it fell into a vacant parking lot and burst into flames; however, the next day, he died from his injuries. The other pilot, Walter Eugene Law, died when his plane burst into flames after crashing into a building following the initial collision. Although Jeanette was saddened by Doyal's death, she immediately signed up to sponsor another pilot.

As much as Jeanette loved her canine family, she loved her country more. In the fall of 1942, she read about Dogs for Defense, an organization formed shortly after the bombing of Pearl Harbor to use dogs for sentry duty to guard against attacks in the United States and its harbors. Eventually, dogs were trained to be scouts, messengers, and mine detectives. People from around the country offered their pets for service. In January 1943, after touring the Dogs for Defense headquarters in San Carlos, California, Jeanette enrolled her Newfoundland, Nick. Gene was against the idea for sentimental reasons, since Nick had been part of their courtship. Patriotism won out and, while most of the dogs were returned to their owners or retired to live with their military partners after the war, it is assumed that Nick gave his life for his country, as Jeanette wore a gold star on her charm bracelet to represent his service. The military realized the importance of dogs; however, since World War II, they used canines belonging to the service, rather than family pets.

Nick wasn't the only sacrifice that Jeanette made. During the war, everyone from a five-year-old girl in Oregon to a farmer in Iowa to a Hollywood movie star had to adhere to rationing, which limited the amount of commodities that consumers could purchase. The federal government introduced programs to control supply and demand to avoid public anger with shortages and so that everyone, not just the wealthy, could buy products. Each American was issued ration stamps for everything from food to gasoline to shoes. Farmers were asked to set aside portions of their fields exclusively for crops that would be used for the troops. All over the country, people planted Victory Gardens so that they could can their own produce and reduce pressure on the public food supply. Commercial products then could be sent to the troops. In large cities, public land was utilized, like the Boston Common, San Francisco's Golden Gate Park, Chicago's Grant Park, and Los Angeles' Griffith Park. Even First Lady Eleanor Roosevelt had a Victory Garden planted on the grounds of the White House. Victory Gardens also helped conserve precious rubber and gas, since trucks were used to transport food to stores.

Like many other war wives, Jeanette planted a Victory Garden to assure that she'd have plenty of vegetables, along with the fruit that already grew on the property. Although she hated bugs and was allergic to pesticides, she took her garden seriously; it wasn't a publicity stunt. When a rabbit began raiding her carrots, she scared him off with a BB gun. During her 1943 fall tour, she complained to reporters about her crops: "My Victory garden [sic] this year was the biggest frost. I planted so much corn—and we only had four ears. We had a lot of squash, wonderful fruit and about—a dozen—tomatoes."[540] Jeanette was too impatient to plant the seeds very deep, which was part of the reason that she wasn't a very successful gardener.

To deal with sugar rationing, Jeanette decided to raise bees so she could have honey, a popular sugar substitute in many recipes. She came up with the idea after bees invaded the rafters at Twin Gables and began going in the house through a ventilator in Gene's closet. The prop man on *Cairo* made a hive for her and she bought a colony of bees to inhabit it. Jeanette shared honey with her friends and even sent a jar to the Honeybee chapter of her fan club.

On February 15, 1943, Jeanette received her first bee sting and, a few days later, she landed in the hospital when her left hand and arm became infected. She ignored the pain in her hand until it spread to her upper arm, making her realize that something serious was wrong. She was given a sulpha drug and, within four days, she was home. Although Gene was concerned, he sent her a silly telegram: "DEAREST PETUNIA DIDNT [sic] I EVER TELL YOU ABOUT THE BEES AND FLOWERS."[541] He had trouble getting the message past the censors, who thought that he was writing in code. In July, Jeanette was stung on the ankle and it swelled to twice its size, forcing her to bed for several days. She didn't blame the bees, insisting that they were kind, as long as no one bothered them. For several years after the war, she continued keeping them, despite the fact that she was so allergic. In 1952, Jeanette told a reporter that, after several trips to the hospital, "Gene decided it would be cheaper and much less painful to buy our honey in a jar."[542]

Chapter Twelve

In 1943, Jeanette continued entertaining at the Hollywood Canteen, military hospitals, and on the radio, while Grace Newell coached her on Charles Gounod's *Romeo et Juliette*, which Jeanette hoped to sing for the Metropolitan Opera, after she gained experience in the field. The opera, which was sung in French, was based on William Shakespeare's tragic play about the star-crossed lovers from feuding families.

For years, there had been rumors about Jeanette receiving offers to sing with various opera companies. As far back as 1928, *The Billboard* reported that internationally known opera director Henry Russell procured an offer for her to sing with the opera in Monte Carlo and the Opéra Comique in Paris. During her MGM years, many magazines said that she received offers from the Metropolitan Opera and she had to refuse them because of her movie contract.

Jeanette said that she came up with the idea to pursue opera after Gene wrote about being cheered up after he attended a July 1942 performance of Giacomo Puccini's *Madama Butterfly* in England. Jeanette explained, "I wanted to do it myself of course, but I wanted also to do it because I knew it would please Gene. I knew it would tickle him to think that I was not only going on with my life as he would wish but that I was trying to do bigger and harder things all the time. It would make him feel that I wasn't worried about him, that I had complete confidence in him. That's pretty important. No matter what a man says, he must be weakened if his wife shows any signs of lacking confidence in him. So—I've been very busy."[543]

In October 1942, during Jeanette's AER tour, she met public relations consultant Constance Hope in Baltimore, Maryland. Helen Ferguson suggested that Hope advise Jeanette on her operatic debut, since Hope handled other classical artists, like sopranos Lily Pons, Lotte Lehmann, and Grace Moore, and tenor Lauritz Melchior. Hope recalled, "Within one hour of conversation we were not star and counsel, but friends. Her knowledge, sincere interest, and determination to acquire all the necessary professional 'know-how' that lay before her to make a successful operatic debut, staggered me. . . . In reflection, I often think of what a 'real trouper' she was—always seriously prepared for work—never slipshod. I was supposed to counsel her and I did, but oftentimes I learned as much from her as she did from me." Hope called Jeanette "a professional in every sense of the term." She explained, "[Jeanette] took that approach to any job she undertook. She could not, and would not, ever compromise!"[544]

Through the years, Jeanette's feelings on opera varied. When she was a child, she dreamed of being an opera singer, but, in 1940, she told reporters that she was "not too crazy about opera" and had "no great urge to sing for the Met."[545] She elaborated: "The 'Met' doesn't excite me as a prospect in the first place. I never was too, too, too crazy about grand opera. I've never had a terrific urge for it. The 'Met' is generally the stepping stone to concerts but the pictures have done that for me. The 'Met' is no lure."[546] During her 1939 recital tour, she answered rumors about the Met. "I've had no time to think of an operatic career much less prepare for it," she insisted. "As long as I can be so happy on the concert stage and in the making of motion pictures there really isn't much incentive in working toward a Metropolitan debut."[547] Ken Richards recalled inviting Jeanette to a Met performance of *Aida* in the 1950s. She declined, insisting that she really was not that fond of opera and would only attend if it was a voice that she wanted to hear.

While Jeanette was in New York in the fall of 1942, she met with Edward Johnson, General Manager of the Met, to discuss singing for the company. Initially, she thought of doing an original American opera, an idea that she found more exciting than singing a well-known work. Among the composers she considered to write it were Erich Korngold, best known for writing film scores, *Rodeo's* Aaron Copland, and cellist/conductor Alfred Wallenstein. She quickly ruled out Korngold because he was German and she wanted the work to be completely American. She decided that Copland's style was "too modern" and "not sufficiently melodic."[548] Jeanette discussed the idea with Jane Cowl, whom Jeanette thought could write the libretto. After Jeanette returned to California, Cowl had lunch with Johnson. She reported to Jeanette that he seemed "very tentative, and very much on the defensive regarding the whole idea and intimated that the Met. would hardly be in a position, financially, to produce a new opera."[549] Jeanette told Constance Hope, "This was, decidedly, not the impression he gave me before I left, and I am wondering just what has brought about the change."[550] She asked Hope if she thought that Johnson overstepped the bounds of his authority and realized that he would have to account to the Met Board of Directors. Instead of a new opera, Johnson suggested that Jeanette study *Romeo et Juliette*.

While Jeanette learned the *Romeo et Juliette* score, she kept busy with other appearances. On January 16, she hosted the AFRS program *Command Performance*, dedicating Charles Gounod's "Ave Maria" to various enlisted men and "my Captain, Gene Raymond, somewhere in England."[551] On January 24, she appeared on an hour-long broadcast of *The Charlie McCarthy Show*, singing "When You're Away" and a medley of service songs, saluting the Marines, the Army Air Corps, the Army, and the Navy with the "Marines' Hymn," "Army Air Corps Song," "The Caissons Go Rolling Along," and "Anchors Away." The announcer said that Jeanette dedicated "When You're Away" to "all husbands and sweethearts who are away, especially one Captain Gene Raymond of the United States Army Air Corps."[552] She also appeared in "Pick Up," a sketch with actor Don Ameche about war plant workers. The show, which usually ran for thirty minutes, was expanded to celebrate sponsor Standard Brands' Peekskill, New York plant receiving an Army–Navy "E" award for excellence in war production. A thirty-minute version of the show was rebroadcast for the Armed Services. Jeanette turned down an appearance on comedian Fred Allen's radio show for March 7, since he offered her $1,500 (now equivalent to about $22,000) versus the $5,000 salary (now almost $73,000) that she received for appearing on the Charlie McCarthy program. "Fred just ain't that much better!!" she reasoned.[553]

On January 27, Jeanette invited a soldier, a sailor, and a Marine to be her escorts at the Hollywood premiere of *In Which We Serve* (1942). The film, written and co-directed by Noel Coward, was about the sinking of the British destroyer HMS Torrin. Proceeds from the premiere went to the combined United Nations Fund, which included British, United China, Dutch, French, Greek, Polish, and Russian War Relief organizations. On January 29, Jeanette sang at inaugural ceremonies at the Naval Hospital in Long Beach.

On February 5, 1943, Jeanette's friend and director, Woody Van Dyke, committed suicide. Three days later, she sang "Ah! Sweet Mystery of Life" and the Christian Science hymn "Oh, Gentle

Presence" at his funeral at the Church of the Recessional at Forest Lawn, Glendale. The service was conducted by Christian Science practitioner Alex Swan. Although some pre-funeral newspaper articles said that Nelson Eddy also would sing, post-funeral reports only mentioned Jeanette. Some contemporary sources erroneously said that Jeanette and Nelson conducted the service. When Gene received the news of Van Dyke's death, he sadly echoed Jeanette's sentiment: ". . . another good guy gone to rest."[554]

Gene knew Leslie Howard since Gene's earliest days in Hollywood. Here, William Gargan (who appeared with Gene on stage in *The War Song* in 1928 and *The Best Man* in 1960), Howard, and Gene sang, while Howard's wife, Ruth, played piano at a 1932 party.

On February 22, Gene and British actor Leslie Howard acted as

Masters of Ceremonies on a radio show for the British observation of American President George Washington's Birthday. The program was broadcast from Sulgrave Manor, the Washington family's home in England, and the London Red Cross Club, and aired in the United States over the Mutual network. It is not known if Jeanette heard the original broadcast, since, at the time, she was hospitalized for her bee sting; however, a 1954 inventory of Twin Gables included a record of the program, presumably sent to her by Gene. Less than three months later, Howard was killed when his plane was shot down over the Bay of Biscay by the Luftwaffe, the German Air Force.

Although Jeanette never presented or received an Oscar, on March 4, 1943, she sang the National Anthem at the fifteenth Academy Awards banquet, which was held at the Cocoanut Grove in the Ambassador Hotel. During the ceremony, a flag was unfurled, listing 27,677 names of Hollywood industry personnel who were serving in the Armed Forces.

A few days later, Jeanette left for New York to prepare for *Romeo et Juliette*. En route, she stopped in Michigan for two wartime presentations. On March 11, she sang for workers at the Willow Run Bomber Plant near Ypsilanti. Nicknamed the eighth Wonder of the World, Willow Run was the largest defense plant in the world, with over 100,000 employees working around the clock, from 1941 to 1945. At its peak, it turned out 650 B-24s per month. Constructed by the Ford Motor Company, Willow Run's floor space was larger than that of Boeing and Douglas Aircraft combined. While Jeanette was at Willow Run, she toured the control tower, tried on a gas mask, and dedicated a B-24 Liberator to her husband, signing the plane in chalk "The 'Captain Gene' from Jeanette." A week later, the plane was transferred to St. Paul, Minnesota. During the war, the Reconnaissance plane patrolled airspace in the United States, assigned to bases in Cincinnati,

Ohio; San Antonio, Texas; and Albuquerque, New Mexico. In July 1945, it was turned over to the Reconstruction Finance Corp.; its ultimate destination is unknown.

On March 11, 1943, Jeanette visited the Ford bomber plant at Willow Run in Ypsilanti, Michigan, where she dedicated a plane to Gene. Photo courtesy of Yankee Air Museum.

On March 12, Jeanette sang "God Bless America" during a national broadcast from the Ford Aircraft plant in Detroit. During the show, the plant received the Army–Navy "E" Award, given for excellence in war production. After the broadcast, the audience, made up of six thousand workers from the Pratt & Whitney Aircraft Engine Division, demanded that she sing "Indian Love Call," "Auld Lang Syne," and other songs, while military brass and Ford Motor Company President Edsel Ford watched. The *Detroit Free Press* reported that she "stole the show" and "when Jeanette finally was allowed to stop singing it took a twelve-man flying wedge of plant police to get her out safely."[555]

In New York, during the lengthy coaching and rehearsal period for *Romeo et Juliette,* Jeanette sublet an apartment from actress Ruth Wilcox Selwyn, which was cheaper than the Sherry–Netherland apartment hotel, where Jeanette usually stayed. In addition to the cost being prohibitive, she feared being "hounded to death." She told Constance Hope, "I should prefer to arrive quite inconspicuously, and do not wish to be seen by the press. After all, my sole purpose this time is to study further the role of Juliet. Besides which, if I am met at the station I will, naturally, be questioned about the Met. debut. I should not like to make a statement to the affect that I am studying the role at Mr. Johnson's request, for that might put him on the spot with his Board of Directors. On the other hand, I am, most certainly, not going to say this was all my own idea. And, so for the sake of not embarrassing anybody, I want to <u>work</u> in New York, and that is all."[556]

Shortly after Jeanette arrived in New York, she began serious work on *Romeo et Juliette.* On the advice of Spanish operatic soprano Lucrezia Bori, Jeanette trained with bass Leon Rothier and her former recital accompanist, Giuseppe Bamboschek. According to *Chicago Tribune* Music Critic Claudia Cassidy, "Rothier told her about Bori's Juliet, and [Geraldine] Farrar's, but . . . he made her sing her own. He ripped her French apart and put it back together in Gallic style, and he taught her Juliet so firmly, so solidly, so irrefutably that not even debut nerves could tangle it up."[557]

While Jeanette was preparing for the role, Constance Hope suggested that Jeanette see Alicia Markova in Sergei Prokofiev's ballet version of *Romeo and Juliet*. Markova's performance influenced some of Jeanette's childlike movements in the opera, depicting the character as feminine and helpless. Hope recalled how, during rehearsals, Jeanette impressed the cast, many of whom had sung with the Metropolitan Opera: "She was prepared—and they had an immediate and instinctive new respect for her. She was a professional."[558]

Flying in raids over Europe as an Intelligence Officer fueled Gene's desire to qualify as a Bomber Pilot; therefore, in late 1942, he transferred from Intelligence to Operations. He wrote to Jeanette, "Make no mistake about it, the guys who are going to win this war are the guys who drop the bombs—and I intend to be one of them."[559] Jeanette was upset, fearing that he would be in more danger. He assured her that he was not, although he became more determined than ever to secure his Military Pilot's rating. Jeanette recalled, "He also wrote casually that there was a new airplane soon to be debuted by the Air Forces, and that he was trying to get assigned for pilot training in the new program. I thought these new planes must be the B-29 Super-Fortresses [sic] I had read about in the news magazines. I knew that this assignment would involve training in this country, and the prospect of his return was gratifying, to say the least."[560] In another letter, Gene hinted about getting an assignment in the United States, but told Jeanette not to count on it, as he didn't want her to be disappointed if it didn't happen. He wrote, "You pray hard for it, and I'll work hard for it!"[561] The prayers and hard work succeeded. On March 28, Gene departed England and, after a stop in Trinidad, on April 3, he arrived back in the United States.

Constance Hope recalled that Jeanette was very anxious for Gene's homecoming. "She and I were together, all that day, waiting for the word that he was back in New York. I never saw any bride more excited about it than she was. And she had everything prepared. . . . She didn't even want to go out of the house. She was afraid she'd miss the call. . . . There was that kind of a close relationship."[562] Despite Jeanette's planning, the Raymonds' reunion didn't go smoothly. When Gene arrived in New York, he didn't know her address so he had to call Anna in California to find his wife.

In the version of Jeanette's autobiography written with James Brough, she said:

> I knew he would be getting leave. He'd told me that, along with the fact that he was desperate for fresh milk, which had been scarce in England. But I had no idea of when to expect him—the telegram he sent me was garbled in transmission. So my face was greased, my hair was in curlers and I'd settled down in an old housecoat to relax before I went to bed when the doorbell rang. There stood Gene, looking like everything important in the world. There stood I, looking like the wreck of the Hesperus instead of the beautiful creature I'd aimed to be when he caught his first homecoming glimpse of me. I couldn't have been more chagrined, but his kiss put an end to that.
>
> Before turning in that night, we observed an old custom of ours and raided the icebox. We made sandwiches, and then Captain Raymond consumed a full quart of milk. After three gusty glasses, he took a final swallow, smacked his lips and regarded the empty glass rather lovingly. "Darling," he grinned, "if I ever leave you, I think it will be for a cow."[563]

Jeanette told a different version of the story in a later draft of her autobiography, written with Fredda Dudley Balling. After receiving a cable that said Gene was arriving soon, she debated the meaning of the word.

So, day after day I waited, working hard, but coaching the role in my apartment, never leaving it unoccupied lest his phone call arrive during my absence. When the phone rang I rushed to answer, and I'd cut all conversations short to be sure he'd not get that tantalizing busy signal. I'm sure that you'll understand, girls, that I even went to bed with my make-up [sic] on—just in case! But after a week of this moment-to-moment existance [sic], I woke up one morning, and decided that more than likely the word "soon" really meant "during the month." The most important thing was that he was on the way. So I removed my make-up [sic], made my breakfast while waiting for Rose, my maid, who would come at nine. Promptly at nine the doorbell rang, and I went to the door to let Rose in, and there stood Gene, grinning in his olive greens and captain's [sic] bars! And there stood I in my oldest robe with a face full of grease and a mouth full of toast! "OH NO! I said unglamourously [sic]. "Oh YES!" he shouted and burst out laughing as he took me in his arms. He got the idea. And if he didn't mind I certainly didn't.

Later when Gene read the cable I'd received he couldn't believe it. "I cabled you from Trinidad, where there are no security restrictions! I wired you in detail the day and time of my arrival in New York and what time I'd be here! All the crew did! I forget how many words, but it cost me twenty-five bucks! Some dam' Four-F must have cut the message down to three words, and pocketed the difference! Between all of us, he made a small fortune that day!"

Before turning in that night, we revived an old custom and raided the icebox. We made sandwiches with which the good Captain consumed a full quart of milk! Savoring the last few drops, he settled back in his chair, smacked his lips and regarded the empty glass lovingly. "Darling," he grinned. "If I ever leave you I think it will be for a cow!"[564]

Movie magazines of the day repeated a story similar to Balling's; however, it isn't known which, if either, version was completely true. In a 1992 interview with Edward Baron Turk, Clara Rhoades said that Jeanette described Fredda Dudley Balling as "too mushy" and James Brough as "distorting the truth for the sake of drama."[565] The telegram seen by this author, sent before Gene departed England, read, "ARRIVING NEWYORK [sic] WILL CALL SHERRY NETHERLAND OR LYTELLS ALL OKAY LOVE=GENE RAYMOND."[566] It is not known if the telegram sent from Trinidad still exists.

On April 5, Jeanette appeared in an all-star benefit at Madison Square Garden, which raised $250,000 (over $3.6 million today) for the American Red Cross. Although she wanted to spend all of her time catching up with her husband, while Gene was in New York, she continued her opera preparation. In between her coaching and rehearsals, the Raymonds found time to take long walks in Central Park and go window shopping on Fifth Avenue. In the evenings, they went to the theater or talked. Columnist Dorothy Kilgallen reported that they were seen holding hands at the Copacabana, "so romantic looking the chorines just sighed and sighed and sighed."[567]

When Gene received leave, he joined Jeanette, wherever she was. Here, they dined in New York in April 1943, finally reunited after Gene returned from serving ten months in England.

During Gene's visit, the Raymonds did some interviews about how the war had affected them. Jeanette philosophized, "It hasn't been a sad year, really, it's been a *thoughtful* one. And I find that, actually, I am happy. Because, I think, I am a naturally happy person. Also because I've been fairly busy, feel that I have accomplished something. And happy, most of all, for what I have had in the past."[568] Gene also put their wartime separation into perspective. "I miss my home just as much as any man in the service does, and naturally, being away from you for a year, more than a year, can't make me terribly happy. And no one really loves the work of war. But I am happier doing what I am than I would be doing anything else. Besides, I am not sure that 'happiness' is any longer the important factor."[569] Both Raymonds repeatedly said that they were grateful for the happy times that they shared in the past and looked forward to resuming their lives together when the war was over.

On April 12, Gene flew to California to visit his brother and Jeanette's family, and take care of some business; six days later, he left to spend the rest of his furlough with Jeanette. En route to New York, he stopped at Barry Field in Nashville, Tennessee to visit Lieutenant Colonel T.B. Herndon of the 20th Ferrying Group. Early in the war, the group delivered aircraft made in Montreal, Canada to British troops and, after the United States entered the war, it delivered aircraft produced in the United States to Allied fronts around the world. Presumably, Gene met Herndon when Gene was serving in England, and wanted to tour Barry Field.

While Gene was gone, Jeanette caught a bad cold, which initially gave her laryngitis. Her doctor ordered her not to talk and she cancelled all appointments. Gene returned to New York, and, on April 22, she left her sick bed to appear on the radio program *Stage Door Canteen* with him. Her voice sounded fine, but in photos, her eyes were noticeably puffy from the cold. She was in a skit with comedian Willie Howard and sang Gene's composition, "Will You?," and "You Are Free." Gene, appearing as a representative of the Army Air Force, instead of as an actor, was in a salute to bombardiers. He appealed to citizens to write to those serving their country and assure them that those on the home front were backing them 100%. After the broadcast, Jeanette sang "The Star Spangled Banner," with the audience joining her, and New York Mayor Fiorello LaGuardia leading the orchestra.

Before Jeanette began her opera tour, she received an offer of $3,000, now equivalent to about $43,600, to do a recital for the Red Cross in Montreal. She turned it down, concerned that the venue may be outdoors and have a poor sound system. She told Constance Hope,

". . . from my own personal, selfish standpoint, it would occur to me that my debut in Montreal must be a personal success, musically, and I should not wish to start at such a disadvantage, and there are times when even the money (assuming a concert were booked on a percentage basis) is of no interest when one's actual artistry is involved. You see, Constance, I am a very serious and sincere singer, in spite of my reputation for being a 'smart business woman.'"[570] Conversely, Jeanette welcomed the opportunity to sing *Romeo et Juliette* in Montreal, no matter the salary, figuring the more times she sang it, the better she would be.

On April 22, 1943, Jeanette and Gene appeared on the radio show *Stage Door Canteen* with actress Cheryl Walker, who also was in the movie *Stage Door Canteen*. Jeanette's eyes were puffy due to a bad cold, but her voice sounded fine.

On April 24, the Saturday before Easter, Gene's furlough ended. Jeanette planned to go to Washington, D.C. with him to spend the holiday and attend some weekend parties; however, her lingering cold prevented her from joining him, as well as from traveling to Montreal with the rest of the *Romeo et Juliette* company. She opened without a dress rehearsal, and her ears were so stuffed up that she barely could hear the orchestra.

Jeanette with bass Ezio Pinza, who played Frère Laurent in *Romeo et Juliette*. According to longtime fan Roger P. Noonan, when Jeanette met Pinza, a notorious womanizer, he hugged her very tight and she told him to stop it. Like her experience with Woody Van Dyke when he tried to get fresh, Pinza realized where he stood. He and Jeanette became friends and, in 1944, she hosted a dinner party for him at Twin Gables and appeared with him in *Faust*.

On May 8, Helen Ferguson attended the opening in Montreal and described Jeanette as "fragile, dainty, graceful," noting "I'm sure both Shakespeare and Gounod would thank her for presenting their heroine with flawless skill and delightful appeal."[571] Conductor Wilfrid Pelletier recalled how Jeanette impressed the *Romeo et Juliette* company: "We travelled together for weeks. She was an outstanding Juliette and an outstanding colleague, refusing at each performance to take a solo bow, insisting that she was one of the company and not the star. It was a great experience and a great lesson of modesty to all of us."[572]

Jeanette was disappointed that Gene did not have enough leave to go to Montreal with her for her opening and further disappointed when, on May 19, two days after she performed in Ottawa, he was sent there on Air Force business. However, to Jeanette's delight, he was able to get another brief leave, and he flew to meet her train in Toronto. At Union Station, Jeanette introduced him to the press as "my lord and master."[573] Gene joked, "It's nice to see the old lady once in a while."[574]

In Toronto, Jeanette talked to the press about wartime fashion, which changed due to restrictions on raw materials and bans of some imported fabrics, leading to more simplistic styles, shorter hemlines, the elimination of cuffs on pants, and the creation of man-made fibers. Silk and nylon were used for parachutes, which forced women to wear cotton or rayon stockings, rely on old ones, or use makeup on their legs. "One thing I don't approve of is the ban on formal dress," Jeanette said. "A lot of people are buying new short dresses to attend some social function, when they could save by wearing last year's evening dress. That would look more patriotic to me! What I'm trying to do is to make my last year's clothes do, adding a few new accessories to make them look different."[575] Jeanette also expressed disappointment over the fact that she hadn't seen any Mounties in the Canadian cities that she visited on her tour.

Gene attended the May 20 and May 22 performances of *Romeo et Juliette*, spending part of the first backstage because autograph seekers kept disturbing him in his seat. At the second, he sat with the Raymonds' longtime friend, Mary Pickford, who was visiting her native city to raise money for the Mary Pickford Bungalow Project. The charity was created to raise $15,000 (currently equivalent to over $218,000) for the Lions British Child War Victim Fund, *The Evening Telegram* British War Victims' Fund, and the Malta War Relief Fund. She started the project by donating a piece of property in Toronto, where a bungalow was built. While the Raymonds were in Toronto, they joined Pickford at an event sponsored by the Canadian Legion Ladies' Auxiliaries.

In Windsor, the last stop on Jeanette's tour, she told the press that Gene was her severest critic. When asked what he said about her performances in Toronto, she teased, "Oh, I can't tell you that. You'd think I was all puffed up, which I am."[576] Jeanette realized that many in her audience were coming to see the movie star rather than the opera singer. "I don't mind in the least," she insisted, "so long as they leave contented with me as an opera star." When told that the Mounties only wore scarlet jackets on parade, she complained, "Oh, I don't want to see a plain policeman. He must have a red coat or he won't be a Mountie at all. He'll just be a man."[577]

Prior to Jeanette's debut, there were many newspaper reports that, in the fall of 1943, she would sing *Romeo et Juliette* for the Metropolitan Opera. In February, the publicity caused Met General Manager Edward Johnson to issue a denial, insisting that no contract had been signed or even discussed. Jeanette explained to Constance Hope how the Met rumors got started upon Jeanette's return from New York in December 1942.

I was met at the train, of course, by photographers and press, and asked what my plans were, now that I was home.

To which I replied, "I am going to concentrate on studying the role of "Romeo and Juliet" for the opera." I was particularly careful to not, under any circumstances, mention anything about contracts, because, after all, who is to be made the fool of by such a misstatement--the Metropolitan or I? I leave you to decide.

However, one by one, our Hollywood columnists have found it exciting news, and, peculiarly enough, by the time Louella Parsons got around to it, she was certain she had a real inside story which no one even suspected (you know how each writer likes to scoop the other.) Poor old Charley Wagner has written a couple of times, suggesting that Helen Ferguson not give out such statements (of course, I told you he dislikes Helen intensely, though why, I do not know, except, it would appear, that he dislikes all female publicists.) Naturally, after a story has broken, it is hardly like Helen is going to call up said columnist and say it is a complete misstatement.[578]

Jeanette was annoyed that the Met issued a statement that no contracts had been discussed when she began studying the role of Juliette at Johnson's request. She told Constance Hope, ". . . I am not a person with sufficient idle time on my hands to waste it on pure speculation. I do not need the Met! And, if the controversy that has arisen, as the result of such an announcement, hasn't indicated a tremendous interest on the part of the press, and they are not aware of the fact that the Metropolitan Opera has already gleaned a tremendous amount of publicity as a direct result, then I can only say they are very shortsighted, and perhaps even stuffy, and that is probably why poor Mr. Johnson has such a difficult problem poking some life into them."[579]

Deciding that she didn't need the Met, in February, Jeanette told Hope that she was negotiating several performances of *Romeo et Juliette* elsewhere, concluding, "I am a lady with a purpose, and when traffic gets too thick, I have been known to honk my horn!"[580] The performances she mentioned were the ones on the Canadian tour.

Johnson planned to see one of Jeanette's Canadian performances, but the continued publicity and rumors about Jeanette and the Met caused him to change his mind. During the tour, Jeanette received a telegram from Johnson, asking if she would give a benefit performance at the Met for Mrs. William Randolph Hearst's milk fund. Jeanette turned down the invitation, but later regretted it, realizing that it was a way to get started at the Met.

In Quebec, Jeanette wrote to Constance Hope about it being imperative for Johnson to see a performance so she would know whether she would be performing at the Met that winter or if she should make a movie. She said, "I really must make up my mind, though frankly it seems to me it is in his hands to make up my mind for me. I have no inclination to become a 'road star' in a touring Company [sic] of 'Romeo and Juliet,' for I can make vastly more money in straight concert. Since I have already devoted six months of my current season to the preparation of this opera (at Mr. Johnson's suggestion) then I do feel that he owes me the courtesy at least of seeing a performance."[581] Jeanette told Hope that she had offers to sing the opera in San Francisco, Los Angeles, and Chicago. Jeanette said that unless she could see the fruition of her plans to sing for the Met, she did not want to invest any more money in preparing. She concluded, "With me it is a very serious step in my career and I cannot allow my entire Season [sic], either financial or artistic, to be tossed about by indecision."[582]

The San Francisco and Los Angeles offers came from San Francisco Opera Company founder/manager Gaetano Merola.

Jeanette was thrilled, hoping that the offer would make the Met take notice after she performed with another esteemed company following her Canadian tour. However, her excitement was short-lived when Merola told her that the San Francisco Opera Company wanted her to sing *Romeo et Juliette* in Los Angeles, but not San Francisco, explaining, "We believe the [San Francisco] critics may be prejudiced against your background of Hollywood!"[583] Jeanette passed on the offer. In 1944, she performed in Chicago.

Unfortunately, Jeanette's Canadian opera tour was a critical success, but not a financial one, leaving her frustrated and depressed. Because the budget needed balancing, she took no salary and paid the company's transportation costs back to New York. Furthermore, with the money she lost financing the tour, she could have bought her way into the Metropolitan Opera, as Edward Johnson had hinted, suggesting that she enroll at the Juilliard School and sing at the Met for a $25,000 donation, now almost $364,000. In a 1959 interview, Jeanette recalled the experience: "Everything about the tour was completely satisfactory, except for one detail—finances. The largest theater on the tour was scaled to $9,000, and the show cost $12,000 a performance. And so every performance started with a minimum loss of $3,000."[584] Today, these figures would be about $131,000, $174,000, and $44,000.

After consulting with Gene, Jeanette wrote to Edward Johnson, asking why the Met did not want her. Johnson blamed internal problems at the Met, insisting "the decisions are always arrived at for technical reasons and never on personal ones."[585] Jeanette was frustrated by the cultural snobbery, prejudice, and political games that she encountered in the opera world. In the past, she could identify a problem with her work and fix it, but she couldn't change others' attitudes. During a January 1944 trip to New York, she met with Johnson again;

however, nothing changed. Through the years, she performed *Romeo et Juliette*, as well as *Faust*, in various American cities, but it remained a disappointment that she never sang for the Met. Jeanette summed up her feelings in an outline for her autobiography: "I made up my mind to sing opera if it killed me. As it turned out, I wasn't killed, but I was crushed. I learned some lessons which are usually not spoken of concerning the operations of the Met and its management. . . . This was another 'unfulfilment,' [sic] another proof that life is always a two-sided affair, bitter and sweet."[586]

In 1974, Emily Wentz talked about Jeanette's opera work and her belief that it affected Jeanette's health. "I never saw anybody work so hard in my life," Emily said. "It was too much. I always thought it was much too much. I think she gave part of her life for that thing and it wasn't worth it," though she admitted that it was worth it to Jeanette, who wanted to try everything.[587]

In May 1943, while Gene was stationed in Raleigh, North Carolina, he made a tour of airfields in the United States and Canada. During his tour, he was asked about public appearances. "My appearance days are over until after this war is won," he answered.[588] He visited several cities in Florida. In Tampa, he spoke to student flyers at MacDill and Drew Fields, giving brief talks on the importance of split-second judgement in being able to recognize enemy or friendly planes. He attended a gunnery conference at Buckingham Field in Fort Myers. In Panama City, he visited the Army Air Forces Flexible Gunnery School at Tyndall Field to study training methods and make recommendations for possible improvements. On May 16, he participated in a program for "I Am an American Day" with singers Bing Crosby and Dinah Shore, and actors Paulette Goddard, John Garfield, and Burgess Meredith, which drew a crowd of 130,000 to Chicago's Soldier Field. In early June, Gene visited the Air Forces School in

Harrisburg, Pennsylvania, where he received Intelligence Officers Training in 1942. Later that month, he reported to Washington, D.C., where he received Heavy Bombardment Training.

With Gene serving back in the United States, the Raymonds were able to see each other and also talk on the telephone, which had been prohibited when he was serving in England. Jeanette wrote to the JMIFC, "He hardly has time to write me very often—he telephones instead, which, I might add pleases me very much more."[589] When a reporter asked Jeanette about her extravagance of calling and sending wires, she said, "Well I can't spend much money on Gene any other way."[590] She admitted to the press, "It's hard, not knowing where he is most of the time, but at least it's comforting to know he's in America—if only for awhile." She continued, "The bravery of other women I meet—women who courageously kiss their husbands good-bye [sic] while holding a two-month-old child in their arms—makes me afraid sometimes that I may not be just as brave as they the next time Gene goes away. But I think one thing we women are learning in this war is to accept what happiness we may have and to fight all the harder for the freedom which will bring happiness for the rest of the world too."[591]

After the *Romeo et Juliette* tour, Jeanette continued her recital and radio work, as well as entertaining the troops. In early June, she made a brief tour with accompanist Stuart Ross, singing a mostly new program that included two of Gene's pieces: "Let Me Always Sing" and "Release." In Tulsa, Oklahoma, Jeanette found herself due at the theater with no car provided and no cab on call in a downpour of rain. She hitched a ride to the theater with a WAVE (the women's branch of the Naval Reserve), fitting for someone who had given so many servicemen a lift during the war.

When a reporter asked Jeanette's plans for her birthday, she pouted that she thought Gene was in San Antonio, adding, "I can't keep track of him, he moves around too much." Sylvia Grogg Wright consoled her by replying, "Well, you move around quite a bit yourself."[592] In Joplin, Missouri, Jeanette took a Red Cross surgical dressing class. She lamented to reporters in Wichita, Kansas, "The captain [sic] and I have been 'skirting' each other in most of our journeys since his return from England. Earlier this week our schedules brought us as close together as Fort Worth[, Texas] and Tulsa[, Oklahoma] but schedules did not permit a meeting. And a telephone call had to bridge the distance." She added, "He is so absorbed in his air duties, sometimes I doubt if he will ever return to pictures."[593]

The Raymonds were thrilled to be together on their sixth anniversary in Washington, D.C., where they dined and danced at the Mayflower Hotel. Jeanette gave Gene handkerchiefs with an aerial design and a Captain's insignia, a photo holder, which she filled with about a dozen snapshots of the Raymonds at different places, and a sewing kit. A few weeks before their anniversary, she confided to reporters, "It's hard to buy anything for him in the service. Gene has everything he needs."[594] She told her fan club, "Even though it was terribly hot and crowded, we had a lovely time, and, needless to say, we were happy to spend our anniversary anywhere, just so long as we were together."[595]

On June 18, Jeanette's fortieth birthday, Gene received orders to take Military Pilot Training at Central Instructors School at Randolph Field in Universal City, Texas. He had a brief leave in California; then, in early July, he reported to Randolph Field. After Basic Training, Gene studied Instrument Training and received his "blind flying" certificate, proving he could pilot a plane in clouds, mist or other conditions that necessitated using only instruments, rather than sight.

Gene's brother, Bob, initially enlisted in the Army, but eventually followed Gene into the Army Air Force. Gene inscribed this photo to Jeanette's mother: "To Maw—From one of your fondest admirers. With love Gene. June 1943."

In July, back in California, Jeanette and Nelson Eddy were among the stars who appeared on *American Forces Program*, a broadcast produced in cooperation with the BBC for American Forces stationed in Great Britain. On July 24, she attended a charitable party at Mary

Pickford's estate, Pickfair, and, two days later, entertained at an all-star show at the Hollywood Canteen, emceed by Louella Parsons. Actors Spencer Tracy, Loretta Young, and Gail Patrick, and singers Lena Horne, Dennis Morgan, and Tommy Dix also were on the bill. On July 10, Jeanette returned to *Command Performance*, singing "Indian Love Call," and, on September 6 (recorded September 4), she appeared again, singing "Will You Remember" and "Battle Hymn of the Republic." Soldiers requested that her RCA Victor recording of the latter song be made available as a V-Disc, a record for United States military personnel.

In August, in between Jeanette's *Command Performance* broadcasts, she sang with symphony orchestras in Milwaukee, Wisconsin, and Denver and Colorado Springs, Colorado. Both Gene, who flew in for the day to see his wife, and his brother, Bob, who transferred from the Army to the Army Air Force and recently earned his wings at Williams Air Force Base in Maricopa County, Arizona, were able to see her off on her tour. In Milwaukee, she shattered attendance records at the Emil Blatz Temple of Music, with forty-two thousand people, topping the existent record, held by Lily Pons, by twelve thousand. The night before Jeanette's Denver concert, she spent Gene's birthday at a dinner party at the home of attorney Wilbur F. Denious, where the guests included Colorado Governor John Charles Vivian. During the party, Gene called her as a gift to himself, and the guests all sang "Happy Birthday" to him. Meanwhile, in San Antonio, Gene had a celebratory dinner with some Army Air Force colleagues and their wives at a hotel dining room. His friends asked the orchestra to play "Happy Birthday," but unfortunately, Gene missed it because he was still upstairs, talking on the phone to Jeanette.

On September 1, Gene flew to California on an assignment with Lieutenant Colonel William Melville "Mel" Brown, which allowed

Gene to have another brief reunion with Jeanette. Two days later, she hosted a party for him at the Mocambo. Guests included their friends, Ben Lyon and Buddy Rogers, both of whom also were in the service. On Labor Day, Jeanette hosted a swimming party and buffet luncheon for her mother and sisters and their husbands, as well as a group of servicemen who were stationed with her brother-in-law, Barney, at Camp Haan, near Riverside, California.

On September 18, Jeanette appeared on the radio program *What's New*, singing "The Merry Widow Waltz" and "Lover, Come Back to Me." Later that month, she shot several scenes for *Follow the Boys* (1944), Universal's all-star film about the Hollywood Victory Committee. She played herself, attending a Hollywood Victory Committee meeting, and singing "Beyond the Blue Horizon" at a camp show and "I'll See You in My Dreams" at a military hospital, scenes that she repeated many times in real life. According to Gary McMaster, Chairman and Curator of The Camp Roberts Historical Museum, some of the film, including Jeanette's performance, was shot in front of a real audience of servicemen at Camp Roberts in San Miguel, California.

Although rumors persist that Jeanette was going to reunite with Nelson Eddy at Universal at this time, she never intended to sign a contract with the studio. She merely did a guest shot in *Follow the Boys*, as did many other stars, because of its connection to the Hollywood Victory Committee. In a letter dated November 1, 1943, Gene commented on how agent Charles Feldman, who produced *Follow the Boys* and was Chairman of the Talent Committee of the Hollywood Victory Committee, had done nothing to help Jeanette's career. Feldman, whose clients included Irene Dunne and Claudette Colbert, was famous for his non-exclusive contracts for stars, where they could make one picture at a studio, rather than be under a long-term, multi-year contract.

To encourage the sale of war bonds, on September 30, Jeanette was on the all-star broadcast *Treasury Star Parade*, where she performed "The Four Freedoms" with actors Thomas Mitchell, Brian Aherne, and Olivia de Havilland. "The Four Freedoms," taken from President Franklin D. Roosevelt's January 6, 1941 speech, were freedom of speech and expression, freedom to worship God in his own way, freedom from want, and freedom from fear. Norman Rockwell's 1943 paintings of "The Four Freedoms" became iconic.

From October to December, Jeanette nearly covered the entire country, from the Pacific Northwest to the South, from the East to the Midwest, on a lengthy recital tour. She was accompanied by pianist Collins Smith and former secretary Sylvia Grogg Wright, who, along with James Davidson, replaced Charles Wagner as Jeanette's concert managers. Following Jeanette's opera tour, Jeanette and Wagner parted ways. He claimed that he quit because Jeanette wouldn't listen to his advice; Jeanette said that she fired him because of an anti-Semitic remark that he made about Constance Hope. During the fall 1943 tour, Jeanette's repertoire included Gene's song "Release." This marked Collins Smith's first tour with Jeanette. He remained her accompanist through 1953, even touring with the Raymonds in *The Guardsman*.

On October 7, Anna attended Jeanette's first performance in Santa Barbara, where Jeanette wore two different gowns during her program. Jeanette explained to the audience that her mother wanted to see both costumes "and my mother's wish is law to me."[596] In Atlanta, Georgia, with a gesture and a bow, Jeanette dedicated "Smilin' Through" to Norma Shearer, who was in the 1932 version of the movie. Shearer, the widow of Irving Thalberg, was in the audience with her second husband, ski instructor and Navy Aviator Martin Arrouge, whom she married in 1942. In New Orleans, Jeanette was so cold that, mid-way through her recital, she put on her mink coat.

During this tour, Jeanette felt more affects from the war. While, in earlier years, most of the members of the press were male, now she encountered many female reporters and photographers. She also found a greater percentage of female musicians when she played with symphony orchestras. At her press conferences, she discussed her problem finding size 3 ½ C shoes, forcing her to wear 4 B. However, her small feet were an advantage when it came to stockings, as she still could find old store stock nylons in her size. While Gene was stationed in Texas, he went across the border to Mexico to buy Jeanette some silk stockings.

Once again fearing food shortages on the road, Jeanette carried honey from her bees, persimmons from her trees, and tomato preserves from her plants, as well as her ration books. Despite her celebrity status, she wasn't given special treatment when it came to wartime restrictions. During a two-hour stopover in Atlanta, en route to Savannah, Georgia, Jeanette told reporters about her two suitcases full of food, which she had to carry herself due to a shortage of porters. In Winston–Salem, North Carolina, she ordered broiled country ham for dinner. She told the press, "At least that will be different from the menu we drew on the train. Eggs—fish—and chicken. I have eaten so many chickens that I feel as though I could cackle."[597] She said that she tried to remain cheerful about travel difficulties, "only sometimes I get awfully hungry."[598] In Richmond, Virginia, she told reporters, "You know, you just don't get on a train and have meals served in your drawing room any more. You take your chance in the diners. It's quite all right, of course, because the servicemen ought to be served first, but sometimes when I have breakfast at the crack of dawn in order to make an early train, and then, I can't get anything to eat until 9 o'clock at night—well, I get mighty empty."[599]

After Jeanette's Portland, Oregon recital, a fan gave Jeanette some venison, which Jeanette had never tasted. She had the hotel chef at her next date in Seattle cook the deer chops, excitedly telling the press that she hadn't had meat for three weeks. While Jeanette was on the road, her housekeeper sent Jeanette an eggplant from her Victory Garden, which Jeanette had a hotel chef cook for her. In Knoxville, University of Tennessee President Ralph W. Frost offered to trade Jeanette twenty red ration stamps, which were used for meat and butter, for an autographed photo to give his mother on her seventy-seventh birthday.

In each city, Jeanette allowed for at least 150 soldiers to sit behind her onstage as her special guests. No dates, civilians, or relatives were allowed. She often asked them to whistle during "The Donkey Serenade," explaining that she didn't bring along a flute.

Jeanette continued to charge civilians for her autograph, donating the money to United War Relief funds. Although signing her eighteen-letter name too much gave Jeanette a literal pain in her neck, she rationalized, "But you know, they say one should worry when people don't want one's autograph."[600] When longtime fan Thelma Buchanan (later known as Thelma Buchanan Short) asked her how she wrote her name so quickly, Jeanette replied, "If you had to sign as many autographs as I do, you would learn how to write fast."[601] She also told Buchanan that she studied the Palmer Method in school, a style of penmanship in which students adopted a uniform style of cursive writing with rhythmic motions.

Jeanette laughed about an experience that happened during her fall 1943 tour when she sold an autograph to a thirteen-year-old boy for a quarter at a train station. He asked which way she was going and she said to the telegraph office. "Then I'll go the other way," he told her. "I resell autographs for the Army Fund and I don't want to compete with you."[602] Many years later, after a 1950 recital in San Antonio,

Jeanette was backstage signing autographs when she felt someone pinch her. William Bass reported, "She turned to chastise the offender, then laughed when an eager[-]faced five-year-old girl looked up at her and said proudly: 'I was named for you!' Jeanette bent down, kissed her and said: 'Oh, my, too bad you have such a long name!'"[603]

When asked if wartime audiences differed from pre-war audiences, Jeanette said that she couldn't see any differences in the way they responded to her program. "But managers tell me that audiences today are quite different in the sense that they always grab up the highest-priced seats first."[604] Although in 1942 she said that servicemen asked for religious songs, during her 1943 tour, she said that soldier audiences most frequently asked for "Indian Love Call." "They usually request classicals [sic] and the quieter songs, but occasionally someone will ask me to sing 'Pistol Packin' Mama.' And then I have to tell them I don't know it," she laughed.[605]

While Jeanette was in Birmingham for a recital, she visited the Jefferson County Anti-Tuberculosis Clinic and bought the first sheet of Christmas Seals sold in Alabama. She had a personal interest in finding a cure for the disease, as her former chauffeur/hairdresser, Henri Coen, husband of her maid, Rose, suffered from tuberculosis. In New Orleans, Jeanette contributed $25 to *The Times–Picayune* Doll and Toy Fund, which provided Christmas gifts for poor children. Today, her donation would be worth about $364.

During the tour, Jeanette's friend, Lily May Caldwell, Entertainment Editor of *The Birmingham News*, broke the story that, in January 1944, Jeanette planned to begin filming a new movie for United Artists. Jeanette described the unnamed picture: "[It] concerns a girl who must choose between a career and marrying the man she loves—and does both."[606] Jeanette later told reporter Ruth Lewis that the movie, *This Moment Forever*, a title Jeanette disliked, would be for MGM. "It's about a girl who has the choice of two careers. The picture shows her taking one . . . and then what would have happened if she had taken the other . . . sort of fantasy . . . no, I won't tell the ending. They'll have to pay to see that."[607] Other reports claimed that the movie would be for RKO, which matched information in the Raymonds' correspondence about a project with writer/producer Edward Kaufman and director Norman Taurog. The film was not made.

While Jeanette was on her recital tour, she proudly discussed Gene's service. "Gene is heart and soul in his air [sic] force [sic] work," she told reporters in Richmond, Virginia. "He has always been air-minded, of course, but the thing that astonishes him most is the wonderful training that he is getting as a pilot. Not long ago he said to me, 'Just think, here I'm getting schooling and training that I couldn't get in four years at West Point, even if I'd been lucky enough to have an appointment in the first place.'" She continued, "When he's through, he'll know everything there is to know about piloting a plane, from the fighters to the big bombers. Of course, he isn't young enough to be a fighter pilot, and I think I'm not very sorry on that score." She reminisced about Gene being cold when he was stationed in England, laughing because he always teased her about her cold feet in bed. "I had to send him flannelette pajamas, and later he wrote that somebody had gotten him some bed socks. Can you imagine anything funnier than a grown man sleeping in bed socks? Anyway, he can't kid me any more on that score."[608]

For the Raymonds, there were advantages and disadvantages to being celebrities. Unlike normal couples, Jeanette generally couldn't pack up and move near the base where Gene was training. She had her own work, both professional and for the war effort, not to mention the fact that, if she lived on or near a base for any length of time, fans would disturb her. She told the press, "This is no time for women to drop their jobs and go running after their husbands to army [sic] posts. This is the time for women to stick to their jobs and work at them harder than ever. The only panacea for these times when we find ourselves alone is work and more work."[609] There were other privacy issues, like the telephone operators who listened to their calls, as Gene noted in one letter. On the positive side, occasionally, Jeanette's tour schedule allowed her to visit Gene when she was crisscrossing the country and, during his leaves, he tried to join her, wherever she was.

During Jeanette's fall recital tour, the Raymonds were able to spend a few days together when she played San Antonio, but even then, they were at the mercy of the Army Air Force. When she arrived on December 2, she had to wait twelve hours before seeing Gene, as he was busy training. While she was in San Antonio, the Raymonds assisted in a recruiting drive for WACs and aviation cadets at Kelly Field and appeared on *The Army on the Air* over WOAI. After her December 4 performance with the San Antonio Symphony Orchestra, Gene hosted a supper party at the St. Anthony Hotel for some of his fellow officers and their wives. He drove Jeanette to Austin for her December 6 concert. On December 8, Gene began a B-25 transition course at Brooks Field in San Antonio; that same day, Jeanette gave a second concert in San Antonio because the first one sold out so quickly. There were over two thousand requests for tickets after the six-thousand-seat auditorium sold out. The sponsor said it was the first time in history that a second performance had to be scheduled to satisfy the crowd.

Since the San Antonio dates would have marked the end of Jeanette's tour, she initially planned to stay with Gene for a few weeks while he finished his training in Texas, spending Christmas there if he couldn't get leave. However, when she had to postpone her November 14 date in Chicago because of a sore throat, she rescheduled the Chicago recital after her San Antonio performances. "I had intended to come to San Antonio for a while and just be a housewife while Gene was here," Jeanette explained to the press. "We had rented a place in Alamo Heights on College boulevard [sic], but Gene thinks he will be graduating around December 15 and will be sent elsewhere, so we decided it would be unwise for me to join him."[610] She told another reporter, "I was just going to move here and be an army [sic] wife and not be a singer, but I have to give a concert in Chicago Dec. 12 and Captain Raymond completes his training Dec. 15, so I'll just have to await orders."[611]

Despite their occasional reunions, the long separations put a gradual strain on the Raymonds' marriage. Jeanette compared their schedules to "ships that pass in the night." She said, "He would be flying back to California just about the time I'd be headed for an engagement in New Orleans, or some such place. And on the rare occasions when we'd manage a couple of days together, we laughingly pretended it was 'like a series of honeymoons,' but it wasn't. It was filled with frustration and anxiety."[612]

On December 20, Gene finished his courses at Brooks Field and was able to get leave for Christmas. He and Jeanette entertained her family at Twin Gables. Elsie surprised them, driving out from Pennsylvania to be with her husband, Barney, still stationed at Camp Haan. Elsie's son, Earle Wallace, his wife, Patricia, and two-year-old daughter, Nanette, also were there. It was the first time four generations of MacDonalds celebrated the holidays together. Unfortunately, Gene's brother, Bob, was unable to get leave. The Raymonds spent New Year's Eve working at the Hollywood Canteen. In early January 1944, Helen Ferguson held a party for them, before Gene was sent to his next assignment.

Chapter Thirteen

On January 7, 1944, Gene reported to Roswell Army Air Field in Roswell, New Mexico to study at B-17 Flying Fortress School and receive Four-Engine Transition Training. Six days later, Jeanette left to work for the Treasury Department to sell war bonds in and around New York. Anna accompanied her, since Emily was ill, as was Rose's husband, Henri, and Jeanette didn't want to take Rose away from him.

In Salt Lake City, Jeanette got off the train to get some fresh air. A group of nurses asked if she would visit the wounded soldiers that they were accompanying on a troop train. Jeanette spent a few minutes with the servicemen and mentioned that she was on a bond tour. They all chipped in and bought her first bond, starting her tour off right. Later, she choked up when she shared the story at a bond rally: "There they were, in that hospital train, those broken, wounded boys. And they wanted to know if I could sell them bonds to back the attack. Good God! They wanted to buy bonds—those boys who had given so much of themselves. Why it would tear your heart out, just to think of their desire to make that last sacrifice."[613]

On January 17, brass bands and a ticker tape heralded the arrival of Jeanette and fellow actors Laraine Day, Brian Donlevy, and Lloyd

Nolan in Times Square. They unveiled a gold chair to symbolize the motion picture industry's goal to sell a bond for every movie theater seat in the United States. For the next few weeks, the quartet campaigned in New York and New Jersey, selling war bonds as part of the Fourth War Loan Drive. After the kick off, Jeanette headed to Albany, where, on January 18, she joined actors Helen Walker and Albert Dekker, and New York Governor Thomas Dewey for the opening of the New York State bond drive. That evening, she made a war bond appeal at the New York State Publishers Association convention, asking for $10 million, equivalent to over $143 million today.

On January 24, Jeanette went to Brooklyn to visit Todd Shipyards Corporation, which had been a virtual battleship factory since World War I. Two ships of great significance to the history of the Second World War were built there: the USS Arizona and the USS Missouri. The USS Arizona, built in 1916, brought the United States into World War II when, on December 7, 1941, it was sunk by the Japanese at Pearl Harbor. The USS Missouri, built in 1944, was the ship where, on September 2, 1945, the Japanese signed surrender papers, officially ending the war. At Todd, Jeanette and Lloyd Nolan previewed the yard's war bond campaign, which launched the following week, and Jeanette sang for the workers.

On January 25, Jeanette joined Brian Donlevy, Lloyd Nolan, Laraine Day, and dancer/actress Vera Zorina on a Fourth War Loan Drive program in Times Square. Coincidentally, Zorina played the angel in the Broadway version of *I Married an Angel*; the character's name, Brigitta, came from her real name. Both she and Jeanette were in the movie *Follow the Boys*, although they had no scenes together.

The next day, Jeanette and Lloyd Nolan traveled to Garden City, New Jersey to address a bond rally at Garden City High School, where students already had sold over $50,000 worth of bonds, equivalent to over $715,000 today. On January 28, Jeanette attended an exhibition tennis match at New York's Seventh Regiment Armory, where the price of admission was the purchase of a war bond. The match pitted professional players against amateurs in conjunction with the Fourth War Loan Drive, in hopes of raising $2.5 million from war bond sales, equivalent to almost $36 million today.

During Jeanette's bond tour, on January 24, 1944, she entertained workers at Todd Shipyards Corporation. Photo from the Eleanor Knowles Dugan collection.

After one bond appearance, a fan reported that Jeanette said that "she knew she didn't have to urge people to buy bonds for she knew they wanted their sons, husbands, sweethearts, brothers, etc., home as much as she wanted her husband, and that they all knew buying bonds was like buying them a ticket back."[614] Following another appearance, Jeanette drank hot chocolate in a restaurant across from where the rally was held. The cup was auctioned off to raise more money for the cause. In addition to Jeanette's war work, she was able to have a little fun while she was in New York, including attending Margaret Sullavan's Broadway play, *The Voice of the Turtle* (1943), with Louella Parsons, who happened to be in the city at the same time.

Jeanette worked so hard selling bonds, not always under the most sanitary conditions, that she caught conjunctivitis (pink eye). While Anna went on to Philadelphia to visit Elsie and some other relatives, Jeanette spent a couple of weeks resting and recovering in Palm Beach. Initially, she stayed at Whitehall, the former estate of industrialist/Standard Oil founder Henry Flagler, which was then Palm Beach's second largest hotel. After her recovery, she visited her friends, Marjorie Merriweather Post and her husband, Joseph Davies, at their home, Mar-a-Lago, now owned by President Donald Trump. While Jeanette was in Palm Beach, she picked out a shell tree for Gene to give her for their anniversary and, on March 1, she entertained servicemen at Reams General Hospital. Jeanette returned to New York for a March 4 radio broadcast, *The RCA Program—The Music America Loves Best*, where she sang "Ah! Sweet Mystery of Life" and "One Kiss."

In mid-March, on Jeanette's way back to California, she stopped in Roswell to visit Gene. During her three-day stay, she gave three concerts for servicemen. In between her performances and Gene's studying, they were able to have a little private time together. While Jeanette was in Roswell, she was over-tired from her tour and caught a cold. Gene asked nose and throat specialist Captain Alex Forrester to look in on her. Forrester's wife, Juliette, was disappointed when all that her husband reported was "She has orange-colored hair and over-developed vocal cords."[615] Although newspaper columns claimed that Jeanette was going to stay in Roswell until Gene finished his course, his letters implied that she only planned to stay a few days, even if she hadn't been sick.

On March 24, 1944, Gene received his diploma for B-17 and Bombardier Training. After a brief leave in California, on March 30, he was transferred to Yuma Army Air Force Flexible Gunnery School in Yuma, Arizona to build up four-engine flying time in preparation for his goal of B-29 Training. On June 7, he was given Command Squadron I, Group I, and on September 12, he was put in charge of Command Group I. On September 23, he was re-rated from Service Pilot to Pilot. The Raymonds' correspondence greatly decreased because Gene could go home on frequent leaves and weekend passes since Yuma is about three hundred miles from Bel Air.

It didn't matter how far away Jeanette was or how recently Gene had seen her; when he received a few days furlough, if able, he traveled to wherever she was to spend whatever time he had with her. When he had a weekend pass, it wasn't always possible for him to join her on the road. During the time that he was stationed in Yuma, one weekend, while Jeanette was on tour in the Southeast, he went home to Twin Gables, but wrote to her, "I don't think I'll come home again until your tour is over – it's no fun this way."[616]

On Easter Sunday, April 9, Jeanette launched her spring recital tour in Phoenix. Gene was able to attend and hear her perform his compositions "Let Me Always Sing" and "Release." She continued to be mobbed wherever she went. Lily May Caldwell noted that crowds waited to catch a glimpse of Jeanette everywhere Caldwell went with her in Montgomery, Alabama. They followed Jeanette to her hotel suite and passed her slips of paper to autograph when she and Caldwell went to see Alfred Hitchcock's *Lifeboat* (1944). Caldwell remarked on Jeanette's sense of humor and utter lack of vanity when Jeanette compared her over-zealous fans to the bobby-soxers who chased the crooners. Caldwell wrote, "She doesn't take the idolitry [sic] seriously; chuckled contagiously: 'I'm a regular [Frank] Sinatra!'"[617]

During Jeanette's five-week tour, she appeared on two radio broadcasts. On April 30, while she was in Asheville, North Carolina for a recital, she was on *We the People*, talking about the city's war work. On May 14, she sang a medley of her movie songs on *Philco Radio Hall of Fame*, broadcast from New York.

Following her tour, Jeanette returned to California, where she burned her hand trying to light a water heater. On June 12, she appeared in an adaptation of *Naughty Marietta* with Nelson Eddy on *Lux Radio Theatre*, their first commercial radio appearance together since they left MGM. Their popularity led to many more broadcasts, causing a radio executive to remark, "Eddy and MacDonald on the radio can stop more parlor conversation than an earthquake."[618]

In 1944, Ernst Lubitsch wanted to collaborate with Jeanette on another project, a film version of the 1922 Broadway musical *That Lady in Ermine*, which was based on Rudolph Schanzer and Ernst Welisch's operetta *Die Frau im Hermelin*. The plot would have allowed Jeanette to play dual roles, a nineteenth century countess and a painting of her great-great-great-great grandmother that came to life. In 1942, when Twentieth Century–Fox acquired the rights, Irene Dunne was announced as the star, but nothing came of the project. Two years later, when Lubitsch became involved, he wanted Jeanette, although, by then, the studio preferred to star Gene Tierney. Because an early script concerned suspicions of adultery, the Production Code Administration deemed it unacceptable and the project was shelved. By the time it finally was produced in late 1947, Betty Grable was the star. It proved to be Ernst Lubitsch's last film, as he died eight days after beginning principal photography. Otto Preminger completed the movie, but insisted that Lubitsch get sole screen credit.

In mid-June 1944, Gene had four days' leave. On June 17, the Raymonds celebrated their seventh anniversary one day late with a star-studded party. The guests included Ernst Lubitsch; Mary Pickford; actress Genevieve Tobin, who was in *One Hour with You* with Jeanette and *The Woman in Red* with Gene, and her husband, director William Keighley; Helen Ferguson; Nelson and Ann Eddy; Marian Nixon and William Seiter; pianist Jose Iturbi; tenor Lauritz Melchior and his wife, Kleinchen; director Richard Wallace and his wife, Mary; and Hedda Hopper. The next day, Jeanette and Gene celebrated Jeanette's birthday with family and a few friends. After Gene returned to Yuma, on June 22, Jeanette performed at the Hollywood Canteen.

That summer, on the advice of Constance Hope, Jeanette hired German soprano Lotte Lehmann to coach her in the role of Marguerite in Charles Gounod's *Faust*. Jeanette paid her $25 an hour, now about $357. After their first two-hour session, Jeanette called Hope and told her that working with Lehmann had been a revelation, "that an hour with her on a role is as if the room is dark, and you open the windows and sunshine flies in."[619] When Jeanette told Lehmann that Gene thought that meeting Lehmann was the best thing that had happened to Jeanette in many years, Lehmann said she was equally pleased to help Jeanette develop her talent. "There is nothing that could give me more satisfaction than to think that I really help you to develop what is hidden in your soul: I cannot *make* you a great artist if you are not one with all your being. And you *are*: it is almost miraculous how quickly you are able to bring to life what has up till now only slumbered in your heart. You have always much too much been concerned about the technique of singing. And also the fear of 'overdo' has held you back. Seeing what you are able to do after such a short time, I don't doubt that the possibilities are almost limitless for you, especially as a concert singer."[620]

In mid-July, Gene had a weekend pass and, on Saturday, July 15, he planned to fly to Los Angeles to meet Jeanette at Twin Gables after one of her Friday sessions with Lotte Lehmann in Santa Barbara.

Wartime dim-outs, which didn't allow drivers to use headlights, only parking lights, prevented Jeanette from driving home Friday night after dark because she'd have to drive too slowly. On July 14, around 10:30 p.m., she returned to her cottage at El Encanto, a deluxe hotel with multiple private guest cottages, and went to bed. A half-hour later, she heard a noise and rose to investigate. A fourteen-year-old bellboy emerged from her closet and came toward her with a blanket. When Jeanette tried to fend him off, he repeatedly hit her, giving her a black eye and multiple cuts on her face. According to reports, the next day, she dropped the battery charges when she learned the attacker, who claimed that he was after a souvenir, was underage and the sole support of his blind mother. Whether this was dramatized by the press or was the truth, Jeanette also probably didn't want the stress and further publicity if the case went to trial, especially with her busy tour schedule. She returned to Twin Gables and got treatment for her swollen right eye and facial cuts. On Saturday, despite her injuries, the Raymonds hosted a dinner party for six for their friend, Joseph Battley, who had been promoted to Brigadier General.

While Gene was busy in Yuma, Jeanette continued to study *Faust*, entertain friends, and appear on the radio. On July 27, she gave a dinner party for her concert manager, James Davidson. Two days later, Jeanette entertained Colonel John Horton and Colonel Anderson and their wives at Twin Gables. Colonel Horton had been Gene's Commanding Officer in Roswell. He later trained pilots at Santa Ana and eventually was promoted to Brigadier General. After the war, the Raymonds continued to keep in touch with him. In 1950, when Jeanette was singing in Montgomery, Alabama, she had dinner at Maxwell Air Force Base with Horton and his wife. It is not known if Gene served with Colonel Anderson. On August 2, 1944, Jeanette hosted a party for her *Romeo et Juliette* co-star Ezio Pinza, the night after he sang at the Hollywood Bowl.

In addition to commercial programs, on August 10, Jeanette was on a broadcast for the Office of War Information and, on August 23, she recorded *Mail Call* for the AFRS, which was broadcast August 30. On the latter, comedienne Gracie Allen tried to break up Jeanette and Nelson Eddy as a singing team, much to the distress of Allen's husband, comedian George Burns. Jeanette sang "Lover, Come Back to Me" and joined Nelson for "Indian Love Call." On September 3, Gene, home on a weekend pass, attended Jeanette and Nelson's rehearsal of a *Lux Radio Theatre* adaptation of *Maytime*. Before the broadcast the next day, Gene had to return to Yuma. On September 9, Jeanette appeared on *The Kenny Baker Show*, singing "Beyond the Blue Horizon" and "My Hero" and joining Baker for "Wanting You." A fan club member reported that, before the show, Jeanette asked if the hitchhiking soldier that she picked up en route to the broadcast was in the audience and if he received the ticket that she left at the studio for him.

In September, Jeanette was the first film star to visit the neuropsychiatric ward at Sawtelle Veterans Hospital in Los Angeles. She sang for forty minutes, accompanied by former Metropolitan Opera conductor/pianist Richard Hageman. He composed "Miranda," which Jeanette sang on *Ford Sunday Evening Hour* in 1945, and "Do Not Go, My Love," which she recorded in 1939 and often sang in her recitals, and won an Academy Award for scoring John Ford's movie *Stagecoach* (1939). Initially, the patients' faces were blank and lifeless; however, before Jeanette left, they looked like different people. She even had them singing "The Donkey Serenade" with her. The hospital sent her a note, saying, "Only we could estimate the enormous amount of good you have done."[621] Helen Ferguson recalled Jeanette's visit to Sawtelle:

"She was so thoughtful and so eager to really <u>help</u> those men and boys. And she did. Music reaches them where all else fails and Jeanette's particular vocal quality and sincerity reached farther than any penetration up to that time. She was very humble amidst the extravagant thanks she received afterwards. And plans to sing there as often as can be arranged."[622] During the 1940s, Jeanette also frequently visited Birmingham Veterans Hospital in Van Nuys, California.

On September 22, toxic vertigo, erroneously reported in some newspapers as tonsillitis, kept Jeanette from acting as an official co-hostess at a tea for the wife of Republican Presidential candidate Governor Thomas Dewey. Jeanette told Mrs. Dewey, "I cannot lift my head off the pillow without immediate dizziness and nausea."[623] It isn't known if Jeanette's toxic vertigo was caused by a viral infection or the medication that she was prescribed to treat her sore throat. Full of concern, Gene came home on a four-day leave to be with her. By October 1, she recovered and sang "My Old Kentucky Home" and "Juliette's Waltz" on *The Standard Hour*.

On October 24, Jeanette left California for her fall tour. She proudly told reporters that, on November 3, Gene was promoted to Major. Between her recital and concert dates, she made her American opera debut, singing *Romeo et Juliette* in Chicago and Milwaukee, and returning to Chicago to sing *Faust*. Jeanette arranged for Anna, Elsie, and Grace Newell to attend her November 11 performance of *Romeo et Juliette* in Chicago. Anna planned to see *Faust* as well, but illness prevented it, much to Jeanette's disappointment. Even the always-hard-to-please *Chicago Tribune* Music Critic Claudia Cassidy praised Jeanette's performances. "From where I sit at the opera, Jeanette MacDonald has turned out to be one of the welcome surprises of the season," Cassidy wrote. "Her Juliet was decorative, intelligent, and well sung within her vocal scope, and last night her Marguerite was better than her Juliet. It was a stagewise [sic] performance as French as Yvonne Gall's, beautifully sung with purity of line and tone, a good trill, and a Gallic inflection that understood Gounod's phrasing."[624]

When Gene was home on leave, the Raymonds often visited the nightspots. This shot was taken at the Mocambo in 1944. The piece of paper in front of them apparently was a Christmas list. It read: "One Bottle of Scotch for Everyone, One Case Haig & Haig Scotch, One John-Frederics Hat, One Koret Handbag, One Elizabeth Arden Makeup Kit, Six Pairs Nylon Hose."

Jeanette called her Chicago opera experience a "noble experiment." She was upset when *Life* magazine did a story about her American debut and quoted from her only negative review. She said, "A great deal was expected of me because of my work in movies and I was barging into a new field where some people might say I don't belong. We had to be very careful, for people were ready to say we were bringing Hollywood to the opera."[625] The *Faust* production also caused Jeanette a lot of stress, as she had no rehearsals. She told a reporter, "I didn't meet the tenor until 1 o'clock and our performance was at 8 p.m., so our voices had never been heard together until the actual performance. I only had one orchestra reading, but I knew the part so well that I was able to keep my own rhythm. It was an awful ordeal though."[626]

Jeanette spent Thanksgiving 1944 singing in Washington, D.C. and had holiday dinner at Hillwood, the home of Marjorie Merriweather Post and Joseph Davies. By this time, Jeanette had grown weary of touring, yet realized how important entertainment was to building morale. She told reporters in Springfield, Massachusetts, "Concertizing is not as much fun as it used to be because traveling accommodations are not what they used to be before the war." She also bemoaned the cuisine on the road. "After my performances I'm ravenous and most of the time sandwiches is [sic] all that I can get at that late hour. And oh! I'm so sick of them, especially chicken sandwiches."[627] Jeanette discussed the perils of touring with violinist Jascha Heifetz: "I don't know why we put up with it. Concert tours mean bad, dirty hotels, bad food, bad hours and they scare you to death. Why do we do it?" Heifetz replied with a grin, "I know why. The house is sold out, isn't it?"[628] The tired Jeanette grinned back, realizing it was the happy fans and the money that kept her touring.

In the fall of 1944, there was talk of Jeanette returning to Broadway in 1945 in a new operetta produced by Michael Todd, featuring unpublished music by Victor Herbert, whose songs were used in her films *Naughty Marietta* and *Sweethearts*. However, Jeanette changed her mind about appearing in the show, which eventually was titled *Three Shamrocks* (1945). In a letter to the JMIFC dated March 29, 1945, she said that there were too many complications getting the music rights from the Victor Herbert estate and she could not waste any more time with it. She was replaced by Jane Farrar, who, coincidentally, had been in *The Phantom of the Opera* with Nelson Eddy. The show never opened on Broadway.

There also were rumors that Jeanette and Nelson would reunite on screen in *East Wind*, an RKO Technicolor musical based on the 1931 Broadway show, with songs by Sigmund Romberg, whose music was used in *Maytime* and *New Moon*. The original plot concerned a singing soldier and a café owner's daughter who married the soldier's brother and lost her husband to the village cooch dancer. Presumably, Nelson would play the soldier and Jeanette the daughter. Both stars disliked the script for *East Wind* and, eventually, the project was cancelled. According to screenwriter DeWitt Bodeen, the 1946 death of RKO Chief of Production Charles Koerner was part of the reason it was not rewritten and filmed later.

On November 26, 1944, Jeanette appeared on the radio program *Music America Loves Best*, singing "A Little Love, A Little Kiss," "Summer Serenade," "Annie Laurie," and, with Thomas L. Thomas, "We Will Always Be Sweethearts" from *One Hour with You*. She told the JMIFC that, while she was on tour, she was unable to do much shopping because she was afraid of catching cold, going from the warm stores to the frosty temperatures outdoors.

Much to Jeanette's delight, Gene received a furlough and was able to spend Christmas at Twin Gables. If he hadn't been able to go home, she planned to join him in Yuma for the holidays. On Christmas Eve, they entertained Jeanette's mother, Blossom and Elsie and their husbands, nephew Earle (then in the Marines), his wife, Patricia, and their daughter, Nanette. The entire family spent the night with the Raymonds, making Twin Gables very crowded. Aside from Mrs. Kipling, who seldom saw Gene after his engagement announcement, the only one missing was Gene's brother, Bob, then flying a B-17 somewhere in England.

Gene gave Jeanette a Skye Terrier that she named Misty. Jeanette reported, ". . . he has taken a great shine to Tray (Gene's Irish Setter) but seems afraid of Gene. We strongly suspect the uniform awes him, but hope he will outgrow his timidity. He is awfully cute."[629] Later, Misty and Gene became great pals. The Skye Terrier sometimes accompanied Jeanette on her recital tours and went on the road with the Raymonds during their 1951 tour of *The Guardsman*. Jeanette and Gene frequently traveled by early morning trains so they could obtain a compartment and Misty wouldn't have to ride in the baggage car. On short distances, they traveled by car. When the Marriott in Indianapolis refused to allow a dog, Jeanette joked that they were evicted, and the Raymonds moved to another hotel. In 1954, Misty was put to sleep because of continual fluid buildup in his abdomen; he was Jeanette and Gene's last dog.

The Raymonds rang in 1945 at Helen Ferguson's house and, on January 1, attended the Rose Bowl game. In early January, Gene left for his new assignment at the headquarters of the Western Flying Training Command in Santa Ana, California, where he was Staff Officer in Operations, in charge of the Flexible Gunnery and Co-pilot Training Program. His duties included attending Flexible Gunnery Meets and observing training on bases around the country. Flexible Gunnery Training involves swivel guns used in airplanes. His travels took him from Texas to Florida. Now stationed about fifty miles from Twin Gables, this allowed the Raymonds to spend much more time together than when he was stationed in Yuma, and he had frequent weekend passes and furloughs at Twin Gables. Except for when Jeanette or Gene was traveling, this ended the Raymonds' wartime correspondence.

On January 4, 1945, Jeanette left for New York to make a two-year backlog of recordings for RCA Victor. During much of the war, she had been unable to make records, due to the musicians' union ban on commercial recordings that lasted from August 1, 1942 through November 11, 1944. In New York, she recorded "Italian Street Song," "Summer Serenade," and six pieces for an album titled *Religious Songs*.

In August 1944, it was announced that, as soon as the ban ended, Jeanette would record songs from Richard Rodgers and Oscar Hammerstein II's Broadway musical *Oklahoma!* (1943) with tenor James Melton and baritone John Charles Thomas. Unfortunately, that never occurred and, when Melton and Thomas made an album of songs from *Oklahoma!*, it was with soprano Eleanor Steber. Instead, Jeanette recorded an album of selections from the Sigmund Romberg/Dorothy Fields Broadway musical *Up in Central Park* (1945) with baritone Robert Merrill. The songs, which included the romantic "Close as Pages in a Book," the wistful "It Doesn't Cost You Anything to Dream," and the amusing "The Fireman's Bride," were among Jeanette's most delightful recordings. *Up in Central Park* was produced by Michael Todd, whom Jeanette almost worked for in *Three Shamrocks*. Since Jeanette chose her songs for RCA Victor, one can't help but wonder if this was her way of making it up to Todd for not doing his operetta.

Robert Merrill recalled how generous Jeanette was when working with other artists. He appreciated her kindness to a newcomer: "Her charm and friendly manner put me at ease at once. And, although it was a busy and tiring day for her, she found time to show me all the little tricks of recording. . . . Throughout the first exhausting afternoon she patiently explained recordings [sic] cues and principles so that I would know what was happening. The reason came a week later when, in response to a query by me, she explained, 'Everyone needs some help. And remembering how grateful I was for the encouragement I received when I was starting, I, in turn, like to help newcomers in any way I can.'"[630] When rehearsals were over, she was even more generous. Merrill recalled, "At recording time, we faced each other across the mike, but she faced the conductor, Robert Russell Bennett. I was, as usual, ill at ease. Hell, I thought why do they always maneuver me like this? . . . She must have read my eyes, for she asked me to change places with her, so that I could face the conductor."[631] Merrill also was one of many who said that Jeanette was even more beautiful off screen.

While Jeanette was in New York, she did radio interviews with actress/producer Paula Stone and Jane Cowl. Columnist Ben Gross noted that the interview with Cowl sounded more like two old friends chatting over old times than a scripted program and that their intimacy and casualness made the broadcast a real treat for listeners. Jeanette's childhood friend, Peg Watson, then a WAC, spent a weekend with Jeanette and Emily. After Gene completed his tour of gunnery schools, he also received a furlough and joined his wife in New York. Gene's leave happened to fall during the same weekend in February as Peg's, which limited Jeanette's time with her. Jeanette joked to their mutual friend, Marion Smith Glendening, "Naturally, Gene being a Major outranked her!!"[632]

On February 13, Jeanette returned to California. She spent March 9 through March 12 in San Francisco and Oakland, California, entertaining patients at Treasure Island, Oak Knoll, and Shoemaker Naval Hospitals, and Dibble Army Hospital. At Oak Knoll, she sang twenty songs to a packed audience in the hospital auditorium. They included eleven nurses who had spent three years imprisoned at Los Baños, an internment camp in the Philippines, and had just returned to the United States. At their request, Jeanette sang "Battle Hymn of the Republic" and the audience joined her. When Jeanette asked the audience to sing along with "Rose Marie," she was so impressed with a sailor's voice that she invited him onstage to sing two solos.

The Oak Leaf reported, "Throughout the evening, Jeanette's superb singing was matched only by her graciousness and poise."[633]

Jeanette and Gene at the Stage Door Canteen during a visit to New York. They did all that they could to entertain the troops and keep up morale. Once again, she wore her favorite pin.

In a March 29 letter to her fan club, Jeanette said that Gene had been home almost every weekend, except when he was going around the country on inspection tours. "I don't mind so long as he stays in this country," she wrote. "I have all my fingers crossed, but that, of course, is up to Uncle Sam."[634] She told Lily May Caldwell, "On the occasions when Gene is able to get in from Santa Ana I try to be home otherwise I join him there. We are being pretty selfish about it these days, but feel everyone understands. We are so grateful for our chances to be together that we are trying to take full advantage of it."[635]

On April 12, President Franklin D. Roosevelt passed away, sending the country into mourning. Three days later, Jeanette and Nelson Eddy paid tribute to the President on a special memorial broadcast on Nelson's radio series, *The Electric Hour*. Jeanette sang Charles Gounod's "Ave Maria" and "I Think When I Read That Sweet Story of Old." Jeanette told Lily May Caldwell, "The last news-reel [sic] I saw of him I commented on how dreadful he looked. He has obviously been a sick man for some time, but I am sure he died the way he wanted. . . . Perhaps he is now where he has learned the answer we are all seeking."[636] The following week, Jeanette returned to *The Electric Hour*, singing "Italian Street Song" and joining Nelson for "Sweethearts" (also known as "Sweetheart Waltz") and a medley of songs from their movies.

On May 6, Jeanette helped kick off National and Inter-American Music Week, singing "Ah! Sweet Mystery of Life" and "My Hero" on the steps of City Hall in Pasadena, California. During the program, which was broadcast over Pasadena's KPAS, William R. Richardson, Los Angeles Chairman of the Music War Council of America, presented her with a plaque for her war work. Los Angeles Mayor Fletcher Bowron proclaimed May 6 to May 13 "Los Angeles Music Week." In a speech before a crowd of over two thousand, Bowron said that he hoped to use music "to break down race barriers, to prevent juvenile delinquency, to make Los Angeles a better place in which to live, because music is the language understood by everyone."[637] When Bowron thanked Jeanette for her work entertaining the troops in hospitals and camps, she said that she did it because of the great love she had for America and the boys. Bowron added that, if he had his way, Jeanette would be given a citation every time she sang.

On May 8, eight months after Italy surrendered, the Allies formally accepted Germany's surrender, marking the end of the war in Europe, celebrated as V-E Day. That afternoon, Jeanette, who was fluent in French, recorded a broadcast for France for the Office of War Information. Later that day, she appeared on an all-star *Hollywood Victory Show* broadcast, where she sang "Land of Hope and Glory" and "Beyond the Blue Horizon" and joined the cast for "The Star Spangled Banner" finale.

On May 14, Jeanette sang "God Bless America" and "Battle Hymn of the Republic" with the U.S. Coast Guard Band on a broadcast from Riverside, California, celebrating the launch of the ten thousandth water buffalo, a landing vehicle tractor used in invasions of Pacific islands. On June 3, she appeared on *Music America Loves Best*, singing "It Doesn't Cost You Anything to Dream," "Vilia," and "Battle Hymn of the Republic." On June 9, she was part of an all-star broadcast from the Los Angeles Coliseum, welcoming home General George S. Patton and General James H. Doolittle. She sang "The Star Spangled Banner" with her friends, Ezio Pinza and Lauritz Melchior.

On June 17, Gene was home on a five-day leave for a birthday/anniversary barbecue. He grilled hamburgers, and Jeanette made peach ice cream. It was a particularly noteworthy celebration, as Gene's brother, Bob, now a Captain in the Army Air Force, was back from England, after taking part in thirty missions over Germany.

During another leave, on June 28, Gene attended a zoning meeting with Jeanette. Bel Air residents convinced the City Planning Commission to change the district from a C–3 commercial category to an R–1 single-family residential district. The Raymonds and other celebrities wanted to preserve the community's country atmosphere and were concerned about proposed expansion of the Hotel Bel-Air, which had taken over the former Bel-Air Stables.

Very little was said about Mrs. Kipling in Jeanette and Gene's wartime correspondence, although Gene and Bob each arranged for her to receive $100 a month out of their service pay, now about $1,400 each. In 1945, Mrs. Kipling contacted Gene through her attorney, trying to reconcile with her son. "I do not believe that she wishes to 'bury the past misunderstandings,'" Gene replied. "In her letters, and I have received hundreds of them, she continues to villify [sic] my wife, and there is no indication of any affection for me in either her letters or her actions. I believe she is still primarily interested in causing discord in my marriage – though this statement would probably be vigorously denied."[638]

Jeanette continued to study German lieder with Lotte Lehmann, perform on commercial radio programs, entertain at military hospitals, and sing recitals and concerts. Since Elsie's school usually closed for the summer, she spent July and August in California with her family, arriving on July 3, in time to celebrate Anna's birthday three days later. On August 21, Elsie and Jeanette hosted a fiftieth birthday party for Blossom.

In between, Jeanette was on the road. In July, she sang *Romeo et Juliette* and *Faust* in Cincinnati, Ohio as part of the Cincinnati Summer Opera at the Zoo. She opened her rehearsals to members of her fan club, as well as a group of patients from the Ft. Thomas Army Air Force Convalescent Hospital from near-by Ft. Thomas, Kentucky. The servicemen were charmed by the way Jeanette refused to hurry her chats with them and seemed genuinely interested in their injuries, their families, and their future plans. They also were impressed when she stopped to talk to a group of nuns from St. Francis, who attended the rehearsal because they were not allowed to be out at night.

Jeanette's performances at the Cincinnati Summer Opera at the Zoo overflowed the facility's seating. *The Cincinnati Enquirer* reported on *Faust*: "Total paid attendance of 3,164 exceeded fixed seating capacity by 264 and special chairs were provided to jam the pavilion and parquet to capacity. Servicemen and women were given free admission to standee areas."[639] The newspaper estimated five hundred standees, including some zoo visitors who parked on benches and walkways near the pavilion so they could hear the opera, even if they couldn't see it. Jeanette's performances of *Romeo et Juliette* drew even bigger crowds. She later recalled that the management even sold the chair from her dressing room and she had to put on her makeup, balancing precariously on a folding hunting stool.

In July 1945, Jeanette posed with soldiers from the Army Air Force Convalescent Hospital in Ft. Thomas, Kentucky during a rehearsal at the Cincinnati Summer Opera at the Zoo.

In between Jeanette's opera appearances in Cincinnati, she performed at the Robin Hood Dell in Philadelphia, giving her a chance to sing for wounded veterans at Philadelphia Naval Hospital while she was in her home city. When her July 19 outdoor recital had to be postponed a day because of rain, Jeanette invited a group of fans to

Michael's, a West Philadelphia ice cream parlor. Later that summer, rain also postponed her Milwaukee recital for a day. On August 1, an estimated 16,005 customers filled the outdoor Emil Blatz Temple of Music in Milwaukee, with an additional eight thousand listening outside the venue's fence, despite the threat of more rain.

On July 26, the Allies called for an unconditional surrender of the Japanese Armed Forces in the Potsdam Declaration, but the Japanese ignored it. On August 6, the United States dropped the first atomic bomb on Hiroshima, Japan, following up on August 9 with a second atomic bomb on Nagasaki, Japan, killing an estimated 129,000 people and virtually ending the war. Two years earlier, when a reporter asked Jeanette what she would do on the day the war ended, she said, "Well, I'd be so happy, I think I'd . . . well, I think I'd sing."[640] Little did she know that, after spending the war entertaining at Army camps, hospitals, and countless auditoriums, large and small, that she would spend the unofficial ending of the war at one of the most famous venues in the United States, making her Hollywood Bowl debut, singing to a crowd of over twenty thousand. Leopold Stokowski led the Bowl Orchestra for Jeanette's program; pianist Paul Ulanowsky accompanied Jeanette for her encores. Gene was able to get leave and attend. After the performance, he hosted a reception for her at the Beverly Hills Hotel. Guests included Governor Earl Warren; Mayor Fletcher Bowron; Louis B. Mayer; Irene Dunne; Johnny Mack Brown; Ezio Pinza; Gertrude and Robert Z. Leonard; Rouben Mamoulian and his wife, Azadia; and Mary Pickford, as well as Anna, Elsie, and Blossom. Ever gracious, Jeanette insisted that Grace Newell stand in the receiving line with her.

Columnist Florabel Muir noted, "You could feel the intense pride [the film actors in the audience] took in Jeanette's triumph." Jeanette proved that she was not just a movie star, but a serious singer. When

Muir talked to her at the party, she said that Jeanette "glowed with little girl pleasure." Muir continued, "Looking at her, I couldn't help thinking of a wise saying of the actress, Mrs. Fiske: 'To be a really great artiste, one must first be a great human being.' . . . The first claim on an artiste of Jeanette's stature does not belong to Hollywood and the people of the picture world but to the men and women whose hearts she has gladdened in a fine career. Hollywood will understand that and rejoice with her."[641]

On August 9, 1945, Jeanette and Gene chatted with Louis B. Mayer and actress Penny Singleton at the party following Jeanette's Hollywood Bowl debut. Photo from the Fay La Galle collection.

On August 15, 1945, Japan time, two days before Gene was to report to B-29 school, the Japanese surrendered. Because of the time zone difference, in the United States, V-J Day was celebrated on August 14. On August 31, Gene was relieved from active duty at Army Air Forces Western Flying Training Command at Santa Ana and, on September 2, he passed through the Fort MacArthur Classification

Center in San Pedro, California. It was the same day that the Japanese signed surrender papers on the USS Missouri, officially ending the war. Gene was put on a fifty-day terminal leave, after which he was allowed to resume his movie career.

During the war, both of the Raymonds gave their all for their country. Although Jeanette did not serve in the Armed Forces, she consistently did whatever she was called upon to do, be it entertaining the troops, visiting wounded soldiers in hospitals, selling war bonds, or keeping up morale on the home front with recitals and broadcasts. For most of the war, she was on the road more than she was at home. Her strenuous schedule affected her health, just as the lengthy separations took a toll on the Raymonds' marriage. The post-war years would prove to be a struggle for them on many levels. The coming years saw the demise of the studio system and radio as they knew it, the advent of television, and the rise of rock 'n roll. Hollywood went from making screwball comedies, operettas, and happily-ever-after family films to serious dramas with messages and dark noir pictures, leaving many actors, including Jeanette and Gene, questioning their place in the industry. Peacetime brought many changes to the world, as well as to the lives of all returning soldiers, those who served on the home front, and their families who faced an unknown future.

Endnotes

1   Kieran, John. "'A lilt and a loveliness' writes John Kieran about Jeanette MacDonald." *Words and Music: Comments by Famous Authors about the World's Greatest Artists*. RCA Victor. 1950.

2   Rhoades, Clara and Williams, Tessa. "Jeanette MacDonald Super Star." *American Classic Screen*. July/August 1978.

3   *MGM: When the Lion Roars*. PBS. 1992.

4   Taviner, Reginald. "How to be Naughty But Nice." *Photoplay Magazine*. September 1934.

5   Kobal, John. *Gotta Sing, Gotta Dance: A Pictorial History of Film Musicals*. Hamlyn. 1970.

6   "The Golden Comet Question Box." *The Golden Comet*. Spring 1964.

7   MacDonald, Jeanette. Draft of Jeanette MacDonald's unpublished autobiography, collaborator unknown. Undated.

8   Rogers, Ginger. Letter to Edwina Hatfield dated February 26, 1962. *The Golden Comet*. Spring 1962.

9   Cassidy, Susan Rogers. "Confessions of a New Member." *Retrospect*. Vol. 9, no. 2.

10 "Number One Leading Man – Gene Raymond." *The Golden Comet*. Summer 1970.

11 "Question Box." *The Golden Comet*. Fall 1958.

12 MacDonald, Jeanette. Revised pages of Jeanette MacDonald's unpublished autobiography. 1963.

13 Raymond, Gene. Foreword for Jeanette MacDonald's unpublished autobiography. Undated.

14   Bass, William. Untitled incomplete draft of Jeanette MacDonald biography. 1981.

15   "Remembering Blossom MacDonald Rock." *The Golden Comet*. Summer 1978.

16   Rock, Blossom. Letter to Jeanette MacDonald dated February 5, 1962. *The Golden Comet*. Spring 1962.

17   Rock, Blossom. Letter to Clara Rhoades. September 21, 1966.

18   Williams, Neva L. "MacDonald Sidelights." *The News–Sentinel*. Fort Wayne, Indiana. April 14, 1939.

19   Turk, Edward Baron. *Hollywood Diva*. University of California Press. 1998.

20   Bass, William. Untitled incomplete draft of Jeanette MacDonald biography. 1981.

21   Wright, Charles A. "My Little Cousin—Who Became a Movie Star." *Pennsylvania Magazine*. Spring 1985.

22   Wright, Charles A. "Jeanette M'Donald 9 Hours In Bathtub." *The Evening Bulletin*. Philadelphia, Pennsylvania. July 23, 1932.

23   Bass, William. Incomplete draft of *The Iron Butterfly*. 1978.

24   Ibid.

25   Gilbert, Douglas. "Blossom MacDonald, Waiting Chance in 'Dead End,' Gets 'Crazy Ideas,' Now Trying Writing as Side Line." *New York World–Telegram*. New York, New York. February 29, 1936.

26   MacDonald, Anna. "My Daughter, Jeanette MacDonald." *Hollywood*. September 1936.

27   Bass, William. Incomplete draft of *The Iron Butterfly*. 1978.

28   Ibid.

29   Hall, Gladys. "'Men Friends Are Important!' Says Jeanette MacDonald." 1936. Gladys Hall Papers, Margaret Herrick Library, Academy of Motion Picture Arts and Sciences.

30   MacDonald, Jeanette. Letter to Florence Gleason. June 18, 1920.

31   Bass, William. Incomplete draft of *The Iron Butterfly*. 1978.

32   Lee, Laura. "Jeanette MacDonald Comes Home to Sing Again." *The Evening Bulletin*. Philadelphia, Pennsylvania. July 26, 1950.

33   "Jeanette MacDonald and Betty Garde Here for Reunion but Graduation Year Is a Secret." Unknown newspaper. Philadelphia, Pennsylvania. March 1952. Reprinted in *The Golden Comet*. Christmas 1965.

34   Parish, James Robert. *The Jeanette MacDonald Story*. Mason/Charter. 1976.

35   Fidler, Jimmie. *San Francisco Chronicle*. San Francisco, California. November 13, 1937.

36   "The Love Parade Girl." Reprinted in *The Magazine Of The Jeanette MacDonald British Fan Club*. Summer 1949.

37 MacDonald, Jeanette. Letter to Gene Raymond. October 1, 1935.

38 Zeitlin, Ida. "'I'm No Prude!' says Jeanette MacDonald." *Screenland*. November 1938.

39 Dinan, Patsy. "Jeanette Voices Her Superstitions." *Amarillo Globe–Times*. Amarillo, Texas. June 4, 1956.

40 "Romantic Film Star Gives Concerts Here. *The Edmonton Journal*. Edmonton, Alberta, Canada. October 14, 1952.

41 Martin, Mildred. "Camera Angles on Film Folk." *The Philadelphia Inquirer*. Philadelphia, PA. March 2, 1937.

42 *Luncheon at the Music Center*. Tom Cassidy interview with Emily Wentz. Circa 1965.

43 "Will You Remember?" *The Golden Comet*. Winter 1972.

44 Bass, William. Untitled incomplete draft of Jeanette MacDonald biography. 1981.

45 Ibid.

46 Bass, William. Incomplete draft of *The Iron Butterfly*. 1978.

47 Ibid.

48 Bass, William. Untitled incomplete draft of Jeanette MacDonald biography. 1981.

49 MacDonald, Jeanette. Outline for Jeanette MacDonald's unpublished autobiography. Undated.

50 "Let's Talk It Out!" *Movie Mirror*. December 1939.

51 Seymore, Hart. "When A Girl Falls In Love Should She Follow Her Family's Advice?" *Photoplay Magazine*. September 1936.

52 "Rest, Reading And Rehearsal Put Miss Jeanette MacDonald In Trim For Concert Tonight." *The Beaumont Enterprise*. Beaumont, Texas. February 14, 1941.

53 Bass, William. Untitled incomplete draft of Jeanette MacDonald biography. 1981.

54 MacDonald, Jeanette and Balling, Fredda Dudley. Draft of Jeanette MacDonald's unpublished autobiography. Fall 1960.

55 Bass, William. Incomplete draft of *The Iron Butterfly*. 1978.

56 Ibid.

57 Howe, Herb. "Jeanette Takes Paris!" *The New Movie Magazine*. February 1932.

58 Bass, William. Incomplete draft of *The Iron Butterfly*. 1978.

59 Rutledge, Fred. "Make Way For Melody, part one." *Radio Mirror*. December 1937.

60 MacDonald, Jeanette and Brough, James. Draft of Jeanette MacDonald's unpublished autobiography. Spring 1960. Cinematic Arts Library, Doheny Memorial Library, University of Southern California.

61 Rhode, Edward. "The Man Jeanette Is Marrying." *Film Pictorial.* June 19, 1937.

62 Bass, William. Incomplete draft of *The Iron Butterfly.* 1978.

63 MacDonald, Jeanette. Outline for Jeanette MacDonald's unpublished autobiography. Undated.

64 "Jeanette MacDonald's Wish." *The Film Weekly.* September 19, 1931.

65 "Thrills on the High 'C's.'" *The Lion's Roar.* October 1942.

66 Shawell, Julia. "Jeanette MacDonald The Girl Who Plays Queens." *Pictorial Review.* September 1933.

67 MacDonald, Jeanette and Brough, James. Draft of Jeanette MacDonald's unpublished autobiography. Spring 1960. Cinematic Arts Library, Doheny Memorial Library, University of Southern California.

68 Kobal, John. *Gotta Sing, Gotta Dance: A Pictorial History of Film Musicals.* Hamlyn. 1970.

69 Sharon, Mary. "Hollywood Has Always Spelt [sic] Good Luck for Me." *Silver Screen.* October 1934.

70 "Jean M'Donald Sues Critic Who 'Counted Eyelashes.'" *Daily News.* New York, New York. July 12, 1933.

71 "Hollywood Is Real Loveless Colony, Claim." *The Evening News.* Wilkes–Barre, Pennsylvania. July 26, 1933.

72 "Dog Damage to Star's Home." *Los Angeles Examiner.* Los Angeles, California. March 14, 1936.

73 Bass, William. Incomplete draft of *The Iron Butterfly.* 1978.

74 Eyman, Scott. *Lion of Hollywood.* Simon & Schuster. 2005.

75 Hall, Gladys. "'Men Friends Are Important!' Says Jeanette MacDonald." 1936. Gladys Hall Papers, Margaret Herrick Library, Academy of Motion Picture Arts and Sciences.

76 Pryor, Nancy. "No More 'Nighties' for Jeanette." *Motion Picture.* February 1933.

77 Hay, Peter. *MGM: When the Lion Roars.* Turner Publishing, Inc. 1991.

78 McBride, Joseph. *How Did Lubitsch Do It?* Columbia University Press. 2018.

79 Ibid.

80 Rickey, Carrie. "Saucy Jeanette Is a Joy." *Boston Herald.* Boston, Massachusetts. March 29, 1984.

81 Barrios, Richard. *Must-See Musicals.* Running Press Adult. 2017.

82 "Jeanette Eats Her Spinach." Reprinted in *Retrospect.* Vol. 6, no. 3.

83 Wilson, Elizabeth. "On Tour with a Prima Donna." *Silver Screen.* June 1940.

84   Albert, Dora. "If Jeanette Didn't Like You..." *Modern Screen*. Circa 1936.

85   Burke, Marcella. "Jeanette MacDonald Fights Her Own Battles!" *Screen Play Magazine*. Reprinted in *Retrospect*. Vol. 9, no. 3.

86   Hagensen, Leslie. "Elizabeth (Betty) Bradley Oral History Interview Regarding Jeanette MacDonald." Philadelphia, Pennsylvania. October 7, 2001.

87   Behr, Edward. *The Good Frenchman: The True Story of the Life and Times of Maurice Chevalier*. Villard. 1993.

88   Berle, Milton. *B.S. I Love You: Sixty Funny Years with the Famous and the Infamous*. McGraw-Hill. 1987.

89   MacDonald, Jeanette. Outline for Jeanette MacDonald's unpublished autobiography. Undated.

90   Reynolds, Roberta. "Memories of Jeanette" sent to Dolores Baird. 1965.

91   Ketcham, George and Fist, Allene. "Gracious Jeanette Has Chat With Press: Hall Sold Out." *Tulsa World*. Tulsa, Oklahoma. June 1943.

92   Roderick, John. "Chevalier Turns 70 in Theater on Third Career." *Independent*. Long Beach, California. September 12, 1958.

93   Scheuer, Philip K. "MacDonald, Eddy Enjoy Renaissance." *Los Angeles Times*. Los Angeles, California. January 18, 1963.

94   MacDonald, Jeanette. "So I'm in Love with Nelson Eddy!" *Hollywood*. June 1935.

95   Adams, Marjory. "Jeanette MacDonald Observes Thanksgiving on N.E. Basis." *The Boston Daily Globe*. Boston, Massachusetts. November 29, 1940.

96   "MacDonald, Eddy Reunited in Song." *The Minneapolis Star*. Minneapolis, Minnesota. December 20, 1956.

97   Blake, Marie (Blossom Rock). Letter to Clara Rhoades. March 25, 1941.

98   Handsaker, Gene. "Nelson Eddy Was Singer First." *The Times*. San Mateo, California. March 10, 1967.

99   Bodeen, DeWitt. Letter to Eleanor Knowles Dugan. July 17, 1965. Eleanor Knowles Dugan collection.

100   Hall, Gladys. "The True Life Story of Nelson Eddy, Part 2." *Modern Screen*. November 1935.

101   Cohen, Stephen. "Nelson Eddy, the serious opera singer." www.theoperacritic.com.

102   Coons, Robbin. "Hollywood Sights and Sounds." *The Corsicana Daily Sun*. Corsicana, Texas. May 16, 1938.

103   "Hollywood DAY by DAY." *The New Movie Magazine*. August 1933.

104   "'Love on a Bet' Farce at Earle." *The Philadelphia Inquirer*. Philadelphia, Pennsylvania. February 22, 1936.

105 Halsell, Grace. "Jeanette Sings Tonight: Being Late Meant Start Of Two Stars' Romance." *Star–Telegram*. Fort Worth, Texas. November 1, 1950.

106 Mereto, Lucille. "Screen Guild Review March 25, 1946." *The Nelson Eddy Golden Notes*. Summer 1946.

107 *Toast of the Town*. CBS. August 5, 1951.

108 Johnson, Susanne and Erdwurm, Donna Lee. "Toast of the Town." *The Golden Comet*. Fall 1951.

109 *Toast of the Town*. CBS. August 5, 1951.

110 *Juke Box Jury* review. *The Shooting Star*. Anniversary 1957.

111 "Picwood Appearance" transcribed by Dorothy Cassidy. *The Golden Comet*. Summer 1963.

112 MacDonald, Jeanette and Brough, James. Draft of Jeanette MacDonald's unpublished autobiography. Spring 1960. Cinematic Arts Library, Doheny Memorial Library, University of Southern California.

113 Lenz, Elita Miller. "A Glimpse at Life Thru [sic] the Eyes of a Fourteen-Year-Old Equity Player." *The Billboard*. March 10, 1923.

114 Raymond, Gene. Foreword for Jeanette MacDonald's unpublished autobiography. Undated.

115 "Spotlight on Gene Raymond." *The Golden Comet*. Summer 1980.

116 Slater, Carl. "Gene Raymond's Complaint About Hollywood." *Movie Classic*. May 1935.

117 Daly, Maury. "Gene Raymond: Renaissance Man." *Classic Images*. November 1995.

118 Dietz, Edith. "Blond Bachelor." *The Detroit Free Press*. Detroit, Michigan. September 2, 1934.

119 Grayson, Charles. "Indifferent to Girls." *Motion Picture*. November 1932.

120 Raymond, Gene. "Gene Raymond Replies to J. Eugene Chrisman." *Hollywood*. December 1934.

121 Foster, Iris. "'I Won't Get in a Rut,' Says Gene Raymond." *Film Weekly*. January 26, 1934.

122 Samuels, Lenore. "Gene Takes a 'Termer.'" *Silver Screen*. May 1936.

123 Torre, Marie. "Jeanette Is No Has-Been." *Akron Beacon Journal*. Akron, Ohio. October 30, 1958.

124 Cavalluzzo, Gina. Letter to Gene Raymond. November 30, 1990.

125 Dietz, Edith. "Blond Bachelor." *The Detroit Free Press*. Detroit, Michigan. September 2, 1934.

126 Ibid.

127 "They Wouldn't Let Jeanette Sing." *Shadowplay Magazine*. May 1935.

128 MacDonald, Jeanette and Brough, James. Draft of Jeanette MacDonald's unpublished autobiography. Spring 1960. Cinematic Arts Library, Doheny Memorial Library, University of Southern California.

129 Spensley, Dorothy. "Like to Read Other People's Mail?" *Modern Screen*. July 1942.

130 Hall, Gladys. "Their First Dates." *Photoplay combined with Movie Mirror*. October 1942.

131 Rohlfing, Joan Halford. Email to author. September 20, 2014.

132 MacDonald, Jeanette. Outline for Jeanette MacDonald's unpublished autobiography. Undated.

133 "Jeanette in Real Romance." *Boston Daily Record*. Boston, Massachusetts. August 23, 1936.

134 Kerr, Martha. "He's Looking for a Sweetheart." *Modern Screen*. October 1935.

135 MacDonald, Jeanette. Draft of Jeanette MacDonald's unpublished autobiography, collaborator unknown. Undated.

136 MacDonald, Jeanette and Balling, Fredda Dudley. Draft of Jeanette MacDonald's unpublished autobiography. Fall 1960.

137 MacDonald, Jeanette. Outline for Jeanette MacDonald's unpublished autobiography. Undated.

138 MacDonald, Jeanette. Undated notes for autobiography.

139 MacDonald, Jeanette and Brough, James. Draft of Jeanette MacDonald's unpublished autobiography. Spring 1960. Cinematic Arts Library, Doheny Memorial Library, University of Southern California.

140 Spain, Nancy. Excerpt from *"Teach": The Story of Eleanor "Teach" Tennant* reprinted in *The Magazine Of The Jeanette MacDonald British Fan Club*. May/December 1953.

141 Ibid.

142 MacDonald, Jeanette. Undated notes for autobiography.

143 MacDonald, Jeanette. Letter to Gene Raymond. September 23, 1935.

144 MacDonald, Jeanette. Letter to Gene Raymond. October 1, 1935.

145 MacDonald, Jeanette. Letter to Gene Raymond. September 21, 1935.

146 MacDonald, Jeanette. Letter to Gene Raymond. October 8, 1935.

147 MacDonald, Jeanette. Outline for Jeanette MacDonald's unpublished autobiography. Undated.

148 MacDonald, Jeanette and Brough, James. Draft of Jeanette MacDonald's unpublished autobiography. Spring 1960. Cinematic Arts Library, Doheny Memorial Library, University of Southern California.

149 MacDonald, Jeanette. Outline for Jeanette MacDonald's unpublished autobiography. Undated.

150 Pack, Harvey. "TV Keynotes: Nelson Eddy Returns." *The Morning Call.* Allentown, Pennsylvania. January 26, 1966.

151 Ibid.

152 Brown, Peter Harry and Brown, Pamela Ann. *The MGM Girls: Behind the Velvet Curtain.* St. Martin's Press. 1983.

153 Munn, Michael. *Jimmy Stewart: The Truth Behind the Legend.* Skyhorse Publishing. 2013.

154 Johnson, Erskine. "Jeanette MacDonald Is Back and Jose Iturbi's Got Her." *The Salisbury Times.* Salisbury, Maryland. November 29, 1946.

155 Lane, Jerry. "Salute to Jeanette and Gene! Their Dreams Came True." *Screen Play.* November 1936.

156 Ibid.

157 *Jeanette MacDonald Story According to the Movie's Fan Magazines.* Self-published collection of movie magazine articles compiled by an anonymous fan. Undated.

158 MacDonald, Jeanette. Outline for Jeanette MacDonald's unpublished autobiography. Undated.

159 MacDonald, Jeanette and Brough, James. Draft of Jeanette MacDonald's unpublished autobiography. Spring 1960. Cinematic Arts Library, Doheny Memorial Library, University of Southern California.

160 Raymond, Gene. Letter to Jeanette MacDonald. Postmarked February 9, 1936.

161 MacDonald, Jeanette. Letter to Martha Farrington and Club Members. *The Golden Comet.* Fall 1949.

162 MacDonald, Jeanette. Draft of Jeanette MacDonald's unpublished autobiography, collaborator unknown. Undated.

163 Taylor, Ariel Yvon. Numerology charts for Jeanette MacDonald and Gene Raymond. February 27, 1936.

164 Rhoades, Clara and Williams, Tessa. "Jeanette MacDonald Super Star Pat II." *American Classic Screen.* November/December 1978.

165 MacDonald, Jeanette and Balling, Fredda Dudley. Draft of Jeanette MacDonald's unpublished autobiography. Fall 1960.

166 Kipling, Mary. Letter to Robert Ritchie. June 20, 1936.

167 Kipling, Mary. Letter to Neil McCarthy. November 8, 1936.

168 MacDonald, Jeanette. Draft of Jeanette MacDonald's unpublished autobiography, collaborator unknown. Undated.

169   Raymond, Gene. Letter to Mary Kipling. April 29, 1936.

170   Kipling, Mary. Letter to Jeanette MacDonald. June 4, 1936.

171   Kipling, Mary. Letter to Robert Ritchie. June 18, 1936.

172   Sharpe, Howard. "What Matters Most In Life?" *Photoplay Magazine.* November 1935.

173   Hall, Gladys. "Gene, Marry? Well –." *Modern Screen.* July 1936.

174   MacDonald, Jeanette. Draft of Jeanette MacDonald's unpublished autobiography, collaborator unknown. Undated.

175   "Extract from 'The Weekly Post.'" *Musical Echoes.* March/April 1947.

176   Lane, Jerry. "Salute to Jeanette and Gene! Their Dreams Came True." *Screen Play.* November 1936.

177   MacDonald, Jeanette. Draft of Jeanette MacDonald's unpublished autobiography, collaborator unknown. Undated.

178   Smalley, Jack. "How Hollywood Tried to Spoil the Jeanette MacDonald-Gene Raymond Marriage!" *Movie Mirror.* August 1937.

179   Kipling, Mary. Letter to Jeanette MacDonald. August 11, 1936.

180   Lane, Jerry. "Salute to Jeanette and Gene! Their Dreams Came True." *Screen Play.* November 1936.

181   Whitaker, Alma. "Sugar and Spice." *Los Angeles Times.* Los Angeles, California. September 25, 1936.

182   MacDonald, Jeanette. Draft of Jeanette MacDonald's unpublished autobiography, collaborator unknown. Undated.

183   Raymond, Gene. Letter to Mary Kipling. October 18, 1936.

184   Kipling, Mary. Letter to Neil McCarthy. November 8, 1936.

185   Kipling, Mary. Letter to Lillian Garrick Malmsten. December 9, 1936.

186   Raymond, Gene. Letter to Neil McCarthy. January 18, 1937.

187   McCarthy, Neil. Letter to Daniel F. Cohalan, Jr. February 16, 1937.

188   MacDonald, Jeanette and Balling, Fredda Dudley. Draft of Jeanette MacDonald's unpublished autobiography. Fall 1960.

189   MacDonald, Jeanette. Draft of Jeanette MacDonald's unpublished autobiography, collaborator unknown. Undated.

190   Zeitlin, Ida. "The MacRaymond Bride Comes Home." *Movie Mirror.* November 1937.

191   Eddy, Nelson, as told to Reid, James. "Gene Raymond Is a Lucky Guy." *Screenland.* January 1937.

192   "A Bit of This and That." Reprinted in *Retrospect*. Vol. 15, no. 1.

193   MacDonald, Jeanette. Draft of Jeanette MacDonald's unpublished autobiography, collaborator unknown. Undated.

194   *Maytime* Notes from MGM Archives. 1936.

195   "Jeanette Eats Her Spinach." Reprinted in *Retrospect*. Vol. 6, no. 3.

196   Cuthbert, David. "Jeanette MacDonald Has 'The Old Sentimentality." *The Times–Picayune*. New Orleans, Louisiana. January 10, 1971.

197   *Nelson and Jeanette: America's Singing Sweethearts*. PBS. 1992.

198   Rhoades, Clara and Williams, Tessa. "Jeanette MacDonald Super Star Pat II." *American Classic Screen*. November/December 1978.

199   "One Hollywood Hard-Worked Artist." Reprinted in *Retrospect*. Vol. 13, no. 1.

200   Zeitlin, Ida. "'I'm No Prude!' says Jeanette MacDonald." *Screenland*. November 1938.

201   "Questions for Miss MacDonald." *The Golden Comet*. Spring 1959.

202   Rhoades, Clara and Williams, Tessa. "Jeanette MacDonald Super Star Pat II." *American Classic Screen*. November/December 1978.

203   "Questions for Miss MacDonald." *The Golden Comet*. Spring 1959.

204   Lane, Jerry. "Salute to Jeanette and Gene! Their Dreams Came True." *Screen Play*. November 1936.

205   Manners, Dorothy. "The Romantic Love Story of Jeanette MacDonald and Gene Raymond." *Photoplay Magazine*. November 1936.

206   Davies, Reine. "Jeanette MacDonald Tells Me." *Los Angeles Examiner*. Los Angeles, California. January 4, 1937.

207   Hill, Mary. "Jeanette Dances." *Screenbook*. September 1937.

208   Ibid.

209   Ibid.

210   1989 Clan Clave banquet speeches. June 24, 1989.

211   Ibid.

212   Jones, Jack. Tweet on January 24, 2014.

213   "Quotes from Here and There." *The Golden Comet*. Summer 1986.

214   Kipling, Mary. Letter to Louis B. Mayer. April 28, 1937.

215   Raymond, Gene. Letter to Louis B. Mayer. May 26, 1937.

216   Selznick, Daniel Mayer. Email to author. October 30, 2018.

217   MacDonald, Jeanette. Calling card to Gene Raymond. June 1937.

218   Nielsen, Ray. "Ray Nielsen's Ray's Way: Gene Raymond and Red Dust." *Classic Images*. March 1985.

219 Morin, Relman. "Jeanette MacDonald Gives Up, Asks Studio to Run Wedding." *The Minneapolis Tribune.* Minneapolis, Minnesota. June 16, 1937.

220 "Jeanette's 'I Do' Held Up an Hour." *Cleveland Plain Dealer.* Cleveland, Ohio. June 17, 1937.

221 Ibid.

222 MacDonald, Jeanette. Draft of Jeanette MacDonald's unpublished autobiography, collaborator unknown. Undated.

223 Rutledge, Fred. "Make Way For Melody, part four." *Radio Mirror.* March 1938.

224 Eddy, Nelson. Letter to Jeanette MacDonald. April 15, 1937.

225 Carr, Barbara. "The News Corner." *The Golden Comet.* Christmas 1966.

226 Turk, Edward Baron. "Jeanette MacDonald and Gene Raymond: The Golden Couple's Honeymoon House in Bel-Air." *Architectural Digest.* April 2000.

227 Phillips, John with Jerome, Jim. *Papa John: A Music Legend's Shattering Journey Through Sex, Drugs, and Rock 'n Roll.* Dolphin Books. 1986.

228 Raymond, Gene. Letter to Jeanette MacDonald. February 9, 1947.

229 Hamilton, Sara. "Jeanette—On the Spot! Things We Like about Jeanette MacDonald." *Movie Mirror.* September 1939.

230 Lindeman, Edith. "Critic Finds Miss MacDonald More Charming Than in Films." *Richmond Times–Dispatch.* Richmond, Virginia. February 26, 1940.

231 Peak, Mayme Ober. "Jeanette MacDonald Has Insured Her Marriage." Unknown newspaper. Boston, Massachusetts. Circa December 3, 1939.

232 Hendrickson, Phyllis. "Jeanette MacDonald, Singer, Quizzed By Tattler Member." *Woodward Tattler.* Woodward High School. Toledo, Ohio. March 29, 1940.

233 Raymond, Gene. Letter to Jeanette MacDonald. August 18, 1955.

234 Raymond, Gene. Note to Jeanette MacDonald. January 8, 1962.

235 Rhoades, Clara and Williams, Tessa. *Lookin' in! and Cookin' in! with the MacRaymonds at Twin Gables.* Jeanette MacDonald International Fan Club. 1984.

236 "A Bit of This and That." Reprinted in *Retrospect.* Vol. 15, no. 1.

237 "'I Would Make a Rotten Husband,' Says James Stewart." *The Picturegoer Xmas Annual.* November 13, 1937.

238 Field, Eunice. "Jeanette MacDonald: Golden Voice of the Thirties." Reprinted in *The Golden Comet.* June 1966.

239 Rhoades, Clara. Letter to Sue (last name unknown). December 1989.

240 Raymond, Gene. Calling card to Jeanette MacDonald. June 23, 1937.

241 Hall, Gladys. "Has She Anything Left to Want?" *Modern Screen.* May 1938.

242   Makarius, Cordelia B. "The Stars Play Games." *The Family Circle*. September 1, 1939.

243   Tyron, Pat. "Singer Thinks Our Pat 'Nice.'" *The Province*. Vancouver, British Columbia. October 27, 1952.

244   Bodeen, DeWitt. "Jeanette MacDonald." *Films in Review*. March 1965.

245   Tildesley, Ruth. "Camera Romance!" *Screenland*. September 1937.

246   Ibid.

247   MacDonald, Jeanette, as told to Zeitlin, Ida. "How to Be Happy in a Man's World." *Movie Mirror*. November 1938.

248   "Philadelphia Music Foundation Hall of Fame Awards Dinner." *The Golden Comet*. Summer 1988.

249   Parish, James Robert. *The Jeanette MacDonald Story*. Mason/Charter. 1976.

250   Dahl, Arlene. "Music Hath Charm to Smooth Beauty's Brow, too, Dahl Told." *Chicago Daily Tribune*. Chicago, Illinois. June 6, 1952.

251   Ibid.

252   MacDonald, Jeanette. Letter to Clara Rhoades. November 7, 1964.

253   Ibid.

254   MacDonald, Jeanette. Letter to Elsie Scheiter. April 3, 1947.

255   Wentz, Emily. Letter to Martha Farrington and JMIFC members. *The Golden Comet*. Christmas 1949.

256   Phillips, Michelle. *California Dreamin'*. Warner Books. 1986.

257   "(2) Comebacker Movie Stars Bring (2) New Husbands." *The Honolulu Advertiser*. Honolulu, Hawaii. July 2, 1937.

258   "Stars Greeted By Huge Crowd." *Honolulu Star–Bulletin*. Honolulu, Hawaii. July 1, 1937.

259   Wilson, Elizabeth. "Projections—Jeanette MacDonald." *Silver Screen*. October 1937.

260   Balling, Fredda Dudley. "The Love Song Is Ended." *Motion Picture*. April 1965.

261   Whitaker, Alma. "Newlyweds Talk From Honolulu." *Los Angeles Times*. Los Angeles, California. August 1, 1937.

262   Harrison, Martha. "Miss M'Donald Admits Stage Fright." *Jackson Daily News*. Jackson, Mississippi. March 29, 1939.

263   Hall, Gladys. "Mrs. Gene Raymond to You." *Radio Stars*. December 1937.

264   Carroll, Harrison. "Behind the Scenes in Hollywood." *Los Angeles Evening Herald–Express*. Los Angeles, California. September 17, 1937.

265 Hall, Gladys. "Has She Anything Left to Want?" *Modern Screen*. May 1938.

266 Ibid.

267 MacDonald, Jeanette. Letter to Glenna Riley and members dated April 10, 1963. *Musical Echoes*. April/May/June 1963.

268 Fitch, Laura Ellsworth. "Can Jobless Gene Hold Jeanette?" *Movies*. February 1940.

269 Keene, Harold. "The Truth about Jeanette and Gene." *Movie Mirror*. May 1939.

270 1989 Clan Clave banquet speeches. June 24, 1989.

271 Keene, Harold. "The Truth about Jeanette and Gene." *Movie Mirror*. May 1939.

272 MacDonald, Jeanette. "My Frankest Confession." *Screenland*. January 1940.

273 "Let's Talk It Out!" *Movie Mirror*. December 1939.

274 Ross, Marilyn T. "A Nostalgia Trip With Jeanette MacDonald & Nelson Eddy." *Movie Stars*. February 1972.

275 Raymond, Gene. Letter to Clara Rhoades. March 15, 1966.

276 Rhoades, Clara. Various undated notes for unpublished book on Jeanette MacDonald.

277 "She Has Everything." Reprinted in *Retrospect*. Vol. 1, no. 2.

278 "Warm Reception Pleases Miss MacDonald." *Peoria Journal–Transcript*. Peoria, Illinois. April 17, 1939.

279 Scheuer, Philip K. "MacDonald, Eddy Enjoy Renaissance." *Los Angeles Times*. Los Angeles, California. January 18, 1963.

280 "Question Box." *The Golden Comet*. Winter 1958.

281 "Miss MacDonald on First Concert Tour." *The Pittsburg Headlight*. Pittsburg, Kansas. March 16, 1939.

282 Stoneham, Eddy. "Remembrances of Jeanette." *The Golden Comet*. Summer 1963.

283 Bray, George. "Famed Singer was His Favorite." *The Golden Comet*. Winter 1973.

284 Hudson, Richard M. *60 Years of Vamps and Camps*. Drake Publishers. 1973.

285 "She Has Everything." Reprinted in *Retrospect*. Vol. 1, no. 2.

286 Leo, Estelle. "Jeanette's Double Life." *Screen Life*. December 1941.

287 Field, Eunice. "Jeanette MacDonald: Golden Voice of the Thirties." Reprinted in *The Golden Comet*. June 1966.

288 Madle, Dorothy. "Jeanette MacDonald Charms People 'Cause They Charm Her, She Says." *Milwaukee Sentinel*. Milwaukee, Wisconsin. August 1, 1945.

289 MacDonald, Jeanette and Brough, James. Draft of Jeanette MacDonald's unpublished autobiography. Spring 1960. Cinematic Arts Library, Doheny Memorial Library, University of Southern California.

290 MacDonald, Jeanette. Outline for Jeanette MacDonald's unpublished autobiography. Undated.

291 *Luncheon at the Music Center.* Tom Cassidy interview with Sharon Rich and Emily Wentz. February 26, 1974.

292 MacDonald, Jeanette and Brough, James. Draft of Jeanette MacDonald's unpublished autobiography. Spring 1960. Cinematic Arts Library, Doheny Memorial Library, University of Southern California.

293 MacDonald, Jeanette. Letter to Marion Smith Glendening. August 9, 1938.

294 "Movie Star Peeved By Snowbound Train Flouts Photographers." *Waterloo Sunday Courier.* Waterloo, Iowa. April 10, 1938.

295 MacDonald, Jeanette. Letter to Marion Smith Glendening. August 9, 1938.

296 "Jeanette, Gene Here;—Shh! It's a Secret." *Daily News.* New York, New York. April 14, 1938.

297 Mariam, E.A. Letter to Gene Raymond. April 18, 1938.

298 Raymond, Gene. Note to Foxy Jack of Wissaboo. December 1938.

299 "Jeanette MacDonald Talks of Fads and Films." Reprinted in *Retrospect.* Vol. 11, no. 4.

300 "'Lady' $26G, 'Heaven'–Raymond $22G, 'Moto'–Vaude $12G, 'Polo' $15,000, Chi; 'Robin'–Vaude Smash $30,000, 2d Wk." *Variety.* May 25, 1938.

301 "As Gene Raymond Reached City." *The Pittsburg Sun.* Pittsburg, Kansas. March 17, 1939.

302 Peak, Mayme Ober. "Jeanette MacDonald Has Insured Her Marriage." Unknown newspaper. Boston, Massachusetts. Circa December 3, 1939.

303 Raymond, Gene. Letter to Jeanette MacDonald. June 16, 1938.

304 Hopper, Hedda. "Hedda Hopper's Hollywood." *Los Angeles Times.* Los Angeles, California. September 23, 1938.

305 Ibid.

306 MacDonald, Jeanette. Letter to Marion Smith Glendening. August 9, 1938.

307 Heimbuecher, Ruth. "Marriage Success Old Hat to Jeanette." *The Pittsburgh Press.* Pittsburgh, Pennsylvania. September 19, 1960.

308 "Next Sunday at the Logan." *The Logan Daily News.* Logan, Ohio. April 20, 1939.

309 MacDonald, Jeanette. Twin Gables guest book. 1938–1963.

310 Peak, Mayme Ober. "Jeanette MacDonald Has Insured Her Marriage." Unknown newspaper. Boston, Massachusetts. Circa December 3, 1939.

311 "Raves and Raps." *Los Angeles Daily News.* Los Angeles, California. June 27, 1939.

312 MacDonald, Jeanette. "This Is What I Want…" *Screen Stars*. January 1947.

313 Williams, Chuck. "The story of the World War II-era Hollywood starlet and a Columbus furniture store." *Ledger–Enquirer*. Columbus, Georgia. December 10, 2016.

314 Gabriel, Grace. "Jeanette's Concert in Bloomington, Indiana." *Chevalier–MacDonald News*. July/August 1939.

315 Cendow, Jeanne. "La MacDonald Takes Time Out for Tea-Time With Our Jeanne." *The Classen Life*. Oklahoma City, Oklahoma. March 1939.

316 "Screen Star Arrives For Dallas Concert." *Dallas Times*. Dallas, Texas. February 14, 1940.

317 Entertainment Schedule, Mr. and Mrs. Gene Raymond Community Account. 1938.

318 Harrison, Martha. "Miss M'Donald Admits Stage Fright." *Jackson Daily News*. Jackson, Mississippi. March 29, 1939.

319 Peak, Mayme Ober. "Jeanette MacDonald Has Insured Her Marriage." Unknown newspaper. Boston, Massachusetts. Circa December 3, 1939.

320 MacDonald, Jeanette. Letter to Glenna Riley. *Chevalier–MacDonald News*. July/August 1939.

321 "MacDonald Proves Popular With Concert Crowd; Big Guards Needed." *Stillwater News*. Stillwater, Oklahoma. March 21, 1939.

322 Harrison, Martha. "Miss M'Donald Admits Stage Fright." *Jackson Daily News*. Jackson, Mississippi. March 29, 1939.

323 Logan, Floyd. "Jeanette MacDonald, Gracious And Charming, Delighted With First American Concert Tour." *The News–Sentinel*. Fort Wayne, Indiana. April 14, 1939.

324 Ninman, Eleanor Evalyn. Letter to Jeanette Macdonald. April 18, 1939.

325 Hughes, Elinor. "Jeanette MacDonald, Here for Boston Debut, Discusses Contrast Between Concert and Films." *Boston Herald*. Boston, Massachusetts. November 29, 1940.

326 Farman, Irvin. "Her Fear Is Two-Fold: Jeanette MacDonald Still Jittery at Curtain Time." *Star–Telegram*. Fort Worth, Texas. October 31, 1950.

327 Ibid.

328 Hawkins, William. "Jeanette Sings into Gotham." *New York World–Telegram and Sun*. New York, New York. October 3, 1950.

329 "Raves and Raps." *Los Angeles Daily News*. Los Angeles, California. June 27, 1939.

330 "Jeanette MacDonald Strolls Around Tulsa Southside Area." Unknown newspaper. Tulsa, Oklahoma. March 1939.

331 Walker, Helen Louise. "Jeanette On Tour." *Movies*. October 1939.

332 Harrison, Martha. "Miss M'Donald Admits Stage Fright." *Jackson Daily News*. Jackson, Mississippi. March 29, 1939.

333 "Vivacious and Gracious Jeanette MacDonald Captivates Listeners In Her Concert Debut at College." *The Pittsburg Sun*. Pittsburg, Kansas. March 17, 1939.

334 Herndon, Booton. "Jeanette, Gene peep out of shell." *New Orleans Tribune*. New Orleans, Louisiana. April 4, 1939.

335 Ibid.

336 Ibid.

337 Bryson, Frances. "Gene and Jeanette joke about disguise to dodge admirers." *New Orleans Tribune*. New Orleans, Louisiana. April 5, 1939.

338 Penn, Penelope. "As a Woman Thineth [sic]." *The Indianapolis Star*. Indianapolis, Indiana. April 23, 1939.

339 Anonymous. Letter to Jeanette MacDonald and Gene Raymond. Postmarked April 24, 1939.

340 "Stars' Brief Interlude Ends, Jeanette, Gene Part Again." *New Orleans Item*. New Orleans, Louisiana. April 7, 1939.

341 Ibid.

342 Myers, Fran. "Broadwalk [sic] Tatler [sic]." *The News–Gazette*. Champaign, Illinois. April 19, 1939.

343 "Jeanette MacDonald, in City for Concert, Asserts She's Just an Old-Fashioned Girl." *Rochester Post–Bulletin*. Rochester, Minnesota. April 19, 1939.

344 "Beauty Plays." *Los Angeles Times*. Los Angeles, California. November 13, 1938.

345 MacDonald, Jeanette. "My Frankest Confession." *Screenland*. January 1940.

346 Harrison, Martha. "Miss M'Donald Admits Stage Fright." *Jackson Daily News*. Jackson, Mississippi. March 29, 1939.

347 "S.L. Fans Mob Singing Star, Husband." *Salt Lake Telegram*. Salt Lake City, Utah. April 29, 1939.

348 MacDonald, Jeanette. Letter to Glenna Riley. *Chevalier–MacDonald News*. July/August 1939.

349 MacDonald, Jeanette "Our Question Box." *The Golden Comet*. Spring 1949.

350 "Famed Stage and Screen Soprano Here." *The Daily Province*. Vancouver, British Columbia. May 8, 1939.

351 MacDonald, Jeanette. Letter to Howard Strickling. Circa April 9, 1939.

352 MacDonald, Jeanette and Balling, Fredda Dudley. Draft of Jeanette MacDonald's unpublished autobiography. Fall 1960.

353 Peak, Mayme Ober. "Jeanette MacDonald Has Insured Her Marriage." Unknown newspaper. Boston, Massachusetts. Circa December 3, 1939.

354 Zeitlin, Ida. "Jeanette Sends Her Man to War." *Photoplay Magazine.* June 1942.

355 Dietz, Edith. "Blond Bachelor." *The Detroit Free Press.* Detroit, Michigan. September 2, 1934.

356 Raymond, Gene. Letter to Roy Guyon. October 14, 1939.

357 MacDonald, Jeanette. Letter to Marion Smith Glendening. Circa fall 1939.

358 "Jeanette MacDonald Escapes Autograph Fiends in Albany." *The Knickerbocker News.* Albany, New York. March 13, 1940.

359 Raymond, Gene. Letter to Marion and Frank Glendening. January 19, 1940.

360 Hughes, Elinor. "Jeanette MacDonald, Here for Boston Debut, Discusses Contrast Between Concert and Films." *Boston Herald.* Boston, Massachusetts. November 29, 1940.

361 Lindeman, Edith. "Critic Finds Miss MacDonald More Charming Than in Films." *Richmond Times–Dispatch.* Richmond, Virginia. February 26, 1940.

362 Raymond, Gene. Handwritten draft of telegram to Jeanette MacDonald. April 8, 1940.

363 Raymond, Gene. Telegram to Jeanette MacDonald. November 8, 1940.

364 Sheridan, Jack. "Sheridan's Ride." *Lubbock Avalanche–Journal.* Lubbock, Texas. January 17, 1965.

365 Hopper, Hedda. "Hedda Hopper's Hollywood." *Los Angeles Times.* Los Angeles, California. April 30, 1940.

366 Carroll, Harrison. "Behind the Scenes in Hollywood." *Vineland Evening Times.* Vineland, New Jersey. April 17, 1940.

367 Macoubrey, Carol. "Jeanette MacDonald Charms School Editor." *St.Paul Central High Times.* St. Paul Central High School. St. Paul, Minnesota. April 5, 1940.

368 Hall, Gladys. "Has She Anything Left to Want?" *Modern Screen.* May 1938.

369 Raymond, Gene. Letter to Jeanette MacDonald. November 22, 1940.

370 Hunter, Marjorie. "Jeanette MacDonald Described As 'Lovely Lady' By Interviewer." *Redbird.* Lamar College. Beaumont, Texas. February 20, 1941.

371 Richards, Ken. Notes from conversation with unnamed fan. April 15, 1990.

372 Windham, Amasa B. "Hundreds Throng Station To Greet Singing Film Star." *The Birmingham Age–Herald.* Birmingham, Alabama. February 26, 1940.

373 Sharon, Mary. "Hollywood Has Always Spelt [sic] Good Luck for Me." *Silver Screen.* October 1934.

374 MacDonald, Jeanette. Photo inscribed to Vivien Leigh. Fall 1964.

375 Rhoades, Clara and Williams, Tessa. "Jeanette MacDonald Super Star Pat II." *American Classic Screen*. November/December 1978.

376 Hartzog, Tom. "Look Who's Coming To Dinner." *The Golden Comet*. Summer 1973.

377 Holleran, Scott. "Turner Classic Movies' Robert Osborne." Online interview. 2006.

378 "Potpourri." Reprinted from *Stereo Review*, February 1979. *The Golden Comet*. Summer 1979.

379 White, Betty. *In Person*. Doubleday. 1987.

380 Ibid.

381 Merrill, Dina. Memorial tribute to Jeanette MacDonald. 1965.

382 Rhoades, Clara. Various undated notes for unpublished book on Jeanette MacDonald.

383 Wentz, Emily. Answers to questions from Clara Rhoades. September 6, 1976.

384 MacDonald, Jeanette. Notes from letters to Elsie Pyette. Undated.

385 Truman, Bess. Letter to Jeanette MacDonald. Postmarked August 23, 1956.

386 Lindsay, Lesley. "Defending Jeanette." *Film Weekly*. November 13, 1937.

387 Start, Clarissa. "Husband–Wife Team in 'The Guardsman.'" *St. Louis Post–Dispatch*. St. Louis, Missouri. March 2, 1951.

388 MacDonald, Jeanette. Notes from letters to Elsie Pyette. Undated.

389 Lee, Sonia. "Private Letters of Jeanette MacDonald." *Hollywood*. September 1940.

390 Bradley, Edgar. "Thank You, Jeanette." *The Golden Comet*. Spring 1962.

391 Ferguson, Helen. Army Emergency Relief Tour Press Book. Fall 1942.

392 MacDonald, Jeanette. Envelope for celebrity correspondence.

393 Beatty, Jerome. "The Girl Who Sang in the Bathtub." Reprinted in *The Golden Comet*. Winter 1971.

394 Barnard, Harold D., M.D. Letter to Webster, Atz and Company. December 20, 1937.

395 Fisher, Marjory M. "Singer Finds Tour Is Dream Come True." *The San Francisco News*. San Francisco, California. April 19, 1940.

396 Zeitlin, Ida. "Jeanette Sends Her Man to War." *Photoplay Magazine*. June 1942.

397 MacDonald, Jeanette, as told to Zeitlin, Ida. "How to Be Happy in a Man's World." *Movie Mirror*. November 1938.

398 MacDonald, Jeanette. Letter to Marion Smith Glendening. August 15, 1949.

399 Wilson, Elizabeth (credited as Liza). "Yes! They Have a Heart." *Screenland*. September 1940.

400 Raymond, Gene. Letter to Roy Guyon. May 23, 1940.

401 "Jeanette MacDonald Likes Concert Work Better Than Movies." *Arkansas Gazette*. Little Rock, Arkansas. November 11, 1940.

402 Parsons, Marjorie. "Noted Star of Screen and Stage In City for Recital." *Muncie Evening Press*. Muncie, Indiana. November 19, 1940.

403 "Miss MacDonald Foresees Filming of American Opera." *The Buffalo News*. Buffalo, New York. November 23, 1940.

404 Mull, June. "Glamorous Singing Star Of Screen Arrives In City." *The Muncie Morning Star*. Muncie, Indiana. November 19, 1940.

405 "Jeanette Surprised That Nelson Is Of Pawtucket, Not Providence." *The Times*. Pawtucket, Rhode Island. November 27, 1940.

406 Penland, Jake. "Jeanette MacDonald's Hubby Dyes Hair Blue, Then Brown; She will Sing Here Tonight." *The State*. Columbia, South Carolina. February 8, 1941.

407 Raymond, Gene. Telegram to Jeanette MacDonald. January 15, 1941.

408 Hughes, Elinor. "Jeanette MacDonald, Here for Boston Debut, Discusses Contrast Between Concert and Films." *Boston Herald*. Boston, Massachusetts. November 29, 1940.

409 MacDonald, Jeanette. Letter to Grace Smyth. Circa December 1940.

410 "Jeanette's Journey." *Movies*. June 1941.

411 Isenhower, Ernest. "Afternoon Walk Will Relax Jeanette For Concert Here." *Columbia Record*. Columbia, South Carolina. February 8, 1941.

412 Foster, Dorothy Todd. "Singer Is 'A Little' Sentimental." *The Columbus Dispatch*. Columbus, Ohio. January 18, 1941.

413 Browne, Marguerite L. "Girl Editor of Weekly Trails Star To Miami, Gets Exclusive Interview." *The World News*. Miami, Florida. January 28, 1941.

414 Hunter, Marjorie. "Jeanette MacDonald Described As 'Lovely Lady' By Interviewer." *Redbird*. Lamar College. Beaumont, Texas. February 20, 1941.

415 *Person to Person*. NBC. October 31, 1958.

416 Hall, Gladys. "The Most In Love Couple In Hollywood!" *Silver Screen*. October 1941.

417 Ibid.

418 Ibid.

419 Ibid.

420 Ibid.

421 Ibid.

422 Rhoades, Clara. Various undated notes for unpublished book on Jeanette MacDonald.

423 MacDonald, Jeanette and Balling, Fredda Dudley. Draft of Jeanette MacDonald's unpublished autobiography. Fall 1960.

424 Raymond, Gene. Letter to Roy Guyon. June 10, 1941.

425 Raymond, Gene. Tribute to LeRoy Guyon. July 1941.

426 Nickel, Reverend Frank. Obituary for Roy Guyon. July 31, 1941.

427 MacDonald, Jeanette. Letter to Lily May Caldwell. August 18, 1941. Lily May Caldwell Papers, Manuscript Collection 15, UAB Archives, the University of Alabama at Birmingham.

428 "'Date–Leaves' [sic] with the Mac-Raymonds [sic]." *Movies.* January 1942.

429 Henderson, Jessie. "Men in Service Get Standing Invitation. To Dine in Homes of Hollywood Stars." *The Philadelphia Inquirer.* Philadelphia, Pennsylvania. April 19, 1942.

430 Peak, Mayme Ober. "Hollywood Has Soldier Party." *Decatur Herald.* Decatur, Illinois. November 8, 1941.

431 Proctor, Kay. "How to Entertain a Soldier." *Stardom.* May 1942.

432 Wilson, Elizabeth. "Jeanette Falls in Line." *Silver Screen.* August 1942.

433 Peak, Mayme Ober. "Hollywood Has Soldier Party." *Decatur Herald.* Decatur, Illinois. November 8, 1941.

434 Ferguson, Helen. "Jeanette Should Have a Medal." Press release sent to Muriel Babcock for *Movies.* 1941.

435 Peak, Mayme Ober. "Hollywood Has Soldier Party." *Decatur Herald.* Decatur, Illinois. November 8, 1941.

436 "Questions & Answers." *The Golden Comet.* Fall 1959.

437 Mola, Mario. Letter to Clara Rhoades. June 5, 1992.

438 Ferguson, Helen. "Jeanette Should Have a Medal." Press release sent to Muriel Babcock for *Movies.* 1941.

439 Turk, Edward Baron. *Hollywood Diva.* University of California Press. 1998.

440 Roosevelt, Franklin D. *The Infamy Speech.* December 8, 1941.

441 Marsh, Paul. "Jeanette Reconsiders." *Silver Screen.* August 1947.

442 Zeitlin, Ida. "Jeanette Sends Her Man to War." *Photoplay Magazine.* June 1942.

443 Grogg, Sylvia. Letter to Lily May Caldwell. January 2, 1942. Lily May Caldwell Papers, Manuscript Collection 15, UAB Archives, the University of Alabama at Birmingham.

444 Hall, Gladys. "You Don't Know My Address." *Screenland.* September 1943.

445 MacDonald, Jeanette. Draft of Jeanette MacDonald's unpublished autobiography, collaborator unknown. Undated.

446 "1980 Mid-Year Conference...." *VFW Auxiliary*. May-June 1980.

447 Carroll, Harrison. "Behind the Scenes in Hollywood." *Los Angeles Evening Herald–Express*. Los Angeles, California. January 29, 1942.

448 "Harvard Lampoon Flays Six Stars in Worst Films Review." *Los Angeles Times*. Los Angeles, California. January 24, 1942.

449 Johnson, Erskine. "Hollywood in '49 Did Its Best To Retain Its Reputation." *The Daily Register*. Harrisburg, Illinois. January 4, 1950.

450 "Friend Is Gone; A Hush Falls on Hollywood." *Chicago Tribune*. Chicago, Illinois. January 18, 1942.

451 Raymond, Gene. Letter to President Franklin D. Roosevelt. February 5, 1942.

452 "Movie Singer Thrills 5000." *Marine Corps Chevron*. February 14, 1942.

453 Hall, Gladys. "You Didn't Know My Address." *Screenland*. September 1943.

454 Ibid.

455 "Gene Raymond A Lieutenant Now." *The Philadelphia Inquirer*. Philadelphia, Pennsylvania. March 5, 1942.

456 Raymond, Gene. Letter to Marion and Frank Glendening. March 13, 1942.

457 MacDonald, Jeanette. Letter to Gene Raymond. March 13, 1942.

458 "Happenings of the New York Chapter." *Musical Echoes*. November/December 1942.

459 Frankenstein, Alfred. "Jeanette MacDonald: An Impressive Concert With A Feeling of Purpose." *San Francisco Chronicle*. San Francisco, California. March 26, 1942.

460 McClain, John. *Cairo*. MGM. 1942.

461 Reagan, Ronald. Letter to Clara Rhoades dated March 30, 1965. *The Golden Comet*. May 1965.

462 Hall, Gladys. "You Didn't Know My Address." *Screenland*. September 1943.

463 1993 Clan Clave banquet speeches. July 29, 1993.

464 MacDonald, Jeanette. Revised pages of Jeanette MacDonald's unpublished autobiography. 1963.

465 Wentz, Emily. Letter to Clara Rhoades. October 11, 1976.

466 Hall, Gladys. "You Didn't Know My Address." *Screenland*. September 1943.

467 Rohlfing, Joan Halford. Email to author. September 23, 2014.

468 Raymond, Gene. Letter to Jeanette MacDonald. August 7, 1942.

469 Stage Door Canteen plaque on 44th Street. New York, New York.

470 "Will You Remember." *The Golden Comet*. Winter 1987.

471 "Will You Remember?" *The Golden Comet*. Summer 1993.

472 Ibid.

473 Ibid.

474 MacDonald, Jeanette. Revised pages of Jeanette MacDonald's unpublished autobiography. 1963.

475 Raymond, Gene. Interview with Clara Rhoades and Tessa Williams for Edward Baron Turk. July 14, 1993.

476 Hall, Gladys. "You Didn't Know My Address." *Screenland*. September 1943.

477 "Famed Singer Says Sacrifice and Love Are Necessary Now." Unknown newspaper. Springfield, Ohio. Circa October 27, 1942.

478 MacDonald, Jeanette. Revised pages of Jeanette MacDonald's unpublished autobiography. 1963.

479 Hover, Helen. "Hollywood's War Effort: Salute to Jeanette MacDonald." *Hollywood*. December 1942.

480 Ketcham, George and Fist, Allene. "Gracious Jeanette Has Chat With Press: Hall Sold Out." *Tulsa World*. Tulsa, Oklahoma. June 1943.

481 Hover, Helen. "Hollywood's War Effort: Salute to Jeanette MacDonald." *Hollywood*. December 1942.

482 Lewis, Ruth. "Army Duties May Keep Hubby Gene Raymond From Coming to Austin With Miss MacDonald." *The Austin American*. Austin, Texas. December 3, 1943.

483 Wilson, Elizabeth. "Jeanette Sings for the Soldiers." *Screenland*. December 1942.

484 Ibid.

485 Hart, Russ. "Jeanette M'Donald Arrives Wearing New Hat, New Title." *Chattanooga News–Free Press*. Chattanooga, Tennessee. September 21, 1942.

486 Wilson, Elizabeth. "Jeanette Sings for the Soldiers." *Screenland*. December 1942.

487 Rheam, Florence Lee. "Jeanette Will Give a Good Performance Here, But She Really Prefers Soldiers." *The Tulsa Tribune*. Tulsa, Oklahoma. June 4, 1943.

488 Wilson, Elizabeth. "Jeanette Sings for the Soldiers." *Screenland*. December 1942.

489 "Soprano Has Sung in Army Camps in South and West." Unknown newspaper. Syracuse, New York. October 1942.

490 Wilson, Elizabeth. "Jeanette Sings for the Soldiers." *Screenland*. December 1942.

491 "Men in Camp Prefer 'Ave Maria' to Jazz." *Pittsburgh Post–Gazette*. Pittsburgh, Pennsylvania. September 17, 1942.

492 Wilson, Elizabeth. "Jeanette Sings for the Soldiers." *Screenland.* December 1942.

493 Ibid.

494 Kelley, Andrew R. "Prima Donna Discovers Religious Note in Army." *Washington Times–Herald.* Washington, D.C. Circa 1942.

495 "Miss MacDonald Here for Concert, Says Army Life Brings Out Serious Side of Young Men." *The Springfield Union.* Springfield, Massachusetts. September 29, 1942.

496 "Facts about Jeanette." *Musical Echoes.* November/December 1942.

497 MacDonald, Jeanette. "I'm proud I believe in God." *Albuquerque Journal.* Albuquerque, New Mexico. August 9, 1942.

498 "Phoenix To Hear Famous Prima Donna." *Casa Grande Dispatch.* Case Grande, Arizona. March 24, 1944.

499 "Soprano Star Talks Venison." Unknown newspaper. Seattle, Washington. October 16, 1943.

500 Rheam, Florence Lee. "Jeanette Will Give a Good Performance Here, But She Really Prefers Soldiers." *The Tulsa Tribune.* Tulsa, Oklahoma. June 4, 1943.

501 Marsh, Paul. "Jeanette Reconsiders." *Silver Screen.* August 1947.

502 Wilson, Elizabeth. "Jeanette Sings for the Soldiers." *Screenland.* December 1942.

503 Norton, Elliot. "Movie Star Scared at Her Grand Opera Debut." *The Boston Post.* Boston, Massachusetts. November 29, 1944.

504 Parsons, Louella O. "Studio to Reissue Gehrig's 'Rawhide.'" *The Philadelphia Inquirer.* Philadelphia, Pennsylvania. September 2, 1942.

505 Hopper, Hedda. "Looking at Hollywood." *Chicago Tribune.* Chicago, Illinois. November 3, 1942.

506 Frazier, George. "Reporter's Bark Irks Singer." *Boston Herald.* Boston, Massachusetts. October 1, 1942.

507 "Star Spangled Singer." *The Golden Comet.* Winter 1991.

508 "Jeanette MacDonald." Press release reprinted in *Retrospect.* 1998 Annual.

509 Stevenson, L.L. "Television Terrifies Veteran of the Concert Stage." November 1951. Reprinted in *Retrospect.* Vol. 5, no. 3.

510 Patrick, Corbin J. "Charming Jeanette MacDonald In City With Song In Heart and Ear to Radio." *The Indianapolis Star.* Indianapolis, Indiana. September 13, 1942.

511 Swann, Rita. "Jeanette MacDonald Here to Sing at Lyric." *The News American.* Baltimore, Maryland. October 15, 1942.

512 Frazier, George. "Reporter's Bark Irks Singer." *Boston Herald.* Boston, Massachusetts. October 1, 1942.

513 Ferguson, Helen. Army Emergency Relief Tour Press Book. Fall 1942.

514 Parish, James Robert. *The Jeanette MacDonald Story*. Mason/Charter. 1976.

515 Adams, Marjory. "Jeanette MacDonald Will Sing Army Camps' Favorite Tonight." *The Boston Daily Globe*. Boston, Massachusetts. October 1, 1942.

516 "Miss MacDonald Here for Concert, Says Army Life Brings Out Serious Side of Young Men." *The Springfield Union*. Springfield, Massachusetts. September 29, 1942.

517 Maddox, Ben. "Jeanette's Back." *Screenland*. July 1947.

518 Patterson, Robert P. Letter to Jeanette MacDonald. October 6, 1942.

519 Battley, Colonel Joseph F. Letter to Gene Raymond. October 9, 1942.

520 Ferguson, Helen. Army Emergency Relief Tour Press Book. Fall 1942.

521 Johnson, Erskine. *Los Angeles Daily News*. Los Angeles, California. November 18, 1942.

522 Springer, John. "Great Movie Stars Jeanette MacDonald." *Screen Stories*. August 1965.

523 Hawkings, Claire Evans. "Jeanette MacDonald Staunch Champion of American Music." *The Post-Standard*. Syracuse, New York. October 14, 1942.

524 Ramon, Florence. "A Short, Enlightening Visit With Jeanette." *The Morning Telegraph*. New York, New York. November 5, 1942.

525 Creelman, Eileen. "Picture Plays and Players." *The New York Sun*. New York, New York. November 10, 1942.

526 Thirer, Irene. "Cash for Autographs." Unknown newspaper. New York, New York. Circa November 1942.

527 Ramon, Florence. "A Short, Enlightening Visit With Jeanette." *The Morning Telegraph*. New York, New York. November 5, 1942.

528 Brocksmith, Charlotte and Gabriel, Grace. "Stage Door Canteen." *The Golden Comet*. December 1942.

529 "Wartime Happenings." *The Golden Comet*. Winter 1991.

530 Ibid.

531 Coward, Noel. "I'll See You Again." *Bitter Sweet*. 1929.

532 MacDonald, Jeanette. Letter to Constance Hope. December 10, 1942. Constance Hope papers, 1931–1975, Rare Book & Manuscript Library, Columbia University in the City of New York.

533 "This and That About Jeanette." *Musical Echoes*. March/April 1943.

534 "Singer on Army Tour Returns." *Los Angeles Times*. Los Angeles, California. December 3, 1942.

535 "Famed Singer Says Sacrifice and Love Are Necessary Now." Unknown newspaper. Springfield, Ohio. Circa October 27, 1942.

536 MacDonald, Jeanette. "Jeanette MacDonald's Tips to Girls on the Home Front." *Movie Stars Parade.* December 1942.

537 MacDonald, Jeanette. Letter to Constance Hope. December 29, 1942. Constance Hope papers, 1931–1975, Rare Book & Manuscript Library, Columbia University in the City of New York.

538 Raymond, Gene. Letter to Jeanette MacDonald. December 26, 1942.

539 MacDonald, Jeanette. Letter to Elsie Scheiter. January 5, 1943.

540 Harrison, Emma Mae. "Bees and War Chest Get Singer's Main Attention." *The Oregon Daily Journal.* Portland, Oregon. October 14, 1943.

541 Raymond, Gene. Telegram to Jeanette MacDonald. February 20, 1943.

542 Kesselring, Margaret. "First Visit to Regina for Glamorous Singer." *Regina, Saskatchawan Leader–Post.* Regina, Saskatchawan, Canada. October 1952.

543 St. Johns, Adela Rogers. "Women Who Wait." *Photoplay Magazine.* May 1943.

544 Hope, Constance. Unused liner notes for *Jeanette MacDonald Opera and Operetta Favorites* LP. 1967.

545 "Screen Star Who Sings Tonight at Auditorium Meets the Press." *Springfield Daily Republican.* Springfield, Massachusetts. March 11, 1940.

546 "Sings Tonight in Auditorium." *The Springfield Union.* Springfield, Massachusetts. March 11, 1940.

547 Logan, Floyd. "Jeanette MacDonald, Gracious And Charming, Delighted With First American Concert Tour." *The News–Sentinel.* Fort Wayne, Indiana. April 14, 1939.

548 MacDonald, Jeanette. Letter to Constance Hope. January 20, 1943. Constance Hope papers, 1931–1975, Rare Book & Manuscript Library, Columbia University in the City of New York.

549 Ibid.

550 Ibid.

551 *Command Performance.* January 16, 1943.

552 *The Charlie McCarthy Show.* January 24, 1943.

553 MacDonald, Jeanette. Letter to Constance Hope. February 25, 1943. Constance Hope papers, 1931–1975, Rare Book & Manuscript Library, Columbia University in the City of New York.

554 Raymond, Gene. Letter to Jeanette MacDonald. February 26, 1943.

555 "Behind the Front Page." *The Detroit Free Press.* Detroit, Michigan. March 18, 1943.

556 MacDonald, Jeanette. Letter to Constance Hope. February 25, 1943. Constance Hope papers, 1931–1975, Rare Book & Manuscript Library, Columbia University in the City of New York.

557 Cassidy, Claudia. "On the Aisle." *Chicago Tribune.* Chicago, Illinois. November 12, 1944.

558 Hope, Constance. Unused liner notes for *Jeanette MacDonald Opera and Operetta Favorites* LP. 1967.

559 "Grace Notes." *The Golden Comet.* Summer 1943.

560 MacDonald, Jeanette and Balling, Fredda Dudley. Draft of Jeanette MacDonald's unpublished autobiography. Fall 1960.

561 Raymond, Gene. Letter to Jeanette MacDonald. February 26, 1943.

562 Parish, James Robert. *The Jeanette MacDonald Story.* Mason/Charter. 1976.

563 MacDonald, Jeanette and Brough, James. Draft of Jeanette MacDonald's unpublished autobiography. Spring 1960. Cinematic Arts Library, Doheny Memorial Library, University of Southern California.

564 MacDonald, Jeanette and Balling, Fredda Dudley. Draft of Jeanette MacDonald's unpublished autobiography. Fall 1960.

565 Turk, Edward Baron. *Hollywood Diva.* University of California Press. 1998.

566 Raymond, Gene. Telegram to Jeanette MacDonald. March 24, 1943.

567 Kilgallen, Dorothy. "Voice of Broadway." *Shamokin News–Dispatch.* Shamokin, Pennsylvania. April 9, 1943.

568 Hall, Gladys. "You Don't Know My Address." *Screenland.* September 1943.

569 Ibid.

570 MacDonald, Jeanette. Letter to Constance Hope. February 25, 1943. Constance Hope papers, 1931–1975, Rare Book & Manuscript Library, Columbia University in the City of New York.

571 Ferguson, Helen. Letter to Glenna Riley dated June 28, 1943. *Musical Echoes.* July/August 1943.

572 Pelletier, Wilfrid. Letter to Clara Rhoades. October 14, 1965.

573 "Movie Star Captain Gene Greets Movie Star Jeanette In Toronto." *The Toronto Daily Star.* Toronto, Ontario, Canada. May 19, 1943.

574 "Opera Debut Thrilling To Jeanette MacDonald." *The Globe and Mail.* Toronto, Ontario, Canada. May 19, 1943.

575 Ibid.

576 Martin, Francoise. "Wonders If 'Mounties' Movie Myth." *The Windsor Star.* Windsor, Ontario, Canada. May 24, 1943.

577 Ibid.

578 MacDonald, Jeanette. Letter to Constance Hope. February 25, 1943. Constance Hope papers, 1931–1975, Rare Book & Manuscript Library, Columbia University in the City of New York.

579 Ibid.

580 Ibid.

581 MacDonald, Jeanette. Letter to Constance Hope. May 12, 1943. Constance Hope papers, 1931–1975, Rare Book & Manuscript Library, Columbia University in the City of New York.

582 Ibid.

583 MacDonald, Jeanette and Balling, Fredda Dudley. Draft of Jeanette MacDonald's unpublished autobiography. Fall 1960.

584 Mossman, Josef. "Detroit Charms Miss MacDonald." *The Detroit News.* Detroit, Mchigan. September 15, 1959.

585 MacDonald, Jeanette and Balling, Fredda Dudley. Draft of Jeanette MacDonald's unpublished autobiography. Fall 1960.

586 MacDonald, Jeanette. Outline for Jeanette MacDonald's unpublished autobiography. Undated.

587 *Luncheon at the Music Center.* Tom Cassidy interview with Sharon Rich and Emily Wentz. February 26, 1974.

588 "Screen Star Capt. Gene Raymond Arrives in City." *The Ottawa Evening Journal.* Ottawa, Ontario, Canada. May 19, 1943.

589 MacDonald, Jeanette. Letter to Marie Waddy and JMIFC members dated August 26, 1943. *The Golden Comet.* Fall 1943.

590 Rheam, Florence Lee. "Jeanette Will Give a Good Performance Here, But She Really Prefers Soldiers." *The Tulsa Tribune.* Tulsa, Oklahoma. June 4, 1943.

591 "Songstress Jeanette MacDonald Bubbling Over with Patriotism." Unknown newspaper. Wichita, Kansas. June 12, 1943.

592 "Charming Jeanette MacDonald In Concert Thrilled Patrons Who Packed Convention Hall." *County Democrat News.* Sapulpa, Oklahoma. Volume 32, number 31. June 1943.

593 Henderson, Harold. "Jeanette M'Donald Returns to Wichita." *The Wichita Beacon.* Wichita, Kansas. June 12, 1943.

594 Ketcham, George and Fist, Allene. "Gracious Jeanette Has Chat With Press: Hall Sold Out." *Tulsa World.* Tulsa, Oklahoma. June 1943.

595 MacDonald, Jeanette. Letter to Glenna Riley dated June 24, 1943. *Musical Echoes.* July/August 1943.

596   Linderman, Verne. "Local Audience Captured By Jeanette MacDonald." *Santa Barbara News–Press*. Santa Barbara, California. October 8, 1943.

597   Wilson, Mary Lib. " 'The Name Is Raymond,' Miss MacDonald Smiles." *Winston–Salem Journal*. Winston–Salem, North Carolina. October 28, 1943.

598   Lindeman, Edith. "Jeanette MacDonald Relates Plans Here for New Picture." *Richmond Times–Dispatch*. Richmond, Virginia. November 20, 1943.

599   Ibid.

600   Hazen, David W. "Singer Brings Food Supplies." *The Oregonian*. Portland, Oregon. October 14, 1943.

601   Belcher, Shirley. "Local woman remembers date with stars." *Middletown Journal*. Middletown, Ohio. Circa 1999.

602   "Concert Nov. 7 Stars M'Donald." *The Atlanta Constitution*. Atlanta, Georgia. October 24, 1943.

603   Bass, William. Untitled incomplete draft of Jeanette MacDonald biography. 1981.

604   "Jeanette MacDonald Quick to Pledge Doll, Toy Fund Aid." *The Times–Picayune*. New Orleans, Louisiana. November 25, 1943.

605   "Jeanette M'Donald Just Army Wife in S.A." *San Antonio News*. San Antonio, Texas. December 2, 1943.

606   Caldwell, Lily May. "Lovely Jeanette MacDonald Arrives." *The Birmingham News*. Birmingham, Alabama. November 5, 1943.

607   Lewis, Ruth. "Braving Wartime Travel With Her Own Kitchen Kit, Jeanette Keeps On Singing. *The Austin American*. Austin, Texas. December 3, 1943.

608   Lindeman, Edith. "Jeanette MacDonald Relates Plans Here for New Picture." *Richmond Times–Dispatch*. Richmond, Vrginia. November 20, 1943.

609   "More For Victory." *Montreal Herald*. Montreal, Quebec, Canada. May 25, 1943.

610   "Jeanette Almost San Antonian." *The San Antonio Light*. San Antonio, Texas. December 2, 1943.

611   "Jeanette M'Donald Just Army Wife in S.A." *San Antonio News*. San Antonio, Texas. December 2, 1943.

612   MacDonald, Jeanette and Balling, Fredda Dudley. Draft of Jeanette MacDonald's unpublished autobiography. Fall 1960.

613   "Try to Match It." *Plainfield Courier–News*. Plainfield, New Jersey. January 25, 1944.

614   "As Told to Pat Smith by a Pal Who Saw Jeanette on a Bond Tour." *Musical Echoes*. March/April 1944.

615   Smith, Katherine T. "Louisville Author Had Gay Trip." *The Courier–Journal*. Louisville, Kentucky. July 16, 1944.

616 Raymond, Gene. Letter to Jeanette MacDonald. April 30, 1944.

617 Caldwell, Lily May. "Jeanette MacDonald Anxious to End Tour, See Her Husband." *The Birmingham News*. Birmingham, Alabama. April 1944.

618 "A Look Back to Yesterday." Reprinted in *Retrospect*. Vol. 5, no. 1.

619 Parish, James Robert. *The Jeanette MacDonald Story*. Mason/Charter. 1976.

620 Lehmann, Lotte. Letter to Jeanette MacDonald. August 11, 1944.

621 Parsons, Louella O. *The Philadelphia Inquirer*. Philadelphia, Pennsylvania. September 20, 1944.

622 Ferguson, Helen. Letter to Glenna Riley dated March 13, 1945. *Musical Echoes*. May/June 1945.

623 MacDonald, Jeanette. Letter to Mrs. Thomas E. Dewey. September 22, 1944.

624 Cassidy, Claudia. "Miss M'Donald Stars; 'Faust' Is Superbly Sung." *Chicago Tribune*. Chicago, Illinois. November 16, 1944.

625 "Opera Debut Is Described By Film Star." *Pittsburgh Post–Gazette*. Pittsburgh, Pennsylvania. November 21, 1944.

626 Ibid.

627 "Jeanette MacDonald Takes All-Night Train Trip in Stride." *Springfield Republican*. Springfield, Massachusetts. November 26, 1944.

628 Shipp, Cameron. "Encore!" *Modern Screen*. September 1947.

629 MacDonald, Jeanette. Letter to Marie Waddy and JMIFC members dated January 11, 1945. *The Golden Comet*. Spring 1945.

630 Merrill, Robert. "Impressions of Miss MacDonald." *Musical Echoes*. March/April 1948.

631 Merrill, Robert. *Between Acts: An irreverent look at opera and other madness*. McGraw–Hill. 1976.

632 MacDonald, Jeanette. Letter to Marion Smith Glendening. April 2, 1945.

633 "Jeanette MacDonald Charms Hospital with Beautiful Singing, Personality." *Oak Leaf*. Alameda High School. Oakland, California. March 1945.

634 MacDonald, Jeanette. Letter to Marie Waddy and JMIFC members dated March 29, 1945. *The Golden Comet*. Spring 1945.

635 MacDonald, Jeanette. Letter to Lily May Caldwell. April 19, 1945. Lily May Caldwell Papers, Manuscript Collection 15, UAB Archives, the University of Alabama at Birmingham.

636 Ibid.

637 Jones, Isabel Morse. "Music Week Has Start at City Hall." *Los Angeles Times*. Los Angeles, California. May 7, 1945.

638 Raymond, Gene. Letter to Avery M. Blount, Esq. April 9, 1945.

639 "Overflow Crowd Attends Opera At Zoo; MacDonald Makes Her Debut In 'Faust.'" *The Cincinnati Enquirer*. Cincinnati, Ohio. July 16, 1945.

640 "Songstress Jeanette MacDonald Bubbling Over with Patriotism." Unknown newspaper. Wichita, Kansas. June 12, 1943.

641 Muir, Florabel. "Just a Little Story about Our Jeanette." *Hollywood Citizen–News*. Hollywood, California. August 10, 1945.

642 Selznick, Daniel Mayer. Email to author. October 30, 2018.

643 Peak, Mayme Ober. "Jeanette MacDonald Has Insured Her Marriage." Unknown newspaper. Boston, Massachusetts. Circa December 3, 1939.

Index

Some people are referred to by their relationships (i.e. mother or brother); occasionally, places, like the Raymonds' home, Twin Gables, are inferred. Every effort has been made to include them in the index whenever they were mentioned, whether by name or not. States are listed for Army and Army Air Force bases, camps, and forts. Cities and/or cities and states usually are listed for other places. Twin Gables is noted as West Los Angeles, instead of Bel Air, California, since the area was called West Los Angeles during the period covered in this book.